Multimedia
AND THE WEB
FROM A TO Z

DISCARDED

WITHDRAWN

MULTIMEDIA AND THE WEB FROM A TO Z

2ND EDITION

by Patrick M. Dillon
and
David C. Leonard

Oryx Press
1998

The rare Arabian Oryx is believed to have inspired the myth of the unicorn. This desert antelope became virtually extinct in the early 1960s. At that time several groups of international conservationists arranged to have 9 animals sent to the Phoenix Zoo to be the nucleus of a captive breeding herd. Today the Oryx population is over 1,000, and over 500 have been returned to the Middle East.

© 1998 by The Oryx Press
4041 North Central at Indian School Road
Phoenix, Arizona 85012-3397

Published simultaneously in Canada
Printed and Bound in the United States of America

∞ The paper used in this publication meets the minimum requirements of American National Standard for Information Science—Permanence of Paper for Printed Library Materials, ANSI Z39.48, 1984.

Library of Congress Cataloging-in-Publication Data

Dillon, Patrick M.
   Multimedia and the Web from a to z / by Patrick M. Dillon and
David C. Leonard
   Includes bibliographical references.
   ISBN 1-57356-132-0 (alk. paper)
   1. Multimedia systems. 2. World Wide Web (Information retrieval
systems) I. Leonard, David C.
QA76.575.D548   1998
006.7—dc21   98-34083
                                                        CIP

DEDICATION

As one gains in wisdom, which is of greater value than knowledge, it becomes clear what is most important in life: our families. This book is dedicated to our wives, Sheri Dillon and Linda Leonard, and to our children: Nikki and Shane Dillon, and Emily and Christian Leonard.

CONTENTS

Foreword ix

Preface xiii

Introduction xv

A–Z Terms 1

Annotated Bibliography 325

Acronyms 348

FOREWORD
A Turbulent Vocabulary for a Restless Industry

The first edition of this work was entitled *Multimedia Technology from A to Z.* We were compelled to change the title for this second edition, even though the act of doing so leaves us with an uneasy feeling. A slang term at loose in the information technology (I/T) industry is "Internet years." It refers to the accelerated rates of change that have characterized every manner of I/T for the past several decades. Though only three years have passed since our first edition appeared, at least a decade of Internet years have transpired, exploding major change on top of major change and inducing us to cannibalize the title of our own book.

Though we have acquiesced to the powerful forces for change unleashed by the sudden rise in Web use, we have done so with some trepidation. In constructing our first edition of this book, we were motivated by the desire to help formulate an established vocabulary—a nomenclature—for the emerging and highly interdisciplinary field of multimedia. That desire has not changed one bit. Indeed, the continued ascent of multimedia as a powerful new form of communication has done nothing but encourage and strengthen our commitment to this goal. At the core of that goal is the belief that no human endeavor can be successful at achieving its full potential unless it bases itself upon a robust and stable language. The professionals of any industry seeking to impart the magnitude of social and economic change that is being contemplated for multimedia must be able to communicate with one another in the most efficient ways possible.

Thus, the notion of "Internet years" is filled with paradoxical elements. The ascent of the Web is a force of enormously positive change for those seeking to advance the many causes of multimedia. It satisfies, in fact, the most urgent need that confronted multimedia practitioners at the time we were writing the first edition. It provides a cost-effective and potentially pervasive means to distribute digital media content. For multimedia, it is the equivalent of Gutenberg's printing press.

But the meteoric rise of the Web is not without its problems. The most serious of those problems may have to do with the Internet's impact on language. Just as our technological infrastructure has been subjected to the pace of "Internet years," so too has the language surrounding multimedia. The term "multimedia," itself, is now considered to be somewhat passe. New words and phrases are being shoved into our vocabulary on a daily basis, and many have "Web" or "net" affixed to them. It is as if language—which is, after all, the bedrock of culture—has gotten caught up in a fashion cycle.

The impact of the Web has been enormous and, for the most part, extremely positive. Surprisingly, however, it has not changed the nature of the multimedia revolution. In fact, it has simply come to occupy a niche in the overall infrastructure that had a need to be filled in the first place. From the outset, digital media needed a far better, far more efficient means of distribution than could be supplied by the optical storage media of laserdisc or CD-ROM. From its inception, multimedia cried out for the same ease of access that has characterized the other major new communications media of the twentieth century: telephony, radio, and television.

With the advent of the Web, multimedia got its necessary angel for distribution. Other than filling a huge—even momentous—need, however, the Web has not changed the essential forces in multimedia at all. The central issue of multimedia continues to be the search for, and exploitation of, new opportunities based on the digitization of the traditional analog media. The central challenge of multimedia remains the intellectually demanding one of designing new and highly interactive modes of communication. Even with the Web—and, actually, because of the Web—the central obstacles facing multimedia are twofold. First, the chronic and always critical shortage of bandwidth remains, which the Internet will do nothing to resolve until our NII (National Information Infrastructure) undergoes substantial reinvestment and renewal. Second, the ongoing crisis of interdisciplinary collision, which some still refer to as "convergence," has not been resolved.

The issues, the challenges, and the obstacles of multimedia remain the same. And the opportunities are of much the same character; only they are larger in stature and more urgent to the business community. This is primarily because the Web has brought them closer—has brought the dream dust within reach. Thus, the need to communicate is also more urgent now, even though the essential concepts that need to be communicated have remained largely the same. The Web has fulfilled a critical need that only three years ago was the subject of much puzzlement. But it would be foolish, if not dangerous, to permit this achievement to overstep its privileges before we establish how–and with what words and phrases—to communicate about it.

Thus, as with this protean industry that we so gratefully and willingly embrace, our essential commitment for this second edition is no different than it was for the first. The Web has heightened the call to action for multimedia practitioners in general, and we want to contribute by helping to establish a nomenclature at what is the most interdisciplinary crossroad in history.

We have added approximately 500 new terms. A good portion of these owe their semantic origins to the Internet. As with the first 1,000 terms, we have tried to balance our entries across a wide range of topics and subtopics. In particular, we have focused on such areas as the technologies of internetworking; the new design issues associated with building Web sites; the broad panoply of legal issues related to creating Web content; the great challenge of making the Internet a more navigable and "search-friendly" place to go; and the rapidly expanding group of new communication genres made possible by the Web.

Still, much of our work for this new edition was focused on rewriting the original terms. In this regard, it is interesting that many of the terms are still at home in the present-day context of multimedia and the Web; but it is clear that in most cases the intellectual furniture has been rearranged. For instance, almost every major interactive communications genre that was there "in the beginning" (circa late 1970s to early 1980s) is still very much alive in the here and now, only their present "gestalt" is being redefined in terms of how they relate to the Web. Many of those genres are still here and doing quite well, but have been subjected to the linguistic ignominy of being completely renamed. Take computer-based training, for example. It is now Web-based training (WBT), even though the majority of its value is still predicated on the fact that a *computer* has been programmed to exhibit pedagogical intelligence.

Additionally, many of the new entries expand the categories of knowledge that anchored our first edition. Again, this a tribute to actual—as opposed to linguistic—stability. The industry's root structure is growing nicely, and in directions that were well anticipated by its conceptual sprigs. For example, we were impelled to create a number of new entries in the areas of instructional technology, information design, graphics development, software engineering, and computer design. As evidence of a dynamic and maturing industry, most of the initial contributory disciplines of multimedia continue to experience a heyday.

The substantial scope of change that motivated us to create this second edition is nothing, if not a sign of extremely good health. To sustain that good health, however, we believe that there is a need for continuity. There is a need for those of us who are happy to inhabit this new industry of multimedia to carefully grow its emergent vocabulary. This need is all the more urgent because the inertia of our educational bureaucracies will likely sustain multimedia's status as an academic orphan— albeit an attractive one tugged at by all.

But an academic tug-of-war is not what this economic and cultural prodigy needs. The risk under this scenario is that each discipline will want to spoil the *Wunderkind* with its own linguistic wealth—a noble gesture in its own right, but certainly not in the best long-term interests of anyone. Rather, what the language of multimedia needs most is a stewardship that ensures a balanced cross-fertilization of ideas from every discipline having a legitimate interest in the enterprise. This continual, almost incessant hybridization is, after all, what is most responsible for giving multimedia its enormous present—as well as anticipated—value.

Of course, this hybridization is also the thing most responsible for destabilizing the language of multimedia. We will consider our efforts here more than successful if we can contribute in a meaningful way to the delicate goal of stabilizing the language of multimedia, while at the same time helping it to stay on its current interdisciplinary course. For us, the goal can be stated in this way. The vocabulary of multimedia needs to grow at whatever pace and in whatever directions are dictated by its actual evolutionary path. If this means that it must experience, from time to time, the convulsive growth that results from having to absorb huge segments of another new discipline's nomenclature, then so be it. However, the speakers of this language should not succumb to the thrill of reinventing that language every time some overpowering new technology happens along.

PREFACE

This book defines for you over 1,500 terms related to multimedia and the Web. Generally speaking, these terms were selected from sets of professional functions that relate to multimedia in one of two ways. They either belong to one of the major contributory disciplines that provide the bases for this new industry, or they belong to a set of competencies that owe their origins to the birth of multimedia.

For example, as video becomes "just another data type," the considerable language surrounding the century-old industry of film and video production has become a justifiable concern for those who speak the language of multimedia. Thus, we have included a large number of film and video terms, though we have not tried to duplicate that industry's entire nomenclature.

Instead, we have made an effort to include those terms that will be of greatest use to developers who are working to incorporate video in their multimedia content, and particularly for those who are producing CD-ROM or DVD (digital video disc) titles—which is now the most intense locus of video activity in this young industry. Since most of these developers are not blessed with Hollywood-sized budgets, but rely heavily on stock footage and other forms of predeveloped video, our most concentrated effort in the video realm is in the area of postproduction. This is where the general move toward all-digital, computer-based tools provides us with a reinforcing motive to include these terms. Thus, you will find a cluster of terms around such areas of video postproduction as digital video effects, which has earned itself the status of an acronym—DVE.

We also selected terms centered around areas of professional competency that owe their very origins to the birth of multimedia. For example, certain software tools that owe their newborn existence to this industry are called "authoring systems." These software toolsets have many dimensions and subclasses, and we have made an effort to be as inclusive as possible with regard to the rapidly growing language that describes their emergent richness and diversity.

As with any professional nomenclature, the semantic network that is the language of multimedia is centered around an overlapping system of conceptual nodes, many of which owe their origins to earlier sources and centers of meaning, and many others of which owe their genesis to the birth and growth of the multimedia profession. Because so many terms are interrelated, the reader will find a large number of cross-references within the entries in this dictionary.

Within definitions, words in italics are those that are defined elsewhere in the dictionary. Sometimes two or more defined terms are part of a compound word, and the reader may have to look up two terms instead of one. For example, the term "digital *video*" is not defined, but *digital* and *video* are defined as separate terms.

Please note that this dictionary does not serve as a style guide for capitalization of terms. Many terms with acronyms contain irregular capitalization to aid the reader in identifying the acronyms.

The entries themselves are arranged in alphabetical order by word, which differs somewhat from the letter-by-letter style used in many dictionaries. Thus, the entry *auto iris* comes before *autochanger*.

In many instances, we introduce a new, and often esoteric, term as part of another term's definition, but we have elected not to define it, typically because that esoteric term lies below what we have determined to be a sort of threshold of interest. Based on our judgment, any terms lying below that threshold do not carry enough weight in the industry, or perhaps lie so far from its fringe that they do not merit their own entry. In such cases, we have enclosed those terms in quotation marks, and made an attempt to define them insofar as they contribute to the definition of the entry in which they appear.

If you were to pursue the cross-references, and all of our embedded definitions, as if riding the associative trails of a hypertext document, you would eventually start to see the multi-nodal pattern of meanings by which this young and vibrant industry is erecting its own language. It is our hope that you will enjoy and be instructed by our efforts to define the elements of the industry.

Acknowledgments

As with any book, we are indebted to many individuals. In particular, for providing us with professional vision, we are indebted to Nicholas Negroponte of the Media Lab at MIT and to George Gilder, noted author of multimedia and virtual reality works. We also wish personally to thank Mike Vollmer and Pam Schaepe, both of whom make substantial contributions to multimedia on a daily basis; L.W. Leonard and T.P. Rud of IDC Information Design Corporation; and Dr. Marjorie Davis, School of Engineering, Mercer University, Macon Campus. Thank you.

INTRODUCTION
The Multimedia Industry

After spending the 1970s and 1980s cloistered in the great technology incubator, the phenomenon we have grown accustomed to—multimedia—has exploded onto the technological landscape in the 1990s with a force that even its most vocal advocates had not imagined possible. But what is it? Most of the authors of the considerable volume of what is being written about the subject are downright bewildered when pressed on this blunt question. It would appear that, in spite of abrupt and blaring pronouncements in the media, the identity of this new medium is poorly understood. The coming of the Web in the past few years, which has been so incredibly beneficial to everyone engaged in any segment of multimedia, has done nothing to clear the conceptual fog that envelops the fundamental definition of multimedia.

Could it be that the future of multimedia is now happening so fast that we have totally lost our place in the procession of technological history? Probably. But there are a number of reasonably cogent things that can be said about multimedia and about where this emergent medium is heading. Based upon the reflections of a handful of industry leaders and early conceptual pioneers, it is possible to round up at least a thimbleful of useful ideas. We offer them here as a provisional explanation of what's happening.

Three Industry Segments

The early market for multimedia applications appears to have divided itself into three fairly distinct segments:

1. **The Home Market,** which owes its origins to the likes of Sega, Nintendo, and the other adolescent video games, is now on the verge of blossoming into a much more robust enterprise. The games are becoming more sophisticated and intelligent and are now offering some of the first genres capable of attracting and holding an adult audience. Just around the corner looms the promise of interactive television, WebTV, the teleputer, the network computer (NC), etc. Whatever we end up naming it, one thing is

certain: its injection into the home will threaten to turn the standard American couch potato into the newly rejuvenated couch commando.

2. **The School Market,** which owes its origins to the small-scale, curriculum-based programs that ran on Apple IIs, has recently played host to the large-scale integrated learning systems that rank among the most sophisticated forms of instructional software yet created. These systems integrate the electronic delivery of course content across broad, multi-grade spans of content and deliver that content via network-based client/server systems that monitor learner performance in specific, objectives-level detail. The advent of the Web promises to infuse this industry with even more positive energy. With all of the great debate over the declining quality of the American education system, the pressure to explore various forms of instructional technology will keep this market growing at a rapid pace into the future.

3. **The Business Market,** which is, ironically, the most underdeveloped segment of the interactive market, has great growth potential. The tremendous pressure to reengineer business practices and processes in almost every sector of our economy will likely elevate the attractiveness of interactive training solutions. Corporate America is seeking ways to quickly and efficiently train large and geographically dispersed workforces as never before, and now that the corporate desktop is coming to be occupied by MPCs (multimedia personal computers), and these machines are being attached to insightfully constructed corporate intranets, the inclination to use interactive multimedia is beginning to grow dramatically.

In sum, every segment of the multimedia market should continue to grow vigorously into the first decades of the next millennium. The business market will be driven by the need to constantly train and retrain a diverse workforce. The school market will be fueled by mounting pressures to modify—if not overhaul—an antiquated instructional delivery system. And the home market will likely be the liveliest of all, as the twitch-and-shoot design model of first-generation electronic games matures into several successor genres, including the first interactive forms of fiction and cinema.

The hype is not unfounded. The wave of mergers and acquisitions we have witnessed between previously segregated portions of the information economy are early harbingers of an explosively innovative future. The massive and cash-rich telecommunications firms are buying entertainment and computing companies. Print publishing firms are seeking alliances with software companies. In fact, virtually every permutation of linkage between these various stewards of information is being pursued with almost frantic vigor. The maturation of the Web, and the enormous expectations associated with e-commerce, should keep the cross-pollination of information industries going for some time to come.

All of these enterprises must be positioning themselves for something. But for what?

Multimedia Is about Converging Industries and Technologies

In 1978 Nicholas Negroponte, one of the true savants of multimedia, used a Venn diagram and his intellectual track record as an MIT professor to raise $70 million to launch the Media Lab—an organization dedicated to contemplating the far-flung technological horizons of communications. In the Venn diagram, Negroponte showed that three industries were converging to form a single technological powerhouse, one that would dominate the future of human communications. Those three industries were the printing and publishing industry, the computer industry, and the broadcast and motion picture industry.

He projected that the overlap between these three industries would approach a near union by the end of the century. And while many futurists would have us forget their projections when their foretold future has arrived, Negroponte's premonitions seem more and more worthy of acknowledgment the closer we get to the year 2000. Clearly, these industries are converging.

If anything, that convergence is ahead of schedule. And the multifarious outcomes of that convergence are a large part of what we are calling multimedia. They involve new products, new services, and new genres of art and entertainment. In fact, the impact that can be attributed to the inter-industrial convergence that is multimedia seems to broaden with each passing year (and certainly with each new journalistic interpretation). For one, Negroponte's anticipation of personal TV—a class of high-bandwidth and content-rich communication that is tailored to the individual—is now essentially with us in the form of push technology and WebTV. That portion of the information age that can be associated with multimedia is—it would appear—just slightly ahead of schedule.

The span of topics covered in the trade and academic presses by articles that feature either of the principal terms in our title—"multimedia" or "Web" —is still staggering. Much of what is written focuses on the enabling technologies, such as networking, transmission, the new forms of mass storage, the playback environments, and the ever-expanding array of authoring tools. Many of the articles claim that, in the final analysis, content is king, and then proceed to spray the journalistic canvas with widely diverging interpretations of what exactly constitutes multimedia content.

Many writers think of multimedia as videoconferencing and its various derivatives, such as document conferencing, distance learning, and video mail. Others see multimedia content as a new form of publishing, and therefore view many of the new media as probable candidates for cannibalizing their paper-based and linear counterparts from the long history of analog media. These new interactive replacements include electronic catalogs and brochures, which will likely replace their passive and inferior ancestors of the same name (sans the "interactive"). They also include electronic encyclopedias and computer-based training programs, which are expected to replace the static encyclopedia and textbook, respectively. In the arts, there are the more speculative interactive fiction and fantasy games, which some anticipate will replace the most venerated form of document in our cultural history—namely, the novel.

Still others see multimedia technology as a natural step in the direction of increasingly sophisticated and immersive media. These writers and thinkers are prone to let their thoughts drift among such topics as 3-D audio and video, motion platforms and force feedback, even into the exotica associated with cyberspace and virtual reality.

Regardless of how one chooses to judge these various attempts to describe and classify the elements associated with multimedia, one thing is absolutely clear: multimedia is a serious phenomenon. It connects to our most salient historical arcs. The merging of computers and media now permits the author—or, as in film, the authoring team—to enlist and engage the audience as never before. Rather than watching the performance of a protagonist from a detached and safe-harbor seat in the theater, the listener-reader-viewer must now become something new and unprecedented in the history of the narrative arts. The audience member must now become an active participant, must now become the very protagonist whose performance is the thing that is judged.

The convergence of publishing with computers and media means that shoppers and learners and explorers will be able to take control of their media in ways that enable them to find just the right advertisement relative to their immediate needs. By accessing large, Web-based curricula, they will be able to individualize their training experiences by matching instructional content to personal skill and knowledge deficiencies. And, by participating in multiplayer, real-time games across the Web, they will be able to challenge themselves in ways not possible even a few years ago.

As we contemplate the consequences of the converging technologies that are now being called multimedia, it is prudent to take stock of a lesser known, but highly appropriate, quote from Marshall McLuhan:

> The hybrid or meeting of two media is a moment of truth and revelation of which new form is born. . . . The crossings of media release great force.
>
> *Understanding Media*, 1964.

As we further devote our thoughts to the proposition of responding to a steady flow of new, hybrid forms of media, it is also prudent to ask . . .

Why Bother?

Imagining—for just a moment—that it might be possible for us to seize control of the innovation fuel line that feeds our capitalist engine, what type and amount of pressure would we want to place on the nozzle that regulates the pace of new media? Imagining that ours might become the invisible hand of Adam Smith's economy, how would we adjust our grip when it came time to determine the rate at which we permit our traditional media to transform themselves via the synthesizing force of digitization?

To inform the grip in our thus deified hand, it would be appropriate to ask the larger question: what is the value of these new forms of media? In other words, what are the advantages of multimedia? In framing the answer to this question, we must first conjure at least a working definition of the proper scope of the term. In other words, we must first answer the question: over what span of human interests will this upstart and wildly hybrid medium have a significant impact?

Even at this relatively early juncture, the answer to this question seems obvious: the impact of multimedia will be global, in both a literal and a figurative sense. Like all previous major forms of communication, multimedia will—in the fullness of time—have a significant impact on every industry and population segment.

Using this perspective to frame the question "why bother?" and, thereby, informing our decision making with regard to our imagined control over the rate of appearance for new media, it would seem appropriate to respond by looking at two broad divisions of our economy: the arts and entertainment industries and the remainder of the business world.

What beneficial impacts will multimedia have on the arts and entertainment industries, particularly now that is has a wide-area deployment mechanism in the form of the Web? More to the point, what benefits will multimedia bestow on the creators of artistic and entertainment products—or on what is being broadly referred to today as "content"? Stated with just one more minor twist: why would our most gifted creators of content take leave of the venerable media of our ancestors and contemporaries (novels, film, painting, etc.) to risk their highly valued time and effort on producing the emerging artifacts of multimedia?

To provide at least a provisional answer to these critical questions, we would like to turn to the insights of an individual whose career predated multimedia, but who remains important because he is the man who many would consider to be perhaps the most credible practitioner of the avant-garde in the twentieth century. That person is Alain Robbe-Grillet, the French novelist who experimented more on the narrative form than any other writer in this century. Though very much on the fringe of the mainstream, Robbe-Grillet captured much critical attention, particularly with works such as *The Voyeur* and *Last Year at Marienbad.*

During his career, Robbe-Grillet penned several essays on the transformation of the narrative form, a subject on which—as we have stated—he had unparalleled expertise. He understood the restless nature of art, particularly in this, our most restless of centuries. Several of these essays were gathered together into the little-known 1965 volume *For a New Novel.* In analyzing the motivating forces that are currently driving us in the direction of new, interactive forms of art, it is appropriate that we exhume some of the thoughts expressed in this mid-1960s collection.

More than anything else, Robbe-Grillet—in both his novels and his philosophical reflections—believed that the great historical arc of our storytelling tradition is the trend toward increasing levels of realism.

It has always been the same: out of a concern for realism each new literary school has sought to destroy the one which preceded it; this was the watchword of the romantics against the classicists, then of the naturalists against the romantics; the surrealists themselves declared in their turn that they were concerned only with the real world.

Central to this trend toward greater realism, in Robbe-Grillet's mind, is the ability for the author to gain increasingly direct access to the audience. In a comment that anticipates the dawn of interactive art forms—though it is clear that he was not specifically thinking of anything like interactive multimedia or virtual reality at the time—Robbe-Grillet states: *"far from neglecting him, the author today proclaims his absolute need of the reader's cooperation, an active, conscious, creative assistance."*

Reading a Robbe-Grillet novel today, two to three decades after its release, is still a strange experience. Many people find his works impossible to penetrate. This is not the time or place to explore the specific attributes that make them seem so out of the ordinary, but what is appropriate to mention here is their most stunning attribute. What Robbe-Grillet is trying to do is eliminate the usual gulf that separates the reader's psyche from that of the main character. He is laboring to place the reader as far *into* the action of the novel as is possible via a literary instrument. In a sense, Robbe-Grillet is trying to make the presence of the author disappear, and thus bring the reader into direct and naked contact with the protagonist's experience.

Robbe-Grillet speaks so directly to the issues surrounding the emergence of new media, because he did not foresee those media in any specific detail. Rather, he saw the larger forces and trends, of which they are a part, that are a natural extension of the late–twentieth century. Like its immediate predecessor, film, an interactive multimedia program provides the author with a leap forward in terms of the power to re-create the scenes and dramas of humans, and thereby extends our storytelling tradition's venerable drive toward greater realism.

Interactive forms of storytelling and entertainment force the audience into the work of art by making them active participants in the creative process. When an audience member plays the role of a protagonist and makes decisions that influence outcome, something fundamental and powerful has happened. As in a Robbe-Grillet novel, the consumer of an interactive fiction experiences direct contact with the narrative circumstances of the story.

The forces motivating the emergence of interactive and increasingly immersive forms of art and entertainment are powerful. They are deeply rooted in much larger historical trajectories and, therefore, must seem inevitable to us no matter what fits and starts and skepticism may greet them during their initial stages. But what of more practical applications? What of the role of multimedia in the world of commerce and industry?

Again, we see powerful trends, but they issue from a different set of motivating forces. Multimedia will play a large role in the business world, but the forces that write the history of interactive media in this market segment will not be the same as in the arts and entertainment world. Here, the key motivating factor appears to be something that we might refer to as *the velocity of information.*

If we follow the major themes that have appeared in business literature over the past few decades, we see that there is wide agreement on what the key trends are: the globalization of the world economy, leading to increased levels of competition in almost every industry segment; the need to compress every aspect of the product life cycle, from R&D to manufacturing, and especially into sales and marketing; the penetration of microprocessor-based forms of machine intelligence into almost every type of product and service, leading to an amplification of the forces behind technology-driven change; and, most critical of all, the need for organizations to employ a dynamic and flexible workforce, thus enabling them to change course quickly in response to sudden opportunities and/ or competitive threats.

All of these themes relate directly to the need for organizations to change quickly, which means they need to increase the rate at which they are able to learn and absorb new processes and technologies. This whole manner of thinking has recently received a great deal of attention under the moniker of the "learning organization." As never before, the pressure to increase the velocity of information beats down on us, both from an individual and an organizational standpoint.

Thus, any technology that can make this acceleration more bearable, that can speed our rates of learning without breaking the bank, will hold great appeal. And while the first generation of interactive training programs has had its fair share of disappointments, there is no doubt that the long-term potential of interactive media in the business world is great.

In fact, a number of studies have appeared over the past few decades that document the power of well-designed interactive training programs. It has been validated that a well-conceived interactive product can be more effective than any other form of instruction, save perhaps the one-on-one mentoring that occurs between learner and expert in the heat of corporate battle. But experts are almost always scarce, and, therefore, they are very expensive resources. They can be leveraged somewhat by using a seminar format. However, this form of instruction reduces the reach of the training, while at the same time abandoning the intense levels of interaction that make one-on-one mentoring so valuable in the first place.

The features of interactive multimedia that make for an effective instructional delivery platform are abundant and are by now fairly well known. They include the ability to offer learners an appropriate level of control over the learning experience; to ask questions of learners, thereby forcing their direct involvement; to track the performance of learners over a range of questions and other interactive challenges, thereby building up profiles of learner knowledge and skill; to prescribe entire learning sequences on the basis of objectively determined skill gaps; to use multiple and appropriate forms of media to meet the unique needs of particular instructional challenges and student populations; to track learning preferences, as well as performances, thereby enabling programs to match delivery formats to learning styles; and to link a diverse database of training resources to the even more diverse learning needs of large audiences, thus providing the long-awaited power and promise of individualized instruction.

The benefits of an effective piece of interactive multimedia to a business organization—especially when it can be delivered across the Web—are both numerous and potentially profound. It enables an organization to leverage the knowledge and skills of its strongest performers by encoding their expertise into the pedagogical logic of the program. It makes it possible for large and geographically dispersed companies to significantly reduce—if not eliminate—the high travel and lodging costs associated with offering seminars. It offers learners the ability to take the training wherever and whenever they need it, a phenomenon called just-in-time learning. It enables organizations to discern knowledge levels in their workforce and, thus, be able to address specific strengths and weaknesses. And it offers managers the ability to track the effectiveness of their investments in training, and to better allocate their future training expenditures.

Though the business world has been slow to adopt interactive solutions, the mounting evidence that these programs can deliver some powerful benefits is beginning to reduce the resistance. The advent of the Web has further diminished the opposition to serious corporate investments in instructional technology, because it single-handedly destroys the biggest existing obstacle to interactive training—the lack of a mechanism for quickly and efficiently deploying content across the enterprise. However, more important than even these forces is the pressure on organizations to increase the velocity with which information travels through their ranks. Many executives are realizing that this need to constantly accelerate the acquisition of new knowledge and skill is the most urgent business requirement to which they must now respond. And, this realization will make interactive forms of instruction a necessity in the near future.

But Will It Be Easy?

Increasingly, interactive forms of media appear destined to stand in the same relationship to the twenty-first century as film and TV have to our own. The current floodtide of journalistic interest is almost "willing" the transition from linear to interactive. But many factors will make the transition difficult, expensive, and painful. In fact, at least two of the most significant problems have already made themselves quite apparent.

The most fundamental aspect of the interactive revolution is its most problematic— the digitization of audiovisual forms of information. This relatively straightforward process holds the potential for unleashing some of the most powerful change agents in the history of the capitalist world. Unfortunately, there is no question about its having unleashed a tremendous set of technological problems.

If we consider the past three decades to be the formative years of computer technology—as most experts do—then it can be said that the formative period in the history of computing was all about the processing of symbolic forms of information, i.e., of text and numbers. As it turns out, digitally encoded forms of symbolic information are very compact, though this was certainly not the prevailing sentiment even just a decade ago when personal computers were only capable of storing and manipulating a few million characters—or about the equivalent of a few healthy books. With the subsequent advent of multi-gigabyte hard drives, and the optical wonders of CD-ROM and DVD, we can now comfortably state that computers have swallowed our books and accounting records. The lone remaining problem lies in getting this information better organized.

But when we move on to the task of digitally encoding the audio and video sources of information, we reenter the domain of the humble—

the very humble. One second of uncompressed, television-quality video requires over 27 megabytes of storage and transmission bandwidth. Pursuing this equation to some of its more painful conclusions, we find that the mighty CD-ROM player is capable of handling just about 30 seconds of uncompressed video, and that a full-length motion picture would require close to 200 gigabytes, which is way beyond what even the most robust standard for DVD can handle. Put another way, an hour of uncompressed, TV-quality video requires approximately the amount of storage that one would expect to find handling the entire data processing needs of a medium-sized corporation. Cough.

The digitization of media—of audio, image, and video—has created a crisis in the computer *and* the communications industries. The appearance of the Web—though wonderful for having provided us with our first public transmission infrastructure for digital media—has done nothing but accentuate the magnitude of the bandwidth crisis. Most of the Web-surfing public must wait for their digital content as it crosses the ever-so-narrow portal of their 28.8 Kbps modem.

Though a multitude of compression/decompression schemes have entered the marketplace in the past half-decade, the problems associated with displaying, storing, and transmitting the volumes of data needed to encode media are still immense. Computers are not fast enough. Storage devices do not have enough capacity. And the networks do not have nearly enough bandwidth, particularly along the now-infamous "last-mile loop" (i.e., the copper telephone line that connects your home to the phone company's central office).

If you look at a multimedia title or Web site and wonder at the relatively poor quality of their media assets, consider them to be a manifestation of this larger problem. Barring some unforeseeable innovation, the challenge of mastering this undercapacitation will be at the center of the multimedia industry for at least the next decade. Satellite and other wireless forms of communication hold the promise of at least partially satiating our enormous appetite for bandwidth, as does the gradual deployment of fiber optic cabling. But the ability to deliver Madison-Avenue quality digital content into the office and the home will likely take some time.

The bandwidth crisis is not the only one that threatens our transition into the age of multimedia. Perhaps it is not even the most difficult. As one contemplates the convergence of media—of print and publishing with computers, and of both of these with film and television—the most tumultuous proposition would appear to be the imminent collision of the cultures that preside over these various media with decisively differ-ent styles, values, and knowledge sets.

Take, for example, the separate cultures that preside over multime-dia—the computer industry, on the one hand, and the film and TV in-dustry, on the other. Both are global leaders. Both require extremely large numbers of finely specialized and highly talented individuals. Both are proud to a fault, even ethnocentric. Neither tribe will take too kindly to the inevitable turf intrusions of the other. And it is impossible to imag-ine that there will be many safe passages across the corporate battle-field, which has already witnessed so many aggressive acquisitions and takeovers. As one contemplates the near future of the multimedia indus-try, the inevitable rivalries between organizations and professions are among the most troubling of the expectations.

Yet another substantial problem has recently reared its head. Ironi-cally, this problem did not become fully manifest *until* the Internet grew so rapidly in popularity. Curiously, it is a problem that the library sci-ence community has known about for quite some time; and it has a wide variety of colorful names, the two most common being "information overload" and "infoglut." When people perform an innocent query on the Internet using one of today's search engines, and receive feedback from the system informing them that they have received 5,000–10,000 responses, or hits, then they have come face-to-face with this problem. They have come face-to-face with the problem of high recall, but very low precision. The knowledge that is needed is probably out there, but no one seems able to find it efficiently.

There is no easy answer to the problem of "infoglut." With particu-lar reference to the Web, it is resulting from the accumulated placement of untold millions of complex, document-like objects onto Web sites around the world. Few of these potentially valuable objects have been indexed in any meaningful way, and among those that have, the kind of sophisticated standard that will make the Internet a truly navigable place to visit is not yet available.

As with its sister problems of bandwidth scarcity and professional collision, the problem of information overload is drawing a great deal of attention. One can only hope that a great deal of investment from the business community will also follow. Several major research initiatives have already been funded by the federal government, and an organiza-tion known as the Online Computer Library Center (OCLC) is doing much creative and very promising work in an area known as metadata.

History may well record that the first decade of the next millennium earned the headlines: "Revenge of the Librarians."

It Will Be All of These Things

The coming decades will see the rise of multimedia, replete with opportunities and pitfalls. The convergence of multiple industries of the most powerful sort will further accelerate the forces of technology-associated change. New forms of media—electronic brochures, interactive fictions, Web-enabled simulations, even virtual reality—will appear with clockwork regularity. Some of them will quickly ascend to the role of major social change agent, much as telephony and television have done in our century.

There is no reason not to feel the same sort of excitement about the prospects of multimedia that one indulges in over such phenomena as genetic engineering and major space exploration programs. This enthusiasm, however, should be tempered by some equally legitimate anxieties. As individuals with careers that will be impacted by these new media technologies, how should we govern our career path decisions? As organizations, which of these risky and expensive technologies should we commit to, and when? And, as a society, how should we manage (regulate) these new industries to minimize some of their potentially destructive influences?

We have written this present and humble volume in an effort to make our contribution to easing the anxiety and conflict that will no doubt accompany the coming of multimedia. As we stated in the foreword, one of the most substantial conflicts will appear early—has, in fact, already appeared. It is the clash of professional vocabularies, of nomenclatures. If we can help some of these contributory industries understand and appreciate the language and concepts and potential of the others, then we will have hit our mark.

If interactive breaks through the barriers between entertainment and the entertained, the next step may be to break down the wall between the real world and the artificial computer world.
— **The Hollywood Reporter**

A/B roll editing: This process of splicing and combining two or more videotapes, the most common of editing functions, is now being made far more flexible and easy to do by the advent of *digital video production tools*.

accelerator board: This term refers to a class of *expansion board* used in personal computers to speed up their performance, usually in relation to processing the display of visual information. Machines built to process alphanumeric forms of information now need to process *mixed media data types* (e.g., audio, image, *video*). These accelerator boards, directly connected to the computer's monitor, process the movement of *pixels,* taking the burden off of the computer's *CPU* (central processing unit). High-end, high-performance *boards* use a special type of memory known as *VRAM* (pronounced "vee-ram," and stands for video random access memory), which allows the computer to write new information to a memory location while the old information is being read.

acceptable use: Very important in the emerging culture of *cyberspace,* this term refers to the guidelines for acceptable online behavior required of users by most *ISPs* (Internet service providers). These guidelines vary from one provider to another.

access key: With the advent of the massive storage capabilities made possible by *DVD, CD-ROM,* and *optical storage* in general, an increasing number of application developers are making use of this technology, which is a software-*encoded* key allowing access to a group of files protected by a file protection code. With large *clip media* libraries, for example, by using this technology the developer can enable users to pay for only those portions of a particular library that they need.

access provider: From the *Internet,* this term refers to a company that sells Internet connections. Other synonyms include Internet service providers (*ISPs*) and Internet access providers (*IAPs*). You contact an ISP when you first determine that you wish to be connected to the *Web*.

access rights: A general term used in the area of computer security, it refers to the authorization needed for a specific level of access to some form of electronic resource, such as a corporate database containing all sales transactions.

access time: Refers to the location and recovery time of information requested by a user on the computer.

accuracy aids: From the realm of computer graphics, this term refers to various preprogrammed techniques, such as *snap-to grids,* that enable a designer to achieve positioning accuracy on an interactive display.

acoustic coupler: A nearly obsolete piece of *data communications* hardware, an acoustic coupler functions as a *modem* by converting a computer's *digital signals* into chirps to be sent over the telephone line, and, conversely, by converting the chirps received back into digital signals intelligible to the computer. As an historical footnote, the acoustic coupler represents the first technology to make connection between nontelephonic devices and the telephone system possible. In 1966, a small Texas company called Carterfone invented a simple device that used acoustic coupling to make it possible for two-way radios to connect to a telephone line. For some time now, this basic function has been served by the *modem.*

active display: Relative to the handling of *digital video* in memory, this term refers to that portion of the video memory currently being displayed, as opposed to screen contents being held in memory for later display (if needed).

active learning: Almost synonymous with *discovery learning,* this term refers to the learning approach that facilitates the self-motivated, mature adult, who, in a course of instruction, is actively engaged in putting together content with his or her colleagues and the instructor. The opposite approach is "inactive," traditional learning, in which the instructor stands in front of a standard classroom lecturing to a passive audience that is often assumed to be relatively ignorant of the subject matter. Active learning has become a very important principle in the *instructional design* of multimedia-based training (*MBT*), where it is employed to keep learners involved and in control of their learning experiences.

active window: With graphical user interfaces (*GUIs*) based on the *desktop metaphor* (such as the Apple Macintosh or the Microsoft *Windows interface*), it is always possible to have several *windows* open on the desktop at any one time. However, for the sake of maintaining order, it is only possible to have one of those windows active at any one time. Thus, the window where the user's actions are directed at a given moment is referred to as the active window.

ActiveX: This is Microsoft's third-generation component architecture (VBX and OCX were the first two). ActiveX objects, known also as "ActiveX controls" or "ActiveX components," are units of code that serve a range of functions. These functions can include creating specific application items as trivial as a single *button* on a graphical *interface,* all the way to creating more complex and comprehensive items such as building an entire application. It is not a language, but a set of rules for how applications should share information. They can be programmed in Visual Basic, C++, or *Java.* ActiveX objects supply precoded reusable functionality for use in any programming application, especially *Web pages.* An ActiveX object can reside on any computer and be accessed over any *network,* i.e., a *LAN,* a *WAN,* or the *Internet.* If an object is not available on a machine, it can be automatically *downloaded* when required. ActiveX controls differ from Java *applets* in two ways. First, ActiveX components can make use of all the facilities of the *Windows* operating systems, which Java cannot do. Unfortunately, this privilege raises the risk of damaging the system. To counter this risk, Microsoft provides a registration service for verifying ActiveX controls before downloading them. The second main difference is that ActiveX controls are only available in Windows, whereas Java is available across most *platforms.*

A/D converter: A device that samples an *analog signal* at regular intervals and *quantizes* each sample. An A/D converter stands as the primary translator between the real world of analog phenomena and the computer world of *digital* phenomena. The most important aspect of the A/D conversion process is the *sampling rate,* which measures the *frequency* with which the analog phenomena are *converted* into digitally *encoded* numbers, and, therefore, expresses the *resolution,* or quality, of the A/D conversion. The higher the sampling rate, the more accurately the digitally encoded data represent the analog phenomena being measured or *captured.* Any type of probe or sensor that *interfaces* to the computer (e.g., a *digital thermometer*) is an example of an A/D converter. As the world becomes increasingly computerized, A/D converters will be widespread.

ADC: Stands for Analog-to-Digital Conversion of data.

address: With regard to data processing, this term refers to a character, a group of characters, or other *bit* patterns that occupy, and can be accessed through, a particular storage location in computer memory. With regard to electronic mail, the term refers to the location used to specify the source or destination of an *e-mail* message. The form of the address is usually the name of the *mailbox* followed by @ and the *host name*. An example is the address: jan.smith@mercer.edu. With regard to the *Internet,* the term refers to the location that allows access to programs, files, computers, and other resources. An example is an *IP address* that refers to a precise location within specific *networks.*

ADF: Stands for Automatic Document Feeder, a mechanism that attaches to a *scanner* and allows unattended scanning of multiple images. This relatively simple device is a great labor-saver for the emerging document imaging industry.

Adobe Photoshop: Adobe Photoshop is a *paint* program, which was developed first for the Macintosh, but is now available on the PC as well. It has been, and continues to be, the industry standard against which other paint programs are measured.

ADPCM: Adaptive Delta Pulse Code Modulation is a technique for translating *analog* audio into *digital* audio. As the term "delta" implies, this technique belongs to a large family of digitization techniques that rely on correlating patterns of *amplitude* over time. It is a direct descendent of *pulse code modulation* (PCM).

ADSL: Otherwise known as the Asymmetrical Digital Subscriber Line, and often referred to by the shorter acronym of *DSL.* This technology was developed by Bellcore, which is the research arm of Bell Labs dedicated to the interests of the so-called baby bells, e.g., Bell Atlantic. ADSL enables the providers of telephone services to supply *video* services for the residential market over the copper wire *transmission* lines that have been traditionally used for providing *POTS* (plain old telephone service). This is a strategic technology for the telephone companies. At present, the telephone companies may be at a competitive disadvantage to the cable operators with regard to providing *multimedia* services like the videophone to the home market. Cable operators own the coaxial cable used to deliver cable TV service to the home market, which provides them with a sizable *bandwidth* advantage over the copper lines that telephone companies own for delivering their *signals.* ADSL may neutralize this comparative disadvantage. It uses specially designed transmitters and receivers that reduce the interference and *noise* normally experienced on a copper line. The technology makes it possible to transmit television-quality, compressed video over ordinary copper wire.

Before the advent of ADSL, the goal of merging the switching capabilities of the *public-switched telephone network* (PSTN) with the ability to carry a video signal would have required the telephone companies to provide curbside optical fiber lines to every home, which is an enormously expensive proposition. This technology is directed at eliminating that need.

Advanced Interactive Video: Also referred to by its acronym, "AIV," this term refers to a *laserdisc* format developed in 1986 by Philips UK and a number of other media and computer interests. The format accommodates *analog video, digital* audio, and digital data on the same laserdisc surface. Also referred to as *LV-ROM,* this format is suffering from the same fate that has befallen the other laserdisc formats: namely, a diminishing popularity in comparison to the all-digital formats associated with *CD-ROM* and *DVD*.

Advisory Committee on Advanced Television Service: This ad hoc committee was established to recommend from among competing technologies a single set of functional specifications to the FCC for an *HDTV* (high-definition television) standard.

aftertouch: Also referred to as "pressure-sensitive," this is an attribute of more sophisticated *MIDI* (musical instrument digital interface) keyboards with which the amount of pressure placed on a key is *encoded* as part of the MIDI data stream. In other words, when a player presses a key on the MIDI keyboard, not only is the code for that particular key generated, but so too is an additional code that describes how much pressure was employed in pressing the key. Obviously, this attribute enables the MIDI standard to encode a finer set of distinctions into its *digital* representation of music.

age of interactivity: This term is slowly emerging from the trade journals and carries with it some probability that it will replace the currently popular phrase "information age" as the label du jour for describing the technology-intensive era in which we live. The term age of interactivity bears many important connotations: that we will soon see the mass media of broadcast TV and film turn to interactive forms of presentation and entertainment; that ye olde technology of *telephony* will soon be revitalized by the *video dial tone;* that the classroom model of education—dominant for the entire history of public education—will begin to give way to interactive forms of instructional delivery, such as we are now calling *educational software* (a.k.a. *CAI, CBT, IVD,* etc.); and that *interactive cinema* and a number of the other *cyberarts* will gradually replace linear, one-way forms of narrative, such as fiction and film, as the dominant modes of storytelling and mass entertainment.

agents: This is a relatively new type of software module that implements technologies to understand the user's spoken or written requrests, and then, in servant-like fashion, to comply with them. This term is roughly synonymous with *interface agents,* varying from that term only in the sense that it represents the more general and abstract machine intelligence that lies behind, and makes possible, the functioning of an interface agent.

AIFF: Stands for Audio Interchange File Format, which is one of the earliest file format standards for *digital* audio. Originally developed by Apple Computer for the Macintosh family of personal computers, AIFF files can be spotted on *disk* directories by looking for the slightly truncated .aif file extension.

alerts: From the world of graphical user interface (*GUI*) design, these *interface* elements, also referred to as alert boxes, notify the user when an unusual, or possibly damaging, condition has occurred.

alias: A shortened, substitute name for a file or device on a computer or *network.* These shortened names can be depicted as *icons* instead of as character text.

aliasing: These are unwanted visual effects in *raster images,* especially jagged lines and edges (*jaggies*) caused by improper or low-quality *sampling* techniques. Aliasing (pronounced "Ollie-oz-ing") is one of the most common visual *artifacts* in the era of *digital media.*

AltaVista: Digital Equipment Corporation at its Palo Alto research labs began with the huge mission in 1995 to index the entire *Internet* and provide a *search engine* for *WWW* users. AltaVista was the result of this effort, and is now one of the most prominent directories of information on the Internet along with *Yahoo!* and Lycos.

ALU: Arithmetic Logic Unit refers to that specialized part of the *CPU* that performs arithmetic and logic operations.

Ames Research Center: Located along Route 101 in Silicon Valley, this NASA research center is responsible for pioneering many of the foundational technologies of *virtual reality* (VR) and *simulation* systems. Home to noted VR inventor Scott Fisher, this center is responsible for developing, among other creations, the *Convolvotron* directional audio system, the *virtual* planetary exploration (VPE) system, and the virtual interactive environmental workstation (VIEWS).

amplitude: With regard to audio and/or *video signals,* amplitude refers to the strength of a given signal. Amplitude is measured in various units depending on the application. For example, with audio signals, the measurement is in *decibels,* which is a logarithmic scale based on human hearing sensitivities. For audio, amplitude is a measure of volume; for video, it is a measure of image contrast.

analog: In electronics, analog is a continuously variable *signal.* Analog signals are often depicted as waveforms, and in the computer world are always held in contrast to the discretely variable *digital* signals, which represent separate datapoints in space and time. Analog phenomena in nature include waves, time, temperature, and voltage.

anchor: A very important term in the world of the *Internet,* an anchor is a *HTML* code that indicates the beginning and end of a *hypertext link.* For example, <a href="www.ibm.*com*">IBM</a> is the HTML code necessary for an anchor link that takes one to a destination *Web site.* The HTML code <a href="www.ibm.com"> indicates the beginning of the anchor and </a> indicates the end of an anchor. In this example, clicking on the anchor source (IBM) takes you to the anchor destination, which is the IBM Web site. Without anchors and anchor HTML code, the universal behavior of *hyperlinking* on the Internet would not be possible. On the *Web pages* of Web sites, anchors are highlighted to differentiate them from the normal text. This lets users know that they can link to another site by simply clicking on the anchor.

animated blobs: Created by Carnegie-Mellon University's Joseph Bates, these creations represent one of the first attempts at automated storytelling using the principles of *object-oriented programming.* The blobs are self-contained, intelligent objects, programmed according to the rules of behavioral theory. The way blobs encounter each other sparks emotional responses that, in chain-reaction form, cause additional reactions so that they appear to be creating their own spontaneous drama.

animated map: A series of maps strung together to create a moving image, typically used to show spatio-temporal patterns such as the distribution of population in the United States over the course of several decades. This presentational technique is part of a large trend in *multimedia* known as *scientific visualization,* where structured data sets are drawn upon to create imagery that enhances the process of communicating complex concepts.

animation: Is the process of displaying artwork over time to simulate motion. Most animation belongs to one of two types: graphic or character. "Graphic animation" is generally composed of a single piece of art whose position changes over time (e.g., a moving logo). To create movement, one piece of art has intermediate positions rather than intermediate drawings. Graphic animation is relatively easy to master, does not require drawing skills, and, in a computer environment, requires only modest storage and processing power. "Character animation," in contrast, entails generating a different piece of art for each *frame,* as is done for film and TV cartoons. In traditional character animation, an artist works at a light table, creating each frame by transferring a drawing from paper to acetate (called a *cel*) and hand coloring it with paint. Two key drawings—which are the principal points of movement for each frame—punctuate several "inbetweens," which, as the name implies, are the intermediate drawings between *key frames.* With *desktop* animation tools, many of the more arduous tasks of traditional animation, such as *inbetweening,* are automated, leaving open the potential for an enormous growth in the use of character animation for many purposes, such as *edutainment* products.

ANSI: Stands for the American National Standards Institute, a standards-making body for the computer industry, most famous for its *ASCII* standard format for encoding characters in the PC environment.

answer analysis: From the realm of *educational software,* this term refers to the simplest, lowest level of *performance tracking,* where the programmer writes code to analyze a learner's response to a single question. The most common form is the multiple-choice question, where the program simply branches on the basis of whether or not the learner answered the question correctly.

anti-aliasing: *Aliasing* is perhaps the most commonly cited visual *artifact* of computer graphics, whereby boundaries take on a stair-step pattern, often referred to as the *jaggies.* Anti-aliasing refers to techniques designed to sharpen the image by switching *pixels* to intermediate intensities along either side of otherwise jagged diagonal lines. Anti-aliasing techniques are particularly important with displays that feature relatively low *resolution.*

AO/DI: Stands for Always On/Dynamic ISDN, which is a form of *ISDN* designed to facilitate *persistent connections* and scalable *bandwidth.* Under AO/DI, the *D-channel* is always open to accommodate data *transmissions.* Because the D-channel has such limited bandwidth (16 *Kbps*), it is only capable of handling modest transmissions, such as those associated with incoming *e-mail,* and trickles of information from *push technology* vendors. However, through a *protocol* called *BACP* (bandwidth allocation control protocol), AO/DI opens the much broader *B-channel* (64 Kbps) when it detects that the D-channel is at full capacity. In this way, AO/DI can actually reduce the overall costs of the communication line by provisioning, and then releasing (i.e., by scaling) bandwidth in conjunction with variations in data traffic.

API: Stands for Application Programming Interface, a general term used in *software engineering* to describe the point at which software modules, layers, or components meet and interconnect. When software engineers speak of APIs, they are typically referring to the standards and *protocols* that govern communication between two or more independently designed software programs.

applet: These are programs created within the *Java* programming environment that can be inserted within the *HTML* code of a document available on a *Web site.* Java works in conjunction with certain *browsers;* however, not all browsers support Java applets.

application program: Refers to the most common and visible form of business software in use today. Word processors, spreadsheets, and *e-mail* programs are all types of application programs. Most individuals and organizations buy their application programs from commercial vendors, who are often referred to as *ISVs* (independent software vendors). Many large organizations also build several of their own critical application programs using their own internal development resources, a challenging process referred to as "application development," or AD.

archie: From the *Internet,* this term refers to a program developed at McGill University School of Computer Science that searches *FTP archives,* compiles indexes, and serves user requests for particular files. To use this program effectively, the user needs to know the exact file name or a substring of it. Given the advent of *browsers* and *search engines* on the *World Wide Web,* archie is now somewhat dated.

architectural walkthrough: A subtype of the *surrogate travel* genre, *walkthroughs* are also a form of *virtual reality,* wherein the user can control a simulated passage through an architectural structure such as a hallway in a building. The underlying or *enabling technology* of architectural walkthroughs is the *CAD* (computer-aided design) program. In the coming age of interactive art forms, the capabilities and techniques made possible by walkthroughs will become a tool within the larger toolkit for those making highly immersive forms of *electronic games, interactive fictions,* and *training simulations.*

archival storage: This term refers to the process of storing *archive* copies of *digital* files that enterprises need for historical purposes. Archival storage allows enterprises to save space on their *network* by storing these seldom-used files on a backup tape or other *offline* storage device.

archive: Is a storage or backup file that is compressed so that it takes up less storage space than the original file. Archives are typically represented by files that are no longer in regular demand, but that cannot be entirely discarded. In most organizations, they are usually stored automatically on a scheduled basis by *archiving software.*

archiving software: Enables an enterprise to have scheduled *archival storage* backups on a regular basis of historical and other information. It also enables an enterprise to manage more easily the *archive* retrieval process. Archived files must be unarchived before re-use on the *network.*

ARM: Otherwise known as the Argonne Remote Manipulator, this prototypical telerobotic device was developed at the Argonne National Laboratories. The ARM is a long, multi-jointed arm suspended from the ceiling. The device provides basic control and *force feedback* to the user's hand, wrist, elbow, and shoulder along three axes and three *torques.* It is designed to give the user control of a remote robotic arm and was developed initially for handling radioactive materials. Many of the techniques and devices used in the construction of the ARM are now finding their way into the design of *virtual reality* systems.

ARPA: Stands for Advanced Research Projects Agency, which was the agency of the U.S. Department of Defense responsible for funding the creation of the *ARPANet.*

ARPANet: Stands for Advanced Research Projects Agency Network, which was the precursor for the *Internet.* In the 1960s and 1970s, the U.S. Department of Defense was seriously concerned about the effect that a major catastrophe, such as a thermonuclear war, might have on information systems. It commissioned a project to develop a wide area network (*WAN*), which would be robust, decentralized, and redundant. The theories and software that now form the bases for the Internet were first tested on ARPANet. The hardware used was individual *packet switching* computers connected with leased *T1* lines. It became operational in 1968, linking government sites, academic research facilities, and industrial sites around the world. *FTP* and *Telnet* were early *protocols.* It became the *backbone* of the Internet while it was being developed. Later, the military communications part split off and became MILNet, while ARPANet became NSFNet.

art director: A key figure throughout much of the history of the collaborative fictional enterprises, such as theater, film, *video,* and feature *animation,* the art director is one role that, if anything, will be enlarged by the advent of *interactive multimedia.* The primary responsibility of the art director is to create the total visual look of a media product, which requires a highly creative and artistic sensibility. Many art directors from the film and video sector have made excellent contributions to the discipline of *interface design.* Their skills at manipulating color and lighting, translating functions into metaphors, and metaphors into *button* designs, as well as specifying *spatial* relationships, have made their presence welcome on many interactive projects. Art directors are often assumed to be good *illustrators,* which is not necessarily the case, though they are certainly dependent on good illustrators to implement their vision. In the interactive world, art directors design the visual aspects of the *interface,* while illustrators execute their designs; i.e., they create the artwork for the buttons, graphics, animations, etc.

artifact: This term is widely used to describe flaws that can be detected in all forms of media, both *analog* and *digital.* More precisely, though, it is used to describe a flaw—a random sound or visual effect—that was not present in the original source *signal,* but that has been introduced by one of the components in the recording or reproduction chain. For example, *flicker* is a common artifact in the analog *video* world, while *pixellation* is one of the most common artifacts found in digital video.

artificial intelligence: This term refers to the part of computer science concerned with designing machines that exhibit human characteristics and that do things in a way that would require intelligence if done by people. The classic measure of "AI," more relevant today than even perhaps when it was conceived, is the *Turing Test.* Named after its author, Alan Turing, this test is passed by a machine if its ability to carry on a conversation is indistinguishable from that of a human, as exemplified by "HAL," the fictional computer in Stanley Kubrick's (director) *2001: A Space Odyssey.*

ASCAP: Stands for American Society of Composers, Authors and Publishers, an organization that has become best known for working out a detailed set of licensing specifications for recording artists that helps ensure that royalties and other usage fees get paid to the *copyright* holders and artists. Many people feel that this set of specifications—or something very much like it—will be in great need in the *age of interactivity,* where, for example, the widespread use of *clip media* will make it difficult to track and manage the payment of royalties to all of the contributing artists.

ASCII: Stands for American Standard Code for Information Interchange (pronounced "ask-ee"), and represents one of the most important and enduring standards of the personal computer market. The standard version of ASCII uses 7 *bits* representing 128 different alphanumeric characters. These characters are the digits 0–9, the uppercase and lowercase letters in the English alphabet, and the standard punctuation marks. This set of codes does not include accented letters or letters other than those used in English. Extended ASCII uses 8 bits, giving it another 128 codes to represent non-English characters, graphics symbols, and mathematical symbols. This widely adhered-to standard makes it possible for the vast majority of PC software programs to exchange information at a basic text-and-number level. *ISO* Latin 1 is a more universal standard used by many operating systems, as well as *Web browsers,* and EBCDIC is a set of codes used on large IBM computers.

aspect ratio: In the most general sense, the aspect ratio is the width-to-height ratio of a rectangular object. With respect to computer displays, this can refer to either the screen shape or the *pixel* shape. *Video* has a screen aspect ratio of 4:3, and film has an image aspect ratio of 3:2. Converting from one presentational medium to another—the classic example being from motion picture to television—can be problematic, often forcing some form of distortion.

asymmetrical codec: Refers, for the most part, to *interframe* forms of compression-decompression, where the encoding (compressing) side of the process is much more time-consuming and expensive than the decoding (decompressing) side. Both *DVI* (Digital Video Interactive) and *MPEG* (Motion Picture Experts Group) are asymmetrical, *interframe codecs.* The primary reason for the asymmetry rests on the arduous computational tasks associated with finding the patterns of temporal change and stability in *video sequences.* Once these patterns have been found and subjected to the *delta encoding* techniques, it is not nearly so difficult to decompress (reconstruct) the original image.

asynchronous: With regard to data processing, asynchronous refers to processes or interactions that occur at various points in time, as opposed to those that occur simultaneously—thus in *synchronous mode.* Sometimes, *distance learning* is referred to as either asynchronous or synchronous, depending upon whether the instructor and learners are communicating via the *Internet* at the same time (synchronous), or through *chat* sessions and *e-mail,* where the communications take place at different times (asynchronous).

ATM: Stands for Asynchronous Transfer Mode, a term which everyone interested in the networking of *mixed media data types* should commit to memory. This technology possesses several traits that make it the favored networking *protocol* for the future of high-*bandwidth, multimedia, data communications.* It works by splitting data into small chunks or *cells* of 53 *bytes,* giving it the key attributes of a *packet switching* protocol. But instead of routing each *packet* individually, as is characteristic of most packet switching systems, ATM establishes a *virtual* circuit between origin and destination so that it can accommodate the time-sensitive *streaming data* associated with *digital video.* Thus, ATM also possesses the essential characteristic of a circuit switching system. Because of this combination of attributes, ATM is noted for its ability to allocate bandwidth on demand, a trait often referred to by the popular computer term *scalability.* Because it is scalable, and because it can handle ultra-high capacities, ATM is favorably viewed by media futurists for its ability to scale up in response to a request for transmitting digital images or video. This allows it to be responsive to the needs of networked multimedia, as well as giving it the ability to scale back down after the multimedia *transmission* is complete, thus saving the user from having to pay for such high bandwidth when it is not needed.

atmospheric effects: This term refers to a family of *DVE* (digital video effects) that render such atmospheric conditions as fog, smoke, and haze.

audiographics: This term refers to an early form of *picturephone* that features two-way audio on a *voice*-grade telephone circuit with computer and/or *video* still images sent over the same line or a second line. Synchronization of the audio and visual components is not sought with audiographics, since the time required to send the visual components (an image, for example) is often delayed in the range of several seconds to several minutes, whereas the audio is transmitted in typical, *real-time* fashion.

augmented reality: Perhaps the most practical branch of *virtual reality,* this term refers to technologies that are used to enhance the real world with computer-generated displays. For example, a mechanic using augmented reality would wear a see-through variety of a head-mounted display (*HMD*). This display would allow a clear view through to the outside world, and thus to the engine on which the mechanic is working, but it would also project an image of an engineering diagram onto an appropriate section of the display. Thus, the mechanic could reference the diagram without having to look away from the engine. The military has been a leader in developing augmented reality technologies.

authoring system: This term is given to systems that contain software tools designed to empower individual developers and development teams to produce various types of *multimedia applications.* Though considerable variation exists from one system to the next, the categories of tools provided in most of these applications include media integration tools, i.e., tools for digitizing *mixed media data types* and for interfacing to the *Internet* or to media peripherals such as *CD-ROM* players; media production tools, such as *paint systems* and other routines for building and managing screen objects; *answer analysis* and *performance tracking* routines; a high-level programming *interface* designed for ease of use, such as the time-line interfaces featured in such programs as Macromedia's Director; and some form of programming or scripting language, such as HyperCard's HyperTalk or Netscape's *Javascript.* Though virtually every authoring system sells the idea that it can be used by computer-neophyte authors, this claim is only true in a limited way. Most authoring systems can be used in a restricted fashion by uninitiated authors. In general, though, the development of sophisticated multimedia products is a highly collaborative undertaking that requires numerous specialists, several tools, and expert direction.

auto assembly: In the world of *video production,* this term refers to the penultimate portion of the editing process whereby a master tape is constructed from the *EDL* (edit decision list) under the control of a computerized editing system.

auto iris: From the world of film and TV *production,* this device is useful when filming a scene during dawn or dusk. It is a camera lens function that automatically adjusts to compensate for changes in light levels.

autochanger: This term refers to the critical component of an *optical juke box* (or any other form of *juke box*) that is responsible for fetching and loading optical *discs* using some form of robotic device.

avatar: From the world of *virtual reality,* this term refers to 3-D graphical images created to represent an individual as a character placed or projected into a *virtual* environment. The term was originally coined by Neal Stephenson in his futuristic novel, *Snow Crash.*

AVI: Stands for Audio Video Interleaved, Microsoft's movie file format. The *interleaving* refers to the fact that under this file format, *video* and audio files that relate to the same *captured* media event are interleaved with one another so that synchronizing them (*lipsynching,* for example) can be more readily accomplished.

back buffer: From the realm of computer graphics, this term refers to a hidden drawing *buffer* used in the process of *double buffering.* Graphics are rendered into a back buffer so that the drawing process can be hidden from the user. When the drawing is complete, the front and back buffers are switched, thereby creating a smoother form of *animation.*

back plane: From the world of *DVE* (digital video effects), this term refers to the lower of two visual planes used in *two-plane effects* to create transitions from one screen to the next.

backbone: From the world of telecommunications and *networks,* this term refers to a high-capacity network connection generally used to handle *voice* and data traffic between smaller networks. For example, most universities have a backbone that connects their building-level *LANs* to the rest of the *CWIS* (campus-wide information system). The *Internet* has its own backbone, which originated out of the high-speed networks that connect the *NSF* (National Science Foundation) supercomputers. This *Internet backbone* is one of the most powerful in the world, and consists of high-capacity telephone links, *microwaves, lasers, fiber optics,* and satellites that connect networks, computer sites, and people all over the globe.

backchannel: In the emerging world of *interactive television,* this term refers to the *channel* over which users (home consumers of interactive programming) will communicate back to the entity from which the programming initiates. Because TV has historically been a one-way medium, with programming that originates with the broadcaster and then is sent to the home user, there has never been an infrastructure in place to handle backflows of data from the user to the broadcaster—other than informal channels that lie outside of the cable system. In other words, cable users can pick up their phones and call their local cable operators, but this communication channel is not part of the cable system per se. With the perceived need for *interactivity* at an all-time high, cable operators are now experimenting with various ways of supplying their users with backchannels so that they can potentially interact with the programming. At present, these backchannels possess relatively low *bandwidths,* but this should change in the near future.

backdrop: From the realm of *digital video,* this term refers to the background image plane displayed when all other *picture planes* are made transparent.

backfile conversion: When an organization contemplates the conversion of its various documentation (e.g., paper documents, microfiche, and slides) to a *digital* format, and then to long-term storage on one or more of the many emerging optical mass storage technologies, it must confront the (often massive) chore of converting all of its historical records. With paper document sources of information—by far the most common case—the process usually involves scanning, touch-up, indexing, and then, finally, transfer to *disk.* This whole process is called backfile conversion, and it represents one of the meat-and-potatoes applications of the age of *multimedia.* The primary advantage to organizations that undertake this process is that it brings all of their historical sources of information under the control of some form of information storage and retrieval system. The *converted* sources of information can then be searched and retrieved in an automated fashion, as well as subjected to various forms of statistical analysis. In contrast, with traditional sources of *archival storage,* such as microfiche, the user must first read an index—which may be computerized—and then manually fetch the target information from the archival storage unit, a procedure that backfile conversions seek to eliminate.

background task: This is a task that a computer performs while the primary, or foreground, program is not using the *CPU* (central processing unit). In a true multitasking environment, the user is typically unaware that a background task is being processed.

back-of-the-book index: In the world of traditional book publishing, this term refers to the index that appears at the back of the book, with which we all have great familiarity. It is of importance to the dawning era of *multimedia* because it is now viewed as part and parcel of a thing called document design, which in turn is attached to such emerging media as electronic reference documents (ERD) and other *DLOs* (document-like objects). With many desktop publishing systems, the construction of back-of-the-book indexes can now be automated by simply tagging the terms in the body of the text that one wants to appear in the index. The program then tracks the location of these terms as the document changes in size, and automatically writes their respective page numbers to the index upon command. Going one step further, with many ERD *authoring systems,* especially with those meant for use on the *Internet* or an *intranet,* these indexes can be made "live," meaning that by clicking on one of the entries in an electronic back-of-the-book index, one is immediately transported to the indexed location (page number) in the body of the text.

BACP: Stands for Bandwidth Allocation Control Protocol, which is a *protocol* of *AO/DI* that opens up the *B-channel* (64 *Kbps*), when the *D-channel* (16 Kbps) is at full capacity for an *ISDN* connection.

bandwidth: This term is of such wide applicability to our emerging era of *multimedia* that it now rolls off the tongues of technological babes, "wannabe" business tycoons, and hardcore telecommunication wizards. In its widely used contemporary sense, bandwidth refers to the information-carrying capacity of a *transmission link* between any two devices. In its more traditional sense, it means the range of frequencies, usually measured in cycles per second, that a piece of audio or *video* equipment can *encode* and decode. Video uses higher frequencies than does audio, and so is said to possess a higher bandwidth. In the field of information processing, the stream of digitally encoded alphanumeric characters that dominated computer usage before the era of multimedia represents one of the smallest forms of bandwidth. Thus, from a technical standpoint, one of the great struggles of the era has to do with transforming the computer so that it can gracefully handle the higher bandwidth sources of information—namely, audio, image, and video. With regard to the transfer of information over the *Internet,* this term loosely refers to the amount of data that can be transferred.

bandwidth reduction: In the television industry this term is commonly heard, especially among those who are wrestling with the *transmission* demands and constraints of *HDTV* (high-definition television). It is roughly equivalent to the term *compression,* in that it refers to the host of techniques that can be employed to reduce the overall *bandwidth* requirements of a television broadcast. *RLE* (run length encoding), *DCT* (discrete cosine transform), and *motion compensation* are just some of the compression techniques enlisted in the overall effort to reduce bandwidth.

Banff Center for the Arts: This Canadian institution is considered by many to be the leading organization in the world for exploring how *virtual reality* can be used within the arts.

bar sheet: Used extensively in *animation productions,* this diagrammatic form is employed by the director to make a blueprint of the action, music, dialogue, and sound effects for the entire picture. It illustrates how all of these elements are to be timed, and unfold in parallel, as each scene progresses. Perhaps most important, though, the bar sheet deserves a bright historical footnote, as it has served as the basis for the time-line metaphor that has informed so many of today's *multimedia* presentation and *authoring systems.*

baseband: From the world of telecommunications, baseband refers to a *digital transmission* medium (wire) allowing only one communication *channel* at any particular time. This term is often contrasted with *broadband,* which refers to technology that endows a single wire with the ability to handle multiple digital *signals* at once.

batch processing: From the world of traditional mainframe data processing, this term refers to a form of information processing that is typically held in contrast to *real-time* processing. With a batch process, information is gathered and stored before being processed or analyzed. Thus, when a bank stores up all of its transactions for the day and then updates all of its customer records at night, this process is said to be batch processing. The data is gathered up into a "batch" before anything meaningful is done to it. In contrast, with real-time processing the data is analyzed or processed immediately upon receipt. In the era of *multimedia,* most applications demand real-time, as opposed to batch, processing, because when users are interacting with media—as when they are playing *video* games—they want their processed data now, not later.

baud rate: From the world of telecommunications, this term refers to the data *transmission* speed over a communication *channel,* such as a telephone line. The term was first made popular through its association with *modems,* where it remains of substantial importance to the world of *multimedia* since most home computer users still connect to the *Internet* using their standard telephone lines. Even today, the highest baud rate most home users can attain without purchasing special *data communications* equipment is that of 28,800 bits per second, which only amounts to about 3,600 text characters and makes the receipt of *rich media* very problematic.

BBS: Stands for Bulletin Board System, and is an electronic message center, or large database, open to the public, where customers can read existing messages and post or submit their own messages. It gives people the ability to discuss an issue without having group members present either at the same place or at the same time. A BBS may be focused on a single area of interest, or it may have many interest groups. Some are very small, running on a PC with one or two phone lines; others are very large involving a throng of participants.

B-channel: One of the fundamental components of an *ISDN* connection, the B-channel is a 64 *Kbps channel* that carries *voice* or data *transmissions*. With a basic rate interface (*BRI*), the most common type of ISDN connection, there will be two B-channels.

bed: This term emanates from the world of film and TV, where it is used to describe the instrumental portion of music that serves as an underscore to the visual proceedings.

benchmark: This is a task used for measuring some aspect of a computer's performance.

beta-test: It has long been the practice of software developers to send prerelease versions of their programs to expert users who get some form of consideration (like discounts or free licenses) for testing out those products before they are released to the general public. Given the extremely complex nature of most software programs, it is to be expected that the developers will be unable to catch all of the "bugs" (technical flaws in the code). The process of beta-testing helps clean up the code. As entertainment developers begin to produce interactive products—which, after all, possess a strong software component—they will need to adapt this methodological innovation of data processing to their own development processes.

binary file: This is a file that contains special codes (based on "1s" and "0s") with arbitrary combinations of letters and numbers rather than printable text, such as *ASCII*. Binary files cannot be displayed on a *browser,* but can be *downloaded* to be used with particular applications on the PC that can handle the binary files. A binary file could be a program, a spreadsheet, or a graphic.

binaural fusion: From the world of perception, this is the process by which the brain compares information received from each ear and then translates the differences into a unified perception of a single sound issuing from a specific region of space. Any manufacturer of *3-D sound* equipment must take this phenomenon into account.

bit: The smallest unit of data, a bit refers to one of the on-off signals stored in computer memory.

bit map: This refers to a software object that represents visual data in a form where each *pixel* location corresponds to a unique memory location accessible by the computer *CPU.*

bit resolution: With *digital* forms of media, bit resolution is a measure of the quality of the *digitized* audio, image, or *video*. Bit resolution represents the number of *bits* used to represent each sample taken in the *ADC* (analog-to-digital) process to form a data stream of digitized media. Thus, with reference to digital audio, the industry standards are 8-bit, 12-bit, and 16-bit audio, with the higher bit lengths representing a higher quality form of digitized media.

bit specifications: From the realm of computer graphics, this term refers to the number of colors or levels of gray that can be presented by a *video* display at one time. An 8-*bit* specification is capable of displaying 256 colors or levels of gray; a 16-bit specification, up to 64,000 colors; and a 24-bit specification, up to 16.8 million colors.

BITC: Stands for Burned-In Time Codes and is pronounced "bit-see." This term refers to a characteristic of *video* required in video editing and other *postproduction* activities whereby the *time codes* for each video *frame* have been burned into a set location, or field, on the frame. Time codes are very important in editing, because they represent the logical equivalent of a memory *address,* enabling users to move quickly to the locations in the video stream they wish to be working with at a particular moment. In the *analog* world of videotape, these time codes are actually "burned" into the surface of the tape. In the *digital* world of *nonlinear video,* the time codes are also digital and are embedded in the video datastream. Though fundamentally different, the digital time codes appear to the end user much as their burned-in forebearers of the analog era.

bit-mapped displays: Are made up of tiny dots, called *pixels,* and stand in contrast to the older generation character displays, which are only capable of representing information out of the *ASCII* character set. Bit-mapped displays are capable of much higher *resolution* than character displays and represent the primary instruments of graphical user interface (*GUI*) design. Bit-mapped displays have manipulation capabilities for both *vector* and raster graphics, which allow presentation of information appearing in the final paper form. Owing to the prevalence of

GUI design in today's computer marketplace, very few displays are manufactured anymore that are not of the bit-mapped variety.

blind: From the realm of digital video effects (*DVE*), this term refers to a *two-plane effect* in which the image on the *front plane* becomes like a Venetian blind that opens to reveal the image on the *back plane*.

BLOB: Stands for Binary Large OBject, a term that belongs to the language of relational databases and is often referred to as a *memo field*. The best way to understand what a BLOB is, is to compare it to standard relational database fields. The standard database fields, because they must fit into a tabular model, have a fixed length. Thus, a relational database always has some intrinsic limit on the amount of information that a single text item, or field, can store. In contrast, a memo field uses the fixed-length part of a table only as a *pointer* to a large body of information with a virtually unlimited size. Thus, a memo field can be used to store a paragraph, a page, a book, ad infinitum, all using, in the database proper, only the amount of space required to hold the pointer (memory *address*). This data structure is ideal for *hypermedia* forms where an orderly, navigable structure must be maintained (which corresponds to the database), but where numerous large information objects (*digitized* images, *animations,* film clips) of widely varying size must be made available.

block: This is an amount of data moved or *addressed* as a single unit within the computer's memory.

BLT: Stands for Bit-aLigned block Transfer, a term used for describing the process of copying *pixels* or other data from one place in memory to another. *Software engineering* specialists dealing with *multimedia applications* are often called upon to facilitate major BLTs.

BMP: Stands for Bit-MaPped file, and refers to the internal picture file format used by Microsoft *Windows,* versions 3.0 and higher. This *raster file* format is also supported by OS/2, the IBM operating system.

board: This term is synonymous with "circuit board" or "card." The primary function of a computer board is to hold the chips and wiring that control either some essential function of the computer's *CPU,* or that of a peripheral device such as a *CD-ROM* player. Throughout the volatile history of computing, boards have been used as a vehicle for scaling up the capabilities of computers, adding, for example, audio capabilities to a computer that was manufactured before such capabilities were a standard part of the computer's "motherboard" (built-in). Thus, boards should be thought of as a major source of *scalability* and *extensibility* in the computer world.

bookmark: Also referred to as an electronic bookmark, this graphical user interface (*GUI*) design/navigational feature is employed to facilitate *multisession* uses of electronic documents, interactive *multimedia applications* for training, and *hypermedia applications* for reference. Bookmarks simply record or save the point at which one decides to exit a program, making it possible to reenter at that exact point when one starts the next session. As the size and use of *electronic forms* of publishing continue to grow, bookmarking is becoming a standard feature of most forms of electronic documents. With reference to the *Internet,* the bookmark has become an important *user interface* feature of *browsers.* By adding a bookmark, the location of a particular *URL* can be saved as a bookmark item. By later viewing the bookmark list and clicking on the item, the user can quickly return to this previously saved URL at some time in the future.

boundary detection: This is considered one of the key problems associated with *virtual reality* environments, where a user's body may interact with, or actually pass through, a *virtual* object, such as a chair or wall. It presents a perceptual problem because these objects should have a solid consistency but, in the "VR" environment, may put up no resistance at all, thereby taking on a ghostly character. The emerging technologies associated with *tactile feedback* are considered to hold the ultimate solution to this problem, enabling the user to move around in a virtual environment and, when the system is appropriately cued by boundary detection logic (or devices), to generate the appropriate sensations when that user bumps into things. Virtual reality research is a long way off from perfecting such systems. In the meantime, designers are experimenting with a number of ersatz solutions, such as sound systems that correlate varying sound effects with the detection of different types of boundary collisions.

boundary representation: From the realm of computer graphics, this term refers to one of the main methods of "solid modeling," in which the object is described by its geometry and *topology.*

BPS: This term stands for Bits Per Second and is a standard measure of *transmission* speed or *transfer rate* in the computer world.

branchpoint: The basis of machine intelligence relies on the computer's ability to change its preset *sequence* of instructions, a most common phenomenon in programming known as "branching"—the code branches from one location in the program to another. A branchpoint is, quite simply, a location within a program where a branch occurs. With regard to interactive forms of entertainment—*video* games, *edutainment* programs, and the like—most of the branchpoints are dedicated to giving the user (learner, gamer, etc.) some element of control over what happens next in the program.

BRI: Stands for Basic Rate Interface, which is the most common form of *ISDN interface* available in the United States. BRI is made up of two *B-channels,* each with 64 *Kbps* capacity, and a single *D-channel* with a 16 Kbps capacity. The B-channels are used to carry the data payload of an ISDN connection, while the D-channel is used for carrying technical control information. This BRI *channel* configuration is also commonly referred to as "2B+D."

bridge: Is an *internetworking* device that relays *frames* of data from one *network* segment to another, making multiple segments appear as one contiguous *LAN.* To improve overall network performance, bridges are often used to segment networks based upon patterns of network traffic. Segmentation divides the network into logical subsets, keeping traffic from workstations that communicate with one another on a common LAN segment, while separating those groups of workstations that do not communicate frequently.

brightness: Along with *hue* and *saturation,* this is one of the three fundamental dimensions of color. Brightness refers to the differences in the intensity of light reflected from or transmitted through an image.

broadband: This term is used frequently in communications to refer to *transmission media* and *channels* that possess relatively larger carrying capacities or *bandwidth* than, for example, *baseband.*

broadband technology: In the field of *data communications,* this term refers to a class of *transmission* technologies that provide greater *bandwidth* than can be obtained across the traditional *POTS* (plain old telephone system) infrastructure. *Web*-accessible *multimedia* and *videoconferencing* applications are frequently cited as key demand drivers for broadband technology. *Frame relay, SMDS,* and *ATM* are examples of broadband technologies in common use today.

broadcast PC: This hybrid term refers to any home computer possessing a TV tuner card that can receive *digital* television broadcasts. The presence of this TV *expansion board* makes it possible for the computer to receive data *transmissions* simultaneously with broadcast *video* and audio. Thus, the user watching a political speech could view biographical data about the politician in a pop-up *window* while the speech is being delivered. It would seem obvious that this type of personal computer represents a steppingstone to the *teleputer.*

browser: A browser is a *hypertext* reader, a program that interprets a file marked with *HTML* tags and displays the contents on a screen or printer. It can communicate with the *Internet* to activate or bring up on the screen embedded hypertext *anchor links.* There are many browsers available which can be *downloaded* from the Net. *Navigator* by Netscape Corporation and *Internet Explorer* by Microsoft Corporation are two of the better known browsers.

browsing: In a *hypertext* and *hypermedia* environment, this term describes the oft-practiced user behavior of meandering through the available electronic information, looking simply for interesting associations. The metaphor corresponds with paying a desultory visit to your favorite bookstore to peruse the stacks. With regard to the *Internet,* the term refers to looking at documents and sites with a *Web browser.* A more casual type of browsing on the *World Wide Web* is often referred to as *surfing the Net,* in which the user meanders from page to page, from *Web site* to Web site, with no specific goal necessarily in mind as one wanders about—in a *virtual* way, that is.

browsing path: Based on the *browsing* behavior of users, this term refers to the specific *sequence* of *hyperlinks* that a particular user selects while moving through a large *hypertext* or *hypermedia application.* Keeping track of this type of information can be very useful, especially if the designer of the hypermedia application wants to establish usage patterns relative to the content, and preference patterns relative to specific user profiles. Likewise, browsing paths on the *Internet* are stored as a series of *URLs,* which mark the user's sequence of hyperlink steps. This stored information can be used, like the proverbial breadcrumbs dropped in the forest, to retrace one's path through *cyberspace.*

brush: With reference to computer *paint systems,* a brush is a marker that draws a line or pattern on the *display surface,* thereby emulating the action of a real paintbrush.

buffer: Is a small part of a computer's memory that temporarily stores data. Buffers can compensate for a difference in data flow rates when transmitting data between two devices; or they can be used to temporarily hold data that is likely to soon be needed somewhere else in the computer system.

BUFR: This term stands for Binary Universal Form for Representation, a standard *digital* imaging file format used by meteorologists to represent the visualizable aspects of weather data.

burst: This term has become popular for describing one of the dominant characteristics of data flows. In this regard, it acknowledges an almost universal aspect of reality: namely, that phenomena are not evenly distributed in time, but rather tend to occur in bursts, separated by periods of relative quiet.

bursty traffic: From the world of *network management,* this term refers to the types of data flow experienced with respect to traditional, alphanumeric (i.e., character) forms of data. On the traditional *network,* traffic is said to be bursty because, for the most part, the network is clear of traffic and so single data conversations are able to be quickly established and released without degrading the overall performance of the network. From time to time, though, the volume of requests for access to the network surges, which in turn leads to the need for invoking some sort of contention *scheme* to determine who has access, and in what order. Owing to this variable traffic pattern, the traditional PC network is said to experience bursty traffic.

bus: This commonly used computer term refers to the circuit or pathway through which data is transmitted. It most often is used to refer to the main such pathway that serves to connect the major components of a computer system to the *CPU.*

bus interface: From the realm of computer design, this term relates to the fact that everything in a computer is attached to the *CPU*—that is, every device that is a part of the computer must communicate with the CPU in some way. To do this, these devices (e.g., *disk* drives, monitors, and printers) must be connected to the computer's *bus* so that they can exchange data. This point of connection is called the bus interface.

button: An important term in graphical user interface (*GUI*) design, a button is a relatively small screen object, usually labeled with text or an *icon,* or both, and typically used to initiate instantaneous actions, such as completing operations defined by a *dialog box* or acknowledging error messages. Buttons represent *hot spots* on the screen—by clicking or touching them, one initiates some computer-mediated action. In designing buttons, the traditional wisdom has it that the label of the button should describe the result of using (clicking, touching) the button, rather than some abstract term about the function that is being performed.

buyer agents: From the realm of *intelligent software agents,* this term refers to programs that can search the *Web* for products that match the criteria set by their human owners. After a buyer agent collects the information, it can review and make recommendations to its owner. Venturesome owners may even let the agent place orders on their behalf. Buyer agents have natural counterparts, called *seller agents,* and typically must interact with them to consummate business deals, no matter how trivial or insignificant. These two types of *agents* are destined to play an important role in the future of *e-commerce.*

byte: In the world of computers, the ubiquitous byte is a unit of measure of 8 binary digits (i.e., 8 *bits*) representing either two numbers or one character.

bytes per second: Again, in the world of computers, this is a unit of measure for the speed of *digital transmission* of information.

The problem . . . is that most of the people who have the trades of screenwriting, cinematography or whatever are utterly ill-equipped to build nonsequential, highly interactive programs.
—Nicholas Negroponte, Director, the Media Lab at MIT

cable headend: This term belongs with the emerging language of the in*formation superhighway,* as it represents one of the key distribution *nodes* on the *network.* Within that segment of the highway dedicated to cable TV, the cable headend is the central point at which TV *signals* are *downlinked* from satellites and are modulated onto the cable by local stations, en route to our television sets. In other words, it is a key port of entry for the distribution of *video content.*

cable modem: One of the hot technologies associated with the *Internet,* the cable modem makes possible a quantum leap in *data rates* for home computer users when compared to the speeds of standard *modems,* and even of *ISDN.* Whereas the conventional modem is only capable of speeds up to 28.8 *Kbps,* and the *BRI* option of ISDN goes up to only 128 Kbps, the cable modem can reach data rates of up to 27 *Mbps.* It is able to reach these much higher speeds because it takes advantage of the much greater inherent *bandwidth* of the coaxial wire that serves as the basis for the cable TV physical infrastructure. In contrast, it is the twisted-pair copper wire that makes up the *last-mile loop* of the telephone infrastructure, the much lower bandwidth of which is responsible for constricting the data speeds of traditional modems and ISDN.

cabling: Any discussion of the technical aspects of communications—*telephony, data communications, LAN,* and *WAN*—usually makes reference to one of its most fundamental features: the type of cabling, or *transmission media,* being used. There are three major forms of cabling in use today. In order of lesser-to-greater capacity, they are the following: Twisted-pair is the copper-wire medium that connects the household telephone to the *public-switched telephone network* (PSTN). It is the oldest cabling technology and can be either shielded or not. Reliance on this largely outdated medium is what is considered to be the largest disadvantage for the telephone companies in the heated competition to control *home interactive media.* Coaxial cable has long been used for cable television connections because of its ability to handle a relatively large number of *signals* or, in other words, different *channels,* simultaneously. "Coax," as aficionados like to call it, has four basic parts: a solid metal wire forms the core of the cable, surrounded by insulation; a tubular piece of metal screen surrounds the insulation; and an outer plastic coating completes the cable. Coax is capable of high *bandwidths* and is therefore a popular choice for LANs that must carry a large amount of *network* traffic. *Fiber optic* cable is considered the transmission medium of the future, for fiber carries light pulses rather than electrical signals. Fiber has several advantages: immunity from electromagnetic interference, enormous bandwidths, and the ability to carry signals for a very long distance. Fiber cable consists of a core fiber enclosed in glass cadding, with a protective outer coating that surrounds the cadding. *LEDs* (light-emitting diodes) are used to send the signal down the optical fiber. At the receiving end, a photodetector is used to receive the signals and *convert* them into a *digital* computer format. Owing to its very large bandwidths, fiber is the core *transmission* technology of the integrated services *digital* network (*ISDN*), and is considered by many experts to be a necessary ingredient in the future extension of *multimedia applications.*

cache: In its traditional usage, cache is a temporary storage area for data requiring very quick access. Most contemporary *CPUs* (e.g., Intel's 80486, Motorola's 68040) carry a specification for their cache size, which denotes the size of the memory held on the CPU itself. This CPU cache is the location where frequently accessed code and data from the current application are stored. But the CPU is not the only "place" in a computer system where the strategy of supplying a cache is commonly employed. As a process, caching is now a commonly employed strategy for building *bridges* between every form of memory and its next-slowest, but higher capacity, companion. Thus, caching is done between optical and hard *disk* storage, between hard disk and RAM, and between CPU cache and RAM. In the coming era of *multimedia,* where extremely large amounts of *digital* data will need to be moved on a constant basis, the importance of using caches will grow dramatically. In this usage of the term, a cache is roughly synonymous with the term *buffer,* and the process of caching is synonymous with "buffering."

CAD: Otherwise known as Computer-Aided Design, it is a widely used term most typically associated with engineering and architectural applications for computer graphics. With the advent of *virtual reality* systems, especially those that *render* visual scenes and *virtual worlds* in *real time,* CAD is taking on a new role as an integral support component in these complex programs. In a very real sense, CAD is becoming a core *enabling technology* for the virtual reality industry.

CAI: Stands for Computer-Assisted Instruction; along with *CBT* (computer-based training), this is one of the early acronyms for describing programs that use the computer as an instructional tool, rather than as an automation machine. As the computer becomes the *teleputer,* future historians may come to view CAI as a truly seminal use of the first generations of computing machines.

calibration: In the world of graphics and *multimedia,* calibration is the process of adjusting the display of images to ensure that the colors and gray tones will be output to various *digital media,* while accurately reflecting the colors. *Scanners,* monitors, printers, and software should be calibrated to ensure consistent rendering of colors and tones.

camera field: In film and *video,* this is the area being photographed by the camera. The camera field constitutes what is visible to the audience at any given moment.

CAP: Stands for Competitive Access Provider, a new breed of phone company that competes with the *RBOCs* (baby bells) for your local exchange telephone service. See also *CLEC.*

capture: In the world of graphics and *multimedia,* capture is the process of creating a graphic file of some computer-displayed image, usually a screen or *window.* The screen or window is usually captured with a *screen capture program* that takes a snapshot of the image and saves it as a *bit map.* These bit maps can then be used to represent the screen or window in any application, such as a *CBT* program designed for application training, or a *Web page* seeking to depict some element of another software program.

carrier: A carrier is a continuous *signal* that connects two computers for *data communication.* It is a single *frequency* that can be modulated by a data carrying signal. The presence of a carrier can be seen on a *modem* when the CD (carrier detect) light is on. A carrier is also a government regulated organization, such as AT&T and Sprint, that provides telephone services to the public. Most public carriers also offer an *e-mail* service for transmitting messages and files.

cataloging: Though cataloging has been an integral part of human cultures since the advent of record keeping, the sudden rise of the *Internet,* writ large (a.k.a. *NII*), has dramatically escalated its importance as a rigorous and disciplined practice, both in the academic and business domains. To the professional library science specialist, cataloging refers to the creation of surrogate descriptions and access records in accordance with formats, rules, and standards. The US*MARC* and AACR2 are two standards of substance that are now being advanced by the library science community as being the best available candidates upon which to build a powerful search architecture for the *information superhighway* (a.k.a. the Internet). The need for this type of cataloging standard has never been greater. The explosion of new media types (e.g., *interactive multimedia, Web sites, electronic games,* and *online databases*) has added an unprecedented burden to our traditional cataloging systems. The result is that individuals have difficulty finding the information they need, when they need it. In this context, cataloging refers to the struggle against, and prospective antidote for, the looming problems of *information overload.*

CATV: Stands for Community-Antenna-TeleVision, which is the separate *transmission* infrastructure that was created to meet the needs of the cable television industry. This infrastructure was needed to serve cable TV, because the copper wire transmission system that serves the ubiquitous residential and business needs of *telephony* is not capable of handling the *bandwidth* (carrying capacity) demands of television broadcasting. Thus, during the 1980s, the cable industry was forced to create its own ubiquitous transmission infrastructure by laying the higher bandwidth coaxial cable into millions of homes and businesses around the country. This higher capacity infrastructure now gives the cable operators a somewhat serendipitous advantage over the telephone companies with respect to offering interactive services, especially to the home market.

CAV: Stands for Constant Angular Velocity, one of two distinct *videodisc* formats (*CLV* [constant linear velocity] being the other). With CAV, the *frames* are laid down in concentric circles. Each frame has its own 360-degree *track* on the videodisc, thereby making it possible for the *laser* reader to jump from one track to the next. This format is the strongest option for providing rapid *random access* to frames, and is thus the preferred format for interactive videodisc applications.

CAVE: A *virtual reality* project conducted at the *EVL* (Electronic Visualization Lab) in Chicago, the CAVE is a room in which a viewer stands and becomes totally immersed in a 3-D audiovisual experience. The visual components of the CAVE are produced by multiple projectors, with each projector being responsible for flooding one of the wall sides. The images are projected in an *interlaced video* fashion, and the viewer wears *stereoscopic glasses.* Fallout applications of the CAVE include biomedical imaging, architectural rendering, interior design, and mechanical design of heavy equipment.

CBR: Stands for Content-Based Retrieval and represents a class of programs that seek to automate the process of searching large information bases. Operating on the grounds of user-defined content characteristics, these programs automatically perform search and retrieval functions against large information databases in an effort to unearth gems of information from the mountains of data. An example of a CBR program would be one that scans the massive flow of stock data that emanates from Wall Street each day and culls from that dataflow just the information that relates to the user's individual portfolio of stocks. Negroponte's concept of *personal television* may be implemented through what we are today calling CBR.

CBT: Stands for Computer-Based Training and represents one of the oldest acronyms in the interactive business. The term was dominant during the early PC era and was used to describe interactive training programs that—owing to the constrained presentational capabilities of early PCs—were limited primarily to text and *ASCII* graphics. By far, the most common application for CBT was the software *tutorial,* where the computer was used to teach end users how to use common computer software applications such as word processors, database managers, and spreadsheets. The term is still alive, and some advocates are trying to migrate it to the more updated, *multimedia*-based forms of interactive training. An updated term for CBT that is offered across the *Internet,* for example, is called Web-based training, or *WBT.* Most of the programs now using the name WBT do not possess any substantial differences from earlier generations of interactive training. For the most part, however, the term CBT is reserved for describing older generation interactive *courseware.*

CCD: Stands for Charge-Coupled Device and represents the dominant technology used in *scanners,* and other related devices, for converting light to electronic impulses, the first step in *digitizing* light sources of information. CCDs consist of a silicon semiconductor and a series of electrodes. When light passes into the silicon, that light frees electrons within the silicon atoms. The brighter the light, at a given point on the image, the more electrons are freed.

CCITT: Stands for Consultative Committee on International Telephone and Telegraph, a former telephone industry standards-making body of considerable importance that is now the *ITU.*

CCITT H.261: Also known as *Px64,* this is a widely accepted *video compression* standard used for *video teleconferencing.*

CD-DA: Stands for Compact Disc-Digital Audio, and represents the earliest standard in the CD industry. Also referred to as the *Red Book* standard, CD-DA is an audio-only standard, specifying how audio CDs should be formatted.

CDF: Stands for Channel Definition Format, Microsoft's *metadata* standard for defining *Web*-based content. In fulfillment of Nicholas Negroponte's (of the MIT *Media Lab*) vision for *personal television,* this metadata standard is designed to enable *content providers* to code their information resources so that end users, or consumers, can be automatically notified when new information of personal interest becomes available. The CDF standard takes the form of page descriptions, both for the *home page,* and for the contents of pages underneath, and contains data elements for detailing how often each section should be checked for new content. In keeping with its central goal of enabling the personalization of the Web-based content, this standard makes it possible for users to specify what parts of a *channel* to retrieve.

CD-I: Stands for Compact Disc-Interactive, a self-contained *multimedia platform* developed by Philips Corporation. One of the early platforms for home multimedia, CD-I possesses its own *proprietary* operating system, known as *CD-RTOS.* As a standard for multimedia, CD-I is also known as the *Green Book* standard. Owing primarily to its proprietary nature, in contrast to the emergence of widely accepted alternative standards for storing multimedia content on optical *discs,* the CD-I format is very much a declining standard, soon to occupy the status of a historical footnote.

CDMA: Stands for Code Division Multiple Access, one of two emerging standards for *digital wireless* communications. CDMA works by splitting a single radio *channel* into a large number of *voices,* using a unique identifier code for each voice. The receiver uses a code book of sorts to detect and *capture* the desired *signal* from the substantial background *noise.* The accepted analogy for CDMA is that everyone in a room filled by many people can hear just the message intended for him or her because each person is concentrating on (is decoding) a single conversation. Along with its sister technology, *TDMA* (time division multiple access), this standard represents a new form of *transmission* capacity, and is therefore able to help address the ongoing *bandwidth* crisis that threatens to thwart the vitality of *multimedia*. In a sense, because digital wireless does not use *cabling,* as do most other forms of *data communications,* CDMA and TDMA represent "found" bandwidth in a contemporary world that is increasingly bandwidth-scarce.

CD-R: Stands for Compact Disc-Recordable, which represents a family of CD players that make it possible for end users to record their own data, albeit only once. CD-R is part of the *Orange Book* standard, which includes most of the CD technologies that enable end users to record (like those that use the magneto-optical technologies).

CD-ROM: Stands for Compact Disc-Read Only Memory and refers to the dominant form of direct access, mass storage for the early years of *multimedia* technology. Refer to *compact disc* for a more complete discussion.

CD-ROM-XA: This is an extended architecture for *CD-ROM* that permits the *interleaving* of sound and data on the same storage *tracks.* By placing the sound and data adjacent to one another, this technology facilitates synchronization when these two data types are merged in motion picture and *animation* segments.

CD-RTOS: Stands for Compact Disc-Real Time Operating System, which is the *proprietary* operating system developed by Philips for its *CD-I platform.*

cel: Short for celluloid, this term actually refers to the sheets of acetate laid down on top of one another to produce a single *frame,* or *exposure,* of an animated feature.

cel animation: Refers to a moving picture produced by displaying a series of complete screen images in rapid succession.

cell: In *ATM,* the cell refers to a fixed-length *packet* that carries data across the ATM *network.* A cell has 53 *bytes,* 5 of which carry a header. The term cell is also commonly used to refer to the smallest component of the cellular *grid* that makes possible cellular communicaitons.

cell relay: This term refers to the communications *protocol* for *ATM cells.*

CELP: This acronym stands for Code-Excited Linear Prediction, and it represents one of the more innovative forms of *digital* audio communication. As *MIDI* (musical instrument digital interface) works with respect to music, CELP works by transmitting an *encoded* representation of the *voice,* rather than a waveform *signal* of the voice itself. The technology is based upon a "codebook" that stores the basic sound elements of the human voice. The transmitting end of the communication decomposes the sounds of the "sending" human voice into its codebook values, and then transmits a set of *pointers,* plus any modifying parameters needed to *capture* the unique characteristics of the speaker, to the receiving station. In turn, the receiver uses the *pointers* to look up the codebook elements, which it then incorporates into a decoded version of the speaker's voice. The primary advantage of this technology—like its MIDI cousin—is that it greatly reduces the *bandwidth* needed to transmit the human voice. In a sense, it is a form of *compression.* Its primary disadvantage is that it is extremely *CPU-intensive,* and typically requires the use of a special purpose *DSP* (digital signal processor).

Center for Creative Imaging: Opened in May of 1991 by Eastman Kodak Company, this training center is designed to help videographers, photographers, and graphic artists make the transition to the new media artforms made possible by the many new and sophisticated electronic imaging products entering the market. Located in Camden, Maine, and founded by longtime Kodak executive Raymond DeMoulin, the Center provides hands-on experience with a broad range of *scanners,* cameras, printers, storage media, and software applications. From a historical perspective, this center represents the type of organizational commitment to *technology transfer* that will be needed to expedite the economic and cultural absorption of *multimedia technologies.*

CERN: Stands for Le Conseil Europeen pour la Recherche Nucleaire, and in English, the European Laboratory for Particle Physics. This organization has played a substantial role in the early evolution of the *Web.* CERN is a research laboratory for high-energy nuclear physics in Geneva, Switzerland. In the 1980s, the scientific community was amassing large quantities of data that they began to make available on the early version of the *Internet.* However, the proliferation of different computer *platforms* and programming languages complicated the accessibility of this information. At the same time, the concept of *hypertext* existed but suffered from a lack of standards. Tim Berners-Lee and his group at CERN undertook the pioneering work of developing what is now known as the *World Wide Web* portion of the Internet. They also developed *HTTP* and *HTML* as common standards for facilitating the sharing of information across disparate computing platforms. Without their work, the Web would not be what it is today—the first legitimate global computing *network* and the first generation of the Global Information Infrastructure (*GII*).

CFD: Stands for Computational Fluid Dynamics, which is one of the most computationally demanding applications in the world. It is used primarily by scientists and chemical engineers to perform various types of fluid flow analysis, in which the motion behavior of liquids and gases is modeled under a variety of environmental conditions. CFD is important to *multimedia,* because it is a strong technical driver of *scientific visualization.* Used as the mathematical basis for generating visual *simulations* of the fluids and gases being modeled, CFD also serves as a seedbed for the visualization technologies that ultimately become a part of the high-end *DVE* (digital video effects) systems, which are used in film and *video production* to simulate such natural phenomena as lava flows and tornadoes.

CGA: Stands for Color Graphics Adapter, a vestigial remnant of the early days of *desktop* computing when any form of graphics was considered a luxury. As some will recall, the original IBM PC came with a monochrome monitor that could display text only. As the forces that would ultimately lead to *multimedia* began to take shape, IBM responded with the first of its graphics adapters, namely CGA. Equipped with a color monitor and a CGA card, the user could display up to 16 colors in *RGB* format with a resolution of 640 x 200 *pixels.* However, to remember how bad a standard this was, to display graphics you had to first go into a thing called "graphics *mode*." And if you wanted to display text while in graphics mode, you had to switch out of 80-column and into 40-column mode. This technical compromise produced some of the least attractive type fonts in the history of communications. Early forms of *CBT* (computer-based training) were particularly haunted by this standard, because if you wanted to incorporate graphics and text on the same screen—which is a pretty compelling combination when you're trying to teach something to somebody—you had to use the extremely blocky and pixellated type fonts necessitated by the 40-column mode. In the lineage of PC graphics standards, CGA comes just after "MDA" (monochrome display adapter) and just before *EGA*, which then gave way to *VGA* and *SVGA*.

CGI: Stands for Common Gateway Interface, a key *enabling technology* of the *World Wide Web*. CGI represents a set of recommendations describing how a *Web server* communicates with other pieces of software located on the same computer, and how those other pieces of software, called CGI programs, communicate with the Web server. A CGI program is typically a small program that takes data from a Web server and manipulates it in some meaningful way.

CGM: Stands for Computer Graphics Metafile, one of the more common file format standards for facilitating the exchange of graphics images.

channel: In the *data communications* world, this term refers to a path or circuit along which information flows. Most channels are measured in terms of how much information they can carry, which is also referred to as their *bandwidth*. In the entertainment world, the more ubiquitous use of the term channel is used to describe a single source of television programming. In the coming era of *DTV* (digital television), these two forms of channel will become the same thing.

channel explosion: This term is now in popular use by observers of the rise of the home media market. It describes the rapid expansion in the number of TV channels that, in the first phase, was made possible by the creation of the *CATV* (cable TV) infrastructure. This first phase resulted in the laying of coaxial cable into cable-connected homes, which provided a form of *transmission media* that has much more effective *bandwidth* than the copper wire of *POTS* (plain old telephone service). With the appearance of a number of other key *enabling technologies,* such as *DBS* (direct broadcast satellite) and *DTV* (digital television), it is expected that increase in channels available to the home viewer will continue to expand at a rapid pace. The channel explosion is a very important part of the evolution toward what Nicholas Negroponte refers to as *personal television.* As the futurists would have it, there will ultimately be so many channels—and so much specialization among *content providers*—that individuals will be able to create highly personalized media diets.

chapter-level entry points: In an effort to join the *age of interactivity,* many film producers are manufacturing interactive versions of their feature films. Many are using the *DVD* format to deliver these *digital* versions. However, as the process is currently being managed, the *interactivity* is "put into" these movies as an afterthought—as a sort of high-tech adornment—rather than being designed into the artworks from the outset. To put the interactivity into these pictures without disrupting their narrative flow, many producers create entry points at obvious locations like the *edit points* between scenes. Using the obvious analogy of text-based narratives, these entry points are often referred to as chapter-level entry points.

character generator: From the realm of traditional *video postproduction,* this term refers to a device dedicated to creating and superimposing text on top of video. Hence, when a person's name appears below his or her talking head in a televised interview, you are witnessing the work of a character generator. In the coming age of *desktop video production,* the function of placing text over video will become almost trivial because all of the content will be in a *digital* format.

character-based applications: This historical term is used to describe PC software applications before the current era of graphical user interfaces (*GUIs*). These applications were said to be "character-based" because they did not make use of *bit-mapped* graphics, the *desktop metaphor,* *mouse* input, or any of the GUI elements that are such an integral part of contemporary computing. Rather, these early forms of UI (*user interface*) were constructed entirely out of *ASCII* characters. For example, many PC users will remember the old, character-based version of Lotus 1-2-3, which is an industry standard for spreadsheets. Most applications have either migrated up to a GUI format or simply migrated into the blissful sunset of extinction.

chat: Is a *real-time* communication via the *Internet.* The fundamentals of chat are simple: with all participants signed on, each types a message that is then sent to the screens of all other participants. Users can be logged into the same computer system or can access a chat session via remote computers with a *network* connection. There are public chats and private chats. At this time, chats involve only typed-in messages, as opposed to true *voice* communication that one might have over an audio-conference line. The present technological limitations of Internet only allow users to conduct text-only chat sessions with two people. In the near future, multi-person voice chats are coming that will allow for Internet audio-conferences. In an era beyond this, the use of *videophone* will enable an even more humane version of chat, which is already referred to as *videoconferencing.*

chat facilitator: Is the person who keeps order during a *chat* session. He or she moderates the chat discussion and seeks to avoid *multi-threaded discussions* in which several different individuals are "talking" about multiple topics all at the same time, leading to something like an electronic Tower of Babel.

check box: With graphical user interfaces (*GUIs*) that are based on the *desktop metaphor* (such as the Apple Macintosh *interface* or the Microsoft *Windows* interface), this is a standard *interface design* element. Used most commonly in *dialog boxes,* the check box is a square structure that operates like a toggle switch to turn particular functions on or off. To activate or deactivate a function, the user simply positions the *cursor* within the confines, or *hot spot,* of the corresponding check box and then clicks the *mouse button.*

check disc: Manufacturing a long run (large number) of any form of optical *disc* (e.g., *CD-ROM* or *laserdisc*) has traditionally been a relatively expensive and, because of its read-only nature, permanent venture. Owing to the risks associated with getting anything wrong on one of these runs, it is customary to proceed with an abundance of caution by first printing one, or a few, test discs that can be thoroughly checked for accuracy before launching the full quantity run. These preliminary discs are usually referred to as check discs.

chroma keyer: A commonly used device in *video production,* a chroma keyer is used to process two *video* sources where one source (referred to as the "foreground") is to be laid down on top of the other source (referred to as the "background"). The device works by first specifying a particular color that plays the role of the "key." Once this key is specified—the most common key being blue—any object in the background that is the same color will drop out and let the background show through. Perhaps the most commonly known use of chroma keyers occurs when they are used to show TV meteorologists apparently standing in front of a weather map, but in fact standing in front of a blue wall. (Is nothing sacred?)

chrominance: This term refers to one-half of the information that typically goes into making a *video signal.* Chrominance is the color portion of the information contained in a full-color electronic image. The other half is *luminance,* or light intensity, that an image requires to make it visible. Of the two, chrominance is the component to which the human eye is less sensitive. For this reason, many of the *compression* techniques employed to handle the *transmission* of *digital* images do more to reduce the presence of chrominance information than they do to reduce the presence of luminance data.

CIE: Also known as *CIX,* CIE stands for Commercial Internet Exchange—a nonprofit trade association providing public *Internet* services.

Cinepak: Considered one of the most popular of early motion *video codec* (compression-decompression) standards, Cinepak was developed by SuperMac—a software developer for the Apple computer environment during the heyday of the Macintosh computer (late 1980s/early 1990s). Typical of early codecs, Cinepak featured a number of physical constraints. It was capable of playback at a maximum *resolution* of only 320 x 240 *pixels,* the same resolution as the first generation of the *MPEG* (Motion Picture Experts Group) standard. Its top playback speed was only 15 *fps* (*frames* per second), and it was viewed as a severely *asymmetrical codec* with the *compression* process taking 300 times longer than *decompression.*

CIRC: This term stands for Cross Interleaved Reed-Solomon Code, which is an error detection and correction method for audio CDs.

circuit switching: A less flexible form of *data communications* than its leading rival, *packet switching,* this term refers to a method of handling data *transmissions* in which a circuit is established for the entire duration of a particular transmission no matter how large the associated files or the amount of time required to complete the transmission. For long data-intensive transmissions, this method is considered quite rigid because it makes no provision for rerouting the data flow even though the availability of *bandwidth* may shift around on the *network* during the time of the transmission. However, in the case of *digital video,* where it is critical that the flow of the *streaming data* not be interrupted in any way, the establishment of a circuit is almost mandatory. Thus, until the aggregate of available bandwidth rises to a point where the transmission requirements of a video datastream can be considered as trivial as *voice* transmission is today, the lifespan of ciruit switching will be temporarily extended.

CIX: Stands for Commercial Internet eXchange, a nonprofit trade association. Its member organizations provide *Internet* services to the public. Their goal is technical research and development for the mutual benefit of suppliers and customers of Internet services. Policies are set by a board of directors who are elected by member organizations. It is open to organizations that offer *TCP/IP* or *OSI* public data *internetworking* services to the general public in one or more geographical locations.

CLEC: Stands for Competitive Local Exchange Carriers. The Telecommunications Reform Act of 1996 opened the way for competition in the provision of local *dial-tone,* or plain old telephone services (*POTS*). This new acronym refers to the class of small company that has jumped into this newly formed market to compete with the *RBOCs,* or baby bells. Many of these smaller firms are providing an innovative array of services in addition to basic dial-tone, including *Internet* and other data connections. These firms are also commonly referred to as *CAPs,* or competitive access providers.

client/server: This term refers to a *network* of computers and processing, whereby remote computers (client) process information and send information to a main computer (server) for updating. In many ways, the *Internet* is a major example of a plethora of client/server networks working together to bring the world of the *Web* to the world of networked computer users.

clip consciousness: This term refers to the growing awareness that original media content—image, audio, and especially *video*—is laced with value in the form of clippable pieces of image, audio, and video. As an example of clip consciousness in action, the well-known *animation* firm Hanna-Barbera turned over some its best known sound effects to Microsoft for inclusion in *digitized* clip audio CDs.

clip media: This overarching term is used to describe the increasing propensity to *cut,* index, store, retrieve, and revise media elements, much as we have done with alphanumeric data during the early decades of the computer age. Common subtypes are clip art, for small pieces of artwork; clip audio, for small pieces of music and speech; and clip *video,* for small, categorizable segments of video. The move to clip media is one that possesses profound implications for society. The primary purpose of *"clipping,* indexing, and storing" these various media elements is so that they can be recombined with other elements for various commercial, artistic, or other purposes. It is just like the boilerplating behavior that occurs with respect to documents, especially with legal documents. One of the most profound social consequences of the continuing maturation of clip media, and the *cut-and-paste* technologies that make it possible, is that it will become virtually impossible to tell real from constructed (i.e., composited) media. Thus, audio recordings, printed images, and recorded video—all traditionally thought of as accurate and unimpeachable sources of information—will now become subject to all sorts of distortion and forgery. As a further source of legal complication, a number of legal issues are already surfacing with respect to the reusability of media elements. These issues will have most to do with the authorship, copyrighting, and licensing of clip media elements. Indeed, the *Internet* is a powerful force in the growing value of clip media, primarily because it lends itself to the accessing, clipping, and re-use of materials developed by others.

clipboard: This term refers to an *interface design* component that is used to supply temporary storage for elements that are being *cut and pasted* from one applicaiton or plac3 in a document to another.

clipping: From the realm of *DVE* (digital video effects), this term refers to the process of removing points and surfaces from a graphics datastream that are outside the *field of view.* For instance, as one circles an object in an *architectural walkthrough,* various dimensions of that object will appear and disappear as the point of view (*POV*) shifts perspective. The software algorithms responsible for automatically removing the points and surfaces that disappear as the POV shifts are referred to as clipping.

clock: In computers, this is a device that marks the time and generates periodic *signals* that control the timing of all computer operations. One of the primary functional specifications for a computer is its clock speed, which is a measure of how fast its clock pulses and, therefore, is also a measure of how quickly it turns over its instructions and other processes.

close-up: From the world of film and *video,* this term refers to a camera *shot* used to establish a desirable level of intimacy between the subject and the viewer. The close-in shot of the romantic interlude represents the exemplar of close-ups. This term is often held in contrast to the *long shot,* which is a camera *POV* (point of view) that is distant from its subject and is typically used to establish the general setting of a scene.

closure: This term refers to a psychological habit of the human mind exploited by every manner of artist—but especially filmmakers—wherein a partial *view* of a subject is provided with the intent that the audience will use its imagination to construct individual versions of a completed subject. In film, for example, a *close-up* of a tapping foot is often used to signify impatience, instead of showing the entirety of the impatient subject. In the *age of interactivity, branchpoints* may be used as a way of getting audience members to externalize their sense of closure. This will be done by providing decision-point options that represent the obvious conclusions that may be derived from performing a closure, e.g., by providing a decision-point option for a scene that one would select if he or she was impatient.

clueless newbie: A slang term from the cyber culture of the *Internet,* this term refers to a new, naive user who somehow betrays his or her ignorance of *Web etiquette,* the most common cases of which occur in the context of *chat* sessions.

CLUT: This term stands for Color Look-Up Table, which is an image encoding method. Under this method, the numeric value of each *pixel* is used to look up an *RGB* (red, green, blue) value in a table of color registers. This reduces the amount of data required to store an image by limiting the number of colors available. CLUT is a method that is usually employed for "computer-style" or "cartoon-style" graphics and *animation*.

CLV: This term stands for Constant Linear Velocity, one of two distinct formats for *videodisc* (the other being *CAV* [constant angular velocity]). With CLV, the information is laid down on the *disk* in one continuous spiral, as opposed to the separate, concentric *tracks* of CAV. For this reason, CLV is the preferred format for videodisc applications with long, continuous *video* plays, such as would be characteristic of a feature-length film delivered under this format.

CNIDR: Stands for Clearinghouse for Networked Information Discovery and Retrieval, an organization devoted to researching information resources on the *Internet*. For example, *WAIS, gopher,* and *archie* are worthy subjects of interest for CNIDR.

CO: Stands for Central Office, which is a very common telephone facility from which basic telephone services are provided to subscribers. In the typical CO, subscriber lines are joined to switching equipment that facilitates the interconnection of phones for both local and long distance calls. In the great debate over who will ultimately control the pipes of the *information superhighway,* the CO is often compared and contrasted with the *cable headend.* Both are the key distribution centers of their respective *networks.* Whereas the CO is given the advantage with respect to facilitating a many-to-many form of *connectivity* through its switching capabilities, the cable headend is given the nod for its superior *bandwidth.* The superior bandwidth of the cable operators results from their use of the more robust coaxial cable, as opposed to the relatively primitive copper-wire media used by providers of telephone services.

codec: A contraction for "compression-decompression," this term describes one of the key technologies of the information age. One of the first applications of codec technology was facsimile *transmission.* With this early form of *digital* transmission, it was realized early-on that the massive amounts of information generated by faxing documents all over the globe would create an urgent need to, first, compress the documents for transmission, and then, decompress them back to their original form once they arrived at their destinations. Using the codec transmission strategy made it possible to increase the effective transmission *bandwidth* by a factor that was directly proportional to the amount of *compression* that could be achieved. For example, a 10:1 *compression ratio*—not at all uncommon—made it possible to increase the transmission carrying capacity of one's communication lines by 10 times without changing any other technical aspect of the *transmission medium.* With the advent of *multimedia,* codec technology has become an even more important area of research and development, underscoring the need to facilitate the dramatically increased bandwidth required by digital forms of the various media—audio, image, and *video.* Reflecting the magnitude of this pursuit, a large number of codec techniques now exist (e.g., delta techniques), as well as an even larger number of commercial codecs (e.g., Apple's *QuickTime,* Intel's *DVI* [digital video interactive], and the industry standard *MPEG*), which are streaming into the market. Much of the debate over today's computer standards has to do with the search for an agreed-upon codec standard.

codes of resemblance: This useful term is one of many invented by the famous French film theorist Andre Bazin. Writing in the first half of the century, Bazin felt as though the primary secret to the power of film was its ability to *encode* reality in ways that resembled reality. Put in simple terms, film is successful because it represents the world in a very familiar form. As we enter an era of increasingly immersive media, i.e., an era dominated by the new forms of *virtual reality,* it would appear that Bazin's term should wear well with time. The new forms of *tactile feedback, motion platforms,* and the like are nothing if not new codes of resemblance.

cold objects: In any type of *hypermedia* system—including the *Internet*—objects that are in low demand are referred to as "cold objects." In a video on demand (*VOD*) system, for example, any *digital* movie that is not requested very often can be accurately called a cold object. In hierarchical storage management (*HSM*) systems, cold objects are typically migrated onto the low-cost, archival portions of the storage subsystem so that they do not occupy expensive, high-quality storage space that should be reserved for *hot objects* (i.e., objects that are in high demand).

collaboration technology: This term involves a group of technologies and behavioral science concepts and approaches that are brought together under the collective goal of facilitating and enhancing the daily work and interactions of people and machines that are pursuing a common business goal, project, or job.

collaborative filtering: This type of software application works by first building a profile of a user's interests, then tracking the information each user requests from servers. Next, the software compares the user's interests with those of others and displays the information one user has accessed to other users with similar interests. This breed of software is often used with *push technology,* where it enables users to see whether others found the information being delivered to be of value.

collision detector: This term comes to us from the realm of *virtual reality,* where it describes the tracking intelligence used to detect when two or more objects are trying to occupy the same coordinates in the three-dimensional space of a *virtual world.* Obviously, when this happens, they are colliding with one another. To remain true to the simulated reality of the virtual world, this tracking intelligence must also be accompanied by *multimedia* software routines that let users know that the objects are colliding. This is particularly the case since in many virtual worlds at least one of the colliding objects will be one of the users. The software intelligence that determines the presence of a collision between objects in a virtual world is referred to as a collision detector.

color space: This term refers to all wavelengths in the electromagnetic spectrum that produce a visible color effect—that is, color perceptible to the human eye.

com: Is a high-level *domain name* generally describing the *domain* as a commercial organization. Com also refers to a class of executable PC programs, usually running under DOS, such as the well-known "command.com," which is the program that manages the *UI* (*user interface*) of DOS.

combination view: From the realm of graphical user interface (*GUI*) design, this term refers to any screen in a windows-style *interface* that has two or more *windows* open at one time. The purpose of seeking such a view is that it permits comparative perspectives on, and/or interchanges of data and information between, the contents presented in the combination of views.

combinatorial explosion: Perhaps the most troublesome aspect of our early days of *interactive fiction,* this term refers to the phenomenon that occurs when an author of interactive content permits each decision point in a *decision tree* or narrative flow to spawn several outcomes. Eventually, the tree-like structure of the program spins out of control, exploding into an insupportable number of branches or combinations of outcomes. This problem was first encountered in the computer world by scientists who were attempting to build problem-solving programs that they thought would lead to *artificial intelligence.* As they attempted to define the ways in which even a simple problem might be solved, these early pioneers discovered that there might be literally trillions of ways in which the computer program could pursue the solution—many leading to incomplete solutions or down blind alleys. This intractable problem is now revisiting the industry by vexing the efforts of those who would attempt to build convincing interactive stories.

command-line interface: This term is used to describe an *interface design* that preceded the now popular graphical user interfaces (*GUIs*), like Microsoft's *Windows.* With the older *interfaces,* the user interacted with the computer's operating system by typing in commands on a rather spartan interface that featured only a drive designation followed by a colon. Often referred to as the "DOS-prompt," this approach to obtaining input from the user has been replaced, for the most part, by a *mouse-*driven world of *desktop metaphors* and the like. A few propeller-heads still prefer the command-line interface to the graphical user interface.

communities of practice: This term refers to groups of people who communicate with one another almost solely on the basis of mutual professional interests. These groups are almost always composed of individuals who belong to different departments or organizations, and who are typically located in different geographies as well. One of the reasons these groups have proliferated recently is that the *Internet* provides a means for all the dispersed members to communicate. Groups of computer artists and systems analysts are just two examples that are of particular relevance to *multimedia.* Communities of practice are of considerable moment because they represent a very strong cultural force promoting a widespread—and highly valued—use of the Internet.

compact disc: Is an injection-molded aluminum *disc* that stores high-density *digital* data in the form of microscopic *pits and lans* that a *laser* beam reads. Conceived by Philips and Sony, it was originally designed to store high-fidelity music, for which *CD-DA* is the accepted worldwide standard. Because of its large capacity compared to magnetic *disks,* the CD was seized upon by the computer industry when it became evident that computers were going to be called upon to process the higher *bandwidth* sources of information—audio, image, and *video.* Thus, *CD-ROM* (compact disc-read only memory) became the first viable direct-access storage standard for the *MPC* (multimedia personal computer).

However, the origin of CD technology as primarily an audio storage device created some early problems for *multimedia* computing, most of which had to do with the standard *transfer rate* of 150 Kbytes between the CD player and the computer. This transfer rate was ideally suited for CD-DA audio, but it did not adequately serve the needs of high-density graphics, digital images, or digital video. Consequently, while it was apparent that *optical storage* would resolve some of the storage needs of *digital media,* it soon became evident that the medium would have to evolve further if it was to sustain itself. As a result, CD technology is now giving way to its immediate successor in the computer realm, *DVD,* which offers the principal advantage of having been designed from the ground up to handle digital video, not just audio.

compiler: This is a computer program that *converts* the source code of a *high-level language* program into the machine code of a computer for processing.

complex information objects: This term is one of several that have appeared in the *Internet* and computer trade literature to provide an umbrella descriptor for the rapid procession of new media data types that are surfacing on the *Web*. Particularly from the perspective of the library science specialist, the various forms of electronic media appearing on the Web are difficult to define and catalog in conventional ways. This difficulty is particularly apparent with the sudden rise of the ubiquitous *Web site* on the Internet, the content of which varies significantly from one site to the next, and can represent anything from a fairly simple set of *HTML* pages, to a very complex *hypermedia* object. The term complex information object is, then, roughly synonymous with the equally general term *Internet resource.*

component video: One of two major types of *video,* the component video stream is transmitted as separate *luminance* and *chrominance signals* to provide a higher quality image. Often compared against *composite video,* which combines all of the video elements into a single signal, "component" pays a price for its higher quality; it requires more than one connector, and it takes up significantly more *bandwidth.*

composite signal: Most *signals* received by the human sensory system are of a composite nature. Reflecting the multisource nature of sensory reality, composite signals consist of many separate components that travel at different frequencies and *amplitudes* but that are perceived in the human mind as a single sensory experience. A simple example of a composite signal is that generated by a pipe organ. Each note produces a single tone, but when several notes are combined—as they typically are when playing an organ—the notes merge to form a complex waveform, which is another way of describing a composite signal. In the era of modern media, the scientific analysis and understanding of composite signals has made it possible to electronically decompose and recompose those signals in ways that enhance their usefulness to humans. In the coming era of *digital media,* this process will reach a new level of abstraction and flexibility through the exploding media manipulation capabilities made possible by *DSP* (digital signal processing) and other media-processing technologies.

composite video: One of two major types of *video,* the composite video signal economizes on *bandwidth* and connectors by combining the *RGB* (red, green, blue) and synchronization *signals* into one. This type of video is used by television and VCRs. It is often compared against *component video,* which transmits the video stream as separate *luminance* and *chrominance* signals to achieve a higher quality image—but at a higher cost.

compositing: Typically thought of as a part of *video postproduction,* this term more generally refers to the practice of layering one media image (sound or picture) on top of another. The practice of building a complex image with multiple layers usually proceeds in phases, with intermediate stages called "pre-composites," and culminates in the last stage, where the finishing element is laid down into what is called the "final composite." In the coming era of *desktop video production,* this practice will become fairly simple. Indeed, with the rise of increasingly sophisticated compositing tools, the much-feared specter of *digital* forgery appears whereby a skilled user can easily create a fraudulent visual or audio recording. These forgeries might then be used for highly dishonorable ends, such as incriminating innocent parties by placing them at the scene of an illegal deed.

compound document: This early term covers business communication's use of *multimedia* and refers to electronic documents composed not only of text and graphics, but also of audio and *video* segments. As an example, tomorrow's business letter as a compound document may contain a textual introduction, followed by video clips taken from a corporate multimedia database. Such video clips might include a set of graphics that depict a business process, accompanied by an executive's *voice annotations.*

compound document architectures: This term refers to an extension of the tagging languages that seeks to govern the structural characteristics of highly formatted (published) documents. These architectures seek ways to *encode,* and therefore make manipulable within the context of a single document, all of the *mixed media data types* that go into making up *compound documents.* The *ISO* open document architecture (ODA) and DEC's CDA (compound document architecture) are two early leaders in the effort to create these standards.

compression: Any effort to understand the technical problems of the emerging *multimedia* industry must start with a simple fact of life: computers were originally designed to handle alphanumeric forms of information, not high-*bandwidth* forms of data such as audio, image, or *video.* That audio, image, and video should have enormous value added to them once they become *digitized,* and therefore become susceptible to computer manipulation, is an absolute revelation, and one that is exerting strong influence over the entire computer industry at present. But the move to *digital* forms of media has introduced one enormous problem. Consider this example: one second of video digitized at a *resolution* (image quality) comparable to today's broadcast television takes up no less than 22 megabytes of storage. One second! That means that a feature length film of, say, two hours would require approximately 158 *gigabytes* of storage. Hence, a huge research and development effort is now underway around the world to find new and better ways to compress digital forms of image and video. The goal of these efforts is to make files smaller—while only throwing away information that will not be visually significant. To understand the magnitude of this effort to find new and innovative compression techniques, consider that a substantial portion of this glossary is given over to terms that name and describe the compression techniques thus far concocted by the industry (e.g., *JPEG, GIF, MPEG, QuickTime, DVI, fractal transform*).

compression ratio: A term of great significance in the *multimedia* industry, compression ratio refers to how well a particular *compression* technique does at reducing the size of a file of *digitized* media. At the low end, compression ratios for fax machines—which work with bit-mapped images of black-and-white documents—average in the range of 10:1. Thus, if an uncompressed *bit map* of a document takes 100 K of storage, its compressed counterpart at this ratio will take only 10 K. The current *JPEG* (Joint Photography Experts Group) standard for compressing color still images ranges up into the neighborhood of 40:1. *Fractal transform* techniques, which are among the most ambitious compression technologies to date, can range comfortably up into the 200:1 range.

computable: This fairly abstract term is used to describe a process by which *complex information objects,* such as images and documents, are made more directly manipulable by computers. Thus, for example, when a *metadata* profile is created for a complex document type, such as a legal will or a divorce agreement, these document are said to become more computable because the metadata provide a means for the computer to quickly access their specific contents. Similarly, when a set of *digital images* are indexed, they are said to be more computable because they can now be easily found through the use of a *search engine.* Obviously, then, the meaning of this term lies at the very heart of *multimedia,* which is all about making the various forms of *analog* media more computable.

congestion: In the world of computer *networks,* congestion occurs on a *network* line when the data being presented for transfer exceeds the capacity of the line, i.e., an electronic traffic jam.

connect time: Is the elapsed time that a user is logged on to a system. Many online services charge users for the time connected. Other services offer unlimited connect time for a monthly fee.

connectivity: One of the grand goals of the information age, connectivity refers to the ability of information systems to allow remotely separated users to communicate in some meaningful fashion with one another. With respect to contemporary forms of computing, the term connectivity is typically used to refer to the exchange of data files, such as *e-mail* messages. In the coming era of *interactive multimedia,* it will be used to refer to the exchange of *digital media,* such as with *digital video* forms of mail.

console cowboy: This term refers to *cyberpunks* who prove their valor by donning *virtual reality* headgear and performing heroic feats in the imaginary world of *cyberspace.* These console cowbows are not to be confused with real cowboys as depicted in John Wayne and Clint Eastwood movies, though many must certainly view themselves as such.

construction visualizer: This term refers to a prime example of the commercial value of *scientific visualization.* It is a program that helps building contractors plan site layouts by visualizing the movement of materials, machines, and trucks for real estate development projects.

consumer software: This popular term used in the business media includes *home interactive* media programs. Of the titles that today would fall squarely into the category of *interactive multimedia* technology, Broderbund's Where in the World is Carmen Sandiego? is commonly thought of as the first major success among this class of program called consumer software.

content provider: In its widest possible meaning, this term refers to any organization that provides some type of information product for general public consumption. Thus, film studios, television broadcasters, music producers, publishers, and other firms that *host Web sites* are all content providers. Indeed, this term has been introduced to our vocabulary for just the purpose of providing a general descriptor for producers of all these types of media. The sudden emergence of the *Internet* and the *World Wide Web* makes the need for this type of term even more timely because these *WAN* standards are accelerating our move into the era in which all forms of media will be *digital* and subject to production processes that use a common set of tools and procedures.

contention protocols: From the world of computer *networks,* this term describes the dominant and traditional form of managing dataflow over networks. Under contention *schemes,* only one data conversation can have control of the network at any given time. However, because most traditional data files are based on alphanumeric (character-based) sources of data, and are therefore of relatively small size, most data conversations are of relatively short duration. Thus, the strategy of limiting flow on the network to one data conversation at a time is highly practical, and only leads to degradation during unusually heavy *bursts* of dataflow. This contention protocol, however, is not well suited to handling the high-*bandwidth* sources of data that make up *mixed media data types.* With the audiovisual data types, networks must be able to handle large, continuously flowing, time-critical streams of data, appropriately referred to as *streaming data.* Consequently, as we enter an era in which *multimedia* data types are of increasing importance, this *network management protocol* is likely to be on the decline.

context-sensitive help: Considered one of the seminal ideas behind *performance support* systems, this term refers to an intelligent extension of the help screen whereby the help is specific to the users' situations at the moment they invoke the help function. It implies that the help system is intelligent enough to interpret what the user is trying to accomplish at any given moment and has given rise to such related concepts as *embedded training* and electronic *job aids.*

continuity: In the film and *video* industry, this term refers to the importance of maintaining the logical order and consistency of what is seen on-screen. With the advent of *interactive cinema,* where the audience may travel a multitude of possible paths through the film experience, maintaining continuity—what Aristotle called "unity"—will be among the most difficult challenges of the enterprise.

contrast ratio: A measure of image quality in *video* playback equipment (e.g., *CRTs* and *LCDs*), this ratio describes the ability of a device to *capture* the differences between bright and dark areas. Generally, CRTs have a much better contrast ratio than LCD screens for they have better *shading* and smoother lines. This concept is somewhat analogous to the audio notion of *dynamic range,* which measures the ability of an audio playback device to capture the differences between loud and soft tones.

controlled vocabulary: From the world of library science, this term refers to any body of strictly controlled words and phrases used to index *complex information objects* for orderly information storage and retrieval. With respect to creating a database of *multimedia* objects (e.g., images, graphics, audio and *video* clips), controlled vocabularies are often used to exert some form of discipline over the indexing of the objects for entry into and retrieval out of the database. Such controlled vocabularies are also often referred to as *subject indexes.* The Library of Congress Thesaurus of Graphic Materials (*TGM*) is perhaps the best-known subject index available to the multimedia industry today.

convert: From the world of data processing, this term refers to the process of translating data from one file format to another. In the world of the *Internet, proprietary* file formats need to be converted to *HTML* so that they may become accessible to *browsers* on the *Web.*

Convolvotron: Based on technology developed at the NASA *Ames Research Center* in collaboration with Crystal River Engineering of Groveland, California, this extremely powerful audio *DSP* (digital signal processor) changes, or convolves, an *analog* sound source using *HRTF* (head-related transfer functions) to create a 3-D *digital* sound effect. Sound that is computer-synthesized, or that is drawn from an external source like a *compact disc,* can be filtered through the Convolvotron and placed in a 3-D space around the listener. The sound-space *resolution* of the Convolvotron is virtually infinite, meaning that it can take *analog* sounds and distribute them to as many sound source positions within the *3-D sound* space as is desired.

cookie: From the world of the *Internet,* this term refers to a small data file that contains information about you and your computer. Advertisers on the *Web* often use cookies to target specific market groups. The cookie is created by an external application and passed to your *browser.* It is checked for length, expiration date, path, and *domain,* and then stored as cookie.txt. The next time you sign on to that application, it uses the information contained in the cookie to present you with a personally tailored screen. For security reasons, a cookie is always restricted in content to data, never containing any code that can be executed. This feature substantially reduces the possibility that a cookie can contain any *viruses* that might damage your computer system. The role of the cookie has quickly expanded. For instance, it facilitates the work of many *servers* by providing steady-state information about your terminal. The server sends your browser a cookie, and each time the browser requests a new page, it sends back the cookie with steady-state information. Cookies are also used in a closed *intranet* to simplify logging on.

copyright: Owing to the rise of the *Internet,* the concept and practice of copyright has become a dramatically heightened source of interest and concern. Copyright is the exclusive right, belonging to the owner, to copy, perform, or display in public or prepare derivative works from an original work. Copyright law has its basis in the Constitution (Art. I, Sect. 8), which gives Congress the authority "to promote the progress of science and useful arts, by securing for limited times to authors and inventors the exclusive right to their respective writings and discoveries." A copyright applies to the author's way of expressing an idea or concept, not the idea or concept itself. A patent is required to protect the idea. Works that can be copyrighted include anything published or unpublished and presented in a tangible medium. These works can include literary pieces, musical compositions, dramatic selections, dances, photographs, drawings, paintings, sculptures, diagrams, advertisements, maps, motion pictures, radio and television programs, sound recordings, and—by special legislation passed by the Congress of the United States in 1980—computer software programs. For works created after January 1, 1978, the copyright belongs to the authors from the time of creation until 50 years after their deaths, but it can be lost unless a copyright notice appears on all publicly distributed copies in one of the following forms: the word copyright, the abbreviation Copr., or the symbol © accompanied by the name of the owner and the year of first publication (for example, © John Doe 1997). To have full copyright protection, the author must file a copyright claim with the Copyright Office in Washington, DC, and pay a fee. For material produced as an employee, the copyright belongs to the employer. The concept of *fair use* allows for copying of copyrighted material in some carefully defined circumstances, including the educational purposes associated with classroom usage.

CORBA: Stands for Common Object Request Broker Architecture, an interoperability standard created by the Object Management Group (*OMG*) to enforce guidelines that enable a wide variety of objects (as in *object-oriented programming*) to interact with one another in a distributed computing environment. CORBA confronts a significant technical challenge by seeking to create standards for a universal form of object-request broker. The purpose of an object-request broker is to manage the interaction between client and *server* objects (as in *client/server* computing), and thereby to enable objects contained in different applications, and even executed on different *platforms,* to interconnect seamlessly. If, for example, you are working with a word processor on your workstation and need to access a spellchecker *applet* from some remote *Web* server, the underlying technology that will make this process seamless will in all likelihood be compliant with the CORBA standard.

couch commando: This slang term is held in contrast to the well-known "couch potato" and is used to signify that an individual belongs to the next generation of viewing audience, who will interact with and participate in the content rather than just sitting passively in front of the television.

courseware: This general term is used to describe programs that embody the convergence of software and instruction. The term *educational software* is a near-synonym, though many purists in the field of *instructional technology* would insist that the term courseware applies to any form of instructional media, including paper-based products, instructional *videos,* etc. However, in general, courseware has become synonymous with educational software. With the rapid growth of the *Internet,* one can now access courseware from a *Web site.* This courseware is commonly referred to as *WBT,* or Web-based training.

CPU: One of the most common terms in the computer industry, this acronym refers to the Central Processing Unit. Also referred to as the processor, the CPU is the brains of the computer, the engine that drives all other aspects of the computer system.

CPU-intensive: As we enter the age of *multimedia,* this term is becoming a veritable catch phrase because so many applications—from *3-D animation* to compression-decompression—are pushing the limits of the current families of processor technology. An application is said to be CPU-intensive when it demands a large number of *CPU* cycles to be performed. The *rendering* of a 3-D animation is a good example of a CPU-intensive application. "Compute-intensive" and "processor-intensive" are widely used synonyms. This term is also at the heart of the *NC* versus workstation argument. Advocates of the NC, or *network* computer, argue that highly sophisticated *desktop* computers will not be needed in the coming era of network-centric computing, because most of the algorithmic sophistication needed to run complex applications will be accessible from *Web servers* across the network. Critics of this view would argue that way too many CPU-intensive applications are still out there for the NC to be a viable option for users of sophisticated applications, such as a high-end computer game (e.g., *Riven*).

cropping: Is a process common to the manipulation of *digital* images. This term refers specifically to discarding unwanted portions of an image. Cropping is most commonly done with freshly scanned images where the *scanner* has picked up unintentional debris around the edges of the target image.

cross fader: From the realm of audio engineering, this term refers to a knob or *slider* that enables the engineer to balance the level of two audio inputs, performing a smooth transition between the two. At one end of the continuum, it passes only one source, and at the opposite end, it passes only the other. In between, it blends the two sources proportionately.

cross-media authoring: Increasingly, creators of *multimedia* content, such as *electronic game* manufacturers and *CBT* (computer-based training) developers, need to produce programs that run on both a stand-alone *MPC* workstation and on the *Web.* Unfortunately, most traditional authoring tools, such as Macromedia's Director and Asymmetrix's ToolBook, were brought to market well before the Web flowered in the mid-1990s. These tools were optimized for developing content that targets MPCs, which have been historically based on *CD-ROMs* for delivering media-rich content. However, given the meteoric rise of the Web as a *channel* for content delivery, most of these *authoring system* vendors have developed tools that enable rapid—and, in some cases, transparent—conversion of content to run on the stand-alone MPC as well as on the Web. Macromedia's Shockwave provides an excellent example. When the authoring environment enables a content developer to create a multimedia program that will run on both an MPC and on the Web with little or no rework, then this environment is said to provide for cross-media authoring.

CRT: This term stands for Cathode Ray Tube and refers to the most common type of *video* display technology, with regard to both computing and television. With this technology, a vacuum tube with an electron gun at one end and a phosphor-coated screen at the other is used to *convert* voltages into patterns of images on the screen for viewing.

Cryptolope: An encryption technology developed by IBM, the Cryptolope is designed to enable forms of *e-commerce* that protect both the vendor and the customer. Known as a "secure container" form of encryption technology, the Cryptolope works by enforcing the following process. The publisher of an information product encrypts the document in which it is contained, stipulating the conditions under which it can be opened. The user, or customer of that information product, *downloads* and opens the encrypted package with the Cryptolope player. The user then sends a credit card number, which is also encrypted by the Cryptolope player, and receives a key to unlock the package. The user employs the Cryptolope players to open, view and print, or view and save the document, as they see fit. In other words, once they have opened the package, they are then free to consume the contents. If the vendor, or publisher, has prohibited the user from saving the document, that user can still pass it along as a Cryptolope to other users.

CSLIP: Stands for Compressed Serial Line Internet Protocol. It is a *protocol* that uses a compressed *TCP/IP* header, reduced from 40 *bytes* to 7 bytes, for data *packets*. It offers a significant and useful saving when a small packet size is all that is required to move the information. It works for *Internet* connections via the *serial,* or communications, *ports*. It has no effect on *UDP,* another transport protocol.

CSS: Stands for Cascading Style Sheet, which is a *style sheet* derived from multiple sources with a defined order of precedence where the definitions of a particular style element are in conflict. Cascading style sheets are rapidly becoming a major design element on *Web sites.*

CSU: Stands for Channel Service Unit. From the world of *data communications,* this *interface* connects a computer to a *digital* communications *channel.* Unlike a *DSU,* the CSU requires that users provide their own digital *transmission* and receive functions.

cue sheet: From the world of *video production,* this form shows the mixer where various sounds on a *track* stop and start. It is used during *postproduction* when combining the tracks (components) of a picture onto one master track. Much of the *production* "logic" communicated by cue sheets is now embodied in the *time-line interfaces* used by several popular *authoring systems.*

CUI: This term stands for Character User Interface and refers to the computer precursor to the graphical user interface (*GUI*), in which the entire *interface* was constructed from alphanumeric characters. Users of earlier generations of personal computers will recall that the CUI phase of *desktop* computing was characterized by the DOS prompt, a total reliance on the *ASCII* character set, and the need to use typed commands to get anything done on the computer.

curator file: This term refers to a use of *hypermedia applications* that is becoming increasingly common, especially over the *Internet.* A curator file is an encyclopedic, *hypermedia* collection of items that represent a museum's stock of *artifacts.* Typically, these hypermedia programs will include *digitized* images of the artifacts, text descriptors, and audio overlays that explain the origins, meaning, and/or significance of those artifacts. Many producers of these programs are now adding *video sequences* that add depth to the meaning of selected artifacts. More and more, museums are building such hypermedia creations as a way of capitalizing on their unique *media assets.* They are also—perhaps unwittingly—adding to the growing canon of *surrogate travel* products, which are designed to eliminate the need to travel to the places where the artifacts originated.

cursor: This refers to a position indicator that can be a symbol on the screen (a screen cursor) or a handheld device for entering coordinate points (a hand cursor).

cursor plane: In the world of *digital video,* this plane is the uppermost *picture plane* used to render the computer screen. It is a small area, typically no larger than 16 x 16 *pixels,* and is used to display the current position of the *cursor.*

curtain: From the realm of *DVE* (digital video effects), this is a *two-plane effect* in which the image on the *front plane* parts or closes like a pair of curtains to reveal the image on the *back plane.*

CUSeeMe: This program, developed by White Pine Software, is a pioneering product that allows for *videoconferencing* on the *Internet* at a reasonable cost. However, no matter how effective and reasonably priced the software may be, low *bandwidth* across the Internet makes for a less-than-perfect *view* of the participants in the Internet videoconference.

cut: From the world of filmmaking, this term refers to the end of a scene.

cut and paste: This is an interactive technique for moving items from one location to another within an electronic document or from one document to another. Originally, this term referred exclusively to the movement—the cutting and pasting—of text segments using a word processor. However, as *mixed media data types* and the *Internet* have found their way into the computing environment, this term has gained much wider application; it can just as easily refer to moving audio, image, graphic, or *video* segments from one place in a *compound document* to another.

cuts-only editing software: Among the slew of new *video postproduction* software tools, this is one of the simplest, specializing in the automation of some of the tedious tasks associated with *A/B roll editing*. Basically, these products offer many of the same controls found on *analog* editing decks, such as viewing, cataloging, and tagging video segments as well as creating *EDLs* (edit decision lists).

cutting room: This is the *editor's* work area, and in traditional filmmaking, the central place of *postproduction activity*. As the world of film and *video production* continues its move into the *digital domain,* the need for a real cutting room, per se, will cease to exist. However, it is highly probable that the notion of the cutting room will live on in a metaphorical way, since the essential postproduction process of editing out the majority of video or film content that is originally recorded will not go away.

CWIS: Stands for Campus-Wide Information Server, a type of networked information system often cited as one of the early prototypes for what is now being called an *intranet*. A CWIS is an information system for a college or university. It typically provides access to a host of resources appropriate for a collegiate community, such as course catalogs, job listings, announcements, campus calendars, and so forth.

cyber mall: An emerging genre of *Web site,* a cyber mall is the *Internet* equivalent of the old Sears & Roebuck mail order catalog. It is a Web site that adds value by aggregating the products of many suppliers, allowing customers to have a one-stop shopping experience on the *World Wide Web.* Cyber malls give small "mom-and-pop" electronic merchants the potential to compete successfully with large retail outlets and other more established brand name "stores" on the Internet.

cyberarts: This is a general term for describing the various emergent forms of interactive entertainment and art, including *interactive cinema* and *interactive fiction,* the various immersive gaming devices associated with *virtual reality,* and a number of entertainment genres that rely on high-*bandwidth* communications to bring geographically dispersed parties together to benefit from some type of shared experience (a.k.a. *cyberspace*).

cybercash: An emergent *enabling technology* of *e-commerce,* this term refers to *digital* forms of currency that can be used over the *Web* to consummate business transactions. Cybercash has the properties of being safeguarded by one or more *network* security features, of being almost infinitely divisible (i.e., as in "microcurrency"), and of being entirely mediated by electronic processes.

cybernetics: This term, which now stands for an entire discipline, was coined by Norbert Weiner of MIT during World War II. At the time, Weiner was designing a system for anti-aircraft guns. During this project, he realized that the key element in a control system of any making—natural or artificial—is a feedback loop that gives a controller information on the results of its actions. He called such systemic considerations cybernetics, a term that has been expanded to refer to the science of communication and control theory. With the prospects of such technologies as *voice* and optical recognition in the offing, the future of this discipline is very bright—and very expansive.

cyberpunk: A term originally used to describe a specific type of individual—a modern-day beatnik of sorts. Yet it has recently expanded to refer to an entire subculture that combines an infatuation with high-tech tools and a disdain for conventional ways of using them—a sort of counterculture including such postmodern phenomena as psychedelics, smart drugs, and cutting-edge technology (especially *virtual reality*). Cyberpunk seems to be part and parcel of the shift from a reverence for the wisdom of the past to the veneration of a technology-driven future.

cyberspace: This now-famous term originated in the cult classic *The Neuromancer,* written by William Gibson in 1984. A basic definition of cyberspace is a 3-D *domain* in which *cybernetic* feedback and control occur. A cyberspace system is one that provides users with a 3-D interactive experience that includes the illusion they are inside a world rather than observing an image. One reason this term has gathered so much popularity is because, in its multiple meanings, it tracks very closely with the concept of *virtual reality.*

Digital technology challenges the traditional relationship between the artist and the viewer/listener. The director will have to give up some of his autonomy . . .

—Paul Schrader, Film Director

DAC: Stands for Digital-to-Analog Conversion. It is the reverse process of *ADC* (analog-to-digital conversion) that occurs on the playback side of the *digital* equation for producing computer-mediated media. For example, with digital audio, the ADC *converts analog,* or waveform, audio into a digital stream of data, and the DAC converts it back to an analog form that can be heard using loudspeakers or headphones.

daemon: Is a program running, but asleep, waiting for a stimulus event to wake it up to perform its function. A prime example of a daemon is the HTTPD (hyper text transport protocol daemon), which is a program found on every *Web server* that waits to fulfill file retrieval requests from the *Web.*

DAG: Stands for Data Acquisition Glove, a device developed at the National Advanced Robotics Research Center in the United Kingdom in conjunction with Airmuscle, Ltd. This device is used in tandem with the *TeleTact Glove,* developed by the same principals. The DAG, as the name implies, is a glove used to *capture* the *force pattern* data associated with grasping various real-world objects (e.g., the gearshift of a racecar). When you put this glove on and grasp a real object, the force-sensitive resistors register distinct *force patterns.* These patterns are, in turn, *converted* to proportional electrical values (i.e., they are *digitized*) and stored in computer memory. Engineers then use this data to create templates of how various objects feel, and, over time, build up a library of *force pattern* templates in much the same fashion that makers of *MIDI* (musical instrument digital interface) *wave tables* build up *patch* sets of musical instrument sounds. These digitized *force feedback* patterns are then used with the *TeleTact Glove,* which is the *output device* used to re-create the tactile sensations associated with a particular *virtual reality* application.

daisy chain: A type of *network topology,* also referred to as a *"bus* topology," in which all network computers are connected to a single *transmission* line. Most local area networks (*LANs*) are based on this type of topology.

DARPA: Stands for Defense Advanced Research Projects Agency, a military organization that has been responsible for funding innumerable research and development projects that have led to advances in the global *Internet,* as well as in the development of many new media prototypes. DARPA originally developed *DDN,* the Defense Data Network, which is a global communications *network* that connects U.S. military installations throughout the world. Another example of an innovative DARPA project is *SIMNET* (Simulated Network), which is a *virtual reality simulation* of an electronic battlefield.

data blade: A concept first made popular by Illustra, a data blade is an object library (see *object-oriented programming*) that contains object implementations for specific categories of applications. This concept is of substantial importance to the evolution of the *multimedia* industry because it represents one of the first concerted efforts to create a data modeling strategy for managing complex information objects. Traditionally, database management technology has only concerned itself with alphanumeric data that can be neatly organized into tables. Data blades are designed on an application-by-application basis to provide database-like facilities for all manner of nontabular information objects. For example, before being acquired by Informix, Illustra developed specific data blades for such complex information objects as 2-D and 3-D spatial objects, *digital* images, and text documents. Consistent with the tenets of object-oriented design, data blades encapsulate both data and software functionality. Hence, the data blade for images contains a wide range of software functions for helping users query and manipulate digital image objects. Functions such as "GetColor," "GetHeight," and "GetWidth" are embedded in the image data blade.

data bus: That part of the internal architecture of the personal computer responsible for transporting data between internal memory (RAM) and the computer's *CPU.* The data bus also provides the "pathway" for moving data among RAM, the CPU, and the various other parts of the computer's architecture, such as the *expansion boards* and the serial and parallel ports (where the PC accesses the outside world of *networks* and peripherals). When a user *downloads* a file across the *Internet,* that file will travel into the computer's internal memory via the data bus.

data capture: This commonly used computer term is nearly synonymous with "digitizing." It refers to the point in the information processing *sequence* where noncomputer sources of information (like pictures of the real world and the real world itself) become digitally *encoded* so that they may be submitted to some form of manipulation by the computer.

data cleansing: An important step in the creation of a *data warehouse* or *data mart.* This is the process whereby the data admitted to the data warehouse or data mart are checked to ensure that all values are consistent and correctly recorded. As *database publishing* becomes a common occurrence on the *Internet,* those charged with provisioning the data need to be sure that the vendors they hire perform an adequate degree of data cleansing to ensure the integrity of the information they are selling.

data communications: This is a broad term used to describe the general phenomenon of exchanging *digital* forms of information between two or more locations.

data conferencing: An enhanced derivative of *document conferencing,* this term refers to a form of all-digital communications in which there is simultaneous *voice* and data *transmission* on the same communications line. With data conferencing, the voice is *digitized* and treated—in *multimedia* fashion—as just one element in the data stream.

data mart: Is considered a scaled-down version of a *data warehouse.* Most data warehouses are very large, and typically contain data from across the entire corporate enterprise. In contrast, data marts are more specialized, and typically will host data that is limited to, for example, a single department within an organization. Like data warehouses, data marts are secondary stores of information derived from the day-to-day production databases of their sponsoring organizations. And, as with data warehouses, it is expected that many commercial enterprises will use their data marts to generate revenue by making them available to paying customers through a practice known as *database publishing.*

data mining: Is a term used to define a variety of techniques for extracting useful information from the large databases for the purposes of making better informed business decisions. Many different data mining techniques are available, most of them based upon advanced statistical algorithms. The ones to use depend on the type of information required and the data available. Some common types are association, *sequence*-based analysis, clustering, classification, estimation, fuzzy logic, fractal-based transforms, *neural networks,* and *decision trees.* Data mining is projected to be a major *World Wide Web* application. It will likely be integrated with *intelligent software agent* technology to assist all types of people in making better business and personal decisions.

data rate: This term refers to the maximum sustainable throughput for an input/output device. In the era of *multimedia,* this rate often determines the fitness-for-duty of a given peripheral device.

data tablet: Also referred to as a "digitizing tablet," this term describes a flat working surface drawn upon by a *stylus* or hand *cursor* to produce an input stream of coordinate data.

data visualization: A technique used increasingly in science and business, this term describes the visual representation and interpretation of complex relationships in multidimensional data. As more voluminous and sophisticated forms of data become available across the *Internet,* designers of *Web sites* will want to take increasing advantage of the techniques of data visualization. They enable the analyst to gain a deeper, more intuitive understanding of the data. This term is nearly synonymous with *scientific visualization.*

data warehouse: Is a special form of database that houses large, well-organized sources of data used repeatedly by corporate enterprises to conduct research and enhance business decision making. To understand the modern data warehouse, it is critical to grasp one very important distinction. Most large commercial organizations in today's world have large databases that house their customer and transaction data. These databases are used heavily in the day-to-day functioning of the business and are typically referred to as "production databases." These databases are highly dynamic and volatile, as they change with every new customer transaction. Additionally, the production databases must be as responsive as possible, since the functioning of the organization depends upon their accuracy and reliability. Given this fact, most organizations do not permit their business analysts to run queries against these production database systems. Instead, for such research-oriented purposes, the organizations create secondary databases that are fed highly filtered, or "cleansed," data from the production database systems. These secondary databases are known as data warehouses. Increasingly, data warehouses are being used to store large volumes of historical data against which business analysts can perform various forms of *data mining.* As data warehouses grow in popularity and sophistication, it is expected that many of their sponsoring organizations will use them to generate revenue through the practice of *database publishing,* whereby paying customers may access and query these rich information stores for their own research purposes.

database publishing: This term refers to what is considered to be one of the biggest and most immediate opportunities for adding end-user value to the stock of *Internet resources.* Most large corporations have in their possession large and long-standing databases, typically focused on customer transaction records and histories, but also covering a host of other business elements. Owing to the fact that these data sets usually reside in rather old database management systems (DBMS), they are often referred to as legacy databases. Database publishing thus refers to the process of making these legacy databases available to interested parties across the *Web* by adding to them, at minimum, access logic with a *browser interface* into the data. Most early forms of database publishing occur across corporate *intranets,* where the communities of interest are strongest, and appropriate security controls can be implemented against what are often privileged stores of information. However, with time and maturation in the market, many companies are expected to find ways to generate new sources of revenue by offering database publishing services to their customers.

DataGlove: A prototypical *virtual reality* (VR) product from VPL Research, this "input" device permits users to reach into the 3-D environment of a *virtual world* while viewing a *virtual* hand corresponding to their own real one. Users can grasp and move virtual objects, and perform various gestural commands. It works through the performance of *fiber-optic* bundles located along the glove's finger, thumb, and palm surfaces. These bundles work by responding to degrees of flexibility and positioning of the various hand features and sending *encoded signal* pulses to the processor. In the short time in which this product was on the market, it took on a generic status. VR aficionados now refer to data gloves as a type of *virtual reality* device, much as the general public uses a term like Kleenex in lieu of "facial tissues."

DataSuit: Produced by VPL Research, this VR concoction makes total immersion possible through the electronic performance of inertial and positioning sensors. The wearer of this suit can move (either freely around a room or on a treadmill) and interact with the *virtual world* through the rull range of the body's movements.

DATV: Stands for Digital-Advanced TeleVision, which is a term recently invented in conjunction with FCC-sponsored efforts to establish a set of *transmission* standards for the soon-to-emerge all-digital television. This standard may eventually replace *NTSC* (National Television Standards Committee), which has reigned as the standard for television in the United States for several decades.

DBS: Stands for Direct Broadcasting by Satellite, which is a rapidly growing technology for delivering entertainment to the home (residential) market. DBS systems are based on the use of satellites to transmit high-power television *signals* directly to homes, where those signals are received via small antennae (also called "dishes"). Primestar and DirecTV are two of the better known providers of DBS services.

DCA: Stands for Directory Client Agent, which is a program that keeps track of *DSA* sites on the *Internet.* DCAs are typically used to search DSAs for names and *addresses* and other resources on the *networks* that a given DSA is responsible for tracking.

DCE: Stands for Data Communications Equipment, which is a term often used by professionals in the field of *data communications.* A DCE is a device that enables data communications to occur by manipulating and/or regulating the flow of data onto and off of transmission lines. *Modems* and *DSUs* (digital service units) are common types of DCEs. Most people connected to the *Internet* rely on some form of DCE to send and receive information to and from the *Web.*

D-channel: One of the fundamental components of an *ISDN* connection, the D-channel is a 16 *Kpbs channel* used for communicating technical control information between the ISDN terminal equipment and the *CO* (central office) switch.

DCT: Stands for Discrete Cosine Transform, an increasingly common *compression* technique used, for example, with the *JPEG* (Joint Photography Experts Group) standard. Essentially, DCT algorithms throw out redundant *pixel* data and analyze the *frequency* of the color data, or *chrominance,* contained in a *video frame* and then use that information to discard the least important visual data.

DDN: Stands for Defense Data Network. It is a global communications *network* for the U.S. Department of Defense. DDN includes *MILNET,* portions of the *Internet,* and classified networks that are not part of the Internet. Originally developed by *DARPA* and presently managed by the Defense Information Systems Agency, the DDN connects U.S. military installations worldwide.

de facto standard: This refers to any standard that arises outside of the formal, standard-setting activities of industry-sanctioned committees. Most commonly, de facto standards come into being because an innovative, entrepreneurial solution appears in the marketplace. Because this previously unheard-of solution is far superior to the current standard being offered up by the industry majors, the invisible hand of consumer selection chooses it to be the standard for its particular industry niche. It is the result of capitalism, and it occurs with almost maddening frequency in the fast world of computer technology and the ultra-fast world of *multimedia* technology. It leads to that most wonderful, yet dreaded, economic phenomenon known as "functional obsolescence." The most common de facto standards for the *Internet* are to be found with respect to the use of *browsers*. At this time *Netscape Navigator* and Microsoft *Internet Explorer* are vying with one another to become the "de facto" standard for browsers.

decibel: This term refers to the most widely used measure of the relative loudness of sound. One decibel is equal to the smallest difference of loudness detectable by the human ear.

decision tree: For those who would attempt to build *interactive fiction,* or any form of *multimedia* like it, the decision tree is a key concept. Drafted into the world of multimedia development from such business and scientific disciplines as management science and *artificial intelligence,* this term captures the notion that a single decision point will have multiple outcomes. Each of those outcomes will spawn additional decision points, and each of those will spawn several more outcomes until the decision-making process being modeled has been completed. This tracking of decision points and their downstream outcomes leads to the creation of a flowchart-like structure that imitates the visual form of a tree—especially a Christmas tree—that has been turned on its side. The decision tree is particularly important to the early theory of interactive design because it offers a graphical representation of the central problem associated with building interactive content. Without any type of reconvergence of decision paths, or other constraining strategy, the natural progression of an interactive fiction or business case study will likely lead to a *combinatorial explosion* of decision points and outcomes. Such a design structure, while conceptually appealing, is virtually impossible to produce, because it simply demands that too many outcomes be constructed.

decision-based scripting: This is another term for interactive scriptwriting, or the writing of scripts for interactive programs. It reflects the fact that scriptwriting in the interactive *domain* must take account of the user's ability and desire to participate in the decision-making process. In this regard, scriptwriters must think in terms of *decision trees,* alternate scenarios, multiple outcomes, and the like.

declustering: Another term for *file striping,* declustering is a high-performance strategy that allows for distribution of a single file over several storage devices. This strategy is important in the age of *multimedia* technology because through its facilitation of pipelining (i.e., the parallel and concurrent processing of different segments of the same file), it permits rapid movement of the enormous files associated with *mixed media data types.*

decoder: This term has a host of meanings in the information age, but is most commonly used to describe a device that is supplied to cable TV subscribers to enable them to receive *signals* to their television sets. Also referred to as a "converter," this device is apt to take on substantially greater functionality as we enter the era of *DTV* (digital television), where it is apt to be called upon to *convert* the TV into an interactive terminal.

decompression: The flip side of *compression,* this term refers to the process by which compressed forms of *digitized* media are reconstructed for presentation or further processing. With many of the simpler *codec* (compression-decompression) technologies, the decompression process is roughly comparable in effort to its compression counterpart. However, for the more sophisticated techniques that achieve higher *compression ratios* (such as *MPEG*), the decompression process takes much less effort. For this reason, these more sophisticated techniques are called *asymmetrical codecs*—that is, they take more time and computing resources to compress the media than they do to decompress it. However, because decompression typically occurs in *real time*—i.e., just before the media is presented to the end user—it is by far the more time-sensitive half of the codec process.

degrees of freedom: This term is commonly used as a gauge of sophistication with regard to the forms of *virtual reality* (VR) that seek to immerse the user in a *virtual world.* The most sophisticated VR systems accommodate up to six degrees of freedom: three in the Cartesian coordinate space of left/right (x), up/down (y), and forward/backward (z); and three having to do with the changes in orientation known as *pitch* (motion around the *x-axis*), roll (motion around the *z-axis*), and yaw (motion around the y-axis).

delivery system: This general term refers to the combination of hardware and software components needed to deliver a particular *multimedia* or *courseware* program. For most of the industry's history, multimedia solutions have been brought to their audiences via *stand-alone systems,* i.e., delivery systems not connected to any *network*. Typical of these traditional stand-alone systems was the *interactive video* workstation, which usually included a *laserdisc,* a personal computer, and a television, all interconnected and controlled by a program developed using an *authoring system.* Rarely were these workstations ever connected with one another over a network. However, as we sail into a future occupied by such technologies as *interactive television* and the *information superhighway,* multimedia delivery systems are increasingly becoming associated with the same sorts of networking features that now characterize advanced data-processing systems in the corporate world.

delta encoding: This term refers to one of the more common strategies for *compression* of image data. With this technique, the actual value of each *pixel* is not what gets stored and/or transmitted. Instead, what gets stored is the amount that must be added to the current pixel value to produce the value of the next pixel in a *scan line.* For each scan line, the true value of the first (leftmost) pixel is stored, but thereafter a series of differences, or deltas, is stored for each subsequent pixel. The assumption underlying this technique for compression of visual data is that the range of deltas will be small relative to the range of the true pixel values.

depth cueing: From the realm of *DVE* (digital video effects), this term refers to a process in which a graphical object's color and intensity are reduced as a function of its distance from the observer.

desktop: As with the use of "environment" in public discourse, the use of the term desktop in the computer industry is gathering so many references that it runs the risk of losing any of the semantic specificity required of useful terms. However, there are two major areas of meaning to which this term may be confined in its contemporary usage: 1) as the central metaphor of the Apple Macintosh and Microsoft *Windows* graphical user interfaces (*GUIs*), and 2) as an adjective for describing various computing devices and functions that have been so thoroughly downscaled in size and price that they are capable of being employed on the individual desktop. Thus, in the first case, we can talk about the Macintosh *desktop metaphor* for graphical *interface design.* In the second, we refer to a personal computer as one's desktop machine.

desktop accessories: With regard to the Apple Macintosh desktop graphical user interface (*GUI*) and the Microsoft *Windows* GUI, these are programs of relatively limited scope that can be opened while other applications are running. Examples are the note pad, alarm clock, and calculator.

desktop entertainment systems: This term relates to the emerging assembly of media production features that enable personal computers to 1) *interface* with the various audio and *video* instruments normally associated with traditional media production, and 2) offer software-driven *postproduction* capabilities covering most of the *mixing,* editing, and refining functions traditionally associated with the large post houses. Together, these *board* and software combinations now make it more affordable for individuals to create their own film *productions* without incurring the great expenses typically associated with such undertakings. It is projected that these emerging capabilities will become standard components in the *MPC* (multimedia personal computer) and will give rise to a whole new class of amateur film authors.

desktop metaphor: One of the early centralizing concepts of graphical user interface (*GUI*) design, the desktop metaphor was first utilized in the marketplace by Apple Computer to serve as the key organizing principle of its Macintosh GUI. It was taken up shortly thereafter by Microsoft in the creation of its *Windows* operating system. This *interface design* has become ubiquitous and has all but completely replaced and outdated the *character-based application interfaces* of *DOS* and the older mainframe, text-heavy, graphically sparse environments predominant in the 1970s and part of the 1980s. Some of the standard components of the GUI desktop interface include the use of *windows* as a visual model for accessing and viewing documents, the use of the click-and-drag method for moving objects about on the desktop, and the use of the trash can as a receptacle for files that the user wishes to delete. As an *interface paradigm,* the desktop metaphor may be falling out of favor, as many feel that a more robust *user interface* is required to handle the *rich data* types of *multimedia.*

desktop video production: This term arises out of the fact that at some point in the near future *desktop* computers will be equipped with all of the electronic tools necessary to perform the essential functions of today's *video production* studio. In other words, the everyday user will be able to do all of the editing, *mixing, titling,* and special effects needed to produce a professional video. This mix of tools will help launch the age of the *compound document,* where professionals communicate with one another by composing documents that have image, audio, and video components.

desktop virtual reality: The low end of *virtual reality* (VR), it is also commonly referred to as "Windows VR." Using the broadest definition, it include: early products like Microsoft's "Flight Simulator," but typically refers to programs that enable one to navigate through 3-D *rendered* worlds. *Architectural walkthroughs* and other *surrogate travel* programs represent common, early examples of this low-end form of VR.

device driver: Refers to the systems-level code, usually written in assembly language or C, responsible for translating high-level instructions from the computer into codes that a particular hardware device can understand. Thus, we often speak of a display driver or a printer driver, these being the codes that make it possible for the computer to work in harmony with specific models of *video* display and printer, respectively.

DHTML: Stands for Dynamic HyperText Markup Language, considered by most industry analysts to be the second generation of the popular *Web site* authoring language, *HTML.* With DHTML, developers can write scripts that change the layout and content of a *Web page* without having to generate a new page or retrieve one from the *server.* This ability to change on the fly is why this latest version of the language has added a fifth letter to its acronym for "dynamic." DHTML also provides additional functionality beyond that of HTML. These functions include pop-up boxes, changing colors and fonts on *mouse-over,* and text and graphics that *scroll* into position.

dialog box: From graphical user interface (*GUI*) design, this is an *interface* element where a windowed portion of the screen is set up to enable the user to more completely specify the details of a particular function before launching it. Selecting the number of copies that one wants before launching a print process provides a good example of how a dialog box might be used.

dial-tone: When you pick up your telephone, the low humming sound you hear is called a "dial-tone." This sound actually indicates the presence of a connection to the *CO* (central office) of your local exchange carrier (e.g., your *RBOC*). In other words, the dial-tone indicates that the CO "knows" you are there, that you intend to make a call or dial a number, and that it (the CO) is ready to process that number. We have always associated the concept of the dial-tone with *voice* connections, for the simple reason that that has always been the only type of two-way connectivity we have had in our lives. However, as we enter the era of the videophone, a new type of dial-tone will come into play, a video dial-tone. This development also implies that the term dial-tone may take on a more general set of meanings—all of which will verify to users that they are "connected" to a system that supplies a two-way, dial-up form of communication.

dial-up connection: In the world of the *Internet,* this is a link between two *modems* over a telephone line, established by a direct-dial call. The very foundation of data communications, the dial-up connection permits remote systems to connect to the Internet through a conventional telephone line, or an *ISDN* line. The *link* is broken when one party hangs up.

DIB: Stands for Device Independent Bit map, an *interoperability* strategy for interactive *video.* In a market that is constantly introducing new *multimedia* devices and *platforms,* a DIB enables the developer to move programs from one platform or device to another without having to redigitize or reformat the images.

DICOM: Stands for Digital Imaging and Communications in Medicine, a standard file format used by the medical industry to represent *digital* images and other forms of medical information.

DigiCipher II: This is a *codec* that was originally designed to compete with *MPEG* 2 for the right to become the standard among cable operators for all-digital TV *transmission.* DigiCipher II has a *compression* quality that is on par with that of MPEG 2, plus it has the additional ability to scramble or encrypt *signals* to prevent piracy. This codec is a product of Chicago-based General Instrument Corporation, a leading supplier of cable TV *decoder* boxes.

digital: This is a term of such wide applicability and appeal that it gets involved in the naming of things that aren't even digital. To be digital, something must be *encoded* in binary format, where all information is ultimately stored in the on-off signals that computers can process.

digital artifacts: This term refers to digital (text, graphics, audio, *video*) records of human communication found in a *digital library.*

digital audio production systems: The aural counterpart to desktop *digital video* systems, these hardware-software creations are now rivaling their *analog,* tape-oriented, studio forebearers in their ability to produce sophisticated, broadcast-quality sound *tracks.*

digital audio special effects: Like their *video* (DVE) counterparts, these *digital* tools now make it possible for audio *editors* to produce entirely synthesized forms of audio special effects such as *reverb, flanging,* and chorusing.

digital imaging: Is an emerging, technology-based art form made possible by the digitization of visual elements, especially the photographically captured image. Perhaps the most powerful form of artistic manipulation made possible by this technology is that of electronic *compositing,* which enables the artist to integrate disparate visual elements into a single imagistic metaphor. Thus, for example, an artist can create a sense of irony by placing a device like a traffic light in the middle of an otherwise all-natural scene like a meadow.

digital library: This term refers to a concept that is in the process of becoming a reality. It can be thought of as a public library on the computer, and is also often referred to by such synonyms as "electronic library" and "virtual library." Numerous groups are working on the concept of the digital library around the world. For example, IBM has a whole family of products associated with this phrase. The key goal of the digital library is that of providing universal access to a *network* of libraries and information services, including a wide range of documents and *artifacts.* To achieve this goal, new technology needs to be developed to enable *links* that remain transparent to the user. Digital libraries will permit rapid access, facilitated by tools for indexing and searching for information. Several research and development projects are under way. The Digital Library Initiative (DLI) is a four-year project exploring the technical requirements of future digital libraries. It is sponsored by the *NSF, ARPA,* and NASA. Six universities have been commissioned to explore various aspects of what constitutes a digital library. Another project funded by Congress and the Library of Congress (LC) is called the National Digital Library (*NDL*). It is currently digitizing *public domain* literary works and early photographs (avoiding complex issues of *copyright*).

digital media: This widely used term describes the group of media types that traditionally were accessed in *analog* format, but during our era in the history of the information technologies are being *converted* to a digital format. Film, television, *video,* photography, and audio are just some of the more prominent forms of traditionally analog media that are undergoing the gradual conversion to digital format.

digital puppetry: This is a new form of puppetry in which the movements of on-screen animated actors are controlled by real-life humans wearing tracking booms and special facial sensors. The most well-known digital puppet to date is the commercially available *PAS* (Performance Animation System) by SimGraphics, which allows actors to control the movements of computer generated 3-D characters in *real time.*

digital thermometer: An example of an *A/D converter,* this is a probe or sensor that performs *sampling* of temperature data to *convert* it from *analog* to *digital* form.

digitize: This widely used term refers to the process by which some form of *analog* media source (picture, slide, audiotape, etc.) is input into a computer by converting it into *encoded signals* that can be stored digitally and processed electronically.

dimmed: In the world of pull-down *menus* and *interface* design, this term refers to the gray tone that is applied to menu items that, for whatever reason, are not available to the user for selection at a given moment. As we move into the era of *interactive cinema,* it is easy to imagine an analogous artistic instrument whereby certain on-screen objects possess dull tones when they cannot be interacted upon by the user (participant).

direct connection: This term refers to a direct connection to the *Internet,* as opposed to a *dial-up connection.* A direct connection is a permanent *link* via *serial port* to the Internet.

direct manipulation: A graphical user interface *(GUI)* design term, direct manipulation refers to the simplification of the *interface* that occurs when the user can manipulate objects directly without having to memorize and use abstract commands. The classic example occurs in the Apple Macintosh or Microsoft *Windows* GUI, where one *drags icons* of files from one place to another to execute the same copy function that, in the old *command-line interface* of the DOS world, required the strict syntactical construction of a "copy" command.

direct neural input: This is one of the most feared and even hated visions being contemplated today for new media. The idea is obvious: to bypass the body's sense organs and send information directly to appropriate areas of the brain. Scary thought.

discovery learning: A term made popular in the educational world by Jerome Bruner, it refers to an approach to learning that emphasizes the intrinsic motivation and self-sponsored curiosity of the learner. Also known as *active learning,* this term has now become popular among *instructional designers* because it matches well with the inherent design characteristics of *hypertext* and *hypermedia* in that both rely upon the associative thinking patterns of a naturally curious learner.

discussion group: This term refers to a form of communal communication, or bulletin board, usually focused on some topic or facet of life.

Individuals interested in the topic subscribe to the group. The computer or *mail server* that supports the group receives messages from any member and distributes them to all other members of the group.

disk, disc: These two terms are often used interchangeably, though the tendency now is to use disk to refer to magnetic storage media, and disc to refer to *optical storage* media. In either case, the term refers to a circular platter used to store *digital* information in a format that makes that information randomly accessible, rather than sequentially accessible (as is the case with sequential media like magnetic tape).

display list: With reference to computer graphics, this term describes a list of display instructions for specifying how an object is to be drawn on the *display surface*. *Vector* graphics, for example, make use of display lists.

display mismatch: One of the principal types of bug found in *virtual reality* systems, it occurs when the visual, auditory, or tactile systems get completely *out of sync* or are otherwise mismatched. For example, if you stepped on a *virtual* gas pedal and got the toot of a car horn as a response, you would be safe in saying that your virtual car had a display mismatch.

display surface: That part of a computer graphics display device (such as a *CRT* or *pen plotter*) that actually displays the graphical data, i.e., the screen itself or the plotting surface.

dissolve: This term refers to a transitional effect between scenes that makes it seem as though one scene has dissolved into the next. With the explosion of PC *paint systems,* there are now virtually hundreds of dissolve routines available for *desktop video production.*

distance learning: A popular term in educational circles, distance learning refers to several options that allow for extension of the geographic span of instruction. This term can refer to the use of broadcast media, *multimedia,* and/or the *Internet* to facilitate interactions between and among instructors and students. One of the initial applications of distance learning had to do with transmitting instruction into rural and otherwise remote geographic areas. A broader and more current application is to allow for "class" interactions to occur between instructors and students who are scattered across multiple locations over a wide geographic area. From this perspective, to a distance learner in New York, New York is "remote" if the other colleagues taking the class are at multiple locations from Maine to Alaska or from Tokyo to Tennessee. The interactions between instructors and students can be both *asynchronous* and *synchronous*. Traditional teaching methods do not always work very well for distance learning. The *discovery learning* method is a popular one for distance learning, for it encourages students to access information via the Internet on their own and to communicate with each other in *chat* sessions and *listservs*, with the instructor acting as a facilitator rather than as a fount of knowledge.

distractor: This term comes from the world of education, where it is used to name an option in a multiple-choice question that is incorrect, i.e., one that is put in place to "distract" the learner. With all forms of computer-based learning, the distractor has become a potentially powerful design tool, often put in place to induce learners to exhibit that most dreaded of learning blocks, the intuitively appealing misassumption. Good *instructional designers* will use distractors to lead learners into alternative pathways that *remediate* these common misassumptions, accelerating the path to enhanced learning. This term even has utility in the field of *video* game design, where it can be used to describe lures placed in the game to challenge the player's ability to exercise sound judgment.

distributed computing: This term refers to the process of providing information across many computers and *networks* with a wide geographic distribution. The *Web* is a huge distributed library of *digital* information representing a massive distributed computing environment spread out worldwide.

distributed system: This system designer's term refers to any computer *network* in which data and machine intelligence are distributed across many computers that work collaboratively with one another over that network. In today's information industry, the *Web* is the premier example of a distributed system. When a corporation builds an *intranet*, it is implementing a distributed system for its enterprise.

dithering: An *anti-aliasing* effect common to most graphics packages, dithering is used to give objects the appearance of higher *resolution* by blending their edges (boundaries) into the background to help remove the unappealing affect also known as the *jaggies*.

DLL: Stands for Dynamic Link Library and represents one of the more prominent elements in software design today. With so many aspects of our lives being automated and *encoded* in software routines, there is an increasing concern about duplication of effort and the needless decrease in productivity it causes for all of us. The dynamic link library is a generic software design concept intended to combat duplication of coding effort, and to make a significant contribution to productivity in the software industry. More specifically, the DLL concept is based on the notion that most applications call on a standard set of routines that are so commonly used that they need to be duplicated in nearly every application. To avoid this duplication, DLLs are created as a way of sharing these routines among their constituent applications. The routines are stored on *disk* in only one place—the dynamic link library—saving space on a computer's hard disk and the effort involved to incorporate them into the compiled versions of the various applications that need to use them. This idea of making a public resource out of widely used elements is as old as the ages, but in computing, and especially in *software engineering*—where localized sources of complexity and uniqueness seem always to foil the best-laid intentions—the concept of the DLL is welcome.

DLO: Stands for Document-Like Objects, and is a term applied by library scientists to define the class of *complex information* objects now appearing on the *Web* whose set of attributes is predominantly that of a document. Most current *Web sites,* particularly those largely comprised of text, can be classified as DLOs. When closely examined, the Web site can be seen to have an internal structure similar to that of a book. In particular, the *home page* often serves the same basic function as a book's table of contents, providing a high-level, author-designed view of the work's entire contents. Many media types (e.g., *digital video,* audio, and image) may be present within a Web site. However, due to current *bandwidth* limitations on the Web, most Web sites rely primarily upon text to deliver the bulk of their information with the printed book as the overriding *interface* and navigational metaphor. Given this context, most Web sites are DLOs. Over time, this scenario will change as bandwidth limitations on the Web decrease. Examples of DLOs on the Web abound. For instance, a large number of scholarly journal articles are being posted to *Internet* sites, many of which are being augmented by *hyperlinks* to related articles and other enriching materials of an electronic nature. Clearly, this genre of the electronic article still owes most of its structure and communication style to its paper-based, document-oriented origins, and would also be most appropriately classified as a DLO. Because so much Internet content currently relies on the design heritage of the document, a great deal of the work being performed by standards committees directed at creating *metadata* conventions for *cataloging Internet resources* focuses upon the indexing of DLOs.

DMA: Stands for Direct Memory Access, which is a technique used to transfer large amounts of data into or out of computer RAM, and off of or onto peripheral storage devices without involving the *CPU* to carry out the operation. This frees the CPU to take on other tasks. In the age of *multimedia,* where vast amounts of *digital* data for representing the various forms of media will be involved, the use of DMA as an architectural strategy will grow increasingly important.

docugraphic system: Is a *network* made up primarily of *scanners* and printers, and the *links* that enable them to function in a collaborative way.

document conferencing: A hybrid form of *interactivity,* this term refers to a type of activity that combines the benefits and features of *videoconferencing* and *groupware.* As two or more geographically separated parties work on a shared document, an embedded *window* is supplied that enables the current speaker to be viewed by others on the team while the communication is directed toward some aspect of the document as a shared-work product.

document exchange format: This term refers to text formatting and styling standards intended to support cross-platform *portability* of highly formatted documents. *SGML* (standard generalized markup language) is perhaps the best known example. The present challenge is to create such formats for files that contain audio, graphics, and full-motion *video,* i.e., the *mixed media data types.* Another example is *HTML,* which is readable by *Internet browsers.* A document prepared in HTML can include audio, graphics, and video, or *links* to these.

document mapping: This term refers to a process by which the contents of a traditional text document are made more accessible, i.e., where those contents are more readily matched to specific user interests and needs. There are now special purpose *authoring systems* that help automate the process of document mapping. These tools help create, among other things, tables of contents with live *links* to the content sections named in the table, *back-of-the-book indexes,* chapter outlines, and maps of *hypertext* links (*hyperlinks*).

dolly: From the world of film *production,* this term refers to a tracking structure that allows a scene to be *shot* by a moving camera. Thus, this cinematographic device is used to create a moving *POV* (point of view). Increasingly, *digital video* software, especially those programs associated with *virtual reality,* are able to create this effect entirely within the software where it is referred to as *flying* (i.e., the user takes control of the POV and flies through the computerized setting or *virtual world*).

domain: A domain is a logical area on the *Internet*. It resides on one computer, which is its *host;* and one host may hold many domains. The domain holds a *Web site*. To access a *Web page* or other document, the client provides the *domain name* in a *URL* (e.g., www.ibm.com). In a technical sense, the Internet only knows about computers or hosts that are identified by *IP addresses* (e.g., 198.105.232.4). When a domain name is registered, it is entered in a domain name table, like a telephone book, giving the domain name and the IP address of its host. When a *browser* requests a particular URL, the *DNS* (domain name server), looks up the domain name to find the IP address. Domain names have two or more parts separated by dots. The last part is the high-level domain name and is one of the following: *gov*—government agencies; *edu*—educational institutions; *org*—organizations (nonprofit); *mil*—military; *com*—commercial business; and net—network organizations; and two-letter country codes: such as ca—Canada; th—Thailand; or ch—Switzerland. Due to the rapid expansion of the *Web,* a new set of high-level domain names was made available in 1997; they include store, Web, arts, rec, info, and nom. The *host name* is often used as part of a domain name for convenience in recognizing its host location. The Internet Assigned Numbers Authority (IANA) has overall responsibility for domain names (as well as for IP addresses, and many other Internet parameters). Day-to-day responsibility is delegated to the Internet Registry (IR) and regional registries. In North America, the domain name registry is *Internic.*

domain name: The *address* of the *host* or *Internet server* computer, also know as the *URL*. The *domain name system* maintains a database for translating domain names in alphabetic form to their numeric *IP addresses* and vice versa. Thus, each *domain* has two domain names. For example, the domain name microsoft.com represents the IP address 198.105.232.4, where the domain name *server* resides.

domain name system: Also referred to by its acronym, DNS, this term represents one of the more important and visible features of the *Internet*. The DNS is the system by which people and organizations maintain their Internet *addresses* on their respective *servers*. Early in its history, the Internet tried to maintain a complete list of all its computers and *networks,* but this tactic quickly failed once the *Web* began its explosive growth. The address lists became unmanageable, both because the size of the list became too great, and because there were too many changes that had to be accommodated. The DNS evolved as a response to this challenge. It works by dividing the Internet into understandable groups, called *domains*. The name of each domain is tacked on the Internet address, starting from the right with the largest domain. *Mil,* for military organizations, *gov* for government agencies, and *com* for commercial establishments are three of the more common *domain names.* Viewed as a system for managing the now-vast name space of the Internet, the DNS is structured hierarchically. Major domains own the responsibility for maintaining lists and addresses for those domains at the next-lower level. In turn, that next level of domains is responsible for the following level, and so on, all the way down to the end user, or the individual computer.

At the most basic level, the DNS maintains a database for translating domain names in alphabetic form to their numeric or dotted quad *IP addresses* and vice versa. Each Internet domain has two name servers. For example, the domain name microsoft.com represents the IP address 198.105.232.4, where the domain name server resides.

Domino: Also referred to by its full name, "Lotus Domino," this is the product name for the application software that has Web-enabled *Lotus Notes*—the popular *groupware* and electronic messaging software from Lotus Development, now a subsidiary of IBM. Domino actually provides a series of applications designed to enable organizations to develop *e-commerce, intranet,* and *extranet* systems.

D1 digital video: This high-end form of *component video* has become a popular input source among the service bureaus that perform *MPEG* (Motion Picture Experts Group) *compression.* Owing to its *digital* format, D1 can be copied any number of times without suffering *generation loss.*

DOS: Now a term for antiquity, DOS stands for Disk Operating System, which was the first widely installed *operating system* for *personal computers.* The original version of DOS was developed for IBM by Bill Gates, and was called PC DOS. Of course, Gates retained copyright for his own version, called MS DOS, or Microsoft DOS, which then grew into the now-famous *Windows* operating system—and as they say, the rest is history. DOS is important to the history of *multimedia,* because its evolution during the 1980s to accommodate ever-increasing graphical standards, and then audio, etc., roughly paralleled and served the convergence of computing, media, and communications that is multimedia.

double buffering: A technique used with regard to *DVE* (digital video effects), this term refers to the use of two *frame buffers* to effect smoother forms of *animation.* With double buffering, the graphical contents of one *buffer* are displayed during the rendering process while updates occur on the other buffer (which is referred to as a *back buffer*). When the updates are complete, the buffers are switched. In this way, only complete images are displayed. As a result, the drawing or rendering of images is always hidden from the user, leading to a decidedly smoother form of animation.

downlink: From the realm of satellite communications, this term refers to the process whereby a broadcast *signal* is sent—or "reflected"—from a satellite's *transponder* to a ground-based antenna. The downlink is actually the second half of the broadcast signal's journey from the *content provider* to the viewer (or user). The first half of that journey, where the signal is beamed from a ground station to a satellite in orbit, is referred to as the *uplink.*

download: In the most general sense, the copying of information from one computer to another. Traditionally, this term has been viewed as the transfer of documents, database files, or other text-oriented data from a larger system to a smaller one. For example, a user would download a desired news item from one of the online information services, such as a bulletin board service or site off of the *Internet.* Increasingly, though, the process of downloading will involve *mixed media data types,* and in the near future it may become common parlance to say that one wants to download a movie.

dpi: Stands for dots per inch, which is a common measure of *resolution* for devices associated with *image processing* such as *scanners.* It represents, for example, the number of *pixels* that a scanner can physically distinguish in each vertical and horizontal inch of an original image.

dragging: This interactive technique, made very common through its use in the *desktop metaphor,* is used to reposition an object on the screen. The most common form of dragging is effected by positioning the *cursor* over the target object, holding down the *mouse button,* and dragging the object through the movement of the mouse until that object is at its destination where the mouse button is released.

draw systems: Used as a term that contrasts with *paint systems,* draw systems are programs that create *structured* or *vectorized graphics* images. Paint systems are programs that create *bit-mapped* graphics images. Draw systems can be simple or very complex: they can range from tools for creating simple two-dimensional images, all the way up to *CAD* (computer-aided design) programs that support 3-D modeling of solid objects with surface *shading*. With these systems, the artist manipulates objects rather than *pixels*. Most programs include, at a minimum, commands for creating various geometric objects (such as circles, rectangles, or boxes), assigning them attributes (such as color), and manipulating their *spatial* properties (such as their location on the screen).

drill-and-practice: From the world of *instructional design,* this term refers to a commonly used design strategy for programming *CBT* (computer-based training). Drill-and-practice programs, as their name implies, are typified by long strings of multiple-choice and fill-in-the-blank types of questions that strive to sharpen the learner's skills with respect to a fairly narrow range of academic concerns. Math programs, in particular, have exploited the drill-and-practice paradigm. For example, a student might be asked to answer a series of short-answer questions regarding the addition of two two-digit numbers. Easy to program, but facetiously referred to by many as "drill and kill," this *mode* of *instructional design* has (thankfully) fallen out of favor with educators over the past decade.

driver software: This is a nearly ubiquitous type of software that provides communications at the machine level between computers and their peripheral devices. For example, one could not use an external *DVD-ROM* player with a computer without first installing that player's driver software in memory. With regard to peripherals that are permanently attached to the computer (e.g., a printer), the driver software becomes a part of that computer's boot (i.e., startup) program and is automatically loaded into memory when the machine is turned on without requiring any user intervention.

drum: This term generally refers to scanning equipment at the high end of the publishing application spectrum. Film or paper is inserted on a drum, which is then *rotated* past a focused light source. Drum devices are generally very high *resolution* machines.

drum plotter: A type of *pen plotter* device in which the paper is *rotated* on a *drum* while the pen moves along the opposite axis.

DSA: Stands for Directory Server Agent, which is a program that maintains the contents of the *white pages* of the *Internet*.

DSL: Stands for Digital Subscriber Line, a relatively high-bandwidth digital *transmission* standard that possesses the advantage of being able to use the existing copper wire physical plant of our historic (*POTS*) telephone system. See also *ADSL*.

DSP: Stands for Digital Signal Processing, a chip-based technology responsible for converting *analog signals* (such as sound) to a computer-readable *digital* format, and vice versa. DSP chips promise to find their way into PCs in a massive way in the near future. In fact, most industry analysts agree that without DSPs, *multimedia* technology would remain a pipe dream, because general purpose *CPUs* simply do not have the horsepower to handle multimedia data efficiently. Thus, DSPs will fast become one of the central components in the emergence of the *multiprocessing* architectures to make the concept of a true *MPC* (multimedia personal computer) possible. A DSP-equipped PC can function as a digital answering machine, a fax *modem,* a CD-quality audio recorder or player, and a file *codec* (compression-decompression), without requiring additional *expansion boards.*

DSS: Stands for Decision Support System, which is a computer-based system to help managers or decision makers identify structure and solve semi-structured and unstructured problems. Its objective is to improve the effectiveness of decisions, not to replace managerial judgment. A typical DSS has an interactive query facility with a query language; and it helps individuals or groups use and manipulate data, apply checklists and *heuristics,* and build and use mathematical models.

DSU: Stands for Digital Service Unit, which connects a channel service unit (*CSU*) to a *DTE* (that is, to a terminal, or to a computer). The DSU provides a standard *interface* between a digital *transmission* line and a user's computer, similar in many respects to the way *modems* handle such functions as *signal* translation, regeneration, reformatting, and timing. Modems and DSUs represent common types of *DCE* (data communications equipment). Most people connected to the *Internet* rely on some form of DCE (a modem or a DSU) to send and receive information to and from the *Web.*

DTD: Stands for Document-Type Definitions, utilized by *tagging languages* such as *SGML* (standard generalized markup language) to define specific processing rules for encoding and decoding a document's structure and the *markup tags* that determine the document's structure.

DTE: Stands for Data Terminal Equipment, and is a term often used in the field of *data communications.* A DTE is a device at one end or the other of a data *transmission,* and typically refers to a personal computer (PC) or network computer (*NC*). Most people connected to the *Internet* are working on some form of DTE.

DTH: Stands for Direct-To-Home, and refers to a set of satellite-based technologies that deliver home entertainment media to the residential market without making use of any of the terrestrial *transmission* infrastructure associated with traditional forms of *telephony* or television. DTH technologies are considered to be of great significance because they afford *content providers* a timely solution to the problem of the *last-mile loop*. Stifled by the limited bandwidth offered by the traditional wireline connections into the home (i.e., the copper wire and coaxial cable connections of telephony and *CATV,* respectively), technologies such as *DBS* (direct broadcasting by satellite) offer a fresh and robust new source of bandwidth for providing such services as *movie-on-demand* and, potentially, *HDTV.*

DTM: Stands for Digital Terrain Model, a *texture mapping* technology for building 3-D, photorealistic landscapes. With high-end systems, scenes may be computed on the fly, enabling the user to freely explore the terrain. DTM could become a powerful tool, or *enabling technology,* for creating the referential context of *interactive fictions* and other forms of *virtual world.*

DTV: Stands for Digital TeleVision, and has also been referred to as *DATV* and ATV (advanced television). DTV is the term used in the broadcast TV industry to refer to *digital* forms of television, which are enabled by the digital *compression, transmission,* and presentation of *video* content. *HDTV* (high-definition television) is another concept often associated with DTV, since it was at the center of the original debates regarding the transition of television from *analog* to digital technologies.

DTVC: Stands for DeskTop VideoConferencing, an emergent use for the PC that relies upon levels of *connectivity* and *network bandwidth* that are not quite in place yet.

dual-resolution displays: This technology is used by *virtual reality* engineers to manufacture wide *field-of-view* systems. These systems create the illusion that the entire, wide area image is projected using a substantial *resolution*. Although, the dual-resolution display conserves enormous *bandwidth* by restricting the high-resolution portions of the image to *windows* that approximate the area of human foveal attention (which is the high-resolution portion of human sight). All other portions of the screen have a much reduced resolution (smaller number of *pixels*) but, in theory, should not be noticed by the viewer because they are only visible to the low-resolution portion of their eyesight or "peripheral vision." This type of display is used in close conjunction with *eye tracking* technology, which works to keep the high-resolution window in front of the user's *fovea* and the low-resolution portions of the image affixed to the user's peripheral vision. The advantage of this technology is that it dramatically reduces the total number of pixels to be used, reducing the computational load and increasing the *frame refresh rate.*

Dublin Core: The *OCLC* (Online Computer Library Center) hosted a library science conference in Dublin, Ohio, in 1995 devoted exclusively to creating *metadata* standards for *Internet resources.* This conference gave birth to a new metadata standard known as the Dublin Core. The standard is named after the location of the conference, which also happens to be the hometown of the OCLC.

ducking: From the world of audio production, this term is used to describe the technique by which the volume (loudness) of a music *track* is reduced to accommodate narration. This process, designed to eliminate sources of competition in a *production's* sound track, is readily handled using numerical methods with *digital audio production systems.*

dumb terminal: A computing device of historical antiquity (at least in computer years), the dumb terminal represented the dominant method for accessing computer resources during the late 1960s and the 1970s, before the personal computer exploded onto the market. Dumb terminals were considered "dumb" because they possessed little or no machine intelligence of their own, but relied upon a *network* connection to a *mainframe* to provide their users with access to meaningful software functionality. The recent emergence of the NC (network computer) has revived interest in the dumb terminal because the architecture of the NC, wherein the bulk of the computing intelligence is accessed across the network from relatively simple and inexpensive *desktop* devices, is very much akin to that of the dumb terminal + mainframe model.

DVD: Stands for Digital VideoDisc. If ever there was a technology that deserved the moniker of "the next thing," DVD is it. A direct descendent of *CD-ROM* technology, DVD takes *optical storage* capacity into the multi-*gigabyte* range. It provides for the scale of storage required by applications that make abundant use of the *rich data* types, and particularly of *digital video.* The initial specification set forth by the *DVD Forum* identifies three levels of DVD storage capacity: a 4.7 GB standard for single-layer DVD, an 8.5 GB standard for dual-layer, and a 17 GB standard for the so-called *flippy disks* that record data on both sides of a dual-layer system. When compared against the 650 MB capacity of CD-ROM, this is a significant step forward—one that is made technically possible by the use of a shorter wavelength form of *laser*. The initial uses for DVD hold explosive market potential. Most of the major film studios are releasing feature films on DVD *encoded* in the relatively high-quality *codec, MPEG* 2. Phone databases, mapping (i.e., atlas) programs, encyclopedias, and games featuring full-motion video and *surround sound* are among the additional early uses of DVD that have substantial promise. Adding to the appeal of DVD technology, their players are able to read both CD-ROM titles and audio CDs and users are able to "protect" their investments in these media.

DVD Forum: Formerly referred to as the "DVD Consortium," this group of companies was responsible for generating the first widely adopted set of specifications for *DVD* (digital videodisc). Six companies are in this group: Hewlett-Packard, Mitsubishi, Philips, Ricoh, Sony, and Yamaha.

DVE: Stands for Digital Video Effects, which refers to the exploding library of digitally constructed visual effects that are being made available to desktop computers through a growing number of desktop *video* products. The most common form of DVE is the transition, or *digital, wipe.*

DVI: Stands for Digital Video Interactive, and it represents one of the earliest technologies to attempt to *digitize video* and compress the resulting datastream. Originally developed by RCA at its laboratories in Princeton, New Jersey, during the mid-1980s, DVI eventually ended up in the hands of chipmaker Intel who purchased it from interim owner GE in 1988. A multifaceted product that revolves around its own *proprietary codec* (compression-decompression) technology, DVI built a fair degree of support for itself in the marketplace. IBM endorsed the technology, while several third-party software houses developed *authoring systems* around it. The technology was also adopted by Microsoft, who created a *Windows* version of DVI known as *Indeo*. However, DVI suffers because it does not conform to any of the widely accepted standards for digitizing visual information: namely, *JPEG* (Joint Photography Experts Group), *MPEG* (Motion Picture Experts Group), and *H.261*. The differences between DVI and, in particular, MPEG and H.261, go to their respective product cores or codecs. Where both MPEG and H.261 are based on the mathematics of *DCT* (discrete cosine transfer), DVI is based on a kind of math called "region coding." (Because JPEG is concerned with still images, it is not appropriate to make direct comparisons.) Many technologists believe that DCT is the superior form of math for doing compression-decompression. The bottom line is that, in spite of the considerable progress that DVI made early in its history, the future of the *digital* video market lies elsewhere.

DXF: A file format that somehow stands for Drawing interchange Format, this acronym refers to a platform-independent format for *CAD* (computer-aided design) files developed by Autodesk. As *virtual reality* brings such phenomena as the *architectural walkthrough* into the mainstream of *desktop* computing, expect standards like DXF and its near-cousin IGES (initial graphics exchange specification) to become increasingly common.

dynamic range: In the world of *digital* audio, this term describes the difference between the loudest and softest sounds that can be expressed by a system. It represents a measure of audio *resolution* and is often expressed in *decibels.*

DYUV: Also known as delta luminance color difference, this image *compression* technique takes advantage of the fact that data for neighboring *pixels* are often similar. Thus instead of recording each pixel separately, it records only the difference between pixels, line by line. Like its *YUV* image-encoding parent, it also exploits the fact that the human eye is more sensitive to differences in *brightness (luminance)* than in color (*chrominance*) and thus saves data space by storing less information about color changes than about brightness changes.

If you want a song in interactive, sing it.
—**John Barlow, Songwriter, The Grateful Dead**

Easter egg: This term comes from the world of *electronic game design.* It refers to a hidden sequence or image that is triggered into the *playfield* by certain combinations of player actions. *Electronic game* developers embed Easter eggs into their products to either reward creative players or to express their own individuality. It is, metaphorically speaking, an electronic carving of one's initials onto the tree of the electronic game.

e-commerce: Short for electronic commerce, this general term refers to the emerging market for conducting business transactions across the *Web.* Though still in its earliest stages, most industry analysts project steady growth for e-commerce over the next several decades. Indeed, many futurists envision a day when the majority of all buying and selling is consummated across the Web.

EDI: Stands for Electronic Data Interchange, which is a general term that refers to the data-communications technology needed for trading partners to conduct business in an automated fashion across a wide area network (*WAN*). More specifically, EDI enables trading partners to transmit various types of business document correspondence—such as purchase orders, bills of lading, and shipping orders—electronically across the *network* instead of sending them physically through the mail. An early form of *e-commerce,* it is expected that this form of electronic communication may increasingly be enhanced by the inclusion of various forms of *mixed media data types,* such as *digital images* and *voice annotations.*

edit point: From the world of film and *video,* this term refers to any place in a video where the *editor* has intervened with respect to the visual flow. An edit point is typically associated with some form of *cut* from one *shot* to another. Producers who wish to make aesthetically appealing interactive programs will need to remember that virtually all points of interaction (*branchpoints*) will also be edit points of one type or another.

editor: From the world of film and *video,* this professional is the one who deletes or adds scenes to a picture by following the instructions of the director, and who also keeps the sound *tracks* in *sync.* It has often been said that it is the editor who actually makes the movie, because it is the editor who controls the overall pacing of the film and determines much of its emotional impact. With regard to *Internet* applications, an *HTML* editor is a program that allows creation of documents and files that can be viewed on a *Web browser.* Some editors are *WYSIWYG* or close to it.

EDL: Stands for Edit Decision List, which in the world of film *production* is a list of instructions for creating a final, single videotape out of multiple source tapes. This particular film production technique is now a popular one among producers of *desktop video production* tools because, from a *systems analysis* standpoint, it represents little more than a straightforward database function of keeping track of *edit points.*

edu: Is a suffix for a top level *domain name* indicating that the *host* computer is run by an educational institution. Until recently, all educational organizations that applied for an *Internet address* were accepted, but now only four-year colleges and universities are accepted due to space problems. Two-year colleges and K–12 schools must register under the country (U.S.) *domain.*

educational software: Nearly synonymous with the terms *courseware* and *CBT* (computer-based training), this growing type of application represents the use of software to educate, rather than automate. Rarely used in the corporate world, this term is much more commonly spoken of in the school market, where it is used to describe what many educators feel will be the next major form of instructional publishing.

edutainment: This contracted term is given to software that merges the functions associated with educational and entertainment software. This new breed of software exploits the media capabilities of the *MPC* (multimedia personal computer) and seeks to expand the home market for software by blending the youth appeal of *electronic games* with the parent appeal of *educational software.* More than just a marketing whim, the concept of edutainment is based on the well-researched overlap between sophisticated, multidimensional games and the higher-order thinking skills associated with problem solving. Manifestations of edutainment applications on the *Internet* have shown the *World Wide Web* to be a popular delivery vehicle for this application.

EGA: This stands for Enhanced Graphics Adapter, which is a vestigial remnant of the graphical ascent of *DOS*-compatible personal computers. Falling in the lineal path just after *CGA* and just before *VGA,* the EGA standard permitted 64 colors with a *resolution* of 640 x 350 *pixels.*

EISA: This term stands for Extended Industry Standard Architecture, a somewhat dated update to the original (and even more dated) *ISA* architecture of the personal computer. The EISA standard provided for a broader data path, or *data bus,* than its ISA forebearer, which became a necessity in 1988 when computer manufacturers began to accelerate their attempts to enrich the computing experience with *multimedia* data types. Because this effort has continued to grow in the 1990s, the EISA standard has fallen behind, and is now being patched by various *local bus* strategies, such as Intel's *PCI* (Peripheral Component Interconnect).

e-journal or e-magazine: Short for electronic journal or magazine, this phenomenon owes its existence almost entirely to the *Internet.* For the most part, these are online versions of print publications that can be viewed from the Internet. Because of this, many social critics consider these to be the latest, best manifestation of democracy. The e-journal embodies the concept that anyone with access to a computer equipped with a *modem* can produce and distribute an electronic magazine through a computer *network.* E-journals are exploding in number and are—predictably—oriented around special topics such as computer law and AIDS prevention. The beauty of e-journals is that they enable many to publish who simply do not have the finances or other resources to bring their ideas to fruition in the print publishing arena.

electronic content: This term from the world of document processing refers to documents stored in the form of electronically *encoded* characters. Each character of the document has its own encoded representation. Documents that have been *converted* to their constituent *ASCII* codes for storage on a personal computer system are an example of electronic content. This form of representing document content is often distinguished from electronic image, wherein the document is represented as a *bit map* of *pixels.* Electronic, or ASCII-encoded, content is more useful because it can be searched on a character-by-character basis (i.e., it can be *parsed*), and is therefore more *computable* than documents stored as electronic images.

electronic forms: Refers to the visual *interface* provided to viewers of information on the *Web* for data entry of information. Many times on *Web sites,* forms are included to request feedback, provide additional information, or gather data on viewers. Forms are used whenever inter-action is required between the viewer and the information viewed on the Web site. Created with special tags in *HTML,* forms serve also as a front end for *search engines.* They are usually written in *CGI* (common gate-way script). In short, electronic forms allow viewers of *Web pages* to send information back to the *host* Web site, while enabling the maintainers of Web sites to gather information on their viewers.

electronic game: By adding the dimensions of computer graphics and soft-ware control to the traditions of board games and television quiz shows, the electronic game has become a ubiquitous new medium—and a pas-time for the 10 year old in all of us.

electronic game design: This is a new field of expertise that represents a microcosm of the converging *domains* of expertise that make *multime-dia* an art form and a commercial medium in its own right. To success-fully perform in this emerging field, the designer must possess a combined knowledge of *art direction, software engineering,* and narrative script-writing. The art direction is required to design the user (or player) *inter-face.* The *software engineering* is required to design the gameplay rules and features (also called the *play-mechanics*), and to fully specify how the scoring and reward system will be executed. The narrative scriptwriting is needed to invest the game with an ability to engage the user in much the same way that stories do. Because few individuals possess all three of these areas of skill at the requisite levels of mastery, most electronic game design is performed as a creative group collabora-tion and team process.

electronic game producer: Analogous to a film producer, this is the role within an *electronic game* development project that carries the greatest authority with respect to business and monetary issues. The game pro-ducer controls the purse strings of the project. As such, the producer has ultimate sign-off authority on all deliverables and is the final arbiter of the *intellectual property* created by the design team. In the final analy-sis, it is the producer who is held most responsible for the business suc-cess or failure of the electronic game.

electronic likeness rights: Related to *intellectual property* rights, this term refers to an emerging trend for *multimedia* content vendors to create animated, or *quasi-video,* representations of famous people—making use of the publicity value that those people possess. These rights help protect the publicity value owned by those people and, in most cases, are used as the basis for establishing some form of royalty arrangement.

electronic publishing: This term refers to the creation and distribution of documents, or *DLOs,* that are meant to be viewed online. Electronic publishing is often used in reference to electronic *digital libraries,* Internet documents found on *Web sites,* and online help information and *CBT tutorials.*

e-mail: Stands for electronic mail and refers to a method of electronic communication, as well as to the programs for sending electronic messages over computer *networks.* Currently, e-mail represents the most popular use of the *Internet.* A standard e-mail system provides a relatively quick and easy means to write new messages, reply to ones that have been received, and forward those messages to others. Messages can also be sent, or "broadcast," to many addressees at one time by simply creating a thing called a "distribution list." As was the case with the historical origins of physical, pen-and-paper mail, e-mail was made possible by the formalized organization of a standard *address* space. For e-mail sent across the Internet, the mailing address is a simple combination of personal identifier and *domain name,* separated by an @ sign. The main disadvantage of today's Internet e-mail is its lack of security. Messages can be easily intercepted in transit, or even forged, making e-mail a less-than-perfect means for certain types of communication such as the exchange of credit information. Most mainframes, minicomputers, and computer networks have some sort of e-mail system. E-mail systems can be used on any kind of computer network from the Internet to an in-house *LAN.* Though today's e-mail messages are primarily a text-only affair, graphics, images, and sound files can be sent as *binary file* attachments, pointing the way to the future of electronic mail.

embedded PC: This term captures the notion that all of the technical components associated with the personal computer can now be embedded in other, traditionally low-tech, devices. Actually, the process of embedding PC-like intelligence in other technologies has been going on for some time: witness the microwave oven, the logical functions of which are based entirely on microprocessor technology. The significance of this term in today's market is that as the PC becomes the *MPC* (multimedia personal computer)—and then the *interactive television* or *teleputer*—media-based applications, such as navigational systems for automobiles, will become commonplace.

embedded training: From the world of *instructional design,* this term refers to use of *CBT* (computer-based training) in small, granular units that are brought as close as possible to, and become "embedded" in, the tasks for which they provide training. This concept is held up as being superior to the traditional form of delivering instruction where all of the training is packed into a single session or period of time, and is separated from the time in which the learner will actually make use of it. Embedded training is used extensively in *performance support systems,* where the embedded training pieces are also often referred to as *job aids.*

e-money: This term refers to the concept of a generic type of electronic money that can be used to pay for purchases on the *Internet.* Many companies have their own trademarked version of e-money. With an e-money system in place that is secure and widely accepted, *e-commerce* can take place—which means that products and services can be bought and sold electronically. "Digital cash" and *cybercash* are just two of the many synonyms that are emerging to describe this nascent form of currency.

emulation: The widespread use of this term in the computer industry in many respects serves as an indicator of the volatility of the computer marketplace in general, and of the *multimedia* market in particular. Emulation occurs when the hardware-software combination that constitutes one delivery *platform* is made to operate like (emulate) the hardware-software combination of another platform. In the computer industry, one of the earliest widespread uses of emulation occurred when intelligent personal computers were made to operate like *dumb terminals* so that PC users could make use of the programs and data stored on large *legacy devices,* such as corporate mainframes. In the current era of multimedia computing, with hardware-software combinations proliferating from every direction, developers of *multimedia applications* are faced with an unprecedented need to emulate all sorts of delivery platforms to make their programs as widely usable and as possible. The rapid ascent of the *Java* programming language is driven by the desire to eliminate such cross-platform problems and, therefore, the need for application developers to devote resources to creating emulation programs.

enabling technologies: Refers to the growing mass of data storage and *transmission* products, computing/media *platforms,* system software, authoring tools, *Internets, intranets,* etc., that altogether make it possible to deliver *multimedia applications* to the end user. Put in a bit more general sense, the term refers to any technology that makes another, more humanly accessible, technology possible. Thus a *fiber optic transmission* line is an enabling technology for *picturephone,* and picturephone is, in turn, an enabling technology for *videoconferencing.* A *Web site* with *courseware* can be an enabling technology for *distance learning.*

encapsulation: Is the technique used to provide the necessary control information to transport data on the *Internet,* or other networks. Data transfer is governed by a series of layered *protocols.* Each protocol attaches a header, which carries that protocol's *routing* data. Taking an example from the Internet, a *packet* of information would carry a protocol header for the physical layer, the *network* layer (*IP*), the transport layer (*TCP*), and the application itself (see *OSI*). A second, widely used definition of encapsulation can be found in the area of *object-oriented programming.* Here, encapsulation refers to the practice of providing the programming specifications necessary for customers to use a set of functions without having to know the details of how they work. Indeed, encapsulation is considered one of the fundamental distinguishing characteristics of object-oriented programming, and involves the bundling together of both the data and the methods (procedures) that act on that data. Once the data and methods have been bundled (i.e., encapsulated) together, then an object has been formed.

encode: This term refers to the transformation of text, graphics, or other forms of information into a predefined *digital* format or code. It involves transforming data from one form to another for a specific purpose. Several different character sets exist specifying the character encoding used by *Web browsers* to display *Web site* information. In America, the Latin 1 character set is the default; in Europe, the Latin 2 character set is used. Chinese, Japanese, and Korean also exist and have their own character sets.

encryption: This term refers to a security feature that involves encoding data in a format that can only be read when decoded or deciphered using a predefined key. Of great moment, encryption provides security for data communications on the *Internet.* With early forms of encryption, sender and receiver used the same key to encrypt and decrypt the data. Today, more sophisticated systems use two keys. In today's business environment, one of the most commonly used encryption methods is "public-key encryption." Public-key encryption relies on two keys: a public key, which the owner can supply to his or her correspondents to encrypt data, and a private key created by the owner, which he or she uses to decrypt messages. *PGP* (pretty good privacy) and DES (Data Encryption Standard) are two public-key encryption systems.

endpoints: In *vector* graphics, these are the points that specify each end of a *line segment.*

environmental systems: This refers to a form of *virtual reality* consisting mostly of externally generated 3-D objects, but ones with little or no body paraphernalia. With this type of system, users move within a real physical space that reacts to cues triggered by their motions and actions.

equalization: From the world of sound engineering, this term refers to the process of reducing or boosting fixed sound frequencies. The most common use of equalization involves the use of tone controls to compensate for some form of *frequency* distortion in the target audio *signal.*

equitagonist: This term refers to a game player who is involved in a multiplayer game that is so rich in nature as to have the feel of a real-life narrative. Thus, it refers to a human player in an *interactive fiction.* The term is derived from the traditional literary terms of protagonist and antagonist and carries the implication that the participants will have their performances assessed (scored) on the basis of criteria that are equally applied to other (both electronic and human) players in the interactive fiction.

ERDAS: Stands for Earth Resource Data AnalySis, a standard file format used for representing remote-sensing (i.e., satellite) images.

Ethernet: This venerable standard for *LANs* (local area networks) is now getting a bit long in the tooth. Capable of only handling 10 *Mbps* (megabits per second), Ethernet is overwhelmed by any substantive effort to network *mixed media data types.* A recent upgrade to this standard called "Fast Ethernet" is capable of 100 Mbps, but represents only a stopgap measure in the face of the multi-*gigabyte* demands of true *multimedia* networking.

Eudora: Is one of the most popular *e-mail* programs on the *Internet,* produced by QualComm, Inc. Eudora allows users to *download* waiting mail from a *mail server* to their local terminal, to prepare messages offline, and to send messages with attached documents that can include text, *video* clips, spreadsheets, etc. It is written to *interface* with *TCP/IP* and works with all the major operating systems.

event loop: One of the key design elements in constructing an interactive program, the event loop is the central routine that, at any given time, determines the range of acceptable user actions. All other things being equal, the broader this range of acceptable actions, the more flexible and interactive the program will appear to be.

EVL: Stands for Electronic Visualization Lab, a branch of the University of Illinois at Chicago dedicated to the development of leading-edge, 3-

D, audiovisual systems for use in *virtual reality* applications. The *CAVE,* a virtual reality environment that features a room whose walls and floor flood the viewer's senses with projected images, is the EVL's leading claim to fame.

expansion board: This term is used to refer to the many plug-in *boards* that expand the capabilities of standard personal computers. Before many of the capabilities associated with *multimedia* computing were migrated to the microprocessor (e.g., *MMX* technology), the rapid onset of market demand for multimedia capabilities caused an explosion in the availability of *video* and audio expansion boards. In general, the expansion board has always been used to accommodate newly demanded capabilities that have not yet been deemed worthy of integration into the native architecture of the *desktop* computer.

experiential prototyping: From the world of practical *virtual reality* (an oxymoron?) applications, this term is a near-synonym for *architectural walkthrough.* It refers to entire environments—such as buildings—that are created by the virtual reality media so that they may be experienced by the user as if they were real.

expert system: From the world of *artificial intelligence,* an expert system is a genre of AI designed to solve problems at the expert level in some scientific, mathematical, or medical *domain.* To date, expert systems have only been successfully used with regard to relatively restricted problem domains. The key step in constructing expert systems is known as *knowledge engineering,* wherein a knowledge engineer works closely with a subject matter expert to untangle the decision rules and sources of knowledge that make the expertise work. As expert systems become joined to *multimedia applications,* taking advantage of such newborn software design techniques as the *interface agent,* their usefulness will likely become dramatically extended.

exposure: In film and *video,* this term refers to one *frame* of film that has been exposed.

extensibility: A term used frequently in *software engineering,* it refers to a desirable system characteristic wherewith new features can be added easily, i.e., without having to undertake major redesigns. Extensible systems help avoid rapid functional obsolescence. Very extensible systems are said to be *future-proofed.*

external viewer: Is a form of *plug-in module* used by a program, often a *Web browser,* to display or interpret file formats and *protocols* that the main program is not designed to read. Examples of external viewers are Shockwave, RealAudio, Adobe *PDF,* and Corel CMX (*vector* graphics). The facility for using external viewers greatly enhances the ability of *browsers* to display different kinds of information, both now and in the future, without increasing the complexity of the browser itself. Netscape *Navigator* and Microsoft *Internet Explorer* have options to allow adding external viewers of the user's choice.

extranet: Is an extension of a company's internal *network,* or *intranet,* to provide access to prespecified sets of external users from across the *Internet.* Such extensions require extremely good security control to prevent unauthorized access from outsiders, loss from damage to the company's information resources due to *viruses,* and unauthorized use of the Internet by employees. In spite of the security risks involved, extranets are becoming increasingly important because they allow customers, mobile workers, and trading partners better access to company data.

extrusion: This is an interactive modeling technique in which a further dimension can be added to an existing definition, e.g., a line can be extruded from a point, a plane from a line, or a solid from a plane.

eye candy: This slang term refers to the richness and *texture* of the computerized image generated on a computer screen, typically as an attention-getting adornment.

eye tracking: This emergent technology, first developed for military applications and now being annexed by makers of *virtual reality* gear, tracks the movement of the human eye for purposes of machine interaction. The primary methods of eye tracking in use today involve bathing the eye in low-intensity infrared light. This light creates a bright image on the pupil and a bright spot reflecting off the cornea, both of which can be captured by a *video* camera focused on the user's eyes. *Image processing* software then analyzes the video image, finds the pupil and cornea, and calculates where the eye is looking. Once the system knows where the user is looking, the computer can be controlled through measuring *gaze duration.* Thus, for example, the user could press a button or select a key by staring at it for a specific length of time. Or, in a virtual reality environment, the user could navigate, or fly, through a landscape by simply staring in the desired direction.

EyePhone: Manufactured by VPL Research, this was the first commercially available stereoscopic *HMD* (head-mounted display) for *virtual* *reality* applications. This apparatus used color *LCD* displays with a *resolution* of 360 x 240 *pixels* to provide a horizontal *field of view* measuring 100 degrees.

e-zine: An even shorter abbreviation for *e-magazine,* an e-zine is an electronically distributed zine. A zine, short for "magazine" or *fanzine,* is a publication typically devoted to some specialized topic of an irreverent, bizarre, or humorous nature. They are often produced by enthusiasts for fun or personal reasons, usually distributed free, and do not carry much advertising except for references to other zines. As you may have gathered, e-zines are nonprofit.

. . . you're building a process . . . not a composition.

**—Randall Packer, Founder,
New Music Theatre**

face armature: Consisting of sensors to track the user's head, face, and lip movements, this piece of *virtual reality* equipment attaches to the head and permits real-life actors to animate corresponding features of animated, on-screen *agents*.

fade in/out: A transitional effect whereby a scene starts as black and is gradually brought, *frame* by frame, to full *exposure* or vice versa. The process of creating fades has been automated by the powerful *pixel* processing routines available in many PC *paint system* programs.

fade margin: From the technical side of communications, this useful term refers to the level of *signal* decay tolerated before communications cease. One of the problems with the emerging forms of all-digital communications is that the distance between a completely valid signal and one that is utterly useless can be both small and abrupt. In contrast to the *analog* forms of *transmission,* there is no graceful degradation of the signal.

fair use: Is a judicial concept applied in *copyright* law to balance an author's right to the control of, and reward for, his or her creative efforts and the public's use of that work to "promote the progress of science and useful arts" (Constitution, Article 1, Section 8). Fair use includes copying for purposes of criticism, comment, news reporting, teaching (including multiple copies for classroom use), scholarship, or research. There exists a large body of case law in which fair use has been raised as a defense. Factors considered in deciding whether a particular case can be seen as fair use are

1. Purpose (commercial, nonprofit, educational) of the use,
2. Nature of the copyrighted work itself,
3. Amount and substance of the portion used relative to the entire copyrighted work, and
4. Effect on the market value of the copyrighted work.

Legal and ethical issues associated with fair use and the display and distribution of *media assets* over the *Internet* are still very much in the process of being worked out by the judicial system.

fantasy role player: From the world of *electronic games,* this term refers to the role that the game player (user) assumes while being involved in some of the more sophisticated types of *video* games. This term points toward the future of electronic games where these interactive programs will seem less like games and more like the next generation of storytelling products, wherein the audience will play a participatory role in an *interactive fiction.*

fanzine: One of several emergent online venues on the *Internet,* this term refers to an underground, do-it-yourself *e-zine* (electronic magazine), typically one that is dedicated to a celebrity, performing rock band, or other popular media figure.

FAQ: Stands for Frequently Asked Questions, a module that has become so common in online help, software *tutorials, CBT* (computer-based training) programs, and *Web sites* that it has earned the status of an acronym. It derives from the widely recognized tendency that, for most products or systems, anywhere from 5 to 20 questions end up representing about 90 percent of all questions asked about that product or system. On the *Internet,* prospective *newsgroup* participants are often encouraged to read FAQs so that they understand the rules of the road and are less prone to generate *flame* mail as an outcome of their participation. FAQ modules exist on a wide range of topics on the *Web,* covering everything from pet grooming to cryptography.

FAT: Stands for File Allocation Table and refers to a common data structure used with erasable storage media, such as hard *disks.* FATs are based on the notion that data sectors are erasable and, therefore, reusable. Generally located on the outermost sectors of the disk, the FAT keeps track of files with regard to the addressable disk sectors they occupy. As a software design element, FATs are generally considered to bring with them a considerable amount of processing *overhead.*

FDDI: Stands for Fiber Distributed Data Interface, and represents an industry standard for *LANs* (local area networks) based on *fiber optic transmission.* FDDI is a token-based standard, which means that a station must have possession of the system's lone token to place an object on the LAN for transmission. There are several advantages of FDDI over the more common copper- and coaxial cable-based LANs. Fiber is high capacity, i.e., it is capable of transmitting up to several gigabits of data per second. FDDI LANs possess electromagnetic isolation properties, which means that they are not affected by external electromagnetic fields that might cause interference, impulse noise, and crosstalk on nonfiber *networks.* These fiber networks also do not emit radiation that can cause interference with other equipment. The FDDI standard is in its second generation, termed FDDI II, which expands the capabilities of FDDI I by supporting *circuit switching* for users who need LAN support for *voice, video (picturephone),* or other *streaming data* applications.

FDX: Stands for Full DupleX, which is a *network* circuit that allows data *transmission* in two directions simultaneously.

feature extraction: From the realm of optical character recognition (*OCR*), this term refers to one of the more common techniques for recognizing characters on source documents. This technique works by analyzing the structure of the character: the angles, slopes, inflection points, holes, etc. The shape of the character is compared with sets of rules (called "operators") about character shapes. For example, a shape with two vertical lines that meet at the top with a horizontal line in the middle fits the rules for the letter A. This technique is often compared with *template matching,* a less expensive but less powerful, alternative for performing OCR.

feelies: What is today being referred to by *virtual reality* aficionados as *tactile feedback* was foreseen by the famous twentieth-century author Aldous Huxley. Huxley wrote about 3-D movies that he called feelies.

fiber channel: This high-speed data *transmission* technology has recently become strongly associated with large *Web sites,* where it is used to interconnect the multiple *server* machines and storage devices that must be integrated to construct a robust site. Fiber channel technology is capable of *data rates* into the gigabit range, and can accommodate *transmission* distances of up to six miles.

fiber optic cable: A transport medium made of microthin (no thicker than human hair) glass or plastic fiber, and capable of conducting modulated light of infra-red or visible wavelengths carrying *digitized* data at very high speeds. It has many advantages: the cable is cheaper to manufacture than copper wire, less susceptible to external noise, and more secure. The trait of superior security owes to the fact that fiber optic cable is a material that provides total internal reflection. Therefore, in contrast to other *transmission media,* it is difficult to monitor from the outside. In the same vein, it is also very difficult to inject invalid data into the middle of a fiber optic *transmission.* Its main disadvantage is that it is more difficult to connect. Fiber optic cable has proven capable of sending data at a rate equal to or greater than 420 megabits per second. At this *data rate,* the entire *Encyclopedia Britannica* can be transmitted in one second. Further, a single fiber can transmit 200 million telephone conversations simultaneously.

fiber optics: This term refers to the use of *an optical fiber transmission* of data by light beam.

field of view: This term drawn from the physiology of human vision is gaining popularity in the world of *virtual reality,* where it is being used to help define the parameters of visual immersion. Large-screen technologies like the *IMAX Theatre,* which seeks to immerse the audience from a visual standpoint, are quite concerned with field of view. Research has shown that to be totally immersive, a screen must cover a 270-degree arc in front of the audience member. This number is arrived at in the following way: when a user is looking straight ahead, each eye is capable of providing visual information as much as 90 degrees away from its central axis. Combining the images from both eyes provides a lateral field of view of approximately 180 degrees. Because you can pivot your eyes to the left and right about 45 degrees, it is possible (even easy) to perceive an additional 90 degrees, making for a total lateral field of view of approximately 270 degrees. Current research suggests that an adequate sense of immersion in an image can be obtained from a field of vision of approximately 90 degrees.

FIF: Stands for Fractal Image Format, the emerging standard for image data that has been *compressed* using techniques derived from *fractal geometry.* This standard was created by Michael Barnsley of Iterated Systems, Inc.

file lock: Relative to the task of managing computer files, this term refers to a software design feature that is used to make sure that only one user can have write access to a file at any one time.

file server: Is a *host* computer that provides storage capacity for and management of data files and/or programs for a *client/server* computing *network,* in which the clients (the PCs) on the network can access the host.

file striping: Also called *declustering,* this term refers to a high-performance algorithm based on the principle of distributing a single file over several storage devices. Each device, then, holds a stripe of the same file. Because these drives can then work in parallel, each one storing and retrieving data in near-simultaneity, striping offers a much higher *transfer rate.* Reads, for example, are performed in a fashion whereby a single read request is broken into multiple requests, each serviced by a different storage device. This strategy holds great currency in the age of *multimedia,* where the challenge of moving enormous files poses one of the industry's enduring problems.

filename extension: This term refers to one of the dominant conventions used in naming computer files. Most filenames include a three-letter extension that is separated from the main body of the filename by a period. This extension is typically used to identify the file type. For example, the filename extension for the *URL* "www.microsoft.com/ie/ie3/features-f.htm" is ".htm" indicating that the file associated with this *Web site* is an *HTML* file.

fill: From the world of computer *paint systems,* this term refers to a widely available feature in commercial packages in which enclosed areas in a picture can be given a gray shade, color, or pattern with a single click of the *mouse.*

film scanner: This type of scanning device specializes in *digitizing* slides and transparencies.

filter: Is a program or subprogram that *converts* a stream of data from one file format to another. It may also produce an error log.

finger: Is a program that identifies users currently logged onto a particular computer system. This term can also be used to refer to the command that executes this user tracking program.

firewall: A *network* security feature that protects a *LAN* from unauthorized access from the external *Internet* (*extranet*), and that also prevents internal users from surfing the external Internet (extranet) without proper authorization.

firmware: This term refers to computer programs stored in programmable read-only memories (PROMs) that can be replaced, but not reprogrammed, by the user. Firmware is common in the various *board* products that are used to increase the media processing capabilities of multimedia personal computers (*MPCs*).

flame: A sad part of the emerging culture of *cyberspace,* a flame is an insulting *e-mail* or *Usenet* post. Flames are often cruel, brutally detailed, and fully intended to defame the unfortunate subject. The term has become so widely used that it is also commonly employed in its verbal form, as in: "If you do thus and such, I will be sure to flame you."

flanging: From the realm of audio engineering, this term refers to an audio effect created by placing two copies of the same sound in and out of temporal phase with one another.

flat panel displays: These are an emerging family of *VDU* (video display unit) that most often use technologies other than the *CRT* to reduce the bulk and power requirements of the VDU. The most popular examples in today's commercial environment are the *LCDs* (liquid crystal displays) and plasma panels that are used with small portable computers.

flatbed plotter: Is a *pen plotter* in which the paper (or film-based material) is held on a flat drawing table where it is traversed by one or more pens in a pen carriage.

flatbed scanner: One of the most commonly used types of *scanner,* it is distinctive for having a flat surface where users place their artwork or documents one at a time for scanning as the light source moves under the item to be scanned. Many flatbed scanners have optional document feeders for scanning multiple pages automatically.

flicker: One of the most common *artifacts* of *analog video,* flicker can be seen as a vibration of the entire screen, the horizontal lines, or the colors.

flippy disks: This is slang for the high-end, 17-*gigabyte,* dual-layer, two-sided standard for *DVD* storage.

flying: This term has been abducted by the *virtual reality* community to refer to movement through a *virtual world* that is enacted by hand gestures (such as pointing one's data-gloved finger in the direction of movement). Thus, with reference to an *architectural walkthrough,* one can say that they are flying through a particular structure.

flying mouse: Is a *virtual reality* version of the *mouse* input device that tracks motion in three, rather than just two, dimensions.

FM synthesis: One of two primary forms of *MIDI* (musical instrument digital interface) synthesis (FM stands for frequency modulation, in case you didn't know). The other primary form is *wave table synthesis,* which is generally considered to be the superior of the two. FM synthesis is the elder of the two, and it is by far the most common among the first generation of add-in sound *boards.* With FM synthesis, at least two digitally generated *sine waves* are required. One of these waves is called the "modulator" because it modulates or changes the *frequency* of the second waveform, which is called the *carrier.* While FM synthesis requires only two sine waves, FM synthesizers typically use multiple carriers and modulators. Each of these sine waves is called an "operator." FM synthesis was invented in the 1970s by Stanford's John Chowning. Yamaha holds an exclusive right to the patent for his invention. Yamaha's first-generation chips used only two operators and produced sounds that were adequate to the early game market. A later Yamaha chip, the *OPL3*, used four operators and was capable of generating more sophisticated sounds.

FMV: Stands for Full-Motion Video and refers to Philips' *MPEG*-compressed full-motion *video* option. OptImage incorporates FMV in MovieStudio, an authoring tool designed specifically for use with *CD-I* (compact disc-interactive) technology.

fogging: From the realm of *DVE* (digital video effects), this term refers to the alteration of the visibility or clarity of an object, depending on how far the object is from the observer. Also known as "haze," this DVE is usually implemented by adding a fixed color (known as the "fog color") to each *pixel* that is effected by a shifting in the user's *POV*.

folder: This term refers to a *GUI* object that is used to represent a subdirectory on a computer's hard *disk*. This particular metaphor is deemed appropriate because subdirectories are designed to contain files in much the same way a physical folder is designed to hold documents. Most PC operating systems, as well as most software applications, use the ubiquitous folder *icon* to indicate the presence of disk subdirectories. In *Eudora,* for example, files that are *downloaded* as attachments within a message are depicted as a folder, entitled Download. From this folder, the user can access the downloaded files later.

foley effects: From the world of film *production,* this term refers to sound effects that are manufactured, usually in a studio, for use in a specific film scene. These effects can be as mundane as someone walking across a linoleum floor, or as spectacular as a volcanic eruption. In traditional film production, foley effects are created in a *postproduction* setting where the appropriately equipped individuals (e.g., foley walkers on sand, wood, or linoleum surfaces) make the sounds while viewing the actual film events with which those sounds will be later *mixed*. This process is similar to looping, which refers to the studio creation of voiceovers to replace dialogue recorded at the live shoot. As *MIDI* (musical instrument digital interface) equipment becomes more common, enabling the digital creation of sound effects and the construction of *clip media* audio libraries, the costs of creating foley effects will be dramatically (no pun intended) reduced since directors will no longer need to incur the costs of original production.

footage: In film and *video,* this term is generally used to refer to film that has been exposed by the camera operator.

footprint: This term has two popular uses in the world of modern communication technology. First, it is used to describe the amount of space that a particular computing device will occupy on the user's *desktop.* For example, a laptop computer has a smaller footprint than a typical desktop computer. The second popular use of this term has to do with satellite communications. The area on earth that is covered by a particular satellite beam is called its footprint.

force feedback: Part and parcel of the effort to master the human-machine elements of *tactile feedback,* this subdiscipline of *virtual reality* is involved with the re-creation of *force patterns* that give users the sense that they are coming into tangible contact with some object from the real world, such as the gearshift of a race car. The most sophisticated force feedback systems to date make use of tables of *digitized* force patterns, with each pattern representing a particular object and/or sensation.

force patterns: Analogous to the sound *patches* stored in a *MIDI* (musical instrument digital interface) *wave table,* force patterns are digitized patterns of *force feedback* that emulate the human experience of interacting with various objects in the real world. Thus, the feel of moving a gearshift from first to second gear might be recorded and stored in a *tactile feedback* database of force patterns.

form factor: This term refers to the physical size and shape of devices, such as computers and *interactive televisions.* With an increasing move toward special purpose equipment—the portable PC, for example—there is a growing move away from a standardized form factor and toward increasingly customized form factors to meet the needs of specific applications.

format longevity: An important economic feature of any media-related technology, this term refers to duration, or length of stay, that a given format may enjoy as a widely used standard. The *NTSC* (National Television Standards Committee) standard for television is now into its fifth decade of format longevity. By way of contrast, the *CGA* standard (the what?) for computer monitors was a mere *flicker* in the technological night, lasting for about two years before it gave way to *EGA* and its successor, *VGA* (video graphics array).

forwarding: In its most common usage, this term refers to the directing of a piece of *e-mail* from one *address* to another. Thus, for example, as an e-mail user you might find occasion to forward a complimentary e-mail sent to you by a client to everyone on your project team.

foundation class: From the realm of *object-oriented programming,* this important term refers to the class library from which all other objects in an object-oriented system are derived. In an object-oriented system, most objects are derived from one object, or a combination of more fundamental objects. It is a principle called "inheritance," and it lies at the very heart of the most significant conceptual movement in the history of *software engineering.* Owing to the practice of inheritance, software engineers are able to reuse "objects" that have been designed and coded by other engineers, and because of this practice, are able to construct reliable programs far more rapidly than previously. But the object-oriented approach is only as good as the object libraries that are in use by a particular organization or programming group. If one is forced to use faulty or poorly designed objects, then most of the programming effort will be devoted to correcting problems and redesigning the objects. However, if designed correctly, the objects making up this class will be the most fundamental and extensible and, as such, will make it possible for the software engineer to quickly design and construct all other objects in the system by either combining foundation objects, or by elaborating on their relatively simple structure. Most major software systems manufactured in the last decade feature a foundation class. Microsoft has produced a foundation class of objects to support its *Windows* operating environment, which is known appropriately as the Microsoft Foundation Class (*MFC*). In turn, Sun Microsystems has created a foundation class for the *Java* programming environment, which is also suitably referred to as the Java Foundation Class, or JFC.

fovea: From the realm of human visual anatomy, this term refers to a region on the rear wall of the retina responsible for one's center of visual attention. This region is both the thinnest part of the retina and the part with the highest concentration of cones. Figuratively speaking, it is the high-resolution portion of the human field of vision. All other portions are low *resolution* and are often referred to collectively as "peripheral vision." Some *virtual reality* engineers involved in building wide *field-of-view* devices are now taking advantage of this foveal concentration of high-resolution vision by building *dual-resolution displays.* These displays reduce the high-resolution portions of their screens to *windows* that roughly approximate the foveal portion of human sight. They keep this portion of the display, or this high-resolution window, in front of the user's foveal line of sight by using *eye tracking* technology that keeps up with the location of the user's pupils. The value of this approach to VR engineering is that it dramatically reduces the overall number of *pixels* that must be projected onto the display, reducing the computational demands placed on the system and making higher *refresh rates* possible.

fps: Stands for frames per second, and represents a primary measure of film quality. The higher the fps, the smoother the flow of motion and, all other things being equal, the higher the quality of the motion *video.*

FQDN: Stands for Fully Qualified Domain Name, which is the complete *domain name* that identifies a specific *host* computer on the *Internet.* The FQDN includes, at the very least, a *host name,* a subdomain name, and a domain name. For example, in the FQDN of <pop_statistics. census_bureau.gov>, the computer hosting the population statistics is the host name, the census_bureau is the subdomain name, and *gov* is the domain name.

fractal geometry: The brainchild of IBM researcher Benoit Mandelbrot, this recent intellectual creation thrives on the notion that nature seems to recapitulate itself at different scales. Thus, large branches scale down into smaller branches, which scale down into twigs virtually ad infinitum. For the *multimedia* industry, fractal geometry has given rise to a number of promising software technologies, including programs that simulate portions of the natural world and routines that are used for *compressing* and *decompressing* images.

fractal transform image compression: This is perhaps the most innovative, and certainly the most promising, form of *codec* technology yet to appear. Pioneered by Michael Bransley and Iterated Systems, Inc., of Norcross, Georgia, this technology can achieve high-image *compression ratios,* with 100:1 being fairly standard. Based on the mathematics of *fractal geometry,* this codec possesses the desirable feature of creating *scalable* images (i.e., images that are *resolution independent*) and can therefore output (*decompress*) images at any *resolution.*

fragmentation: This term refers to the process required by *Internet protocols* for splitting an object into smaller pieces, referred to as fragments or *packets.* Fragmentation is required for the transport of Internet packets, where it is used to accommodate the limitations of the physical linking medium.

frame: An area of film equal to one *exposure,* this is the principal term used to describe the fundamental unit of both *analog* and *digital* forms of *video.* With regard to the *Internet,* a frame divides the *browser window* into multiple regions, each displaying a different document. With regard to this second definition, frames are not supported by all *Web browsers.*

frame accuracy: This term refers to a device's ability to consistently locate any single *frame* on a tape. The *SMPTE* (Society for Motion Picture and Television Engineers) *time code* is, for example, frame accurate. This means that SMPTE is extremely accurate because it can locate and then let the user access any one of the 30 frames contained in a second of *NTSC video.*

frame buffer: This term refers to a very important feature of graphical display systems. It refers to a portion of memory, or RAM, that is dedicated to storing a full *frame* of picture data at one time. Frame buffers are composed of arrays of *bit* values that correspond to the graphical display's *pixels.* Thus, the size of the frame buffer and the number of bits per pixel are two variables that have much to do with determining the richness of the images that can be shown.

frame dropping: A process that often accompanies the give and take of scaling up the size of a *digital video window,* this term refers to the lowering of the *frame rate (fps)* of a digital video stream to maintain a constant *data rate.* The process of frame dropping often leads to a herky-jerky video image, an *artifact* that results because key segments of motion are missing after a certain number of *frames* have been eliminated. The process is required only because of the present *bandwidth* limitations that surround the use of video on today's computers and computer *networks.* In due time, it is hoped, the need for frame dropping will be eliminated by the ever-increasing media-handling capabilities of personal computers and the *Web.*

frame grabber: This is a system component, usually implemented as an *expansion board* with companion software, used to *capture,* or *digitize,* the *video signal* from a motion picture source (e.g., from a TV, video camera, or VCR). Often, the term is used synonymously with a video digitizer.

frame rate: This term refers to the rate at which single *frames* in a motion picture *sequence* are displayed on a screen. With TV in North America, broadcast *video* is displayed at 30 frames per second *(fps);* the 35-mm motion pictures seen in the theater play at 24 frames per second.

frame refresh rate: Nearly synonymous with *frame rate,* this term has taken on a unique importance in the world of *virtual reality,* where each *frame* the user sees is dynamically constructed in *real time* from visual data stored in the computer's memory. It is far easier to create high frame rates when frames are represented by prerecorded images stored on videotape than it is to generate photorealistic images on the fly from visual data. For this reason, it is widely accepted that it will be some time into the future before we have virtual reality equipment that can *render* photorealistic (film-quality) images at anything approaching the frame rates of television or movies.

frame relay: From the realm of *data communications,* this term refers to a form of *broadband technology* in wide use today. Frame relay gets its name from its method of operation—the relaying of *frames* of information. The appeal of frame relay is that it operates at the data *link* layer of the *OSI* model only and, thus, does not include any *network* or higher layer *protocol* functions. As a result, the protocol *overhead*—i.e., the processing overhead needed to handle higher-layer functions—is much lower with frame relay than it is with most other broadband technologies. Thus, the time required to set up connections is also reduced, leading to a streamlined form of data communications. Most industry experts view frame relay as a transition technology to *ATM* (asynchronous transfer mode).

freeware: Is software programming that is *copyrighted* but offered at no cost. Freeware is *shareware* that does not involve a fee. It is made available from a variety of sources, including bulletin boards (*BBS*), online services, *archives* on the *Internet,* and sometimes via *CD-ROM* or floppy *disk.*

freeze frame: This feature, common to both analog and *digital video* devices, is used to hold a single *frame* of video motionless on the screen.

frequency: With regard to the physical characteristics of a *signal,* the term frequency is used most often to describe the number of times that a signal varies per second. In this context, frequency is usually measured in *hertz* or cycles per second.

fringeware: This slang term refers to software of dubious stability and marginal value that is made available as *freeware.*

front plane: From the world of computer graphics, this term refers to the uppermost of two visual planes used in *two-plane effects* to create transitions between one screen and the next.

FTP: Stands for File Transfer Protocol, and refers to a venerable standard for transferring files from one computer to another over the *Internet.*

full-body recognition: This is one of the *enabling technologies* of *full-immersion* VR. It is a dreamed-about capability of *virtual reality* that will make it possible for cybernauts to enter a *virtual world* and have the tracking intelligence of that world recognize what their entire body is doing, e.g., what the arms are doing, what the facial expressions are like, how the body is moving through space, etc. Though this technology is a long way off in any practical sense, early prototypes such as VPL Research's *DataSuit* have already been brought to market.

full-duplex: From the world of *networks,* this term describes a communication *channel* that permits data to travel in both directions simultaneously (see also *FDX*).

full-immersion VR: This is the fullest form of *virtual reality,* wherein one dons head gear, *DataGloves,* and a bodysuit and becomes completely immersed in the *virtual world* (such as it is).

full-text retrieval: This term refers to the most exhaustive form of search and retrieval that can be applied to a large database comprised of text-based documents. With this type of retrieval, users supply target words or phrases (representing the information they are looking for) to the *search engine,* and the search engine scans, or *parses,* the entirety of the documents contained in the database. Under this search strategy, the users can be confident that no incidences of their target words will be missed. However, owing to the massive nature of many document databases (imagine searching through every article of every issue of the *Wall Street Journal*), many designers back away from using this computationally intensive approach. Instead, many opt to perform the far simpler *keyword* search, in which the only text data parsed are a relatively small number of keywords that have been drawn from the target documents to summarize their content.

future-proofing: In our current era of rapid, technology-driven change, enterprises are very concerned with controlling the costs associated with the functional obsolescence of their technology investments. For instance, many firms invest heavily in the development of new software applications, only to discover shortly after completing the first phases of development that the *platform* for which they developed the program is about to—or already has—become functionally obsolete. Technologies such as *Java,* which promote cross-platform compatibility are about future-proofing, because they help protect organizations from the inevitable changes in technology platforms that lie at the heart of this innovative period in history.

Perhaps the central fact and assumption of the information society is that the world of concrete objects is being controlled more and more by a parallel, but separate, world of abstract objects and concepts.

—Kamran Parsaye, Chairman, IntelligenceWare

gaffer: From the world of filmmaking, this term refers to the chief electrician, responsible for the safe and efficient setup of lights, cables, and accessories—an important role in film *production*.

gain: From the realm of sound engineering, this term refers to the increase in signaling power that results when an audio *signal* is boosted by an electronic device (such as a *repeater*). Gain is typically measured in *decibels*.

game engine: In the world of *electronic game design*, this term refers to a set of software routines that can be used to spawn a whole series of related games. Games created from the same game engine possess a similar *play-mechanic* and are likely to be viewed by the marketplace as belonging to the same genre. The well-designed game engine is thus a business asset of enormous value.

gas plasma: This is the technology of the future for large, color, flat-panel displays (such as those featured in the movie *Total Recall*).

gateway: Is a specialized computer program that translates *e-mail* from one network *protocol* to another, through a process known as "protocol conversion." The gateway works by reformatting data so that it will be acceptable to its destination system.

gaze duration: This is the amount of time a human spends looking in a particular direction. This phenomenon is now used as a computer input parameter with *virtual reality* systems that make use of *eye tracking*.

generation loss: Is a characteristic of *analog* forms of media, such as cassette tape audio or VHS *video*, where with each successive copying of the program some of the original quality is lost. Thus a copy of a copy will possess less quality—more generation loss—than will a first-generation copy of an original. Generation loss is often cited as one of the most distinct disadvantages that analog forms of media have relative to their *digital* counterparts. With *digital media*, where the original is stored in the form of a data representation—a binary stream of data, to be exact—no generational loss of quality occurs no matter how many times the information is copied.

genlocking: From the world of *video production*, this term refers to a device's ability to synchronize video *signals* from two tape sources so that they can be recorded together onto a third tape. The term has also been used to describe a signal synchronization technique essential to the process of creating a stable signal when overlaying computer graphics with video.

ghosting: An *artifact* common on *LCD* screens, ghosting refers to the faint continuation of solid lines—also termed "shadowing"—beyond the actual ends of those lines. This artifact is caused by the uncontrolled spread of electricity along the electrodes that turn screen *pixels* on and off.

Gibb's effect: The most common *artifact* for images that have been compressed using the *DCT* (discrete cosine transfer) technique (which is the base technique for the *JPEG* [Joint Photography Experts Group] standard), this effect appears as ripples running out from sharp edges such as street signs or tree trunks, giving an overall impression of blockiness. As one would expect, this artifact becomes increasingly pronounced the higher the *compression ratio*.

GIF: Stands for Graphics Interchange File, a file format defined by CompuServe in 1987 (for which UNISYS holds the patent) to facilitate the exchange of picture files between computer *platforms*. It allows up to 256 colors or shades of gray and is commonly used to post photographic images on bulletin boards. It does not, however, have a high standing with graphics professionals. It is popular on the *Web* because it employs an efficient *compression* technique called the *LZW* algorithm.

gigabyte: Is one billion *bytes*; it is also the next level of common storage capacity, now that *multimedia* technology is making megabytes of storage passé. A gigabyte is typically represented by the initials GB.

gigahertz: Is one billion cycles per second.

GII: Stands for Global Information Infrastructure, and is one of many terms being used to describe the emerging network infrastructure that is projected by futurists to serve as the prime delivery mechanism for bringing *multimedia content* into every home and business around the world. On a more provincial scale, politicians and technologists in the United

States (and other countries) refer to this concept by the acronym *NII* (National Information Infrastructure), which increasingly is being viewed as a national strategic asset. Today's *Internet* is being viewed as the first generation edition of the GII.

glass distortion: This refers to a form of *DVE* (digital video effect) in which the image is altered so that it appears as it would if it were viewed through a piece of unfinished glass.

glyphs: From the world of *scientific visualization,* these are visual objects whose attributes (e.g., shape, position, color, size, and orientation) are bound to independent variables and serve to provide a symbolic representation of some aspect of nature. Spheres in a molecular structure and color patterns in an anatomical graphic to depict tumors represent just two examples of glyph usage.

gopher: Is the information retrieval system developed at the University of Minnesota that preceded the *World Wide Web.* It provides a hierarchically structured *menu* of viewable files. Gopher is a *client/server* application that makes use of the gopher *protocol.* A user with a gopher client can retrieve information from any accessible gopher *server.*

gopher space: Refers to the totality of information that is stored on the thousands of *gopher servers* located around the world. The files are organized in a subject hierarchy, the contents of which can reside on a single server, on multiple servers, or can theoretically span all gopher servers. Gopher space is the *network* of all gopher servers, and it represents a seemingly limitless source of information for the gopher user.

gouraud shading: From the realm of computer graphics, this term refers to a relatively high-end form of *polygon shading.* With gouraud, a lighting calculation is applied to each vertex of a *polygon* face, and is then interpolated in a linear fashion across the face of that polygon to achieve a smooth lighting effect with gradual color transitions.

gov: From the world of the *Internet, gov* is a top-level *domain name* that is reserved for use by branches or agencies of the U.S. federal government.

gradient fill: This is a feature common to commercial *paint systems* in which the user is able to *fill* a specified area of an image with a pattern, gray shade, or color that displays a gradual transition from the foreground of the fill area to the background.

granularity: This term refers to the size of the units by which something is structured. The smaller the units, the more granular the structure. For example, a foot-long ruler that provides tick marks for every tenth of an inch is more granular in its markings than one that only provides tick marks for every inch. Generally speaking, granularity is considered a desirable design feature for *multimedia applications* because it implies that the program has an ability to take greater advantage of the *random access* capabilities of the computer. In the world of *digital libraries*, granularity refers to the ability to designate a small part of a document or set of documents for retrieval, even when the full document or set of documents is quite large.

graphics subroutine packages: The so-called toolbox systems, these packages help programmers build their own graphically oriented application software using prewritten graphics utilities.

graphics tablet: An input device used by graphic artists, this is a touch-sensitive *board* over which the *illustrator* passes some form of hand-held input device, typically a pen. Under its most common form of usage, the pressure from the pen as it moves across the surface causes the tablet to generate a stream of x and y coordinates, which a graphics program will then accept and translate into a line drawing that appears on the computer display.

grayscale: The spectrum, or range, of shades of black an image has. *Scanners'* and terminals' grayscales are determined by the number of gray shades or steps they can recognize and reproduce. A *scanner* that can only see a grayscale of 16 will not produce as accurate an image as one that distinguishes a grayscale of 256.

great electronic machine: This is futurist Joseph Pelton's term for the world's biggest existing machine: the massive, interconnected system of cables, telephones, computers, and broadcasting equipment that constitutes the world's communications *network*.

Green Book: Related to the *Red Book, Yellow Book*, and *Orange Book* standards, this standard for *compact disc* refers specifically to the *CD-I* (compact disc-interactive) technology of Philips. This standard relies upon a specific operating system, called *CD-RTOS,* and sets forth the specifications for the *disc* layout. Like XA of the Yellow Book standard, the Green Book allows *interleaving* of computer data and compressed audio on the same *track*.

grid: This is an invisible layout that divides a screen into separate visual areas. Grids are quite common in *digital video production* tools, such as *paint systems*, where they are used as a tool for enabling artists to blend more than one graphic object on a single *frame*.

grip: From the world of filmmaking, this term refers to the occupation responsible for assisting the camera and sound crews by helping to move equipment, props, costumes, and the like.

grooming: Also referred to as "file grooming," this concept is associated with network file storage systems and describes an automated (defined by algorithm) process whereby files are migrated from *online* to *near-line storage* devices without any operator intervention. As the name implies, the algorithmic intelligence associated with grooming will usually involve some deletion of files (a process traditionally referred to as *purging*). In large scale *multimedia* systems where *gigabytes* and possibly even *terabytes* of permanent storage are involved, grooming is a powerful labor-saving technology.

groupware: This term refers to software designed to enhance the sharing of an information work product (for example, a large document such as a corporate annual report) among members of a work group. This emergent technology typically relies upon some form of networking technology such as *e-mail*, an *intranet*, or the *Internet* to interconnect members of the work team and to provide mutual access to the shared work product. A good example of groupware is *Lotus Notes*. *Document conferencing* is a slightly more advanced application of groupware in which members of the work team communicate via *video windows* embedded in a document work product.

GUI: Stands for Graphical User Interface, and is pronounced "goo-ee." This standard buzz phrase of the late 1980s and early 1990s refers to the *interface design* goals that became predominant in the industry as PCs began to accrue significant graphics capabilities. In essence, a GUI is supposed to make the computer easier to use by providing users with graphical objects, such as *icons, buttons,* and *windows,* that are based on familiar real-world objects (i.e., those that are found on the average office *desktop*). Indeed, the *desktop metaphor* of the Apple Macintosh and Microsoft *Windows interfaces* are the classic examples of GUIs. They replaced the sterile systems of text commands that preceded GUIs in the historical evolution of computer software. With the recent rapid growth of the *Internet*, the GUI continues to be a critical design issue and is a focal point in the construction of Internet *browsers* and most *Web sites*.

GUI painter: This is a standard feature of most of today's sophisticated software development toolkits (*SDK*). The GUI painter enables software developers to create user *interfaces* relatively quickly by *dragging* and *dropping* standard *window* objects onto the application they are developing. The standard windows objects include *dialog boxes*, pulldown *menus*, *radio buttons*, and the like. Thus, with a GUI painter, software developers are able to create a graphical user interface (*GUI*) with relative ease by simply dragging, or "painting," these windows objects onto the "canvas" that is their software application in development.

If something beyond the immediate spatial moment is one of the primal traits that makes us human, then virtual reality can be considered the most natural progression we can imagine.
—Tony Reveaux, Editor,
Computer Publicity News

hachures: In the world of computer graphics, this term refers to a series of lines representing the general direction and steepness of a slope. Gentle slopes are represented by longer, lighter, or more widely spaced lines, whereas steep slopes are symbolized by shorter, heavier, or more closely spaced lines. The use of hachures has a considerable tradition in the field of cartography (map making), where the lines are used to depict relief on topographic maps.

hackers: Are persons who attempt to penetrate the security of a computer system, usually from a remote location, for nefarious purposes.

hacking: When programmers write software code outside the structure of a highly managed development project, they are often said to be hacking. This somewhat derogatory term springs from the generally accepted principle that sound software code can only be constructed under the auspices of a tightly managed development project in which a rigorous *methodology* is practiced. Version control, iterative cycles of testing and debugging, and substantive trials to determine *usability* are just some of the quality control measures practiced during a well-managed software development process. *Hackers* operate outside this type of rigorous and structured environment, and as a result their code is often "buggy" and poorly structured. However, one significant benefit of hacking exists, and it is the primary reason why this renegade method of software development remains a useful tradition in the history of software development. Because programming is such a demanding and creative skill and because programmers tend to be profiled as lone wolves, hacking in the absence of management control often breeds some of the most interesting and innovative programs around.

half-duplex: This term describes a data *channel* that can carry data in both directions but only in one direction at any one time. Half-duplex is often contrasted with *full-duplex* (*FDX*), which permits data to travel in both directions simultaneously.

hand-off function: This term is used to describe the ability found with the *wireless* technologies—such as cellular phone or *RDS* (radio data systems)—to automatically switch from one broadcast source to another as a moving destination (e.g., a car) travels from one geographic zone to another. The latest and perhaps most innovative use of the hand-off function can be found in RDS, where it will soon be possible in the United States for a cross-country driver to have the radio automatically retune itself to another station for nationally broadcast shows as the driver travels from one geographic zone into another.

handshaking: From the world of *networks* and *data communications*, handshaking refers to a procedure carried out by two *modems* to establish a connection. The procedure establishes the connection *protocol* to be used and synchronizes the data *transmissions* to follow.

haptic system: From the realm of human anatomy, this system has taken on sudden importance with the emerging effort to provide *tactile feedback* in association with *virtual reality* products. The haptic system has two major subsystems. The first is called "mechanoreceptors." They are extremely sensitive mechanisms that measure pressure or deformation of the skin. They are critical in providing information about the *texture* of an object. The second subsystem is associated with the term "proprioception," which has to do with how our muscles and tendons work to discover the size, weight, and shape of an object based on how much effort they must exert when encountering that object. Together, the mechanoreceptors and proprioception make up the haptic system and provide haptic cues that convey information to our minds about the tangible environment.

hardware address: Is the physical, or absolute *address*, where a device or document can be located within a computer system. With regard to the *OSI* model, this term is nearly synonymous with the "data link layer address."

HCD: Stands for Head-Coupled Display, which is a piece of *virtual reality* gear that is closely related to the *HMD* (head-mounted display). The HCD is a large device that is connected to a free-moving, pivotal, robotic arm. The arm contains a built-in tracking unit that also supports the weight of the device as the user moves around. Compared to a HMD, the HCD offers an increased *field of view* and superior image *resolutions*, and is, therefore, capable of enabling a highly immersive form of VR.

HDF: Stands for Hierarchical Data Format, a file format developed by the National Center for Supercomputer Applications and intended to serve as a standard for the *scientific visualization* community. HDF is ideal for this role because it is extensible, available in the *public domain*, and capable of handling data and images as well as scaling information.

HDTV: Stands for High-Definition TeleVision, an emerging standard for higher quality television broadcasts. Actually, the term HDTV has been with us for some time and may represent the next generation of television. The term has become increasingly specific, as the Advisory Committee on Advanced Television Service in the United States has begun serious deliberations with the goal in mind of recommending a single HDTV standard to the FCC. HDTV broadcasting was originally intended to begin by 1996 and air concurrently with traditional *NTSC* (National Television Standards Committee) broadcasts until 2008, at which time all *NTSC transmissions* are to be phased out. There are two primary elements of the HDTV standard. First, the new standard offers higher *resolution* in the vicinity of 1,000 *scan lines*, which is roughly twice the *NTSC* number of 525 scan lines. This resolution delivers broadcast quality that is roughly equivalent to 35-mm film (the quality one sees in today's movie theaters). Second, the new standard will include a wider screen *aspect ratio*, another feature that will bring television broadcasts into closer physical harmony with the motion picture industry. The dominant problem facing the various corporate/academic alliances who are in competition for establishing the new HDTV standard revolves around the *bandwidth reduction* that must be achieved to deliver these new capabilities within the *bandwidth* constraints that have been put in place by the FCC.

headend: This is becoming a general purpose term for describing source *nodes* in the architecture of the *information superhighway* that are responsible for storing and serving up the various elements of content that users of the highway want. As the superhighway (i.e., *NII, GII*) takes greater shape, headends will provide mass storage (projected to be in the *terabyte* range) of *multimedia* content within the near future.

heads-up display: This type of display is projected by futurists to become a common part of the radio data systems (*RDS*) that will soon be standard features in most automobiles. With these displays, digitally displayed information is projected onto a small viewing area on the windshield, so that drivers do not have to redirect their line of sight away from the road to see the digitally transmitted information. As with so many advanced technologies, the heads-up display originated in the military, where it is already used by fighter pilots.

heat mapping: From the realm of *scientific visualization*, this visual procedure produces a surface plot in which height and color are used to represent the magnitudes of different variables, such as stress intensity or age of data. The higher the height and the warmer the color, the greater the intensity one adduces to the variables being represented.

helper application: Is a program that enables the user to run various modes of *multimedia* seamlessly from the *Internet*. Usually, the helper application is *downloaded* to the client's (user's) computer to run the multimedia. Often, users must download one or more helper applications (referred to more commonly as "helper apps") before they can properly view a *Web site* that has multimedia.

hertz: A common metric in the world of communications, this term refers to the *frequency* of a *signal* measured in cycles per second.

heuristics: This term is important to the discipline of *artificial intelligence*, where it refers to general rules of thumb that can be translated into *domain*-specific rules to be used in given situations.

hexadecimal: Just as the decimal system is based on 10, and the binary system on 2 (i.e., 0s and 1s), the hexadecimal system is based on 16. In hexadecimal, the numbers are referred to as hexits (as compared with digits in base 10). The hexits 0–9 are used, and are extended by the letters A, B, C, D, E, and F to represent the numbers 10–15. Thus, 1A in hexadecimal is 11 decimal. The hexadecimal system is very important to the world of computer programming, where it is used to conduct all internal mathematical operations. All *hardware addresses* are, for example, ultimately represented in hexadecimal.

hidden-line removal: This technique is used in sophisticated graphics programs whereby lines are removed from view that would normally be hidden on a real object by virtue of being obstructed by the front surfaces of the object.

High Sierra format: The first widely accepted standard for positioning files and directories on *CD-ROM*, this term owes its origins to the fact that it was initially conjured in the mid-1980s at a meeting of industry representatives held at the High Sierra Hotel in Lake Tahoe, Nevada.

high-fidelity simulation: This term represents the convergence of high-end business training applications, such as the flight simulators sponsored by the airline industry, and the use of the immersive technologies of *virtual reality*, such as full *field-of-view video*.

high-intensity amusement attractions: One of the leading edges of new media design and production, these attractions form the *backbone* of the late–twentieth-century theme park (e.g., Disney World and Universal Studios in Orlando, Florida). These attractions use a combination of *3-D sound* and *video*, environmental props, and live actors to create hyper-real experiences for their audiences. The "Back to the Future" ride at Universal Studios in Orlando is one of the best examples of a high-intensity amusement attraction.

high-level language: From the *archives* of software history, this term refers to a family of software tools that came into existence early (circa 1960s) to make it easier for humans to write programs that computers can understand. In the initial years of computing, all programs were written using the binary code of 1s and 0s, a phenomenon called "machine language." This was very difficult and was mastered by only a few (nerds). Thus, a thing called "assembly language" was invented. It enables programmers to use more human-like commands to build their programs. When they (think they) are finished, they simply submit their code to a thing called an "assembler," which translates the assembly language stuff into machine language. This is still very difficult and still attracts mostly nerds. Then along came the invention of high-level languages, which enabled programmers to use an almost-human language to write their programs. Again, when finished, they submit their programs to a piece of software that translates their code into machine language. In the case of high-level languages there are actually two such families of translating programs: one called an "interpreter," the other a *compiler*. Early examples of high-level languages include COBOL and Fortran, both of which are still in fairly wide though diminishing use. More recent and more popular examples of high-level languages include Visual Basic, C++, and *Java*, all of which are commonly used to author *multimedia* creations. In spite of their name, however, high-level languages still require considerable technical training to be able to use them with any proficiency. As a consequence, they are not the end of the road when it comes to pursuing the dream of inventing software tools that enable the layperson to program the computer. There are now software tools called "Fourth Generation Languages" or, more popularly, "4GLs." These programs are also called "code generators" because they enable users to interact with a graphical user interface (*GUI*), which then generates usable code on the bases of those interactions. In many respects, most of the programs that pass for *authoring systems* are 4GLs. However, it must be reported that when you use a 4GL, you give up a considerable amount of control and flexibility and often cannot create what it is possible to produce using a high-level language. This is why many *multimedia* developers still rely heavily upon programmers working with high-level languages.

hit: From the *Internet*, a hit is a successful access to a *Web site*. A hit refers to each access or visit to a particular site. Different *browsers* use different methods to calculate the number of hits a site receives, which can cause confusion about the actual number of people who use Netscape *Navigator* or Microsoft *Internet Explorer*. In a more technical sense, the term hit refers to a successful match made while using some type of query program. When, for example, you use one of the Internet *search engines* and initiate a search by specifying the search terms that are of interest to you, each of the successful matches that are reported back to you by the search engine is a hit.

hit counter: This software feature found on many *Web sites* is used, quite simply, to count the number of times the site is "*hit*," or accessed from the outside world. In practice, these relatively simple code objects operate by incrementing a running total every time somebody (or something) accesses their site. Obviously, these relatively simple programs are used by *Webmasters*, and other stakeholders in a Web site, to determine the levels and patterns of activity on their site. Many Web sites reflect the presence of their hit counters by presenting a *digital* read-out of the running total of hits the site has experienced.

HMD: Stands for Head-Mounted Display, one of the more noteworthy contraptions of the dawning *virtual reality* medium. This device typically houses *stereoscopic glasses* and headphones and is somehow connected to power and processing sources.

hologram: Refers to a 3-D optical image formed by storing 3-D information about an image or pattern of light. Where two beams of *laser* light cross, they produce an interference pattern of microscopic light and dark fringes. If this pattern is recorded, the result is a hologram that contains full information about the two beams that formed it.

home interactive media: This term represents the youngest, but most rapidly growing, segment of the *multimedia* market. The home market, traditionally characterized almost solely by the *video* games that are computer applications disguised as entertainment, is now starting to expand into a host of other applications such as *home shopping*. With the rapid growth of access to and use of the *Internet* in the home, the potential for home interactive media is substantial.

home page: An updated version of the main *menu* that characterized first generation software programs, this *interface design* term refers to the main point of entry into a *multimedia* program. The home page typically possesses *icons* or *buttons* representing the largest categories into which the program's content has been divided. This screen also usually serves the role of being the first and last screen the user sees when entering and exiting the program, respectively. With reference to a document or *Web site* on the *Internet*, this term refers to the first or "main" page of the document or Web site.

home shopping: Considered one of the true prototypes of *interactive television*, this genre is already being exploited in a very successful fashion by mixing the technologies of television and *telephony*. With contemporary home shopping, viewers watch a visual procession of products on TV, any one of which they can order by calling the listed phone number. For future interactive versions of home shopping, it is envisioned that this shotgun type of approach will be replaced by systems that enable viewers to navigate through a *hypermedia* collection of products to view content more specifically related to their purchasing needs. Many industry analysts believe that the ultimate home of home shopping will be the *Internet*, where users can be given the ability to find just those products for which they have a need. Indeed, the main obstacle standing in the way of the migration of home shopping from television to the *Internet* is the lack of adequate *bandwidth* on the latter. Because most homes are not yet equipped with the technology needed to receive full-motion video (*FMV*) across the Internet, the television is still needed to view the quality of message provided by home shopping. But the migration would appear to be fairly imminent. The technology of *Web TV*, for example, makes possible the best of both worlds: it provides the visual fidelity of television, while also offering the *interactivity* of the online world.

hop: From the world of data communications, a hop is the movement of a *packet* from one *router* or connection point to the next across a particular *network*. A hop count, or the number of hops that must be traversed in moving information from source to destination, is a routing metric used to measure the distance between source and destination.

horizontal correlation: Also referred to as "horizontal redundancy," this term refers to the tendency with most *video* images to have a great deal of similarity in the *chrominance* and *luminance* qualities of horizontally adjacent *pixels*. This tendency makes it possible for broadcasters to use various forms of *compression*—for example, *RLE* (run-length encoding)—to reduce the *bandwidth* requirements of their broadcasts and recordings. Horizontal correlation occurs when adjacent *pixels* on the same *scan line* have the same (or similar) color and *brightness* qualities. When this occurs, the broadcast *signal* can be *digitized* in such a way that only one of the values needs to be transmitted or recorded, thus cutting the effective *bandwidth* requirements in half for that portion of the image.

horizontal scrolling: This is a form of user interaction that is called for when the developer of a *multimedia* application or *Web site* loads an image into memory that is wider than the display screen. When this happens, the user may be motivated to move sideways across the image—to *pan* the image—to see what is there. One common application of horizontal scrolling occurs where *Web site* developers have used the image of a town as the primary *interface* metaphor of their *home page*. Often, these cartoon-like renditions of a town present an image that is wider than can be effectively displayed on the screen at one time. With this type of site, users are provided with the ability to scroll left and right (horizontally) so that they can view and access all of the components of the image one screenful at a time.

host: Is a *server*, or repository, for data and services available to other remote computers or clients across some type of *network*. In the world of the *Internet*, a host will have a *direct connection* to the *Web* through an *ISP* (Internet service provider).

host name: Identifies the computer acting as *server* or *host* for a *domain* and is usually, but not necessarily, part of the *domain name*. The naming of *hosts* has provided a fertile field for exercising wild creativity and humor. Classic mythology, cartoon animals, and science fiction have provided sources of inspiration for many a host name. This type of creativity seems to be confined to *hackers*—most corporate sites tend to have more sedate host names.

host number: This is a numeric *address*, which uniquely identifies every computer on the *Internet*. It is assigned according to the *IP* (Internet protocol) addressing *scheme*, and consists of four sets of numbers separated by periods—also called a "dotted quad."

hot list: Is a personal *address* list of *URLs* of *Web sites* one wishes to refer back to. The term hot list is used in *NCSA Mosaic*. Netscape *Navigator* uses the term *bookmark*.

hot objects: In any type of *hypermedia* system—including the *Internet*—objects that are in great demand are referred to as "hot objects." In a video on demand (*VOD*) system, for example, any digital movie that is in frequent demand can be accurately called a hot object. In hierarchical storage management (*HSM*) systems, hot objects are typically migrated onto the high-speed, high-cost portions of the storage subsystem so that they become the most accessible objects in the system. See also *cold objects*.

hot spot: From the realm of graphical user interface (*GUI*) design, a hot spot is an area of the screen that can be manipulated by the user to launch some activity, such as an on-screen action by a graphic character or the triggering of a branch to another screen. To date, most hot spots have been activated by either clicking on them with a mouse-driven *cursor* or by simply touching them if the system has *touch screen* capabilities. On the *Internet*, hot spots are widely used to facilitate *hyperlinks*.

household buy rates: This term, commandeered from *home shopping* by *interactive television* savants, describes the rate at which residential consumers make use of such pay-per-view cable services as *movies-on-demand*. These rates are very important to the cable operators because they determine the capacity that will be required by these new services. In turn, these capacity values indicate the levels of investment in hardware, such as *video PBXs*, that they will need to make to provide those services.

HPC: Stands for Handheld Personal Computer, a device that is roughly synonymous with a host of emerging miniaturized computing devices, such as *PDAs* and *palmtop* computers.

HRTF: Stands for Head-Related Transfer Functions, a term associated with the mathematical modeling of the various sound transformations performed by the human audio perception system. These functions are used extensively by *virtual reality* engineers to create 3-D acoustic pictures of sound. These sound images are then used as interpretive filters that take incoming sound sources and modify them for output to headphones or speakers, such that the user hears an immersive, 3-D form of sound.

HSM: Stands for Hierarchical Storage Management, an emerging discipline for the management of very large repositories of *digital* information. HSM has become particularly relevant to the enormous storage requirements of digital media and *multimedia databases*. Under HSM, large repositories of digital content (e.g., libraries of digital *video* content) are stored across a hierarchy of storage devices. For content that is in immediate demand (*hot objects*), an HSM system will reserve space on high-speed storage devices—probably some form of magnetic disk—that are directly accessible to end users. In contrast, for content that is not in great immediate demand (*cold objects*), an HSM system will take responsibility for migrating that information to lower speed and less expensive forms of storage, such as the *optical juke boxes* associated with *near-line storage*. Thus, the HSM discipline creates an automated form of system administration that takes responsibility for allocating large volumes of digital content to those portions of the storage system that make the most sense based on their current patterns of usage.

HTML: Stands for HyperText Markup Language, which is a formatting script language similar to a typesetting code that was designed specifically for use on the *Web*. HTML comprises a body of *tags* that are inserted into the content portion of a file to define how the components of that content should be displayed. A client program, called a *browser,* reads the script and displays the document. HTML includes codes for specifying internal or external *links*, which the browser uses to *jump* to other locations in the same document or to retrieve any existing documents on the *Internet* for which a *URL* is known. HTML allows for graphics, *video*, and audiovisual links. Standard HTML was originally designed by a group at *CERN*, headed by Tim Berners-Lee, to permit easy accessibility to the wealth of information on the Internet. It was originally written in *SGML* (standard generalized markup language), a language to which it owes much of its design and composition. Currently, the standard for HTML is set by the World Wide Web Consortium. Netscape and Microsoft have each added their own extensions to the HTML codes, which permit more advanced formatting such as *frames*.

HTTP: Stands for HyperText Transport Protocol, which is the principal *protocol* used for moving files across the *Internet*. It is a rapid application *protocol* that is necessary for creating the interactive, distributed environment of the *Web*. HTTP is a communications (*client/server TCP/IP*) *protocol* that works by establishing a connection between a client and a *server* for the purposes of transmitting *HTML* pages to the client's *browser*. The prefix HTTP, which appears at the beginning of a *URL,* defines the document as an *HTML* page and establishes the requirement that HTTP be used for *transmission*.

H.261: Also referred to as *Px64* by the *CCITT* (Consultative Committee on International Telephone and Telegraph), this is the *videoconferencing* standard for *compressing* moving *video* images for *transmission* over telephone trunk lines. Capable of very high *compression ratios*—on the order of 100:1 up to 2,000:1—this is also a very *lossy compression* technique reflecting the still primitive state of *video telephony*.

hue: This refers to that dimension of color that is related to wavelength and the classification of the color as, say, blue, green, or red.

human-centered computing: This phrase was coined by IBM in conjunction with the development of *PowerPC* technology. The idea it conveys is a simple one: computers should be made easier to use by forcing them to conform to how humans communicate, rather than vice versa. Thus, one image of future computing that has been proposed under this conception is an advanced form of graphical user interface (*GUI*) governed by an *interface agent* that possesses speech recognition and works in slave-like fashion to carry out the voice-generated wishes of its user (master?). I dream of computer genie?

human-factors engineering: This design discipline is focused on creating optimal designs for major technologies such as automobiles, airplanes, etc. It is one of the key applications for *virtual reality* systems, wherein designers are allowed to become immersed (*CAD* [computer-aided design] visualizations) in the physical environments they are creating. The primary benefit of such *virtual worlds* is that they reduce the need for costly prototypes and identify human-factor design flaws that might otherwise go undetected. Examples of the issues that can be addressed by such visual models include foot traffic problems, element positioning, and aesthetic concerns.

HyperCard: Introduced in 1987 by Apple Computer, this software program was designed to facilitate the creation of *hypertext* and *hypermedia* applications. Much of the language used by Apple to describe the functionality of this program has become part of the general nomenclature of graphical user interface (*GUI*) design. Terms such as *button*, card, and stack are nearly universal among those who design GUIs and build *multimedia applications*.

hyperfiction: This term refers to what is perhaps the most common form of work to be found in the emergent medium of *interactive fiction*. Based on the *hypertext* model of structuring information, readers cut their own paths through the narrative work. Thus, consuming a work of hyperfiction is more like *browsing* through an interconnected body of information than it is like starting at the beginning and moving in linear fashion to the end, as is the case with traditional fiction. It is a nonlinear, discovery experience. In searching for models to understand this new form of fiction, one is drawn to the 1978 work *Story and Discourse*, by literary critic Seymour Chatman. In that book, Chatman made a distinction between two types of fiction. The first, and by far the most common, is what he terms "the resolved plot" or the traditional narrative that uses rising action and climax to hold the reader's interest. The second, and much more avant-garde, form is what he terms "the revealed plot" or the novel that seeks more to reveal the nature of human experience by bringing the reader close to anecdotal events that do not necessarily have to occur in any particular order. With stories told in the tradition of "the resolved plot," the order in which the events are told has everything to do with the impact of the work—one cannot tamper with its authored *sequence*. For stories told in the form of "the revealed plot," however, sequence is not nearly so critical. Thus, it would appear that this second type of narrative, "the revealed plot," may be the predecessor to hyperfiction and supply us with some form of design model for how these works should be constructed. Indeed, it would probably be fair to classify the *CD-ROM* programs *Myst* and *Riven* as early examples of this emergent medium.

hyperfootage: Currently, most *stock footage* houses organize their libraries with systems that combine electronic and manual elements. The indexes that point to particular clips, or film segments, are electronically *encoded*—and, in most cases, have databases that rely upon *keyword* indexes to enable their users to find the desired *footage*. However, the film clips are still located on tape, and the huge volume of tapes that make up the *stock footage* libraries are stored in vaults. Thus, the electronic indexes point not just to particular titles, but also (and perhaps more importantly) to the locations of the particular tapes within the tape vault. Fetching the tape is still a manual procedure. Though systems of this sort are today considered state of the art, the day will soon come when the film footage will be *digitized* and stored on *disk*, obviating the need for tape altogether and making access to the desired film clips as easy as accessing a record in one of today's many electronic databases. When this occurs, stock footage houses will become hyperfootage houses.

hyperlink: This term refers to the branching logic that connects pieces of related information within a *hypertext* or *hypermedia* program. Hyperlinks are typically implemented through some type of *button* or *hot spot*, both of which enable the user to click on a designated object on the screen to move instantly to another location in the same document or to another document on any site on the *Internet*. Hyperlinks are a very common element on most *Web sites*, and are typically displayed by *browsers* in some kind of easily recognized format such as underlining or color-coding. Most users of the Internet are very familiar with the conventions of hyperlinking and understand that a simple click of the *mouse button* will take them to the target document.

hypermedia: This term refers to a form of *information design* that is an extension of *hypertext*, incorporating other media in addition to text. One of the favored design models for *multimedia* titles, hypermedia permits an author to create an interconnected corpus of material that includes text, static graphics, *animations*, *video*, sound effects, music, voiceover annotations, etc.

hypermedia applications: As the number of *CD-ROM* titles exploded during the first half of the 1990s, *hypermedia* became one of the dominant design models for the wave of new media titles. Hypermedia applications are actually quite simple in design and purpose: they provide a visually coherent form of *navigation* through a thematically interconnected body of material, and they are predominantly exploratory in nature. There are three common examples of hypermedia application in the market today: 1) The electronic encyclopedia: with much the same purpose as our voluminous, book-bound encyclopedias, the electronic version has become the early exemplar of hypermedia. Examples of these are *Compton's Interactive Encyclopedia*, by Compton's New Media, and *Encarta*, by Microsoft. These programs provide visually oriented navigational *interfaces* to content that is presented using all of the *mixed media data types*: image, audio, *video*, and good ole text. 2) The online museum (also called a curator's file): if you change your normal perceptions a bit and think of a museum as a physically embodied database of human artwork, then you will see in an instant why hypermedia is such an ideal design model for bringing the hard-to-reach museum into your home. Many such products use the physical structure of the museum as the interface, permitting the user to view its contents by walking the halls. In this regard, the online museum illustrates the overlap between the *surrogate travel* and hypermedia models of *multimedia application*. 3) The electronic marketing brochure: increasingly, corporations are moving in the direction of building hypermedia programs to serve as powerful marketing information aids. These programs will typically array the company's products, people, and/or services in a thematically oriented fashion, enabling a salesperson or a potential customer to move through the content to find whatever is of interest at the moment. A real estate firm, for example, might have two dominant paths: one that takes the user to visual *treatments* of its prime properties, and a second that introduces key executives and salespersons. Many such brochures are invested with an auto-run logic, which enables the program to flow automatically through selected portions of its content so that it can be used at trade shows in an unattended manner. When they follow this approach, with little or no interaction by the user, they become what is referred to as a *rolling demo*. The principal design features of the hypermedia application have been transferred into the realm of the *Internet*, where they are used to structure most *Web sites*. Thus, it should be fairly easy to find examples of all three of the design models discussed in this definition while surfing the *Web*.

hypertext: In the early 1960s, Theodor Nelson coined this word to describe the idea of nonsequential writing. A hypertext system is one that allows authors or groups of authors to link information together, create paths through a corpus of related material, annotate existing texts, and create notes that point readers to either bibliographic data or the body of the referenced text. In essence, a hypertext system is a tool for creating or following associative trains of thought through a document or body of documents. Hypertext is a powerful tool for exploring large bodies of interrelated documents in areas of expertise or of interest to the user. Hypertext has played an instrumental role in the emergent discipline of *interface design*, because many of the principles of this discipline have been created by individuals and teams constructing various hypertext authoring and viewing systems. Too, the design principles of hypertext lie at the very heart of how the *Internet* is constructed, and how it operates. For example, the ability to easily establish a *hyperlink* from one *Web site* to another by simply specifying a *URL* makes operative the associational *mode* of thinking and exploring that lies at the core of the hypertext design model.

And, as imagination bodies forth
The forms of things unknown, the poets pen
Turns them to shapes, and gives to airy nothing
A local habitation and a name.
—William Shakespeare, Midsummer
Night's Dream

IAB: Stands for the Internet Architecture (or Activities) Board, which is a group of 12 people who act as a technical advisory group to the Internet Society (*ISOC*). Its responsibilities include setting the standards for the *Internet*, discussing outstanding issues, overseeing the Internet Engineering Task Force (*IETF*) and the Internet Research Task Force (*IRTF*), and publishing and managing requests for comment (*RFC*). It was reorganized in 1989 to create research and engineering subgroups. Currently, it copes with its mounting workload by assigning issues to task forces for further study and analysis.

IANA: Stands for Internet Assigned Numbers Authority, an organization devoted to assigning *addresses* and *domain names* to users of the *Internet*. Though the Internet is often thought of in almost mystical terms, the core of its value and functionality relies on the simple concept of giving every *Web site* and user a unique name. At heart, it is exactly the same principle that makes it possible for our modern postal systems to deliver individual items of mail to persons and organizations, quickly and easily, no matter how large the "address space." Though the concept is simple, the practice of keeping everyone's address unique is often very challenging. Working in concert with the Internet Registry in the United States, and with subsidiaries in other countries, IANA acts as a central repository for the massive, and rapidly growing, name and address data associated with the Internet. It uses this centralized control to ensure the uniqueness of each new address, and in this way, to maintain order in what will soon be the largest, most complex address space in human history.

IAP: Stands for Internet Access Provider and refers to the type of firm that sells *Internet* connections.

ICAI: Stands for Intelligent Computer-Assisted Instruction and refers to forms of interactive computer-based training that possess elements of *artificial intelligence*.

ICMP: Stands for Internet Control Message Protocol, which is an extension of the Internet protocol (*IP*). It provides an error detection *protocol* for *packet* processing on the *Internet*. It adds functionality and value by informing other *routers* or *hosts* about routing problems, and by suggesting better routes.

Icon: Is a stylized image that graphically conveys purpose or function in graphical user interface (*GUI*) design. The icon has become one of the most important elements in the field of *interface design.*

Iconic authoring: This term refers to a category of authoring that is performed by using the type of *authoring systems* that rely primarily on the manipulation of *icons* to produce *multimedia* creations. The most popular *icons* in the world of multimedia authoring are those associated with the flowcharting conventions of software programming. Thus, when individuals perform iconic authoring, they do so by manipulating the sequences and interrelationships between flowchart symbols, typically enacted by *dragging* the symbols from a toolbar to appropriate positions on the screen. Two popular commercial authoring systems that rely upon an iconic *interface* are Authorware Professional, by Macromedia, and IconAuthor, by Asymmetrix (originally created by AimTech).

ICW: Stands for Internet Call Waiting, which is a service that is an inevitable part of *Internet telephony*. With ICW, a person using a PC for an Internet session would be notified of an incoming call and its identity through a pop-up *window*. From a technical standpoint, ICW is handled by the *ISP* (Internet Service Provider) through the operation of an ICW server. This server is connected to the phone company's central office (*CO*) through some type of high-speed line, most likely an *ISDN* connection. When a call comes in that is intended for an ISP subscriber, the ICW server extracts the caller's number, as well as the subscriber's current *IP address*. It then looks up the subscriber's *address*, generates a pop-up message to the subscriber's PC, and then accepts a response from the subscriber for call disposition.

Idea map: From the world of *multimedia application* design, this term refers to a type of document that some design methodologies insist should be created near the front end of a development cycle. It provides an overview of a project's proposed content by displaying *links* between the major conceptual components.

Identity theft: In the age of the *Internet*, there are many fears concerning invasion of privacy through electronic means. Identity theft numbers among the most severe of these fears, and involves the unauthorized— and illegal—use of someone else's identity to achieve personal gain. The concern over this threat is particularly strong in conjunction with electronic commerce (*e-commerce*). This is because it is relatively difficult to check personal identities in the absence of face-to-face interaction, and because the very act of consummating e-commerce business requires the *transmission* of sensitive data regarding one's identity (e.g., one's personal account number).

IESG: Stands for Internet Engineering Steering Group, a body composed of the *IETF* (Internet Engineering Task Force) Area Directors and the IETF Chair. It provides the first technical review of *Internet* standards and is responsible for the day-to-day management of the IETF.

IETF: Formed in 1986, the Internet Engineering Task Force is the main standards organization for the *Internet*. Its purpose is to help coordinate the operation and management of the *Internet* and to help resolve *protocol* and architectural issues. It is an important source of proposals for *protocol* standards submitted to the Internet Architecture Board (*IAB*). The IETF resides under the auspices of the *ISOC* and consists of 80 working groups. It is open to any interested individual. Its membership is comprised of a global group of professional network specialists, operators, vendors, and researchers, all of whom are greatly interested in the evolution of the Internet, its architecture, and its efficient operation. The IETF meets three or four times per year and records its activities in a proceedings document.

IFF: Stands for Interchange File Format, which is a file format standard first developed by Electronic Arts (the *electronic game* manufacturer) for the Commodore Amiga. It was designed to allow different programs to share a common file format. It works by appending header information to the file, which describes the amount and layout of the data.

IGES: Stands for Initial Graphics Exchange Specification, a standard file format used to represent data in the *CAD* (computer-aided design) industry.

IGP: Is an Interior Gateway Protocol, which defines the information and procedures used to pass routing information to other *routers* within a closed *network* system. The word *gateway* has been recently replaced by the word *router*. RIP (routing information protocol) is an example of an IGP. Exterior gateway *protocols* also exist.

IICS: Stands for International Interactive Communication Society, a professional organization charged with promoting the exchange of ideas and opportunities between individuals involved in the *interactive multimedia* marketplace. As an example of the types of activities sponsored by IICS, the San Francisco chapter worked to get the city of San Francisco to pass legislation in the mid-1990s that would ensure future investments in the infrastructure needed to support *multimedia* development, e.g., local sources of high-*bandwidth transmission* facilities.

IID: Stands for Interaural Intensity Differences, a highly technical term that comes to us from the land of *3-D sound*. IID is one of the key *HRTFs* (head-related transfer functions) and is based on the fact that sound that originates to one side of the head (as opposed to coming from directly in front or behind) will be received as louder by the ear that faces the sound source. Also referred to as the "head shadowing effect," this phenomenon has become a key element in *virtual realit*y systems that seek to create a consistent sense of sound sources, even while the participant is moving around in the *virtual world* environment.

IITF: Stands for the Information Infrastructure Task Force, which is a committee set up by the president of the United States to formulate and implement a vision for the National Information Infrastructure (*NII*). This task force is made up of the heads of 18 major federal agencies. Working with the private sector, IITF's mission is to develop a comprehensive technology plan, formulate policy for telecommunications and information, and promote applications to meet the needs of the agencies it serves and the United States. As an example of their efforts, one of the IITF working groups is focused on protecting *intellectual property* rights.

Illustrator: Often compared with the role of *art director*, the illustrator on a *multimedia* development project is the person responsible for creating the artwork. An illustrator would, for example, be responsible for drawing the *icons* that go on *buttons* or that serve as *hyperlinks*. Some illustrators are good *art directors*, but more often the two roles are performed by separate people. The *art director* develops the visual design of a multimedia product, while the illustrator is responsible for executing the art director's vision.

IMA: Stands for the Interactive Multimedia Association, an international trade association based in Washington, DC. "The purpose of IMA is to promote the benefits of *multimedia* technology; advance the growth of the industry through public education; develop specifications for hardware, software tools, and applications; develop industry-wide services; and provide government and media relations." Founded in 1987, the IMA's most interesting project to date is its "Cross-Platform Compatibility Project," which seeks to establish industry-wide standards that enable the *portability* of *multimedia applications* across different hardware *platforms*.

image extraction: From the realm of *virtual reality*, this term refers to the high end of *position tracking* systems whereby *video* cameras are teamed with visual recognition systems to keep track of the location of virtual reality participants as they move about within their *virtual world* environments.

image map: From the world of the *Internet*, this term refers to a graphical image that is often placed at the front end of a *Web site*. The image map contains *hot spots* that when clicked upon, *link* to pages below the map. For example, clicking on an image map of the United States may take one to individual sets of information on each of the states.

image processing: This term most generally refers to the science of interpreting *digital* images by using computers and computer graphics techniques. The discipline originated in the relatively specialized area that deals with processing data acquired by remote sensing devices placed aboard satellites or other spacecraft. With the onset of *multimedia* technology, the fruits of this discipline are finding wider usage throughout the computer industry.

image systems: One of the meat-and-potatoes activities of early *multimedia applications* will be that of converting our mass document storage standard from microfiche and microfilm to the eminently more useful— because it is more accessible—medium of *optical storage*. The manufacturing process for achieving this new standard goes by the name imaging system. With such a system, paper documents are passed through a *scanner*, which *digitizes* the document to create a *bit-mapped* image of it. At some point during this process, the bit-mapped image is assigned *keywords*. The purpose of the keywords is to index the document, making it electronically retrievable—making it *computable*. The primary problem with this approach to mass document storage is that the contents of the documents are in a bit-mapped form, and therefore are not themselves searchable. Only the keywords assigned to each image are in *ASCII* (text) format. Thus, the process of assigning keywords must anticipate all of the ways in which future users might wish to search the document base. In other words, all of the meaning that can be associated with the contents of a given document not represented by the keywords become the textual equivalent of a lost treasure.

Image-enabled database: As we enter the era of *multimedia*, one of the first things that large organizations are beginning to do is to enhance their existing database records with all sorts of *mixed media data types*, especially those that are in the form of *digital images*. This term labels that process. Many organizations today are, for example, adding document images of actual invoices to their accounts payable records, *digitized* images of resumes and pictures to their personnel records, and images of correspondence to their customer files. These visual sources add valuable information to the traditional database record, which historically has been based solely on alphanumeric forms of data.

IMAP: Stands for Internet Messaging Access Protocol. IMAP4, the latest version, is a standard for *mail servers* that is expected to become popular on the *Internet*. Its principal advantage over *POP3*, the current widely used standard, is that it allows clients to access and manipulate electronic mail on the *server*. It has all the functionality of local mail managers including creating, deleting, and renaming *mailboxes*, checking for new messages, and deleting messages. Its new facilities include sharing mailboxes, accessing multiple mail servers, and better integration with *MIME* for attaching files. The user can read headers or search text for *keywords* while still on the server and then selectively *download* messages or portions thereof. It uses *SMTP* for communication between the mail client and server. The first iteration of IMAP was developed at Stanford University in 1986.

IMAX Theatre: These theme park establishments use large-format, motion-picture film and huge parabolic, metallic projection screens. They seek to achieve a vivid 3-D, almost holographic, panoramic realism for audiences. IMAX has become synonymous with the concept of creating a wrap-around or surround environment for entertainment purposes.

IMS metadata specification: Initiated by Educom NLII, this important *metadata* specification is now being advanced in the hope of better organizing the *Internet* and its vast number of *complex information objects*. The "IMS" stands for Instructional Management Systems, and the metadata specification is designed to facilitate the discovery of learning resources on the *Web*. More specifically, this metadata standard is intended to help users locate interesting resources, evaluate the appropriateness of any given resource, and determine the availability of a resource for use. Learning resources can include people, educational service companies, content, tools, and activities. In particular, though, this metadata specification is providing the Internet with much needed standards for cataloging such complex media types as computer-based training (*CBT*).

Inbetweener: With traditional *animation*, this term refers to a job role wherein a person is responsible for producing in-between drawings and creating, for example, the sense of a character's motion between a beginning and ending posture. Many of the *paint systems* now provide functions for automating this activity, which is also referred to by the slang word "tweening."

Indeo: A software version of Intel's *DVI compression-decompression* standard, it is delivered in conjunction with *VFW* (video for windows). It is *scalable*, compatible across *platforms*, and compressible in *real time*.

Infoglut: Very similar in meaning to the term *information overload*, infoglut refers to one of the most perplexing problems of the information age. We have more information available to us today than at any time in history, but most of this information is of relatively low quality (i.e., it is often inaccurate or irrelevant) and rarely can we find just the piece of information we need at the moment we need it. *Search engines, intelligent software agents*, and *information filtering* represent the current wave of technical solutions that are being offered to counter the problem of infoglut.

Infomercials: You know 'em when you flip past 'em on the dial. This relatively recent form of television advertising is characterized by a relatively long duration—commonly running up to a half-hour in length— and by a relatively high proportion of in-depth information, often purporting to be scientific in nature. Many media futurists believe that this form of advertising is a prototype of what will be available en masse on the *information superhighway*. The *Internet* is currently full of a variation of infomercial that is made up of text and graphics of all kinds including logos, banners, and various forms of *animation*.

Information agent: This term refers to the *intelligent software agents* that collect and store usage information about the *Web* user. The body of information thus *captured* is also referred to as "user preferences." User preferences are stored and tracked by information agents, which are also referred to as *knowbots*.

Information design: This field of technical communication design exploits the online reference and presentation power of the computer to access and show information to the user in discrete, defined units visually segmented and organized so that information is easy to understand and use.

Information designer: An information designer is a professional technical communicator skilled in the methods, techniques, and tools of *information design*. It is worthy to note that an information designer is capable of working with various forms of *hypermedia applications* and *platforms*, including exploratory libraries of *digital* information created and organized for distribution over the *Internet*.

Information landscape: In the simplest sense, this term describes the use of 3-D graphics to represent data typically presented in the form of tables and 2-D graphs and charts. For example, an information landscape might present a 3-D bar graph representing multiple variables, into and around which the viewer may fly using some form of mobile *POV* (point of view). However, the term is also capable of describing a very interesting and potentially profound movement in the field of user *interface design*, wherein the design goal is to provide a sense of place as a container of information. Thus, a corporate history might be presented as an art gallery in which viewers use a mobile POV to move from room to room. They then find hanging from the walls a set of portraits representing the key players in the company's history, and by clicking on these portraits, the various players deliver their own personal accounts of significant events and trends in the organization's evolution.

Information overload: This term refers to a serious problem confronting the information age. Huge amounts of data and information are available to all of us—through libraries, on TV, in the movie theater, and now across the *Web*. The volume of information on the *Web,* alone, is growing exponentially. However, much of this growing stock of information goes to waste because people cannot find it when they need it. For anyone who has performed a search on the *Internet*, the classic symptom of information overload occurs when a search query returns thousands of items for which the search has found a supposed match. The time taken to access and scan these thousands of items often far outweighs the benefits of finally finding a useful piece of information amid the deluge of data. It is hoped that better cataloging of electronic information and more efficient *search engines* may help alleviate the problem of information overload.

Information superhighway: This is a phrase coined by the Clinton administration to refer to the emerging national communications network—the *NII* (National Information Infrastructure)—which will enable an ever increasing level of communications of every sort: data communications, personal communications, and *multimedia* communications. Most industry analysts believe that the *Internet* is the prototype and origin of the information superhighway.

Information visualizers: A relatively new advance in user *interface design* under development at *Xerox PARC*, this technology strives to take traditional alphanumeric forms of data and *convert* them into 3-D objects that the user can interact with in ways that are perceptually familiar. With visualizers, it is hoped that users can see their information, touch it, and rearrange it, thereby achieving a deeper, almost tactile, understanding of its structure.

Initialization string: From the world of data communications, this term refers to the string of characters that is sent to a *modem* to start a data *transmission* or to retrieve a mail addressing table.

Inline images: An inline graphic is a *multimedia* object (image, sound, *animation*, etc.) that is placed or embedded within a line of text. The object file is *downloaded* to the receiving computer with the carrying or *host* document. A *browser* may have a switch that allows the user to control the automatic download of graphics. If this is the case, images can be viewed by selecting a command to view the images. The objects are only displayed in browsers that have the appropriate capability or have access to a plug-in. An external image is only transmitted when a *link* is activated.

Instruction cache: From the realm of processor design, this term refers to a specialized type of *cache* featured on some microprocessors that enables faster execution by storing frequently used instructions in a form of memory that is physically adjacent to the *CPU*.

Instructional design: This field of communications design exploits the instructional power of the computer. The emergence of instructional design can be directly attributed to the convergence of media, computing, and learning theory.

Instructional designer: An instructional designer is responsible for designing interactive forms of *CBT* (computer-based training) and *multimedia applications*. An instructional designer, for example, works with end users to decompose knowledge and tasks into their constituent concepts, skills, and procedural steps and then use that information to design appropriate forms of programmed instruction. It is worthy to note that instructional designers are currently focused on plying their trade across the *Internet*, adapting the principles of CBT design to the latest generation of programmed instruction known as Web-based training (*WBT*).

Instructional technology: In many respects, this term now has the same expansive meaning with respect to the world of education that the term *multimedia* has taken on with regard to the world of commerce. Instructional technology is an umbrella term that refers to any technology used for training and education. In the literal sense, then, a chalkboard represents a kind of instructional technology. However, when used in the school market, this term generally refers to the burgeoning supply of hardware and software solutions now crowding their way into our schools.

Intellectual property: One of the most explosive topics of the Information Age, this is an umbrella term for the ownership rights that individuals have when they can demonstrate that they have added value to an information product. Actors in a film, composers of music, programmers of software, and *art directors* of *multimedia interfaces* are all examples of individuals who add value. Their recourse for recording and protecting their rights in this respect are embodied in the laws of *copyright*, trademark, patents, or some combination of these. With most multimedia products, because many of the markets are still small and/or poorly defined, the entity that pays for building the product will usually be forced to induce the development talent to sign nondisclosure agreements, most of which contain work-for-hire provisions that transfer all of the ownership rights to that sponsoring entity. Where royalty payments are contemplated, a potential thicket of problems awaits, because *digital media assets* are so fungible, so readily subjected to *electronic forms* of *cut and paste*, that downstream use of those assets will be nearly impossible to track—especially given the growth of the *Internet. Stock footage* houses and purveyors of *clip media* have a partial solution to this problem; they handle all of the royalty arrangements for the various artists and relieve users of any worry about usage fees beyond those that are embedded in the purchase price—unless they willingly give those media assets to others, who then use them for economic gain without paying any purchase price. Expect intellectual property to be a bonanza for the legal profession in the age of multimedia.

Intelligence augmentation: One of the goals of all communications media, but especially appropriate in the age of *multimedia*, this term refers to the general objective of using computer media to increase the capability of people to conceptualize, approach, and gain solutions to complex problems.

Intelligent job aid: Often thought of as an ingredient in *performance support systems*, intelligent *job aids* are *granular multimedia applications* designed to lead learners through an interactive training session that helps them solve a specific type of job-related, procedural problem.

Intelligent software agents: One of the key new *enabling technologies* of the next few decades, intelligent software agents represent a breed of software programs that possess an intriguing mix of attributes. First, they are mobile, that is, they are capable of guiding themselves across the *Web* from one *Web site* to another. Second, they are autonomous—they possess the intelligence needed to govern their own *navigation* as they move across the Web. Finally, depending upon what genre of *agents* they belong to, they are endowed with some substantial form of functional intelligence. For example, *buyer agents* are invested with the intelligence needed to consummate transactions on behalf of their users (or owners). Thus, intelligent software agents are viewed as a form of electronic servant, capable of performing routine tasks across the Web on behalf of their human owners. Today's relatively primitive agents are restricted to conducting simple kinds of transactions, such as the purchase of plane tickets. However, futurists envision a day when agents will be endowed with sophisticated forms of negotiating intelligence and will therefore be capable of conducting complex types of business, such as real estate transactions, in an entirely unattended *mode*.

Intelligent tutoring system: This is an *expert system* whose domain of expertise is instruction. Such systems usually contain an expert system relevant to the subject domain the tutoring system is teaching about. The objective of an intelligent tutor is to enable a machine to process both the concept to be taught, and the concept of how best to present the ideas to the student.

Interactive cinema: This term refers to an interactive form of entertainment that is most closely related to film. While both *interactive fiction* and *interactive television* have abundant prototypes on the market, interactive cinema is very early in its evolution. However, it is worthwhile to note that the New York Film Festival has been offering awards in an interactive category for several years now.

Interactive document: This is a document whose content or sequence of presentation can be altered through direct intervention by the reader at the time of reading.

Interactive fiction: Considered by many to be the next major transformation of our storytelling tradition, interactive fiction refers to the convergence of *interactivity* and narration. Interactive fictions are stories with *branchpoints*, contingent subplots, alternate outcomes, and the like. As the various genres of interactive entertainment take shape, interactive fiction will be seen primarily as text-based content, whereas *interactive cinema* and *interactive television* will be viewed as the interactive forms that make use of high-end forms of media, such as full-motion video (*FMV*). In many respects, then, interactive fiction stands in the same relationship to interactive cinema that *hypertext* stands with regard to *hypermedia*. Still in its embryonic stages, interactive fiction has explosive potential as a new medium, and may well end up standing in the same dominant relationship to the twenty-first century that film has with regard to the twentieth century.

Interactive multimedia: *Multimedia applications* are not necessarily interactive. For example, a *rolling demo* has all the characteristics that we are coming to associate with *multimedia*—audio, image, and possibly *video*, all running on a computer—but, by design, possesses little or no *interactivity*. Thus, because there are some forms of multimedia that are **not** interactive, it is considered by some to be a worthwhile exercise in language to designate those forms that are.

Interactive talk: A form of communication over the *Internet* between two or more users in which all participants are online simultaneously. Comments and responses can be exchanged in close to *real time*. Interactive talk often occurs in c*hat* rooms and represents a *synchronous* form of *Web* communication. Interactive talk groups on the Internet are usually focused on some common interest.

Interactive television: Most media industry futurists agree that this is the inevitable near-term destiny of home entertainment: a single device that merges the capabilities of the computer and the television. Also referred to as the *smart TV*, this device will make it possible for users to do such things as temporarily store films that they have *downloaded* from libraries supplied by public media services; play interactive games on their televisions, without the special attachments required by today's games such as Sega Genesis; and create, edit, and store one's own personal *video productions*. Even though many of the early pilot projects conducted by the large media conglomerates were dismal economic failures, few industry analysts doubt that the long term historical arc of in-home entertainment will ultimately focus on interactive forms of content. Indeed, many of those analysts see the technology of *Web TV* as the communication industry's second attempt at making interactive television a viable enterprise.

Interactivity: The defining characteristic of the emerging forms of education and entertainment associated with *multimedia applications*, this term refers to the ability of users to communicate directly with the computer and to have a consequential impact on whatever message is being created.

Interface: Put in the most general way, an interface is a boundary between two systems. An interface can be between two hardware devices, such as exists between the sockets and plugs that are used to convey electrical current. The term interface can also be used to refer to the boundaries between hardware and software components, between one software program and another, and even between a computer and a human. Most organizations that have to deal with any type of interface as a major element in their business environment are very concerned about establishing some form of standard for governing the flow of information across that interface. Common interface standards include EIA standards RS-232B/C, adopted by the Electronic Industries Association to ensure uniformity among manufacturers; MIL STD 188B, a mandatory standard established by the U.S. Department of Defense; and *CCITT*, the global recommendation for interface, mandatory in Europe and closely resembling the American EIA standard. The human computer interface is one of the most important of the breed, and is now mediated by a set of commands, *menus*, and iconic objects where humans and computers interact. In a command-driven interface, the human types commands to direct the computer. In a menu-driven interface, the human selects commands from a series of menus displayed on the screen. With graphical user interfaces (*GUIs*), the user clicks with a *mouse* on various *windows*, *icons*, and pop-up menus to achieve the intended purpose. A functionally appropriate, well-designed *user interface* is a key to the successful use of any *application program*.

Interface agent: Can be defined as a character, enacted by the computer, who acts on behalf of the user in a *virtual* (computer-based) environment. The use of interface agents implies an authorial effort to create computer-based personae and, through their use, to heighten the naturalness of the *interface* both in terms of cognitive accessibility and communication style. Obviously, the fuller implementation of this *interface design* strategy waits on further advances in the field of *artificial intelligence* known as *natural language processing*, which seeks to imbue computers with the ability to speak on a human conversational level.

Interface design: Also referred to as "human interface design" or "human-computer interface design," this intellectual pursuit is rapidly ascending to the status of an academic discipline in its own right. As the term implies, it has to do with designing computer *interfaces* that make computers easier for humans to use. Originally focused on issues having to do with screen design—e.g., the *desktop metaphor* that drives the Apple Macintosh and Microsoft *Windows* interfaces—the discipline is rapidly extending itself to include all issues having to do with the input and output of information to and from the computer. In essence, interface design encompasses any topic that can be meaningfully related to the process by which humans and computers interact with one another. With the advent of *mixed media data types*, with the coming of *multimedia* and its progression into the marketplace, the potential for extending the purview of this nascent discipline would appear to be virtually without limit. Expect colleges and universities to be acknowledging the legitimacy of this academic pursuit over the next decade by creating subdisciplines or even entirely new departments.

Interface paradigm: One of the truly big terms in the industry, it refers to the dominant metaphor that people encounter when interacting with the operating environment of their computer. With both the Apple Macintosh and the Microsoft *Windows* environments, the dominant metaphor has long been the *desktop*. The designers of these highly similar *interfaces* have tried to represent all of the objects with appropriate metaphors drawn from the common office environment. For example, files are represented as file *folders*, and in the Apple Macintosh environment there is the well-known image of the trash can that is used to delete files. Many industry analysts believe that we will soon be ready for a new dominant metaphor, a new interface paradigm. Some of the early candidates are the *personal newspaper*, which would deliver information tailored to the individual's needs in a prioritized format similar to the headline-and-column structure of the newspaper; the geographic information system (GIS), which would give all information items a geographic location—as they actually have in the real world—and permit the user to *pan* and *zoom* to get about to the desired locations in geographic space; and the 3-D building, which is actually an enlargement of the *desktop metaphor* that would provide a more variegated set of submetaphors with which to access much larger knowledge bases.

Interframe codec: A form of *video* compression-decompression that works on the basis of eliminating the redundant components that occur between (as opposed to within) *frames*. To date, these are the most powerful forms of *codec*, achieving *compression ratios* on the order of 50:1 up to 200:1. The *MPEG* (Motion Picture Experts Group) standard codec is an interframe technology, and works by looking forward and backward in a *video* stream and then recording only the information that changes during a given segment. Interframe codecs are said to be *asymmetrical*, because it is much more time-consuming and expensive to *encode* (*compress*) the video stream than it is to decode (*decompress*) it. This owes to the enormous computational resources that must be expended to define the various visual patterns in a video sequence in terms of their degree of change. Interframe technologies are often compared with the less powerful, but also less expensive, *intraframe* techniques, which are perhaps best exemplified by the *JPEG* (Joint Photography Experts Group) standard.

Interlaced video: This term is used to describe the dominant process by which today's standard (*NTSC*, for one) television picture is created. Interlaced video is a technique that can be described as follows: a television picture is drawn onto the picture tube by one or more electron guns, which fire a stream of electrons at the face of the tube one horizontal line at a time. The horizontal lines that make up the arrays of *pixels* that comprise the TV screen are referred to as *scan lines*. With interlaced video, the electron gun draws all the even lines first, then goes back to the top of the screen and draws the odd lines. This alternating process is referred to as interlaced video for the obvious reason that the even and odd lines are interlaced with one another.

Interleaving: This term refers to a technical strategy for laying down *mixed media data types* on storage media, particularly on *CD-ROM* and *DVD*. With interleaving, as the term implies, one type of information is interleaved with another so that the two types can be physically close to one another on the storage device. The most common example occurs with the *digital video* and audio data types, each of which has its own unique format, and therefore must be stored as a separate file. They are often interleaved when they are laid down on *CD-ROM* or *DVD* because this storage strategy makes it easier to synchronize the picture with the sound—as occurs, for example, with *lipsynching*. This strategy is made necessary by the fact that *transfer rates* on most digital storage devices (especially *CD-ROM*) are still relatively slow when compared against the demand to load both types into computer memory so that they may be played in synchronization.

Internet: Is the successor of an experimental *network* built by the U.S. Department of Defense in the 1960s. This communication system links millions of computers worldwide and is growing at a geometric pace. A good portion of the connections on the Internet initially belonged to universities and research and development organizations, but today the user base has expanded to include a broad range of businesses and individuals. In the contemporary technical environment, many users still connect to the Internet via phone (*modem*) and are therefore constrained by the relatively narrow *bandwidth* that can be obtained through this form of access device. However, huge investments are being made in the technical network infrastructure that supports the Internet, and it is anticipated that the current bandwidth bottleneck will soon be reduced or altogether eliminated. The potential impact of the Internet on social and political thought is enormous. Central to understanding the phenomenon that is the Internet is the realization that whatever it is, it is not a centrally managed or controlled organization. Rather, it is a vast, decentralized collection of computers, each of which is independent and can offer or refuse services in an autonomous fashion. It is, therefore, a quintessentially democratic phenomenon. From an operational standpoint, the Internet is organized in a three-level hierarchy. At the top is the *Internet backbone,* which consists of a series of *nodes* that are linked together around the world. At the second level are the "transit nodes," which are attached to a *backbone* and can transmit between other *networks* on the same backbone. The third level, called "stub networks," are attached to the transit networks. A stub network carries *packets* between the local *hosts* that are attached to it. Access to the Internet can be through online services such as America Online or Compuserve, or more directly through an Internet service provider (*ISP*).

Internet backbone: Is a large high-speed *network* that supports many other smaller, independent networks. It is the main communication pathway in a *WAN* (wide area network). It can span thousands and thousands of miles and provides the means by which to connect regional networks with each other across the *Internet.*

Internet Explorer: Microsoft Internet Explorer is a *World Wide Web browser* that runs under *Windows* 95 or NT. It is the principal competitor of *Netscape Navigator*. Both Netscape and Microsoft have gone beyond the officially recognized *HTML* standard to add their own features, which are generally not supported by the other or by other less-sophisticated browsers.

Internet resource: This term has gained popularity in the library science community as a convenient phrase for referring to any electronic information facility accessible through the capabilities of a *WAN* (wide area network) across the *Web*. Thus, a *Web site* would be viewed as a type of Internet resource.

Internet telephony: Also referred to as "IP Telephony," this new *digital* service offered by *ISPs* enables the user to route telephone calls across the same line that is being used to host an *Internet* session. The first, and most obvious, advantage to this service is that it notifies single-line Internet access users of incoming phone calls while their phone lines are tied up in a net session. Under this type of scenario, if the ISP customer elected to take the call, it would be routed to the PC's sound card and speakers. One immediate benefit of this service is to reduce the cost of *telecommuting* by eliminating the need for a second phone line.

Internetworking: From the world of data communications, this term refers to communication between data processing devices on one *network* and other dissimilar devices on another network. From a technical standpoint, the linking together of dissimilar networks is very challenging, and often involves sophisticated software routines and combinations of special purpose hardware devices, such as *bridges*, *routers*, and *gateways*. The drive to *link* one *digital* network with another is precisely what led, ultimately, to the formation of the *Internet*.

Internic: Is a contraction for "Internet Network Information Center," an organization set up by the National Science Foundation (*NSF*) with the general approval of the *Internet* community. In 1992, the NSF recognized the need to have organized management for the *NSFNet* community. It selected and entered into a cooperative agreement with three organizations to act as Network Information Service (*NIS*) managers. They are General Electric, AT&T, and Network Solutions, Inc. (NSI). Each of these three organizations was given a different set of responsibilities. General Electric is responsible for providing information services, AT&T is charged with providing directory and database services, and NSI is devoted to providing registration services.

Interoperability: This polysyllabic tongue-twister simply refers to the system design feature wherewith a system can operate on several different computer hardware *platforms*.

Interpolation: Used in its most general sense, this term refers to the process of introducing or inserting additional values between the existing values in a series. The process is used frequently in computer graphics, especially in color *shading* and various *codec* techniques. In a more specific sense, this term is now used to describe any form of *motion compensation* (i.e., temporal codec in which a *frame* is constructed during *decompression* based upon the difference in information between the original frame, [which is determined during the *compression* process] and both its previous and subsequent *key frames*.) This process is also known as forward and backward *prediction* and tends to be a very expensive, CPU-intensive process that, until recently, required *off-line compression* using mainframe computers.

Interprocessor communications: This term refers to any data communications that occur between two processors within the same computing system. The integration of *DSPs* (digital signal processors) into the personal computer to handle the onerous processing requirements of the various media types has made the issue of interprocessor communications of particular importance to *multimedia* computing. The future of media-oriented, interprocessor communications seems to be headed toward the use of specialized operating systems (such as Spectrum Microsystems' SPOX) designed to handle the personal computer-DSP connection. Over time, these programming efforts—and the interprocessor communications they make possible—will continue to make it increasingly easy to add new media capabilities (e.g., *voice recognition*) to the personal computer.

Interrupt: From the world of *software engineering*, an interrupt is a procedure whereby a program that is currently running on a computer is temporarily suspended so that the *CPU* can devote its time to processing another program that has been determined to be of higher priority. It is sort of like relaxing in a colleague's office and then being summoned by a superior—the process of relaxing becomes interrupted by the higher priority task of making a living. The interrupting event may be an expected event, such as the completion of an input/output operation, or an unexpected event, such as occurs when an error is detected. Once the tasks associated with the interrupt have been completed, the processor resumes working with the interrupted task.

Interrupt-driven: This is a software structure that uses *interrupts* to determine what tasks can run and/or be given control of the *CPU*.

Intervention: This term is gaining popularity with *instructional designers*, who are now using it to name many of their work products as "*performance* support interventions," "*CBT* interventions," or simply "training interventions." The idea impelling the use of this term is that electronic training media can be invoked closer to the moment of need than can conventional training technologies, such as traditional classroom seminars or courses. Thus, *multimedia* training technologies can be viewed as intervening at the moment of need to aid workers who must learn new job tasks or skills to perform successfully.

Intraframe codec: This is a form of *video* compression-decompression technology that works by eliminating redundant information within the *frames* that make up a *video sequence*. The very popular *motion-JPEG* standard is based on intraframe and achieves *compression ratios* in the range of 20:1 up to 50:1. Intraframe technologies are often compared to the more powerful *interframe codecs*, such as *MPEG* (Motion Picture Experts Group). The interframe techniques are much more expensive because they are asymmetrical, often requiring special purpose processors or even powerful computers (mainframes) to perform the encoding process. In contrast, most of the intraframe codecs can be done in *real time*, i.e., on the fly.

Intranet: A suddenly important concept, an intranet is an intra-organization *WAN* that makes use of the networking technologies of the *Internet* (e.g., *TCP/IP*, *HTML*, the industry-standard *Web browsers*, etc.) to provide for a robust form of internal communications. More specifically, intranets are being put in place by many large organizations to provide facilities for *e-mail*, *groupware*, automated workflow, and access to internal *data warehouses* and *data marts*. Though these types of facilities can be provided by engineering a *client/server* strategy, the technologies associated with the *Internet* provide huge advantages, the most important of which have to do with the global standardization for *internetworking* that are being established in support of the *World Wide Web*. Thus, an intranet that is constructed in true compliance with *Internet* standards will not only be able to forge relatively seamless connections to the Web, but will also be far less susceptible to the cross-platform issues that plague most client/server installations.

I/O: One of the earliest, and still most standard, of computer acronyms, I/O stands for Input/Output. It represents a most fundamental truth about computers, which is that they cannot survive as closed systems; they must receive input from the world and be provided useful input through the magic of *digital* processing and the programmer's intervention. Traditional I/O devices include the keyboard and *mouse* for input and the monitor for output. As we sail into the age of *multimedia*, I/O devices will become increasingly oriented toward the *mixed media data types* of image, graphics, *animation*, audio, and *video*. On the near horizon, *voice recognition* promises to become a major new form of I/O.

IP: Stands for Internet Protocol, and refers to the most important *protocol* upon which the *Internet* is based. Constituting the latter part of the extended acronym *TCP/IP*, the Internet protocol defines how *packets* of data get routed from the source computer to a destination on the Internet. Each computer is identified by an *IP address*, which represents a number that uniquely identifies all devices that are connected to the Internet (in much the same way that your home *address* uniquely identifies your residence to the public mail system, or your phone number uniquely identifies your phone to the *POTS*).

IP address: Is the unique numeric identifier of a computer connected to the *Internet*. Just as your telephone has a unique *address* or numeric identifier, every computer connected to the Internet has a unique address by which it, and it alone, can be identified. Instead of being called a telephone number, this identifier is called an IP address on the Internet.

IRC: Stands for Internet Relay Chat, a system that provides *real-time* chatting over the *Internet*. Participants can type a message on a keyboard and it is relayed immediately to all other participants on the same chat *channel*. To participate in this form of *interactive talk*, users must be in possession of an IRC client software program such as *UNIX* ircii, Windows mIRC, or PIRCH; and they must be registered with an IRC *server*. Efnet and Undernet are two of the largest *networks*, and both have numerous servers. Once engaged in an IRC session, you can *chat* with anyone on the same network even if they are on a different server. Each network has numerous channels, each purportedly devoted to its own topic. However, chats often stray from their intended topic. The conversations that take place during an IRC session may be either public, in which case everyone on the channel sees all messages; or they may be private, in which case only selected members will be communicating with one another. The IRC community overlaps somewhat with the *Usenet* and *MUD* communities. They all have *hackers* and regular folks participating.

Iridium Project: One of the major telecommunication developments of the 1990s, this project is being carried forward by Motorola and involves the development of a system of small satellites that operate in low earth orbit, providing worldwide personal communications services.

It also complements existing systems by providing telephone services where they do not exist today.

IRIS: Stands for Institute for Research on Information Systems, an organization located at Brown University in Providence, Rhode Island. This group has been responsible for a good deal of groundbreaking research in the areas of *hypertext* systems and graphical user interface (*GUI*) design.

Iris out: Is a special video effect (*DVE*) in which a series of masks containing circles of diminishing size are laid down in succession to visually obliterate the action.

IRTF: Stands for Internet Research Task Force, which is chartered by the Internet Architecture Board (*IAB*) to consider long-term theoretical issues for the *Internet*. It has research groups assigned to discuss different research topics, such as *multi-casting,* audio/video conferencing, privacy enhanced *e-mail, TCP/IP*, continuous growth, and emerging technologies.

ISA bus: The ISA stands for Industry Standard Architecture and the term represents one of the foremost bottlenecks in the computer industry today. The ISA bus problem is particularly acute with *mixed media data types*, like *digital video*, and owes its origins to one of the most common of all problems associated with computing: functional obsolescence. Designed during the initial generations of personal computers, the ISA bus was basically the expansion *bus* on a PC into which users plugged *expansion boards* for purposes such as attaching peripheral devices (a *CD-ROM* player, for example) or enhancing machine performance (e.g., *accelerator boards*). Inasmuch as it was designed during the era of alphanumeric computing, the ISA bus has a very limited *bandwidth*: only 8 MHz or so. When trying to accommodate *multimedia applications*, such as digital video or *compound documents*, the ISA bus simply gets clogged up, creating a major performance problem. One of the most common responses to this problem today is the *local bus* solution, which bypasses the ISA bus, routing data through the bus that is attached to the computer's *CPU*.

ISDN: Stands for Integrated Services Digital Network, an end-to-end *digital* service that is standardized throughout the world. As originally conceived in the early 1980s, ISDN was to help do away with most (if not all) forms of *analog transmission*. In particular, ISDN was viewed by its original designers as the telecommunications technology that would replace the *POTS* (plain old telephone service) infrastructure, while ushering in an era of all-digital communications and dramatically expanded forms of *bandwidth*. While ISDN is still an important piece of the *NII* puzzle, and is used by many *ISPs* to provide their subscribers with premium forms of service, the needs of the *information superhighway* have outstripped its original vision. In a world that can now legitimately contemplate such applications as *interactive television* and videophone, *broadband* technologies such as *ATM* (asynchronous transfer mode) are needed that are far more capable than ISDN. Until these more powerful technologies mature, however, ISDN will provide a source of relatively high-bandwidth access to the *Internet*.

ISO: Stands for the International Standards Organization, a group composed of the national standards organizations of its member countries. As the name implies, the ISO seeks to establish worldwide quality standards. The ISO has defined standards for data communications, most notably, the ISO model for *OSI* (open system interconnections).

ISOC: Is the Internet SOCiety, a nongovernmental, international organization whose mission is to coordinate the technologies and applications used on the *Internet*. Its members are companies, government agencies, foundations, and individuals who have created the Internet and its technologies. It is governed by a board of trustees elected by its membership around the world.

Isochronous distribution: From the challenging world of networked *video*, this term refers to *digital* forms of audio and video that are guaranteed to arrive at the same time. It is a strategy for networking video that separates the audio and video *channels* from other data *transmissions* to avoid the kinds of interference that lead to errors and a lack of synchronization.

ISP: Stands for Internet Service Provider, which is an organization that maintains a *server* on the *Internet* and sells Internet *connectivity* to a body of subscribers. ISP customers can typically obtain access to the Internet via a serial telephone line or an *ISDN* line. Larger ISPs offer private hookups with *T1* lines, or other high-*bandwidth links*. Customers are usually billed a fixed monthly rate. ISPs also offer customers the opportunity to create a personal *Web site* with a unique *domain name* and have that service included within the monthly fixed fee. Access to personal *e-mail* is typically included in the monthly fee.

ISV: Stands for Independent Software Vendor, which is a type of commercial organization whose purpose is to develop software *application programs*—also referred to as "shrink-wrapped software"—for sale or resale on the open market. The reason why this term uses the adjective independent is to help draw the distinction between external and internal software application development efforts. Many large industrial corporations develop their own software applications internally through the efforts of their MIS departments. However, most, if not all, of these large corporations also make a habit of buying considerable amounts of software from external software manufacturers—the ISVs—Microsoft, IBM, and Oracle are examples of three large and successful ISVs.

ITD: Stands for Interaural Time Differences, a technical term that comes to us courtesy of the rapidly advancing world of *3-D sound*. ITD is one of the key *HRTFs* (head-related transfer functions) and refers to the obvious fact that sound that originates from one side of the head (as opposed to coming from directly in front of or behind the head) will reach the listener's ear facing the sound source before it reaches the opposing ear. ITD is used to perceive sound direction and has become a critical element in the effort to create realistic sound environments in *virtual reality* systems where the participants are permitted to move around, thus changing the orientation of their heads.

ITU: Stands for the International Telecommunications Union, the foremost international organization responsible for setting standards in the complex and demanding telecommunications equipment industry. The *X.400* messaging standard, the high-*bandwidth* optical *transmission SONET* standards, and the *videoconferencing* standards of *Px64* and *H.261* are among the better known standards put forth by ITU and its predecessor, *CCITT* (Consultative Committee on International Telephone and Telegraph).

IVD: Stands for Interactive VideoDisc and is a term that, historically, has become associated with a particular *platform strategy* for delivering interactive *video*. It refers to a *platform* that combines a personal computer with a *laserdisc*. As such, it also refers to the first generation of interactive video platform. Most industry experts believe that the laserdisc is destined for technological extinction and that *CD-ROM* and its successor, *DVD*, will come to replace it for delivering interactive video.

IXC: Stands for Inter-eXchange Carrier, which is the generic name given to the long distance phone companies such as AT&T and WorldSpan. Their responsibility is to handle the call traffic that occurs between *LATAs* (local access and transport areas).

Silicon Valley is about entrepreneurship, making bets, taking risks. Hollywood is about playing the field, taking your 10%.
—**Hollywood executive, commenting on the clash of cultures taking shape with the advent of multimedia technology**

Jaggies: This slang term refers to *aliasing*, perhaps the most widely recognized *artifact* of *digital* media. This distorting effect is most evident on low-resolution displays, where the outlines of objects take on a jagged appearance that silhouettes the square shapes of the *pixels* that form their boundaries with the rest of the image. In a low-resolution picture of a mountain range, for example, the edge between the mountains and the sky is apt to appear jagged as a result of possessing this artifact.

Java: Is a high-level, *object-oriented programming* language designed and developed in 1995 by Sun Microsystems specifically to facilitate application development for the *Internet*. Java is similar to C++, another *high-level language*, but is designed to reduce common programming errors that occur in some of the more complex languages like C++. It has been widely accepted by major Internet software application developers. Java is an interpreted language, meaning that the code is *converted* into machine language at run time. To accommodate higher levels of *interactivity*, it is designed such that most programs are delivered across the *Web* in relatively small programs called *applets*. It is a secure, *multithreaded*, high-performance language. Most important, though, Java possesses the enormously desirable feature that it is portable across many operating system *platforms*, which means that application developers only need to create one version of a program—"write once, run anywhere" is the motto being proclaimed by its creators.

Javabeans: This *object-oriented programming interface* was developed by Sun Microsystems to facilitate the re-use of code elements, or "components," within their *Java* programming environment. Like *Java applets*, Javabean components can be used to give *Web sites* and other applications interactive capabilities by embedding the components within the *Web page* or application, which then becomes referred to as the component's "container."

Javascript: This interpreted programming or script language was developed by Netscape Corporation to facilitate the design of interactive *Web sites*. Javascript is a variant of *Java* and is touted as providing an easier environment in which to develop code than its counterpart from Sun Microsystems. Javascript can interact with *HTML* code and enable use of dynamic content in Web sites.

JBIG: Stands for Joint Bilevel Image Experts Group; this standards organization is related to, though much less well known, than *JPEG* (Joint Photography Experts Group) and *MPEG* (Motion Picture Experts Group). It was formed to address issues related to compressing "one-*bit*," bilevel, black-and-white images such as a fax machine might send or a *digital scanner* might create from a page containing black text on white paper. The standards that emerge from this group will serve the industry segment focused on the convergence of fax, copier, and *laser* print technologies.

JFC: Stands for Java Foundation Class, which is the library of fundamental software objects that was created to support the *Internet*-enabling software environment of the *Java* programming language. Like any other *foundation class*, the JFC is intended to provide a set of fundamental and extensible objects from which all other objects in the software system can be readily derived.

JFIF: Stands for JPEG File Interchange Format, which is an image file format based on the *JPEG* (Joint Photography Experts Group) standard for *compression* and *decompression* of images.

job aids: From the world of *instructional design* and *CBT* (computer-based training), these are relatively small, *granular* devices designed to prompt user performance relative to specific, job-related tasks. An *instructional designer* may develop job aids, also known as quick-reference aids, to avoid the time and expense required to instill memorized responses in the target learner audience. Thus, job aids are very useful in situations where large organizations are undergoing dramatic and widespread change and must therefore quickly train—or retrain—a significant portion of their workforce.

joystick: This remote control device for a computer, which looks and operates much like the gearshift for a car, is often used in *video* and arcade games. As *home interactive media* come of age, variations on the joystick, such as *CD-I*'s so-called thumbstick, are apt to become increasingly popular.

JPEG: Stands for Joint Photography Experts Group, and has come to be synonymous with the *compression* standard for still images devised by the same organization. This compression technique relies upon *DCT* (discrete cosine transformation) as do many of the other most common *codecs* (e.g., *MPEG* [Motion Picture Experts Group] and *H.261*). JPEG is an *intraframe*, distinct from an *interframe*, codec, meaning that it deals with compressing single *frame* sources of content rather than motion picture sources. While the actual *compression* achieved depends on the *frequency* content (or colors) of the compressed image, *compression ratios* in the vicinity of 20:1 are typical for JPEG encoding. Among graphics specialists, JPEG is preferred over *GIF* for graphical images on the *Internet*.

Juke box: This is an increasingly prominent form of mass storage device often used for *image processing* systems. Multiple CDs or *digital* tapes are held in separate slots on a carousel or elevator type of container, with individual storage units brought under the read head by some form of robotic device as the information it contains is requested by users. In today's market, it is not uncommon for this form of *near-line storage* device to have as much as several *terabytes* of storage capacity. Even with systems this large, *access times* do not typically exceed 10–100 seconds.

Jump: In a *hypertext* system, and on a *Web site*, this term refers to the *link* to another document as well as to the *link* to another related section within the same document.

Jump cut: From the world of film and *video*, this term refers to *edit points* between camera *shots* that change the scene of action either between extremely different or extremely similar shots.

Jump station: A *Web site* whose pages are comprised primarily of *hyperlinks* to other Web sites focused on related areas of interest. Thus, one uses this type of site as a jump station to other selected sites.

JVM: Stands for Java Virtual Machine, the feature of the *Java* programming environment that is most responsible for delivering on the promise of "write once, run anywhere." In essence, the JVM is a set of program elements, each of which is responsible for translating the code written in Java into "*byte* code" that will run in a particular operating system environment. Thus, JVM provides translation programs for *Windows* 98, Windows NT, *UNIX* and OS/2, just to name some of the better known operating environments. Owing to the presence of these translation routines, developers of *application programs* need only write one version of their software, and leave it to the JVM to translate the code for the various operating environments. As intended by its designers, JVM provides the penultimate tool for enabling interoperability.

Somewhere in my education I was misled to believe that science fiction and science fact must be kept rigorously separate. In practice they are so blurred together they are practically one intellectual activity, although the results are published differently, one kind of journal for careful scientific reporting, another kind for wicked speculation.
—**Stewart Brand, Author of The Media Lab**

Kaleida Labs: Established in 1991, this now-defunct joint venture of IBM and Apple was created to execute the mission of developing standards for *multimedia* products that span the personal computer, consumer electronics, and communications industries.

karaoke: Now one of the more popular applications for musically oriented *CD-ROM* and *DVD* titles, this term refers to any entertainment product whose primary purpose is that of inspiring the audience to sing along. The better systems, which might be found on videotapes, *laserdiscs*, *CD-ROM*, or *DVD*, display the lyrics as well as graphics and/or *video* clips.

Kbps: Stands for Kilobits per second, which is one thousand *bits* per second. It is a very common unit of measurement for the low end of data *transmission* speeds across a *network*.

Kermit: Is a popular *FTP* (file transfer protocol) developed by Columbia University. It is system and medium independent and can run under most operating systems. It can be used to transfer text and *binary files* on *full-duplex* or *half-duplex*, 8-*bit* or 7-bit serial connections. Kermit is an open *protocol* available for general use. However, some of the Kermit source code is *copyrighted* by Columbia University. Kermit is not the same as FTP.

key frame: A term used in conjunction with *motion compensation* forms of *video compression*, a key frame is a base *frame* that has not been temporally compressed but serves as a base against which the change, or delta, elements of subsequent frames are measured.

key grip: From the world of film *production*, this term refers to the individual who manages the *grips*—the people responsible for moving equipment, props, costumes, and the like.

keywords: With regard to *hypertext* systems, and specifically to the *Internet*, keywords represent a subclass of *link* where a word is highlighted or in some way denoted as special. By clicking on that word, the user is taken to an item of information associated with it. The most common example occurs where clicking on a keyword opens a text *window* in which that word is given a dictionary-style definition. However, keywords are used for many other purposes, especially those related to connecting (linking) one document section with a related section of another document. A prime example of this is where clicking on a name keyword takes one to biographical information about the named person located at some other place within the hypertext system. Keyword is a term also frequently used in the related area of *text search and retrieval*, where it refers to terms that are drawn from a document to characterize or summarize the overall content of the document. In this search and retrieval context, keywords are placed in some form of header record offered up to the *search engine* as a more compressed and therefore more efficient item to be scanned for matching the document's content against the user's interests. Effective manipulation of keywords is a cornerstone of efficient use of the Internet.

kinesthesia: This is the sensation of movement or strain in muscles, tendons, or joints. This physical sensation is the goal of most of the *high-intensity amusement attractions*.

kiosk: One of the major early applications for *interactive multimedia*, kiosks make use of *multimedia* technology by encasing the necessary delivery *platform* in some sort of architectural structure. Typically deployed in stand-alone fashion (i.e., without any human accompaniment), most kiosks hide everything from the user but the computer screen and employ *touch screen* technology to enable interaction with their programs. The building or campus directory is a typical example of how kiosks are used.

kludge: This is a slang term for an awkward and unsophisticated implementation of technology. Early interactive *video* workstations were, for example, often patched together by joining incompatible devices never intended for such integration with one another. Walks through early computer trade shows (circa early 1980s) would typically yield for the acute listener frequent grumblings about what "kludgey" systems these interactive *video* workstations are—or, thankfully, were.

knowbot: A form of *intelligent software agent*, the knowbot is a personal *search engine* capable of receiving and storing instructions about what kind of information its owner seeks. Once it is equipped with this type of user preference data, the knowbot then has the wherewithal to go out and search across the *Internet* for the specified information required by the owner.

knowledge engineering: This is the art of building *expert systems* by working with subject matter experts to extract, and then codify, their knowledge.

knowledge management: An exciting new concept in the maturation of the information age, this term represents one of the first acknowledgments on the part of the corporate world that knowledge assets and intellectual capital lie at the very heart of what makes an organization of value to society. Though the concept is still in its infancy, the early thinking it has provoked is focused on the methods and processes by which organizations can enhance the *capture*, storage, management, and distribution of their knowledge assets. Knowledge management is of great relevance to *multimedia* because, increasingly, the knowledge assets of most organizations will reside in the various forms of *digital media*. For example, as we move into the future, a commercial organization's success with electronic commerce (*e-commerce*) will in large part be determined by the quality of the navigational *interfaces* and electronic media that make up their online catalogs.

... there is so much worthless information available to each of us that intelligent pre-sorting of it, whether performed by people or by a machine, is an increasingly critical service.
—W.R. Johnson, Jr.,
VP, Telecommunication and Networks,
Digital Equipment Corporation

ladder of challenge: A concept stolen from the world of academe, this term refers to a common gaming strategy whereby as soon as a player masters the challenges presented by a game at one level, the gaming logic automatically upgrades the difficulties of the challenge to a new and heightened level. The purpose of this logic is to sustain interest and induce the player (also covetously viewed as a consumer) to stay with the present game, rather than moving onto another offering from a competitor. Fortunately, this concept has also been extended into the realm of *educational software*, where it is used to produce what are called "adaptive learning systems," which are programs that attempt to match the level of academic difficulty to the learner's demonstrated level of skill and knowledge.

LAN: Stands for Local Area Network, a widely used term that refers to data communications *networks* that span a physically limited geographic area (less than 10 km). They are implemented using some type of switching capability and high-*bandwidth* communications on a relatively inexpensive medium such as coaxial cable and are owned by the user, as opposed to using public (e.g., *public-switched telephone network*) communications facilities. With the onset of *multimedia* and the ever-expanding use of the *Internet*, a great deal of pressure is being placed on the LAN producer community to add both greater *transmission* bandwidth and greater central (*server*) storage capacity.

large-format scanner: This is a type of *scanner* used for scanning engineering drawings and other large documents too big for standard *sheetfed* and *flatbed scanners*.

laser: One of the dominant technologies of the information age, a laser is a device that generates light in which all of the photons are exactly in step and therefore produce a coherent beam. Laser light has one wavelength and is more easily controlled than other kinds of light.

laserdisc: This term refers to a form of *optical storage* that is very much on the wane. During the early 1990s, it was replaced gradually by *CD-ROM* technology. Like CD-ROM and *DVD*, laserdisc stores information in an optical format. That is, it relies on patterns of *pits and lans* burned into the *disc* surface that are read by a head that is sensitive to the reflectance values that occur when a *laser* beam is bounced off of that storage surface. Unlike CD-ROM and DVD, which employ an all-*digital* format, laserdisc stores its information in an *analog* format. Hence, laserdisc is not nearly as compatible with the computer environment as are CD-ROM and DVD.

last-mile loop: This term refers to the *transmission media* that make up the final segments of the telephone and TV networks, i.e., those low-*bandwidth* segments that actually connect the global and national networks to our homes. For a long time, the last-mile loop has been viewed as a prohibitive bottleneck with respect to delivering high-bandwidth, high-quality media services such as *picturephone* and *movies-on-demand* into the home. In the phone system, the bottleneck is that last bit of copper wiring that connects the *public-switched telephone network* to our residences. With regard to cable TV, the last-mile roadblocks are the long cascades of amplifiers that run from the cable company's *transmission* headquarters to the home, boosting the *signal* every quarter-mile or so, and frequently introducing all sorts of electronic *noise*. Traditionally, media futurists have believed that it would take a massive investment in residential *fiber optic* connections to make the likes of point-to-point interactive *video* and *HDTV* (high-definition television) possible. However, recent innovations in *compression* technology have paved the way for possibly using the existing stock of last-mile media to carry at least the first generation of *home interactive media* into our living rooms. Also, the problem of the last-mile loop may be solved by *DTH* (direct to home) technologies that use satellite broadcasting to entirely bypass this aging infrastructure.

LATA: Stands for Local Access and Transport Area, which is the geographic territory used primarily by local telephone companies to determine charges for intrastate calls. As a result of the Bell divestiture, switched telephone calls that begin and end within the same LATA are typically the sole responsibility of the local telephone company. Calls that require connections outside a given LATA are passed on to *IXCs*, or inter-exchange carriers, such as AT&T or WorldSpan.

latency: With reference to *virtual reality (VR)*, this is a measure of the time between when a person moves in a *virtual world* and when the computer governing the virtual world registers that movement. In systems that are primarily visual—as most VR systems are today—this term is closely associated with *frame refresh rates*. The key to success in displaying the computer-generated imagery that these systems rely upon is low latency and high frame refresh rates.

With regard to *data communications*, this term refers to any characteristic of a data *transmission* path that introduces a delay in response time. There are many causes of latency on computer *networks*. One of the most commonly cited delays has to do with the processing *overhead* associated with reading and interpreting data *packets*. This particular source of latency is duplicated for every *hop* in a data transmission path, and so can become quite substantial for data transmitted across complex or long-range paths. There are several other sources of latency: 1) the delays that occur when there is a mismatch in the data speed between the computer processor and its *I/O* devices; 2) the absence of adequate *buffering* by machines sending and/or receiving data; and 3) the need to resend data that has arrived at its destination with some form of error or corrupted information. One of the perpetual goals of network engineering is that of finding ways to squeeze latency out of the network.

LBE: Stands for Location-Based Entertainment, which is the primary use of *surrogate travel* technologies for entertainment purposes. This term is now being applied to the theme-park uses of surrogate travel, such as those embodied in *virtual* rides and *IMAX Theatres*.

LCD: Stands for Liquid Crystal Display, a rapidly evolving form of computer display. LCDs are popular with users and manufacturers of small machines owing to their low power demands and light weight. LCDs differ significantly from *CRTs* (cathode ray tubes), the most common form of *video* playback device, because they are light modifiers, or valves, rather than light producers. They typically consist of two small panes of glass, between which are a vast array of *cells*, referred to as *pixels*, which contain a liquid crystal substance. When no electrical current is sent to an LCD *pixel*, the crystals are oriented in a particular direction, blocking light from passing through and causing that *pixel* to remain dark. When a small electrical current is sent to a *cell*, the crystal's orientation is altered, allowing light to pass. The patterns formed by these electrically manipulated *pixels* are what create the images we see on an LCD screen.

learning organization: Within the business world, the concept of the learning organization elevates the status of learning to one of strategic competitive importance for the enterprise. The phrase was first coined by
Peter Senge in his 1990 business management book, entitled *The Fifth
Discipline: The Art and Practice of the Learning Organization*. Basically, a learning organization is a business entity that gains and then
sustains some type of competitive advantage through the collective and
organized acquisition of knowledge and skills. The concept is important
to the *multimedia* industry because it helps draw management attention
to corporate education at just the moment when the complementary technologies of *WBT* (Web-based training) and corporate *intranets* are making the widespread deployment of interactive training both possible and
profitable. Thus, to the extent that large corporations generate top management support for the learning organization concept, there will be a
sizable and sustainable market to fuel the continued maturation of *interactive multimedia*.

learning styles: From the world of learning theory—and, more recently,
from *instructional design*—this term is used to describe a classification
scheme that is based on the realization that people learn in widely varying ways. One group of people may learn better by working through
related tasks with other people, while others may be better able to master the same content by reading from an instruction manual in solitude.
Some people learn more from what they hear, while others excel in learning from what they see. Being able to determine learning styles by observing learners using a particular piece of *educational software* is one
of the more ambitious goals of contemporary instructional design.
Progress in this area of research will serve the larger goal of individualizing—or personalizing—*multimedia* content relative to the specific
needs of the user.

LED: Stands for Light-Emitting Diode, a device used widely for a broad
number of applications in the world of computing and electronics. LEDs
are basically *transmission* devices, in that they emit pulses of light energy in response to various sorts of stimuli. They are usually coupled
with *photosensors*, which serve to *convert* light energy to electrical energy to be used, for example, to create the logical, *digital* patterns of
computing devices.

legacy device: In our present era of hypersonic change, today's newfangled
and highly fashionable technology becomes tomorrow's old news. Rapid
and sudden obsolescence has become part in parcel of our technology-

driven times and is particularly at home in the world of *multimedia* technology. For example, just a few years ago *CD-ROM* was an exciting, sunrise technology in the field of multimedia, offering *content providers* their first legitimate opportunity to develop media-rich products for the *desktop PC* market. Today—merely five to seven years after its true debut as a commercially viable product—*CD-ROM* is rapidly being eclipsed by *DVD-ROM* and the *Web* as a *technology enabler* for multimedia content. When a technology like *CD-ROM* experiences this form of obsolescence, it is said to be a legacy device.

levels I–IV: Refers to levels of interactive *videodisc*; see *videodisc levels*.

life quality: As Walt Disney was pushing the world of cartoon *animation* to new levels of quality with his feature films (e.g., *Snow White and the Seven Dwarfs*), this term emerged in the press to describe the effect his obsession with realism and detail had on audiences (and critics). For example, he was reputed to have sent all of his animators through seminars and coursework in animal anatomy before making *Bambi*. Thus, life quality is an idea that extends the concept of *codes of resemblance*, wherein media is invested with technological inputs for the purpose of making the audience's experience as true to life as is possible.

light pen: This handheld device detects light emitted by elements comprising the picture on the screen. It can, for example, detect the presence of lines or points.

linear: As in "linear video," this term refers to the dominant *mode* for producing media for at least the last several centuries. In fact, not since the oral storytelling tradition waned as our primary mode of delivering socially sanctioned stories has the linear tradition received any considerable threat to its hegemony. However, with the apparent imminence of *interactive media*, that unchallenged dominion is now in doubt—and the implications are potentially staggering. To understand these implications it is necessary to examine the ingrained habits of mind that dictate the behaviors of those who produce linear media. For example, with linear, all *segue* or branching decisions—such as which scene follows another, or when a particular scene should end and its successor begin—are left entirely under the author's (director's) control. With interactive, most of these branching decisions are transferred to the user, who becomes a participant in a medium that can be characterized as a form of shared authorship. The big question that is raised by this impending challenge to linear media is this: will the same people who have made a living (a fortune, actually) making linear media be well suited to producing interactive media? Think about it.

line driver: From the world of *data communications*, this term refers to a *signal* converter that conditions a *signal* to ensure reliable *transmission* over an extended distance.

line level inputs: From the world of audio production, this term refers to inputs made to a recording device that originate from another electronic source, such as a tape deck, VCR, or CD player. This form of input is often contrasted with *microphone level inputs*, which originate from natural sources and, as the name implies, are *captured* in electronic storage through a microphone.

line segment: In *vector* graphics, this term refers to the portion of a line bound by *endpoints*.

LineMode: A historical tidbit from the evolution of the *Internet*, this is the name of the first legitimate *browser*, invented by Tim Berners-Lee in the early 1990s. At its inception, LineMode was text based, but it was far easier to use than any previous *user interface* to the Internet. It provided the capability for linking to other sources of information, also known as the *hyperlink*. LineMode was eventually superseded in 1993 by *NCSA Mosaic*, the first browser to offer a graphical user interface (*GUI*) with *mouse* capabilities.

link: With regard to *hypertext*, this term has a specific meaning. It refers to an *icon*, or other visible *hot spot*, that makes a connection between one location in a hypertext system and another. Links are based on some sort of association between the origin and the destination. With some interactive design *treatments*, the icon that denotes a link is styled to represent the conceptual basis of the connection. For example, in a geographic portion of a *hypertext* system, a magnifying glass icon might be used to indicate the availability of a *zoom* link, i.e., a link that shows some portion of a map in greater detail. With regard to an *HTML* document on the *Internet*, a link will typically take the user to another location in the same document, or to another Internet site altogether. These types of links are usually underlined or shown in a different color.

linked list: Is a data structure in which each element points to the next element. The trail of *Web pages* that is built—and can be accessed in reverse order by clicking successively on the back *button* of one's *browser*—while *surfing the net* is made possible by a linked list.

lipsynch: From the earliest days of film and TV, lipsynch refers to the synchronization of lip movements on screen with the vocal sounds of the sound *track*. Lipsynching confronts a renewed challenge in the world of *digital video*, where techniques such as the *interleaving* of *voice* and image on *disk* must be used for the computer to access these two disparate, memory-hungry forms of data quickly enough and in close enough proximity to one another to achieve the desired synchronization effect.

listserv: This term generally refers to an *Internet* mailing list. To be more specific, the listserv is a program that forwards messages received from one member to all members of an *e-mail* group who have subscribed to a topic, discussion, or course. Listservs were originally developed for IBM's VM operating system by Eric Thomas. In a listserv, a user subscribes to a topic by sending an e-mail to a listserv@host. Some listservs provide additional functions such as file retrieval from *archives* and database searches. The full range of functions available from a listserv can usually be obtained by sending a message for help to the listserver. At the very least, with most listservs one can subscribe to the listserv, unsubscribe to the listserv, and obtain a listing of all members currently on the listserv.

LMDS: Stands for Local Multipoint Distribution Service, a relatively new entry to the field of *wireless* access to *Internet* services. LMDS (capable of delivering a 500-*Kbps data rate*) uses a part of the radio frequency spectrum, a regional infrastructure of *microwave* facilities, and a granular network of local *transceivers* to deliver Internet services mostly to users located in densely populated urban areas.

local bus: From the world of processor design, this term refers to an emerging tweak of standard personal computer architecture designed to speed the processing of the massive amounts of data that accompany *multimedia applications*. A number of local bus designs have come to the market in an effort to address the processing demands of *multimedia* technology, the two most dominant to date being *VESA's* (Video Electronics Standards Association) VL-bus and Intel's *PCI* (peripheral component interconnect). Local bus circuitry speeds the processing of media-intensive data types by transferring data directly to the system processor using a broader data path so that faster throughput can be achieved than on the traditional system *bus* of PCs (e.g., the 16-*bit ISA* bus). In all likelihood, the local bus will be remembered as a momentary annoyance and minor footnote in the computer's transformation from a computational machine to an *interactive multimedia* machine.

localization: This term refers to the process of adapting text, sound, images, *icons*, and other visual or audio user cues for use with other languages and within other countries and cultures. Thus, localization is a sophisticated form of translation that adds value by applying a heightened cultural sensitivity to all aspects of the work product being translated. For *multimedia* programs that are to be distributed to international markets, the process of localizing the content is a key success factor.

localization cues: This term is used with respect to *3-D sound* to describe the localizing effect created when sound arrives at one ear before the other. These cues enable human listeners to create an audio picture of their environments.

locator: An information source that *links* automatically to other information sources.

LOD: Stands for Level Of Detail, and refers to the capability of *virtual world* products to provide greater levels of detail in the objects they contain as users *zoom* in on them. Thus in a *flythrough* of a virtual world cityscape as you approach a building or other object in the landscape, the virtual world tools will render that building or object in progressively greater detail as you approach it. LOD is an important consideration when dealing with the *Internet*. Issues of limited *bandwidth* call upon developers of *Web content* to reduce, or dynamically filter, the levels of detail so that users can access the virtual world objects without compromising the *frame refresh rates* to the point where the virtual world loses all semblance of its *life quality*.

lofting: This term refers to an interactive graphics technique in which the third dimension of a 3-D image is obtained from a 2-D representation. A good example of lofting would be the creation of a 3-D image from the elevation contours contained in a 2-D topographic map.

logical assets: As opposed to the *media assets* of a *multimedia application*, this term refers to the branching, performance assessment, and other software design features that altogether supply a program with its sense of intelligence. Generally speaking, in today's *multimedia* market, high-end gaming and *simulation* programs possess the strongest logical assets.

logical link control: This term refers to a temporary connection between two *nodes*, i.e., a source and a destination, or between two processes located on the same PC machine.

long shot: From the world of film and *video*, this term refers to a camera *shot* with a vantage point relatively far from its subject. An aerial *view* of a cityscape would be a prime example of a long shot. This type of shot has been most commonly used at the beginning of movie scenes to establish the locale or atmosphere. The long shot is often held in contrast to the *close-up*, which is used to provide intimacy between subject and viewer.

longdocument-handling features: In the early days of desktop publishing, most of the programs advertised under this moniker were ill-equipped to handle large documents such as books, magazines, or lofty proposals; they were better suited to handling the company newsletter. However, with time and market pressure, these programs have taken on a set of features that makes them well qualified to work with large, or long, documents. These features include automatic tables of contents, automatic *back-of-the-book indexes*, facilities for chaining multiple documents, and the like. The appearance of these features represents a maturation of the *electronic publishing* industry. The next major push for this industry segment will be the features associated with ERD (electronic reference documents), such as *hyperlinks* and full-text search.

loop qualification: With respect to *ISDN* services, this is a test performed by the customers' local phone company to determine if they are located within the maximum distance of 18,000 feet from their respective central office (*CO*). If the customer lies outside of that range, then the provision of *ISDN* services will require the inclusion of a signal-strengthening *data communications* device known as a *mid-span repeater*.

lossy compression: Refers to a group of *compression* techniques that sacrifice exact reproduction of data for better compression. A common example of a lossy compression technique is the *MPEG* (Motion Picture Experts Group) standard for motion *video* compression, which achieves ratios on the order of 100:1 up to 2,000:1 but sacrifices quite a bit in terms of image quality. A second common example is the *H.261* standard, which is used for *video teleconferencing*.

Lotus Notes: Also referred to as simply "Notes," this is the brand name for the popular *groupware* and messaging application developed by Lotus Development, now a subsidiary of IBM. Founded on the long-range goal of making complex documents (or *DLOs*) more *computable* and therefore useful to individuals and organizations, the Notes application provides software functionality in the areas of *e-mail*, group calendaring, *replication*, document databasing, and *workflow management*. The functionality of Notes is Web-enabled through the creation of a companion application called *Domino*.

luminance: The intensity, or *brightness* component, of an electronic image. By itself, luminance creates an image in black, gray, and white. With color television, it is combined with *chrominance* to create a color image. Because the human eye is more sensitive to luminance than it is to chrominance, more is done when compressing color *digital* images to reduce the chrominance content than is done to eliminate the luminance information.

lurking: In the context of the *Internet discussion group* or *newsgroup*, lurking means to read and listen to the conversation without participating or posting messages of one's own. The term is not pejorative and newcomers are often encouraged to lurk to learn the history and customs of a particular group.

LV-ROM: This term stands for LaserVision-Read Only Memory, a *laserdisc* format developed by Philips UK in conjunction with a number of other media and computer interests in 1986. The format accommodates *analog video*, *digital* audio, and *digital* data. Like laserdisc technology, though, this format is now little more than a historical footnote in the evolution of interactive video.

LZW compression: This term refers to a *compression* algorithm that is used in *GIF* files, a very popular graphics file format on the *Web*. It was developed by A. Lempel, J. Ziv, and T. Welch at Unisys Corporation.

Technology is sporadic. As in the history of optics, it may take thousands of years to realize a theory.

—Douglas Leebaert,
Professor, Graduate School of Business,
Georgetown University

magnetic positioning systems: This term refers to the primary position-sensing technique used in *virtual reality (VR)* research today. The underlying concept of these systems is simple. Electrical current sent through a coil of wire generates a magnetic field oriented along a single axis. Conversely, when a coil of wire is exposed to a magnetic field, an electrical current is generated that is proportional to the field's strength. The closer to the axis of the magnetic field, the greater the electric charge generated. If you mount three coils of wire at right angles to each other and feed them electrical current, the coils create magnetic fields along three axes. And if you move a second three-coil set through these magnetic fields, it produces three distinct electrical charges depending on its position and orientation. It is then possible to process these values mathematically to provide position (x, y, and z) and orientation (roll, *pitch*, and yaw) information about the sensor. All of this magnetic magic makes it possible for a VR system to track the movement of objects through a *virtual world*. The first and best known example of this three-coil, magnetic system is the *Polhemus Tracker*.

magnetoencephlamography: Possibly one of the longest words in the English language, this term refers to a futuristic, perhaps frightening, form of computer input now being contemplated in some research labs. Based on medical brain scanning, the concept is that scientists will be able to measure the electromagnetic *signals* coming out of your brain and match them with a map of what previous brain scans revealed. One of the hopes is that we might be able to teach computers to recognize certain types of brain activity. Going beyond this, it is theoretically possible that particular thoughts create distinct patterns of brain activity, and that the equivalent of *MIDI* (musical instrument digital interface) *wave tables* could be filled with recorded thought patterns such that the computer could read the human mind. Scary thought.

mail address: This term refers to an *e-mail address* that provides a location to which correspondence from all over the *Internet* can be directed.

Mail Exchange Record: A domain name server *(DNS)* resource record that lists which *host* can handle *e-mail* for a particular *domain*.

mail gateway: This term refers to a machine that connects two similar or dissimilar mail systems and transfers messages between them. The mail *gateway* adds its greatest value when it is facilitating data transfer between otherwise incompatible *networks*. For these dissimilar systems, the gateway maps and translates the data requiring a *store-and-forward scheme*. Under this process, the message is received completely before it is translated and retransmitted. The term *router* is more commonly used than gateway.

mail server: Is a program used to *store and forward e-mail*. In the early days of the *Internet*, mail servers also provided remote services, which now are provided by *FTP* or the *Web*.

mailbox: This term refers to a collection of *e-mail* messages received for an individual *address*. The mailbox may be a special file or a *queue* that collects e-mail messages for that address.

mapping software: Is a program that allows one to create and draw clickable *image maps* on *Web pages* for *Web sites* on the *Internet*. The map data consists of coordinates indicating what portions of the map are clickable, allowing the user to *link* to information content that lies below the map.

MARBI: Stands for MAchine Readable Bibliographic Information, which is an interdivisional committee of the American Library Association including ALCTS (Association for Library Collections and Technical Services), LITA (Library and Information Technology Association), and RUSA (Reference and User Services Association). Its purpose is to update and maintain the *MARC* standard for bibliographic information and to provide a liaison with units within the ALA and with relevant outside agencies.

MARC: Stands for MAchine Readable Cataloging, and is also known as USMARC, to indicate its American origins. Originally developed in 1960 to create electronic standards for the description of printed books, USMARC is still being adapted to provide description, access, and location information for networked resources. It is a highly developed and refined standard, providing individual data elements defined at a very *granular* level, and has gained wide acceptance in the library science community through its long tenure of use. Owing to these strong advantages, many librarians are in favor of extending the *functionality* of the MARC standard so that it can serve as the dominant *metadata* convention for cataloging *Internet resources*.

markup tags: Used by *tagging languages* such as *SGML* (standard generalized markup language) and *HTML* (hypertext markup language), markup tags enable users to embed specialized publishing and document-formatting characteristics within documents.

mass deployment: This general term is now gaining a specific meaning: it is coming to represent that long-awaited moment in our national future when we convert our communications infrastructure—our *NII* (National Information Infrastructure)—from one that is dominated by the traditional *analog* set of technologies to one that is governed primarily by *digital* technologies. When this occurs, all of the now-anticipated forms of information and entertainment—such as *VOD* (video on demand), the *virtual mall*, even the *personal newspaper*—will move from the status of blue sky to reality. Most industry analysts agree that the technologies associated with the infrastructure of the *Internet*, such as *TCP/IP*, represent the first wave of this mass deployment.

mastering: This term is used most commonly in reference to a critical step in the process of producing a *CD-ROM* or *DVD*. As the word implies, it refers to the process of creating the *disc* from which all others will be produced. It involves the burning of *pits and lans*—the optical technology equivalents for binary data—into the photo-resistant surface of the master disc.

matte: From the world of traditional film and *video*, this *production* tool is essentially a mask. There are two types: the female mask, which is the character or object photographed over a black background, and the male mask, which is a silhouette of a character or object *shot* on a white background. When applied to the realm of *DVE* (*digital* video effects), this term refers to the *two-plane effect* in which a defined area of the *front plane* is made transparent revealing the image on the *back plane*.

Mbps: Stands for Megabits per second, which is one million *bits* per second. It is a unit of measurement for computer storage, memory capacity, or data *transmission* speed across a *network*.

MBT: Stands for Multimedia-Based Training, which is a term often used to refer to forms of computer-based training (*CBT*) that have been designed to include substantial *multimedia* content in the form of *digital images*, graphics, *animations*, audio, and *video*. This term is actually a partial reflection of the history of electronic *courseware* or *CBT*. Earlier generations of *CBT* were created for mainframes and then first-generation PCs, and did not incorporate much in the way of multimedia content. Rather, they were composed largely of text and rudimentary graphics. More contemporary generations of courseware, however, have benefited from the rise of the *MPC* (multimedia personal computer) and have been able to present subject matter in ways that can be enlivened with the richer forms of communication, i.e., with images, graphics, audio, etc. Hence, these later forms of *CBT* are now often referred to as MBT, and the use of this latter-day acronym is often a code for indicating that the *courseware* being referenced has been developed more recently to take advantage of today's *multimedia* computer capabilities.

MCC: Stands for Microelectronics and Computer Technology Corporation, a consortium of American high-technology firms established in 1982 to share technological innovations for the purpose of warding off the competitive onslaught of Japanese firms. Located in Austin, Texas, the founding corporations of MCC include Digital Equipment, Motorola, National Semiconductor, Advanced Micro Devices, Honeywell, Martin Marietta, and Bell Communications Research.

MCF: Stands for Meta-Content Format, which is Netscape's *metadata* standard for defining *Web*-based content. In fulfillment of Nicholas Negroponte's (of the MIT *Media Lab*) vision for *personal television*, this metadata standard is designed to enable *content providers* to code their information resources so that end users, or consumers, can be automatically notified when new information of personal interest becomes available. Originally developed by Apple Computer, MCF provides a tree structure for describing a site.

MCI: This term stands for Media Control Interface, and it refers to a *multimedia* software utility embedded in Microsoft's *Windows* operating system. It is used to provide standard methods for accessing the various devices that one associates with multimedia delivery *platforms*, such as *CD-ROM* and *laserdisc*. The facilities of MCI can be accessed through *Media Player*.

media assets: As opposed to the *logical assets* of a *multimedia application*, this term refers to the *video*, audio, and text elements that together convey the media production value of a program.

media integrators: This term refers to the low end of software tools that are used to build *multimedia* presentations. When compared against the high-end *authoring systems*, media integrators seek ease of use as their primary goal. Examples in today's market include Macromedia's Action! and Interactive Media's Special Delivery.

Media Lab: Founded in 1985 at MIT by Jerome Weisner and current director Nicholas Negroponte, this center receives fame for the research it conducts on the future of communications technologies. The founding concept of the Media Lab was a belief in the inexorable merger of three previously separate and distinct industries: broadcast and motion picture, print and publishing, and computer. The Lab is funded mostly by grants from corporations and governments, all of whom are paying to see the future of communications 30 or so years down the road.

Media Player: This is a software utility embedded in Microsoft *Windows* that is the main *interface* to the *MCI*. It uses VCR-like *buttons* to control remote devices, such as the *CD-ROM* player on the *MPC* (multimedia personal computer).

memex: In 1945, Vannevar Bush wrote an article entitled "As We May Think," and many people hold it out as the inaugural work of the Information Age. In that article, Bush described a machine, which he referred to as a memex, that could be used to browse and make notes in a voluminous online text and graphics system. The memex contained a large library of documents, as well as personal items such as notes, photographs, and sketches. This imaginary machine was to have several screens and a facility for establishing a labeled *link* between any two points or *nodes* in the library. The memex is an obvious ancestor of the concepts that we today refer to as *hypertext* and the *Web*.

memo field: From the world of database design, the memo field is a design feature that enables users to place fields in records that can receive data of widely variable size or length. With traditional database design, data fields have a maximum length specified in the database's data dictionary. For example, a name field might be defined in the data dictionary as having a fixed length of 30 characters. This means that the designer of that database anticipates that no name will ever exceed 30 characters in length. Virtually all of the fields specified for the typical database possess this type of length specification, which provides a predetermined structure to the data and makes it easier to manage. The memo field was introduced to account for the increasing tendency of users to want to add information to a database that is of considerable length and varies so much in size that it is nearly impossible to anticipate length with any degree of accuracy. The first such incidence of this must have been "memos" that people wanted to add to data records, as in adding a memo to an accounts receivable record that explains why a particular customer has been extended credit. With the advent of *mixed* *media data types*—audio, image, and *video*—the need to add information that varies widely in size/magnitude is going to grow dramatically. In the absence of any other significant extensions to the design of database systems, the obvious place for putting this type of *rich data* will be the memo field. Thus, to many the memo field is viewed as a historical point of entry for extending the capabilities of traditional database management tools and systems into the age of *multimedia*.

menu: Perhaps the most basic element of graphical user interface (*GUI*) design, the menu is a pull-down list of functions available in a software application.

metadata: This term is drawing great attention as the *Internet* continues its ascendance as the *WAN* (wide area network) of choice. Strictly speaking, metadata refer to information about information, and has long been used in the data processing community to describe, among other things, the data dictionaries that are used to profile the contents of corporate databases. The term has gained much wider attention lately, and is becoming particularly popular with the library science community, as efforts to overcome the tremendous problems associated with *information overload* on the *Web* continue to unfold. Because metadata are used to describe information objects, they represent a form of *cataloging*, no different in essence from the library card catalog. Just like the card catalog, the primary goal of metadata is to help define complex information objects, such as electronic journal articles, so that they can be sought for in a predictable and organized way. In this vein, it is believed that the successful creation of widely practiced metadata standards will ultimately lead to greater precision in the use of *search engines* on the Internet. The text encoding initiative (*TEI*), the *Dublin Core*, and recent extensions of the longstanding *MARC* standard all represent recent efforts to create metadata standards for the Internet.

methodology: In the world of computing, a methodology is a defined, structured approach and process to developing a software application throughout its life cycle. A typical process involves analysis, design, evaluation, development, installation, and maintenance. Within these phases, various roles such as the *instructional designer,* the programmer, and the *information designer* interact with one another to perform the activities specified in the methodology. The primary outcome of their efforts is to create process deliverables, such as the requirements document or the design statement, both of which provide direction as to the character of the final application itself. It is hoped that developers of *multimedia applications* and *hypermedia applications* will follow a methodology to help ensure product *usability*.

MFC: Stands for Microsoft Foundation Class, which is the library of fundamental software objects that Microsoft has created to support its *Windows* programming environment. Like any other *foundation class*, the MFC is intended to provide a set of fundamental and extensible objects from which all other objects in the software system can be readily derived.

microphone level inputs: Refers to forms of audio input that originate from natural sources and are *captured* to storage through a microphone. This term is often contrasted with *line level inputs*, which refer to inputs that originate from other electronic sources, such as VCR, tape deck, or CD player.

microwave: Refers to the following: 1) radio *transmission* that uses very short wavelengths and 2) a high-*bandwidth* facility that provides line-of-sight radio communications and that requires repeater stations to be placed every 40 km or so because of the curvature of the earth's surface.

MIDI: Stands for Musical Instrument Digital Interface and represents one of the most powerful early innovations in *multimedia* technology. MIDI is both an *interface* used for connecting MIDI instruments and a music description language that reproduces instrumental sound (just as *PostScript* by Adobe Systems is a page description language used to create printed and other graphic output). The technology is based on the analytical decomposition of sound into its fundamental and electronically reproducible elements. There are two types of MIDI synthesizers, the devices used for creating electronically generated music: *FM synthesizers*, which use oscillators to reproduce sound waves, and sampled sound or *wave table* technology, which uses digitally recorded samples of instruments. Commands from the MIDI description language tell the synthesizers what to play. MIDI devices assign different instrument sounds to different *channels* and use those channels to play back or record MIDI songs. Because MIDI devices use a symbolic representation of sound that then generates a synthesized version of that sound on the fly rather than the space-hungry, *digitized* equivalent, this technology represents a powerful form of audio *compression*. Using MIDI, an hour of stereo sound can be stored in less than 500 K, which is a fraction of what it would take to store that volume of audio were it recorded in, say, the *Red Book* audio format.

mid-span repeater: With respect to *ISDN* services, this *data communications* device is required to service any customers that lie outside a distance of 18,000 feet from their respective central office (*CO*).

mil: This is a suffix indicating a military *Web site.*

MIINET: Is a contraction for Military Network, which is part of both the Defense Data Network (*DDN*) and the *Internet.* It is managed by the Defense Information Systems Agency (DISA).

MIME: Stands for Multipurpose Internet Mail Extension. It defines a format for converting *binary files* of nontext data such as graphics, audio, and fax into a text-based format for *transmission* within *e-mail* messages.

mips: Stands for millions of instructions per second and is the standard measure of processor speed in the computing world.

mirror: This term refers to a clone or exact copy of a *Web site*, stored conveniently for quick access. Mirroring is a security technique to protect data in case of a *disk* failure on a computer. Data is written to two devices, usually two hard disks. Mirroring is a typical feature of *RAID* systems.

mix: In film and *video*, the mix is a recording session during which all the *tracks* for dialogue, music, and sound effects are combined onto a single master.

mixed media data types: This phrase has emerged as another way of referring to the realization that information processing must now be inclusive of the nontraditional, high-*bandwidth* sources of data—namely, audio, image, and *video*. There are many synonymous terms for this phrase, such as *rich data, multimedia* data, high-bandwidth data, etc.

MMX: Along with *MPEG* and *MPC*, this is one of the key threshold technologies in the history of the *multimedia industry.* MMX technology is an extension to Intel's microprocessor architecture, and represents the movement of multimedia-specific processor features from their original location on *expansion boards* to a more fully integrated location on the core *CPU.* MMX appears on the Pentium and Pentium Pro processor lines of Intel and is designed specifically to enhance a personal computer's *video*, audio, *animation*, and sound capabilities. More specifically, MMX is implemented through the addition of 57 new instructions to the Intel microprocessor instruction set. When working with applications that have been written for MMX-enabled processors, users will experience faster screen redraws and *bit-map* editing and faster and smoother *wipes* and other transitions.

mode: This very general—some would say overused—term refers to "one among several alternative methods of operation." Being a classificatory term, each mode has some characteristic or set of characteristics that sets it apart from another mode.

model sheet: Used extensively in the world of cartoon and feature *animation*, this is a group of drawings that are used to show various views of a character. The model sheet is designed to show the animators and assistants how particular characters are to be constructed. In many respects, the model sheet illustrates an object-oriented approach to *animation*, inasmuch as it isolates the characters as objects from their immersion in a story.

modem: A contraction for modulator-demodulator, this term refers to a *data communications* translating device that *links* a computer to a telecommunications network (usually the *public-switched telephone network*). A modem *converts* the *digital signals* of a computer to *analog* signals for *transmission* over the telecommunications network and then *converts* those analog signals back to digital when they arrive at their destination. It is generally believed that as we enter the age of *multimedia*, the demand for modems may wane as all-digital *transmission media* gradually replace the older stock of analog devices. This trend will be precipitated by the immense demand for carrying capacity levied by the *mixed media data types*, such as image and *video*. Modems are simply not equipped to handle the mammoth files associated with *rich data*.

Modular Windows: A subset of the Microsoft *Windows* graphical environment, this product was developed in the mid-1990s to serve what appeared to be an emerging *CD-ROM*-player TV accessory market. This market never evolved as many thought it would, but the phenomenon that was Modular Windows still offers clues for how software will need to be designed to manage the convergence of televisions and computers (a.k.a. the *teleputer*). Modular Windows was designed to be controlled by a TV viewer wielding a remote control and thus offered larger screen fonts and had a decisively different look and feel than its parent, MS Windows. An early user of Modular Windows was Tandy's *VIS* (Visual Information System) player, which was sold through Tandy's Radio Shack stores as a direct competitor to the Philips *CD-I* system.

moire effect: This term refers to a noticeable pattern of wavy, regularly spaced spots that results from the nearly parallel alignment of the axes of two superimposed dot screens. In the world of color printing, this effect is considered highly undesirable because it reduces the clarity of the printed image.

morphing: A special effects technique of fairly recent vintage, morphing is the now familiar visual process abundantly used in television whereby one object blends into another. Whenever one sees an object such as a face blend quickly and seamlessly into another object, such as another face, the technique being used is that of morphing. Drawn from the word "metamorphosis," this technique is based on very simple principles. To create a morph, one begins by selecting the beginning and ending *key frames*. Each point in the first key frame is associated with a point in the last key frame. The artist also selects a number of points between these two bookend key frames, then specifies the number of *frames* over which the transformation will occur from beginning to end. The more points that are selected for use with this *inbetweening* tool, the finer will be the transition.

Mosaic: Now a historical curiosity, this program was the first popular graphical user interface (*GUI*) standard *browser* application used to access information on the *Internet.* It was developed by the National Center for Supercomputing Applications (*NCSA*) and was also the first *Web browser* available with the same *interface* for the Mac, *Windows*, and *UNIX*. It provided a relatively easy-to-use graphical interface for access to the Internet's massive supply of distributed information. Mosaic met the needs of a new and growing category of customers for the Internet, that is, people outside the scientific and industrial research community. Mosaic was written by Marc Andreesen and Eric Bina at *NCSA*. Andreesen went on to become a cofounder of Netscape Communications and was instrumental in the creation of the *Netscape Navigator,* an industry standard for Internet browsers.

mosaic effects: From the realm of *DVE* (*digital* video effects), this term refers to a family of effects that are used to coarsen a *video* image. These techniques are typically employed as a method for fading out a scene and are most effectively used when the fade coincides with the psychological effect of losing attentional focus, such as occurs when someone is losing consciousness. There are two dominant mosaic effects. The first, *pixel repeat, zooms* in on a portion of the screen without providing any additional detail. The result is that the portion of the screen that is enlarged in the zoom comes to appear increasingly coarser, or out of focus. The second technique, known as *pixel hold*, retains the whole screen (does not zoom) but creates a granulated look by taking the color and tone (*chrominance* and *luminance*) of one *pixel* and extending it to neighboring pixels. Typically, this process is continued until the whole screen seems to break up into a set of increasingly hazy squares.

motion compensation: This term refers to a breed of *video compression* techniques that compress across *video frames* by saving only the differences between them. The *MPEG* (Motion Picture Experts Group) standard is a prime example of this breed. Motion compensation *codecs* are also referred to as *interframe codecs*.

motion parallax: This term is of growing importance in the world of *virtual reality*, where it describes the sensation of changing perspectives as one moves through a space. Specifically, motion parallax is an anomaly of the human visual system that occurs as we move our heads from side to side. Objects closer to us appear to move faster than objects farther away. This is because images of closer objects are larger and move across our retinas faster than the images of distant objects. This phenomenon is exploited by creators of virtual reality programs by simply getting objects in the visual field of action to move.

motion platform: One of the outstanding new features of *high-intensity amusement attractions*, motion platforms are used in conjunction with high-*resolution video* systems to create an immersive sense of motion associated with the action being portrayed in the video or graphic part of the system. As the name implies, the motion platform actually moves in conjunction with the video, artfully using a relatively small amount of movement to create for the audience an amplified sense of motion. The most popular and effective uses of motion platforms are found in our country's high-visibility theme parks (e.g., Universal Studios and Disney World, both in Orlando, Florida).

motion-control photography: One of many technical innovations created by George Lucas's Industrial Light & Magic, this term refers to a family of products that use computers to provide precision control of camera movement. This technology is used, for example, to create multiple *exposures* of the same scene, such that various special effects can be laid down on that scene in a seamless fashion.

motion-JPEG: One of the most popular *codecs* available today, it serves as the core *codec* for Apple's *QuickTime*. Motion-JPEG (Joint Photography Experts Group) is an *intraframe codec*, which means that it is symmetrical and can, for the most part, be performed on the fly (in *real time*).

mounting bracket: A metal bracket found on virtually every *expansion board* for IBM-compatible PCs that is used to secure the card in its slot with a screw.

mouse: Aside from the keyboard, the mouse is currently the most common computer input device. It is a handheld device that inputs coordinate information and is chiefly used as a "pick device" for selecting items from among *icons*, screen *menus*, and the like. The technology for the mouse was first developed at Stanford Research Institute in the 1960s and was later integrated into the seminal *interface* research that occurred at *Xerox PARC* in the 1970s and 1980s. The principle behind mousing is a simple one: a small ball is placed inside a device that is rolled on a table. Sensors measure how far the ball has rolled forward, backward, or side-to-side; and computer algorithms translate these movements into horizontal and vertical coordinate movements of an on-screen *cursor*.

mouse-over: This new verb of the information age refers to onscreen "events" that occur when you move your *mouse pointer* over a given object. For example: please mouse-over this *icon* to get a text bubble containing a description of the program.

mouth action: This refers to the numerous shapes the mouth must make when speaking. With an object-oriented approach to *animation*, these shapes are stored in an object library, available to be inherited (with appropriate modifications) by any character.

moviemap: A subtype of the *surrogate travel* genre, moviemaps are used to enable people to travel the roads and byways of geographically remote areas. The early examples were created by, first, actually filming movement (by foot or by car) through the target geographic area and then by digitizing these travel segments and placing them on some form of *optical storage*, most commonly a *laserdisc*. Points within the moviemap where users can change direction, e.g., turn down another street, are represented in the moviemap by simple *branchpoints* that enable the various street segments to become (seamlessly, one hopes) connected to one another for the purposes of simulating movement. The tedium of capturing a city's geobase of street segments on film is apt to give way in the future to terrain modeling systems that are integrated with geographic information systems to enable dynamic and automated rendering of *virtual* pathways through any target city for which adequate data is available. As these types of capabilities do become available, moviemaps will become part in parcel of the process of building *virtual worlds*. The Aspen Movie Map, created in 1978 by MIT's Machine Architecture Group, represents the proof-of-concept prototype of the moviemap.

movies-on-demand: Made possible by the rapid expansion of the *channel bandwidth* available to cable operators, this media service makes it possible for cable viewers to order films at their leisure. The full implementation of this service is projected to give viewers access to vast libraries of film offerings (e.g., the complete MGM library) and therefore to severely undercut, if not make completely obsolete, the VCR and the home *video* rental industry.

moving viewpoint commands: One of the emerging primitives of *interactivity*, moving viewpoint commands are a subtype of the interactive *branchpoint*. As the term suggests, these *branchpoints* enable participants to change what occupies their field of vision as they move through a particular scene, or *virtual world*. With the more immersive forms of interactive story, or *virtual reality*, these commands will be effected by sensors that correspond directly with the participant's own body movements (e.g., through the technology of the *DataSuit*). Consequently, they will obtain high levels of sophistication with respect to the *code of resemblance*.

Mozilla: Before the now-popular *Netscape Navigator* appeared on the market, there was *Mosaic*, the first *Web browser* to feature a graphical user interface (*GUI*). The creator of *Mosaic*, Marc Andreessen, went on to be a cofounder of Netscape Communications where the product that eventually became *Navigator* obtained the inside nickname of Mozilla. Now, a number of *Easter eggs* commemorating the spirit of Mozilla can be found buried in the Navigator interface.

MPC: Stands for Multimedia Personal Computer, and represents a historically significant market specification set forth by the *Multimedia PC Marketing Council* of Washington, DC. The first generation of the standard was published in 1990, the second in 1993. Its goal is to encourage the adoption of a standard *multimedia* computing *platform*, which stands to benefit hardware and title manufacturers as well as consumers. The council grants a distinctive MPC certification mark to all hardware manufacturers who meet the functional requirements of the specification. In summary, the minimum requirements of level 1 were as follows: 386SX *CPU*; 2 MB of RAM; 30 MB hard drive; single-spin *CD-ROM* drive with 150 KB *transfer rate* and *CD-DA* outputs; *VGA* monitor (640 x 480, 16 colors); and *MIDI I/O, joystick.*

The 1993 level-2 standard was much more robust and included the following specifications: 486SX, 25 Mhz *CPU*; 4 MB of RAM; 65,000-color graphics at 640 x 480 *resolution*; 160 MB hard drive; double-spin CD-ROM drive with 300 KB transfer rate; *CD-ROM-XA* ready; and multisession-capable MIDI I/O, joystick.

MPEG: This acronym, which stands for the *ISO* standards committee known as the Motion Picture Experts Group, has become synonymous with one of the early favorites to become a dominant *codec* for delivering *digital video*. In contrast to its close cousin, *JPEG* (Joint Photography Experts Group), the MPEG standard is an *interframe* or *motion compensation* codec. Like all codecs, MPEG seeks out redundant information that can be removed from a data stream. Because it is an *interframe codec*, MPEG seeks out redundancies that occur between *frames* in a video stream, as well as those that occur within single frames (as is the case with *intraframe codecs* like *JPEG*). The first generation of the standard was called MPEG but is now retrospectively being referred to as MPEG 1. This inaugural version of the standard provides a level of image quality that has been likened to the VHS standard of our VCRs. Technically speaking, the MPEG 1 format, which was finally blessed by its committee in 1993, is capable of presenting a quarter-screen picture at a *resolution* of 352 x 240 *pixels* at the *NTSC* (National Television Standards Committee) standard *frame rate* of 30 frames per second (*fps*). While full-screen implementations of MPEG are common, they are actually *interpolated* from the original quarter-screen data. This first round of the standard is considered most appropriate for presentation on older generations of deliver *platforms*, such as those that feature *VGA* monitors and early-generation *CD-ROM* drives. The second iteration of the standard, MPEG 2, rapidly became the digital *transmission* standard for the broadcast cable industry. In fact, at the time of its inception many industry analysts expected that the 50+ million cable subscribers in the United States would convert to digital *set-top boxes* with MPEG 2 *decoders* by the turn of the century. The MPEG 2 standard bumps the resolution of MPEG to 720 x 480, achieving a full television-quality standard.

MSC: Stands for MIDI Show Control, a language extension to the *MIDI* (musical instrument digital interface) standard that provides for the computer control of a variety of equipment systems used in live performance and large audiovisual *productions*. Motorized stage equipment, pyrotechnical effects, various audio devices, lighting systems, and *videodisc* players are just some of the devices that have been brought under the control of the MSC language. As envisioned by its authors, MSC will provide strong assistance to the traditionally harried *board* operators responsible for launching complex *sequences* of on-stage events in precise order and with precise timing.

MSCDEX: This combination acronym-contraction stands for Microsoft CD-ROM extensions. It is a program that enables the MS-DOS operating system to "talk" to a *CD-ROM* drive.

MUD: Stands for Multi-User Dimension or Dungeon, which is an interactive simulated environment—an exercise in *virtual reality* over the *Internet*. Some use it for fun and personal entertainment, while others use it for serious software creation or for educational uses. MUDs allow users to construct and manipulate objects and move into and around a set of *virtual* rooms. The objects created stay after the author leaves, so that others can interact with the objects in the author's absence *asynchronously*. MUD communication thus has both a *synchronous* and an *asynchronous hypertext* aspect. The *synchronous* component allows users to interact in *real time*, as in *chat* systems. The hypertext, asynchronous component consists of written descriptions of imaginary rooms, objects, and people. Participants can move from room to room and view objects or people whenever they choose to do so. Other variations are MOO, which is an object-oriented MUD; MUSE, which is a multi-user-simulated environment; and MUSH, which is multiple-user-shared hallucinations.

multicast: Analogous to broadcast, this term refers to transmitting electronic messages that may include *multimedia* content across multiple computer *networks* to a specified set of computer *hosts* (*servers*) capable of receiving the messages for further distribution to particular clients on the network.

multidrop line: Also commonly referred to as a "multipoint line," this term refers to a single communications line that is connected to two or more stations. The most obvious examples of a multidrop line are the telephone and cable connections that provide phone and TV services, respectively, to the residential market.

multimbral: From the world of audio engineering, this term refers to a *digital* audio device's ability to produce more than one instrument sound simultaneously.

multimedia: Is the umbrella term that has been coined to cover all of the synergistic uses of text, *voice*, music, *video*, graphics, and other forms of data to enhance the computer's role as a communications device.

multimedia applications: Though the decade of the 1990s has witnessed an explosion in what are being called *multimedia* titles, few have stopped to question what type of content denotes a *multimedia application*. We offer the following three-part taxonomy as a tentative starting point for defining the array of multimedia applications. **1) Structured pathways** are largely training applications—often called *tutorials*—that tightly constrict the user's movement through a series of interactive presentational *sequences* designed to achieve a specific set of learning objectives. This genre of multimedia is most often used with regard to content that requires a large measure of rote memorization. *Drill-and-practice* programs for grade school math and end-user training for software applications are two common examples of this type of *multimedia*. It is best employed with learners who bring very little base knowledge to the learning experience and therefore require that the *scope and sequence* of the content be laid out for them. **2) Exploratory** is probably the most common type of multimedia title coming onto the market today; it lies on the opposite side of the learner continuum from structured pathways as it works best with users that are already quite familiar with the content. The exploratory category is best typified by programs that are termed *hypertext* or *hypermedia*. It provides a navigational *interface* to large volumes of *hyperlinked* or relationally associated content. Electronic museums, electronic encyclopedias, online help systems, medical databases, and *surrogate travel* programs are all examples of exploratory multimedia (i.e., hypermedia). This type of program is fairly easy to build as it does not demand sophisticated software logic. Exploratory programs rise or fall on the merits of two factors: the desirability or appeal of their content and the quality of their navigational interface. **3) Gaming** is the most demanding of the three from the standpoint of software design. Gaming multimedia programs succeed by providing an engaging context in which users are challenged to achieve one or more well-specified goals (e.g., find the buried treasure, slay the appropriate villains, earn the imaginary fortune). Well-constructed games provide abundant feedback and are highly interactive. Most games inspire repeated use by implementing what educators call the *ladder of challenge*: once the player has obtained mastery at one level of challenge, the program automatically upgrades that challenge to a heightened level of difficulty. Though games are frequently scoffed at by those in the corporate world, a deeper look would reveal that the much-respected business *simulation* is, in fact, based on the same software design principles as games. The only substantive difference between the two is that the simulation is placed in a job context with real-world variables and feedback systems.

Multimedia applications have their roots in standard training and education courses with or without exercises, *CBT* (computer-based training) programs for education and training, and *video* games, simulations, and stories for fun and entertainment.

multimedia asset management: As *Web sites* and *e-commerce* grow in importance, many businesses are becoming increasingly concerned with the need to manage their *digital media* assets much as they have historically concerned themselves with managing transactional and other data about customers. Also referred to as *multimedia database*, multimedia asset management is about bringing the various business disciplines of database management to the project of organizing such digital media assets as images, graphics, audio and *video* clips, and the like.

multimedia database: This term has emerged in the nomenclature to pay witness to the fact that most database applications are making it possible to embed *mixed media data types* in their traditional database records. The most commonly cited example of this is a personnel database, where the employee's picture is attached as part of the employee record.

multimedia mail: This term refers to an electronic mail system that allows users to integrate text, graphics, audio, and *video*.

Multimedia PC Marketing Council: This is a nonprofit organization incorporated as a subsidiary of the Software Publishers Association. Using the multimedia PC standard set forth by Tandy Corporation in 1990, this council of 11 members established the standard of what constitutes a *multimedia* personal computer. As a way of enforcing this standard the council makes available to all hardware vendors the option of licensing the *MPC* (multimedia personal computer) trademark, which stands as a validation that any workstation thus trademarked has achieved the level of technical sophistication demanded by the MPC standard.

multiplexing: This term refers to a technique for combining several *signals* for data *transmission* on a shared medium (e.g., a telephone wire) to improve information throughput efficiency. Multiplexing is useful when there are several slow devices and multiple signals. The signals are combined at the transmitter by a *multiplexor* (also called a "mux") and split at the receiver by a demultiplexor. Different methods are used to combine signals: time division multiplexing, frequency division multiplexing, and code division multiplexing are the most common methods. The method used determines *bandwidth* requirements.

multiplexor: This term refers to a device that accepts *signals*, combines them, and sends them on as a single, high-speed stream of data.

multiprocessing: This term refers to an emerging trend in personal computer design to incorporate more than one processor. It is often confused with *parallel processing*, which denotes many small, identically constructed processors working simultaneously. Multiprocessing refers to the somewhat different notion of a computer with two or more specialized processors. In the age of *multimedia*, multiprocessing will play an increasingly important role as manufacturers discover that the most efficient way to handle the various forms of *encoded* media—text, audio, image, *video*—is to supply each with its own specialized processor. This is the approach that the Electronic Arts offshoot, 3D0, took when designing its home interactive multiplayer of the same name. The design approach of 3D0 was to assign to the *CPU* the function of "babysitting" a number of other processors working independently on processing the sound, graphics, and *animation*, respectively. The 3D0 design also incorporated a number of *DMA* (direct memory access) *channels*, which further reduced the processing load of the CPU by making certain that the movement of the various media files operated in a near-independent fashion.

multisession: This term refers to the ability of a certain breed of write-once CDs to record data during multiple sessions. The technology is essentially analogous to the append function familiar to database applications, wherein the physical placement of new data is located just beyond the existing data. With write-once, multisession CDs, this is the only place that new data can be placed. Once a portion of the CD's surface is burned with its *digital* pattern of *pits and lans*, it cannot be changed because there is no currently viable technology for *rerecording* these surfaces. However, multisession is considered a significant step forward, inasmuch as most CDs are single session. This means that any *disc* surface that is unused during the *mastering* process remains forever wasted. The Kodak Photo CD technology was the best known early example of a multisession CD.

multi-threaded discussions: Occurs in *chat* sessions that do not have a chat *facilitator*. In short, too many individuals are chatting at once about more than one topic within a single *chat* session, making it difficult for the participants to perceive a line of thought. Computer processors can "talk" to each other simultaneously, but problems occur when people try to do the same in a *chat* session.

multi-threading: From the realm of operating system design, this feature makes it possible for several processors to run the same code simultaneously. A feature like this is critical to many high-end *multimedia applications*, where the volume of data to be handled creates bottlenecks on most standard systems.

Myst: The best-selling *electronic game* distributed initially on *CD-ROM* by Broderbund. Created by the brothers Rand and Robin Miller, this game sold over three million copies and developed a huge and devoted following. The game is based on a *surrogate travel* model in which players move about in a richly depicted island setting in search of clues and story fragments that enable the piecing together of the underlying narrative. Now succeeded by a much-anticipated sequel, *Riven*, history may well record that Myst was the first legitimate piece of *interactive fiction*.

The prospect, then, is that the intelligence of the human participants in a conversational medium will dominate that of the computer for the foreseeable future.

**—Tim Oren,
Advanced Technology Group, Apple Computer**

NAPLPS: Stands for North American Presentation Level Protocol Standard and is pronounced "naplips." This was one of the earliest standards for sending computer graphics over the television industry *transmission* infrastructure, appearing well over a decade ago. Though it is still maintained by the major online services, such as Prodigy and America Online, it is considered to be seriously out of date. Blocky graphics, slow *transmission*, lack of built-in support for mice, and no audio are just some of this standard's shortcomings. As with so many early *network* communication standards for *multimedia* data, the *Internet* eliminates the need for NAPLPS.

narrowband: In contrast to the term *broadband*, this word describes a *transmission channel* that has a relatively low carrying capacity or amount of *bandwidth*. It typically describes channels with *voice grade* bandwidth (4 khz) or below.

narrowcasting: In contrast to the traditional, mass-market television network broadcasting predominant before cable television, this term describes media services targeted toward relatively small, specialized vertical market segments (also referred to as "interest groups"). ESPN and A&E are prime examples. Narrowcasting is projected to continue as a powerful trend well into the information age as *transmission bandwidths* for media services—and the resulting number of available *channels*—continue their unabated expansion. Also, the use of such customizing features as the *Internet cookie*—which works by posting one's personal preferences for use as an information filter—will help further extend the concept of narrowcasting.

native file format: This term refers to the unique format to which a program saves files. Most databases, word processors, graphics programs, and other software applications have their own file format *proprietary* to that application. This tendency to produce proprietary, native file formats obstructs the ability for people to share files across different application environments. Because of this, most commercial software applications provide conversion utilities that translate from their native format to the formats of other popular applications. Thus, the Microsoft Word word processing program provides conversion utilities for converting documents created in Word into the format of Lotus WordPro. To help combat the need for all of these conversion utilities—which must be updated every time any popular software application has a new release—the *Internet* has sought to create standard file formats that will reduce this balkanization of the data landscape. For example, saving a document from a native file format to an *HTML* format makes it possible for that file to be viewed on any *Web site*.

natural language processing: This term refers to a branch of *artificial intelligence* that specializes in programming computers with the ability to carry on normal human speech. This branch has become tightly connected with the technologies associated with speech recognition (or *voice recognition*).

natural language query: A query expressed in a natural human language such as English, French, or Russian. An example of a natural language query might be: "What sales rep had the highest sales volume in the Northwest in March 1998?" While the human brain easily and quickly grasps the sense of such questions, the complex, irregular nature of human language still poses difficult philosophical problems for *artificial intelligence* programs.

natural media: This term refers to a type of paint program that emulates artists' materials, including various types of canvases, paper, and paints.

navigation: A term that has found its way from seafaring origins to the world of *interface design* and *hypermedia*, it has become a popular design concept associated with building comprehensible structures when assembling large amounts of information into mixed media databases (*hypermedia*). Building the navigable interface is, for the present, one of the great challenges and research foci of the early stages in the age of *multimedia*.

navigator: This term has been offered to describe an emergent software that searches and manipulates content on various databases. Perhaps the outstanding feature of a navigator is its ability to self-navigate the *network*, seeking out the most appropriate information items from the numerous public information databases. This term can also refer to Netscape Corporation's *Web browser*, which some estimates show is used by over half of all people who access the *WWW*. There are versions of *Netscape Navigator* that run on major *platforms* such as Microsoft *Windows*, Macintoshes, and *UNIX*.

NC: Stands for Network Computer, a concept that lies at the center of one of the great controversies of our time. The primary business goal of the NC is to dramatically reduce the cost of desktop computers by shifting the intelligence, complexity, and feature-functionality of today's *personal computers* out of the *desktop* machine and onto the *network*. Thus, the NC is a relatively simple device, but one that matches the functional capabilities of a personal computer by relying upon sophisticated *Web servers* and other network-accessible sources of computer functionality to provide the data and software logic needed to perform the types of intelligent operations that characterize the PC. Price points for the NC are envisioned to be less than $1,000 and substantially less than the long-standing price range standard for desktop computers—$2,500–$5,000. As conceived by Oracle's CEO, Larry Ellison, the NC will dramatically broaden the market for *Internet* users by virtue of its significantly lower price and will pave the way for the highly anticipated future of pervasive *e-commerce*. According to Ellison, the NC will become as ubiquitous as the TV, and in the process, create the kind of broad-based demand needed to support richly intelligent forms of software services across the *Web*. Naysayers of the NC contend that it is nothing more than the second coming of the *dumb terminal*, a type of computing device that was popular during the 1960s and 1970s when the only viable sources of machine intelligence were the mainframes; users accessed computing resources via terminals that possessed little or no local intelligence of their own. In this light, the NC is viewed as a step back, not forward. Naysayers also contend that the appetite for local intelligence—i.e., the kinds of software intelligence that characterize today's personal computers—is insatiable and will remain that way for some time to come. *Multimedia applications* such as *electronic games* and *edutainment* titles are among the many types of sophisticated programs that continue to push for greater capability on the desktop. Thus, as this argument goes, users will not be willing to step back to a less intelligence device even when lured by significantly lower prices.

NCSA: Stands for the National Center for Supercomputing Applications, which is at the University of Illinois at Urbana-Champaign—the birthplace of *Mosaic*. Founded in 1985 with a grant from *NSF* and additional funds from *DARPA*, NASA, corporate partners, the state of Illinois, and the University of Illinois, its mission is to develop and implement a national strategy to create, use, and transfer advanced computing and communication tools and information technologies. Its constituencies are in the areas of science, engineering, education, and business. NCSA released the first version of *Mosaic* in 1992 to give the first impetus to the "gold rush" on the *Internet*. Its Virtual Environment Laboratory is one of the world's most advanced *virtual reality (VR)* research laboratories available to academic and industrial researchers. The lab consists primarily of three projection-based modes of VR: the *CAVE* and the ImmersaDesk (developed by the Electronic Visualization Laboratory [*EVL*] at the University of Illinois at Chicago) and the Infinity Wall (developed by *EVL* in collaboration with NCSA and the University of Minnesota).

NDL: Stands for National Digital Library, which is an important *digital library* project funded by the U.S. Congress and the Library of Congress (LoC). This project is currently focused on digitizing *public domain* literary works and early photographs (and in so doing, avoiding complex issues of *copyright* and *intellectual property* ownership).

near-line storage: From the world of data storage, this term refers to a transitional form of storage between online and off-line media. It differs from online in one simple way: data is not processed directly from near-line devices. Rather, data is migrated from an *online storage* device to a near-line device when it is not needed and is brought back to the online device when needed. Near-line can be distinguished from *off-line storage,* such as traditional magnetic tape systems, in two ways. First, the media onto which the files have been placed is continuously and immediately available (or nearly so) to the end user. There is no need for personnel to fetch and mount the media. Second, no system administrator intervention is required to save files or to retrieve them from storage. Examples of near-line storage include the *optical juke box* and the *tape autoloader*. In the age of *multimedia*, where all forms of storage will be under severe pressure to increase capacity, this hybrid form of storage medium is apt to gain wide popularity if only as a stopgap measure until much higher capacity forms of online storage are made available.

netizen: Derived from the word "citizen," this term connotes the bundle of ethical, personal, and business behaviors that a heavy user of the *Web* needs to possess to be a positive contributor to life in *cyberspace*.

netiquette: Is the etiquette or common courtesy that should be used for polite interaction over the *Internet*.

Netscape Navigator: Is one of the most popular *Web browsers* on the *Internet.* It evolved from *NCSA's Mosaic,* which was developed by Marc Andreesen, among others. (Andreesen and Jim Clark founded *Mosaic* Communications, which was later changed to Netscape Communications.) Several improvements were made to the original *browser* design, such as increased speed and *interface* improvements, and considerable enhancements in functionality, including support for electronic mail, the ability to read *Usenet* news, and the provision of *RSA* encryption for secure communications. The Netscape browser also provides a number of other functionality enhancements, including the ability to load and then interrupt any one of multiple simultaneous text and image objects; native inline *JPEG* image display; the ability to display and interact with documents as they load; and multiple independent *windows*. *Navigator* was first released in October 1994, running on the X Window System with versions for the Mac, *Windows*, and *UNIX* operating environments. Along with Microsoft's *Internet Explorer*, it holds a major portion of the market share for *Web* browsers.

network: Put simply, a network is two or more computers linked together to share resources. Each computer on a network is a *node* connected by *transmission channels*. The term network is also commonly used to refer to the ensemble of hardware and software that connects a group of computers. A network may be private or public, and the physical connections may be facilitated by virtually any form of *transmission media* (see the entry for *cabling*). The *Internet* is a network of networks.

network adapter: Is a printed circuit *board* used to *interface* personal computers to some type of *LAN* (local area network). Also referred to as a "LAN adapter," this device plugs into the expansion *bus* of the PC. It uses a specialized processor and software routines to move data to and from the computer's memory over the *data bus* and to transmit and receive data across the *serial port* connecting the computer to the *network*.

network interface card: A network interface card, or *network adapter*, is a printed circuit *board* that is plugged into a computer. Any computer wishing to connect to a *network* must have one. It controls the exchange of data at the data *link* level or access method (see *OSI*). Network interface cards are connected by a *transmission medium* such as twisted-pair, coaxial, or *fiber optic cables*. On some computers, the network interface card may be an external device instead of a card.

network management: One of the more important forms of computer system applications, network management refers to the body of software system functionality responsible for monitoring and administering the *transmission* lines, computing devices, and peripherals that connect to form computer *networks.* On the typical network, the network management system will be *hosted* on a centralized *server* but will remain constantly in touch with most or all of the devices attached to the network through the operation of *agents* distributed across the *nodes* of the network. Working in concert with one another, these software elements gather statistics on the movement of data and watch for conditions that exceed programmed thresholds. If they detect a problem, they will issue some form of *alert* that can direct certain types of restart or rerouting actions and call for human assistance. To help perpetuate quality standards for the management of computer networks, manufacturers of network equipment have adopted several sets of standards such as *SNMP* for the operation of network management software.

Network Operating System (NOS): This is the software that enables computers to communicate with one another. Its tasks include locking files, allocating resources, controlling errors, responding to multiple requests concurrently, and maintaining security for a multi-user environment. Some network operating systems are self-contained, such as Novell NetWare; others run on top of a main operating system, such as *LAN* Manager on OS/2 or LANtastic on DOS.

neural network: Is a set of computer programs that attempts to emulate the way neurons perform in the human brain. Neural networks enable a computer to learn to recognize patterns in data similar to the way humans can learn to recognize patterns in real-world data. Examples of neural networks are stock futures timing applications, flight control applications, traffic flows, and speech communications applications. Programs that learn the way humans learn or that emulate the way humans learn are truly what is referred to as *artificial intelligence.*

Neuro-Baby: Created by Naoka Tosa of Fujitsu Laboratories in Japan, Neuro-Baby is a computer-generated 3-D character programmed to learn by using voice input and *neural network* software. It reacts to the tone and frequency of a person's voice and, for example, might cry or become angry if a person were to speak loudly to it. As such, this cutting edge technology represents one of the earliest attempts at the creation of an artificial personality.

neutral density filter: From the world of film and *video production*, this term describes a type of filter that is used to reduce the amount of light entering a lens. Because neutral density filters do not change the *hues* or relative intensities of the colors in a scene, they can be used without altering the appearance of what is seen. These filters are available in several degrees of density and are most often used to reduce the *exposure* of very bright scenes such as those that are *shot* in the midday sun.

newsgroup: This term refers to one of many thousands of topics in *Usenet*. It may be unmoderated, which means that anyone can post anything; or moderated, which means that submissions are sent to someone who edits and filters the messages before posting them to the group. Some moderated newsgroups are distributed as digests in which a number of submissions are grouped together with an index to form a single posting. Some newsgroups are available through parallel mailing lists to users who do not have access to that newsgroup.

NFS: Stands for Network File System, which is a *protocol* developed by Sun Microsystems that allows users to access remote files as though they were resident on their local computer. NFS has become a *de facto standard* incorporated into a multitude of products by more than a hundred companies. NFS and *FTP* are both transfer files; the difference between them is that FTP transfers entire files whereas NFS allows the user to transfer only the part required as it is needed. It uses a connectionless protocol (*UDP*) to make it stateless, which means that each request is treated as an independent transaction.

NIC: Stands for Network Information Center, which is any office that provides information for a *network*. *Internic* is the primary NIC for the *Internet*. An NIC provides information about software and support people who supply a set of services. Among their more prominent responsibilities, NIC personnel maintain documents and standards *archives*, and they assign *Internet addresses* and register *network* and *domain names* as well. They also provide "help desk" services for users and an information service providing *host* names and *addresses* accessible by computers using a particular *protocol*.

NII: Stands for National Information Infrastructure and is the officially sanctioned term of the Clinton administration for the so-called *information superhighway*. If the vision for NII is on target, this composite infrastructure of *fiber optic*, coaxial, and *wireless transmission* facilities plus the machine intelligence to manage it will play very big in the future of *multimedia*. The emerging medium of *interactive television*, for one, will be utterly dependent on the viability and vitality of the NII.

NNTP: Stands for Network News Transfer Protocol, which defines the format and procedures for communicating with *Usenet newsgroups*. NNTP defines procedures for distribution, inquiry, retrieval, and posting of *Usenet* news articles. It operates between a news reader and a news *server*. NNTP is an *ASCII* text *protocol*, which can be read without any special reader.

NOC: Stands for Network Operations Center. Its role is to monitor the network and locate and resolve connection problems.

node: Is a single computer attached to a *network* and represents the smallest addressable device on a network.

noise: In the media industry, this term refers to the interference a *signal* picks up as it is transmitted along an electronic circuit. "Static" on telephone lines and "snow" on TV screens are two common examples of noise. Originating from the lofty heights of information theory, noise refers to any random or unintentional form of information that gets embedded in a message and distracts or otherwise degrades the quality of that message.

noise gate: Used by audio engineers, this device makes it possible to erase all sound that registers above or beneath a specified level.

noninterlaced video: This is a high-quality form of *video* offered by many *video* digitizers wherein the original, *interlaced video signal* (a signal painted on the screen in two passes) is *buffered* into memory and merged into a single screen image before being displayed on the monitor. A near synonym is *progressive scanning*.

nonlinear video: This term is used in the *video* industry to describe the *random access* abilities afforded the producer when working in the *digital* format. Frequently used as an off-line tool, nonlinear video editing is a process whereby video is *digitized* in *real time* and stored on a hard *disk*. When video is placed in this *digital* format, the *editor* can go to any single point in the digitized video *sequence* without having to rewind or fast-forward through other material. You might entitle the story associated with this term "Hollywood Discovers Random Access."

NREN: Stands for the National Research and Education Network program, which was initiated as one of four components of the High-Performance Computing and Communications (HPCC) Act of 1991. It was formed to develop and implement multiple, *gigabyte*-capacity, interconnected computer *networks* and make them available to educational institutions and to the private sector, to facilitate the deployment of high-speed data communications in the United States.

NSF: Stands for the National Science Foundation, an independent U.S. government agency that funds science research projects and information technology infrastructure to improve the quality of scientific research. It invests over $3.3 billion per year in over 20,000 research and educational projects in science and engineering and has been an instrumental player in the evolution of the *Internet*.

NSFNet: Stands for the National Science Foundation Network, a high-speed hierarchical "network of networks" with three levels funded by the *NSF*. The highest level, or *backbone,* supports 16 *nodes* spanning the United States. Each backbone node has mid-level or transit nodes to which are attached campus and local *networks*. It also has connections to Canada, Mexico, Europe, and the Pacific Rim. It was the successor to *ARPANet* and served as the backbone for the *Internet* in its early days. It is still a key part of the Internet.

NTSC: Stands for National Television Standards Committee and is used most commonly to refer to the U.S. color *video* standard. This long-standing broadcast standard is represented by a 525-line screen running at a rate of 60 fields/30 frames per second and at a broadcast *bandwidth* of 4 MHz. Most people in the *multimedia* industry equate this acronym not only with the standard, but also with the level of image quality that is associated with television broadcasts.

NTSC safe colors: For those who are creating graphics on computer for eventual transfer to some form of television broadcast, this term refers to a set of constraints that limit the selection of colors to those that reproduce well on *video.*

NVOD: Stands for Near Video On Demand and represents one of the earliest interactive products to be offered through *interactive television*. Most industry analysts view NVOD as a temporary precursor to true *movies-on-demand* or *VOD*. The service will be characterized by movies staggered on multiple *channels* with enough copies always playing so that viewers will never wait more than a few minutes for their selection to start.

NVRAM: Stands for NonVolatile Random Access Memory and refers to a typically small portion of battery-powered computer RAM that is kept from losing its *digital* patterns when the computer is turned off. NVRAM is used to hold data of high priority, such as password information or key last-usage data. With the growing importance of long-play *video* games, NVRAM will be used increasingly to *bookmark* the progress of particular gaming sessions so that users can have the liberty of turning off their machines without having to restart an involved game when they return.

Artificial realities will have the same relationship to the real one that our homes have to the natural environment. Our homes are abstract spaces, partly defined by economics but primarily by our aesthetic sense.

—Myron Kreuger, Author

object-oriented programming: This is the new philosophy of programming. Rather than segregating software procedures from their associated data, as has been typical of the programming discipline for the bulk of its history, object-oriented programming encapsulates procedures and data into tightly structured entities that the industry now calls "objects." Though there are many benefits to this change in approach to *software engineering*, its most notable advantage is that it promotes the re-use of code. This is an enormous leap forward for the software industry, which has been historically characterized by the reinvention of almost every algorithmic wheel ad nauseum. Now, in the Valhalla promised by object-oriented programming, programmers build libraries of objects that can be passed on to both their colleagues and their heirs. Though the impact of object-oriented programming is global to the entire software industry, it has a very specific advantage within the *multimedia* industry: software *simulations* are far more easily coded when using an object-oriented approach. In fact, one of the original programming environments to enforce the various rules and constraints of object orientation was a language called "Simula," which was invented to aid in the creation of simulations by encouraging programmers to write pieces of encapsulated code (objects) that simulate objects in the real world.

OCLC: Stands for Online Computer Library Center. It is a nonprofit organization offering computer-based services and research to libraries, educational institutions, and their users. OCLC runs the PRISM service for cataloging and resource sharing, provides online reference systems for both librarians and end users, and distributes online electronic journals. OCLC manages a library *network* connecting more than 20,000 libraries worldwide providing interlibrary loans, bibliographic verification, and reference searching. This organization has been active in promoting standards for indexing *Internet resources*, a very important goal in view of the endemic *infoglut* that plagues the *Web* in today's environment. Most notably, OCLC hosted a conference in 1995 devoted to creating *metadata* standards for Internet resources. Named after the location of the conference (Dublin, Ohio), which is also the hometown of OCLC, a new standard known as the *Dublin Core* was born.

OCR: Stands for Optical Character Recognition, which is conceptually one of the most attractive and efficient methods for converting printed text to machine-readable character codes. An optical character reader scans a typewritten or printed document, stores it as a *bit-mapped* image, and then *converts* the letter shapes based on some form of *pattern recognition* into *ASCII* codes. OCR is far from being a perfected technology, owing to the difficulties associated with pattern matching against the broad range of font sizes and styles that make up our canon of printed materials. Hence, the typical functional specification for an OCR device will include its average error rate, i.e., the average number of times it will not properly interpret a scanned alphanumeric character.

off-line browsing: Refers to a *mode* of *browsing electronic content* that does not require a *network* connection at the time the *browsing* takes place. Most often associated with *push technology*, off-line browsing occurs after an online connection with a *content provider* (e.g., ABC-News.com) has resulted in a *download* of information to the user's computer. In this way, devices that are often detached from the network, such as laptop computers, can be used to browse popular electronic content even while the user is on the move.

off-line compression: Refers to an expensive, *CPU-intensive* form of *compression* that typically requires users to send their source *video* to a service that uses more sophisticated and time-consuming algorithms than are typically capable of being run on a PC. Off-line compression is the high-end, expensive part of the *codec* equation and is also described as an *asymmetrical codec* because it makes the compression side of handling *digital* video much more time consuming and expensive than the *decompression* side.

off-line editing: The first of two phases involved in *video* editing, the second being *online editing*. During the off-line phase, the *editor* reviews *footage*, makes edit decisions, prepares a *rough cut*, and compiles an *EDL* (edit decision list). As *desktop video production* becomes increasingly practical, many *production* houses are relying entirely upon PC-based video editing tools to carry them through the off-line phase.

off-line storage: A venerable form of mass data storage, off-line is distinguished from *online* and *near-line storage* in that it requires human intervention to make its store of contents accessible to users. By far, the most common form of off-line storage is magnetic tape. Typically, these tapes are stored on racks, and when a particular tape is needed an operator retrieves and mounts the tape on a reader that is online to the computer system. Off-line is impractical for any type of data needed on a frequent or regular basis. For this reason, it is reserved for use with a type of data management known as *archival storage*, where the information being stored is bulky and/or infrequently used. With the *mixed media data types* that characterize *multimedia,* the data sources are by definition bulky, so any indication that a particular source may not be regularly needed almost certainly ensures that it will be transferred to some form of off-line storage.

OLE: Stands for Object Linking and Embedding and refers to Microsoft's utility for *Windows,* which is designed to make interapplication data transfer easy to manage. OLE is intended to enable different applications to communicate and share information. In practice, this translates into the ability of users to construct *compound documents* because, for example, OLE makes it possible for a user to embed a *digital video* movie in a word processor without requiring that the word processor have any native video capabilities. OLE is designed to work in such a way that it is up to one application (called the source document) to take the responsibility for the overall structure of the compound document, while the other contributing applications participate by owning sections of the structure. Once the user has created a *link* to an object located in another application, that user need only double-click on the section in which it is located to invoke any of the needed functionality from its parent application.

OMG: Stands for Object Management Group, which is a consortium of over four hundred computer and software companies formed to create standards associated with the *object-oriented programming* paradigm. Founded in 1990, this group has been responsible for several important standards, probably the most important of which is *CORBA,* the common object request broker architecture.

one-to-one: This is an adjective for describing one of the keenest hopes for our Web-enabled future: the notion of precision marketing. It is the idea that, through the two-way interactive communication capabilities of the *Web,* sellers of mass market products will be able to develop highly personalized relationships with each one of their customers. Thus, automated systems will be able to accurately trace the identity of information requests made to their organization's *Web site(s),* correlate those requests to known patterns of buying, augment these findings with brief and unobtrusive customer surveys, and deduce from all these information sources the precise type and mix of products that each individual customer wants and needs. Anticipated by Alvin Toffler's work, "The Third Wave," the business vision of one-to-one marketing predicts an era in which our economy will be enriched by the mass customization of products and services.

online editing: This term refers to the second of two phases involved in *video* editing, the first being *off-line editing.* During the online phase, the *EDL* (edit decision list) is loaded into an editing system that controls the "playback" and "record" decks. The editing system automatically assembles the final *production* by dubbing the video and audio *sequences* selected from the playback deck onto the record deck. For most broadcast quality productions, producers still rely upon the high-end equipment found only in traditional video production suites. The day approaches, however, when even online editing is done using a PC.

online services: Prior to the blossoming of the *Internet,* online services provided the first commercial networked communities. Services such as Prodigy and CompuServe were among the first online services, and were followed into the electronic marketplace by AOL (America Online) and Microsoft Network. Today, these services provide Internet access, but they also provide private content, which is carried on a separate *network* and is only available to members. Though many Internet users have elected not to pay for these services, they hold several advantages over the plain old *Web.* They are better organized, more secure, regulated, easier to *navigate,* and simpler to install.

online storage: This is the most immediate form of long-term (permanent) storage. A file storage medium must meet two criteria to be considered "online." First, data must be processed directly from the medium, that is, it must be directly accessible to the computer's internal memory (RAM). Second, there should be no operator or user intervention required to access the medium. In today's world, magnetic *disk* is still the most common type of online storage owing to its relatively large capacity, fast access, and data transfer speeds. As *multimedia* continues to exert its voracious appetite for mass storage, the hegemony of the magnetic disk is increasingly threatened by optical *disc* and magnetic tape technologies. Both of these forms of storage can be configured as online media, though they both suffer from decisively slower access and transfer speeds than those associated with magnetic disks.

OPAC: This acronym stands for Online Public Access Catalog, which is a part of our emerging *information superhighway* that provides a place where schools, libraries, media centers, and other institutions can hook up via *modem* to obtain information.

OpenGL: Short for Open Graphics Library, this is an industry standard *API* developed by Silicon Graphics for defining 2-D and *3-D* graphics. OpenGL enables the first form of *platform* independent creation of sophisticated graphics and digital video effects (*DVE*).

optical carrier levels: Also referred to by the acronym OCx, this term refers to the *signal* rate multiples used by *SONET* for transmitting *digital signals* over *fiber optic cable*. The base rate is OC-1, which is 51.85 *Mbps*. All other rates are multiples of OC-1, such that OC-3 is 155.52 Mbps and OC-12 is 622.08 *Mbps*. Given the insatiable appetite for *bandwidth* that is being promoted by the use of *multimedia* technologies and the *Web*, the demand for and popularity of the optical carrier levels is apt to grow quickly.

optical fiber transmission: This term refers to the increasingly critical technology that makes possible the rapid and relatively distortion-free *transmission* of information through fine optical fibers (*fiber optic cable*). With this *transmission medium, digital* data is transmitted as a series of on-off pulses of light representing *bits* of information.

optical juke boxes: These are also known as *juke boxes* and provide large volumes of *near-line storage* that can be used for handling such demanding mass storage applications as large *clip media* libraries.

optical memory: This general term is used to describe forms of storage that rely upon the fundamentals of light, rather than that of magnetics, to record and retrieve *digital* information. *CD-ROM, DVD*, and their ancestor *laserdisc* are the most common forms of optical memory. This type of memory is known for its much greater capacity, a feat made possible by the use of high-precision *laser* beams but suffers in reputation for its slow *transfer rates* and lack of writability.

optical printer: From the world of film and *video production*, this is a machine that is a combination of a projector and a camera. Generally speaking, it is used to combine live action and *animation* and to make fades, *dissolves*, and *wipes*. These devices are also capable of creating split screens, skipping *frames* and superimposing text on film, and rotating *shots* and creating multi-*exposure* scenes. Optical printers are the devices most responsible for creating all sorts of special effects in the *analog video* world. As we move toward an all-*digital* world, however, the importance of these machines may eventually wane.

optical storage: By all indications, optical storage may rapidly become the dominant storage medium in the era of *multimedia* technology. Optical *discs* offer two advantages over other forms of mass storage: they have large storage capacities; and they are removable, providing users with access to many discs per drive. Both of these advantages owe to the fact that optical storage devices use a *laser* instead of a magnetic field to make marks on the medium. Given the vast storage requirements demanded by *multimedia applications* (e.g., *video*, audio, and image), optical storage may grow in parallel with the adoption of *multimedia* technology.

Orange Book: Related to the *Red Book* and *Yellow Book* standards for *compact disc*, this term refers to a set of standards that specify how information is to be organized on compact discs. The Orange Book defines standards that enable the user to write audio and/or data to the *disc*. There are two parts to this standard: 1) compact disc-magneto optical (CD-MO), where data can be written, erased, and rewritten; and 2) compact disc-write once (CD-WO), where data can be written but not erased.

org: Is a top-level *domain* name used by nonprofit organizations on the *Internet*.

organic video effects: This emerging class of *DVE* (digital video effects) simulates natural phenomena as a way of transitioning from one *video shot* or scene to the next. Examples include breaking glass or pouring liquids (e.g., the last shot of one scene breaks apart like broken glass revealing underneath it the first shot of the next scene).

OSI: Stands for Open Systems Interconnection, and is the name given to the architectural model for communications defined by the *ISO* (International Standards Organization). Its primary purpose is to promote standards for data communications throughout the industry. The standards specify the *interfaces* between pieces of hardware and/or software in the form of *protocols* such that if one manufacturer designs products that comply with the OSI model, those products will work with any other manufacturer's products so long as they are also compliant with the model. Thus, a system of mutual compliance is created in which buyers can create their own optimal solutions even though that strategy might lead them to buy from several different vendors.

This OSI model contains seven layers used for comparing and defining computer *network* architectures. The seven-protocol layers provide increasingly fine or detailed definition of the work to be done as a piece of information descends from top to bottom through the seven layers. Thus, when an application generates a request for input from a remote computer, this request is treated first at the top layer, which is also called layer 7 or the application layer. The request is then passed down layer by layer to the lowest level or layer 1, which initiates transfer to the network. It is passed to the destination computer where it is successively processed in reverse order up the layers to the application at the receiving end.

Starting from the top, the seven layers and their functions are as follows:

7. Application: The application layer generates the functional meaning of the transaction, e.g., open file, retrieve data, execute remote job, etc.

6. Presentation: The presentation layer negotiates and manages the data format. It acts as a *bridge* between different formats such as *ASCII* and EBCDIC or different floating point and binary formats. It is also used for *encryption* and decryption.

5. Session: The *session layer* coordinates communication between two parties like a traffic director. It specifies one-way or two-way communication, ensures that a request has been fulfilled before the next one is sent, and marks checkpoints for fast error recovery. In practice, the functions of this layer are not always used or they are fulfilled by the next layer down, the transport layer (4).

Layers 1–4 are collectively known as the "OSI transport services" and together they ensure that messages are delivered completely and error free.

4. Transport: The transport layer ensures the validity and integrity of the data from source to destination. If 12 *Mbps* are sent, then this layer will work to ensure that 12 *Mbps* are received correctly.

3. Network: The network layer establishes the route between the sending and receiving stations. Whereas layers 3–7 may or may not be used from one situation to the next, layers 1 and 2 are required for all communications over a network.

2. Data Link: The data link layer manages the *node*-to-node validity and integrity of the data. The entire stream of *bits* is cut into *frames* as appropriate for the particular network, such as *Ethernet*, Token Ring, or *FDDI*.

1. <u>Physical</u>: The physical layer passes *bits* to and receives data from the *transmission medium*. It is concerned exclusively with the physical characteristics, electrical or mechanical, of the *signals* and signaling methods.

out of sync: This phrase is used to describe a sound *track* running either ahead of or behind the picture.

outernet: Is a *network* or bulletin board that interacts with the *Internet* through a *gateway*.

output devices: This general computer term refers to devices that draw, print, photograph, or otherwise display the information generated by a computer.

outtake: In film, this is a scene rejected by the director.

overhead: The resources required to run a system that do not contribute to the functional purpose of that system. Car insurance is overhead to running a car. On computer systems, overhead can take several forms: space used by the operating system, processing time used for system management functions, and extra *bytes* added to *transmissions* for routing, error control, or *network* status.

overlay: From the realm of *digital video*, this term refers to the process of combining computer-generated graphics with video *signals*. It is particularly useful for adding text on top of the video image, such as when the identity of an on-screen speaker is written over the image, or when the credits are listed at the end of a motion picture.

The kinds of tasks that computers perform for us require that they express two distinctly anthropomorphic qualities: responsiveness and the capacity to perform actions.
—**Brenda Laurel, Author**

packet: From the world of *data communications*, this term refers to a way of organizing data for *transmission* in which the target data (the actual information that the user is sending) is "embedded," or placed, between sets of header and trailer information. These headers and trailers identify key attributes of the enclosed, or "packetized" data, including the *address* of the packet's destination and sender, error control information, request for services, and sequencing information when packets need to be recombined at the destination.

packet switching: With respect to *data communications*, this form of *transmission* is favored for its flexibility over its most common rival, *circuit switching*. Packet switching works by breaking data down into small chunks called *packets*. Because these packets contain addressing and sequencing information, they make it possible to break large files into relatively small units that can be routed across the *network* over different pathways depending upon the ever-changing and shifting availability of *bandwidth*. Thus, packet switching accommodates peak loads in one part of the network by rerouting packets over alternate pathways. Because of sequencing information in the packets, some packets can even arrive at their destination before their predecessors, and the packet switching system will simply resequence the packets into their original order. This flexibility makes packet switching a very popular way of handling data communications. When it comes to transmitting the extremely large and time-sensitive files associated with *digital video*, however, packet switching is often untenable because the processing overhead and network irregularities associated with routing and reassembling the packets can disrupt the video stream.

packet-switched network: This is a *network* that shares communication resources by routing *packets* among the *hosts* attached to it.

paint systems: This is the generic name for computer art systems that produce *bit-mapped* graphic images. They generally are *pixel* oriented, and the artist creates pictures with them by setting pixels to specific color values. Most paint systems are driven by some form or combination of *pointing devices* (e.g., *mouse, graphics tablet*), and provide, at a minimum, functions for changing *brush* size and shape; changing and merging the colors provided by the system's standard *palette;* and cutting, pasting, and merging one *bit map* with others. Paint systems are often held in contrast to *draw systems* that manipulate *structured graphics* (also called *vector* graphics)—mathematically represented objects such as lines, boxes, and circles.

PAL: Stands for Phase Alternating Line and is the TV *signal* encoding counterpart to the North American *NTSC* (National Television Standards Committee) standard. PAL is used in Great Britain, most of Europe, Africa, Australia, South America, and China.

palette: With reference to graphical user interface (*GUI*) design, a palette is a collection of small symbols, usually enclosed in rectangles, which offers the user a quick, visually cued method for switching between a host of related functions. The symbols used to represent the various functions can be *icons*, patterns, characters, or drawings that stand for their respective operations. This term is also used in its more traditional sense with *paint systems* to refer to the particular mix of colors that are available to the computer artists as they create pieces of computer art.

palmtop computer: Referring to a miniaturized version of a personal computer, this term is roughly synonymous with personal digital assistants (*PDAs*). In keeping with their names, these devices possess a *form factor* that enables them to be comfortably held in a single hand. Typically, they feature PIM-type software applications, such as *address* books and calendars. Increasingly, these devices have direct access to the *Internet* through *wireless connections.*

pan: Short for *panorama*, this term refers both to a *shot* where the camera sweeps across a given area, thereby giving the audience a panoramic *view* of the film subject; and to a shot where, in contrast to a *zoom*, the camera pulls away from its subject, thereby placing that subject in its larger social or natural context. As a form of cinematic language, the pan is often used at the beginning or end of a major film segment to place the subject against the larger *backdrop* of its setting. Increasingly, both forms of panning are becoming a part of *desktop video production* systems, which means, of course, that they can be achieved by merely issuing a single command.

parallel processing: Perhaps the next generation in computer design, parallel processing refers to a form of processing where more than one processor is devoted to executing the same program simultaneously, or in parallel. Based on a half-century history of computing, we have come to think of the *CPU*—the brains of the computer—as a single, serial processing device. Although this single device has undergone a steady increase in size and speed, it is still a serial processor, which means it can only execute one instruction at a time. Advocates of parallel processing insist that a wiser direction for many applications is that of having many small processors work in parallel. With the huge file sizes and *codec* processing requirements of *digitized* media, parallel processing seems ideally suited for many of the computing tasks associated with *multimedia*. In fact, many of today's chip developers are hard at work creating the next generation of chips for the multimedia era, and many of their efforts are focused on creating "on-chip parallelism," whereby groups of small processors team up to do such inherently parallel tasks as *decompressing* a screen's *pixel* map of incoming *digital video*.

parallel protocols: This term describes the emerging standard for *multimedia* networking in which two *network protocols* coexist on the same physical *network*. Historically speaking, *contention protocols*, which handle the *bursty traffic* associated with traditional alphanumeric data, have always exsited. More recently, and with the appearance of *mixed media data types*, new *stream management* protocols are being used with the large, continuously flowing streams of data necessary to play compressed *digital video* or other high-*bandwidth* audiovisual data types.

parallel transmission: This term is used to refer to a *mode* of data transfer in which all 8 *bits* of a *byte* are transmitted simultaneously over parallel communication lines (such as the ribbon cable found inside many computers). This form of *transmission* is typically held in contrast to serial transmission, where data are communicated over a single communication line one bit at a time.

parity: This term refers to a classical method of checking for computer errors that occur during data *transmission*. There are two types of parity checking, odd or even. This very simple method uses an extra *bit* in the encoded message of a data transmission to validate that either an odd or even number of bits have been transmitted. If the encoded message does not conform, then an error condition is established, indicating that the message has been corrupted.

parse: From the realm of *software engineering*, this term refers to the very common practice of scanning a list or sequential file of uncertain length, one character or element at a time, to determine its contents. Thus, for example, the common word processor accessories known as spell checkers typically work by parsing the text files to seek out misspelled words.

party-line games: This is a type of online interactive game that is played over a *network* by two or more players.

PAS: Stands for Performance Animation System, which is an object-oriented software toolkit developed by SimGraphics that enables developers to create *real time* character-animation applications. It is an authoring tool for creating *digital puppet* applications.

pass-through video: This term refers to a way of presenting *video* on a computer in which the video *signal* is not handled by (or integrated with) the computer's graphics subsystem, but rather is simply passed through to the computer's monitor in its original *analog* format. Pass-through video is the simplest form of computer-related video technology.

patch: With respect to *wave table synthesis*, which is the highest quality technology now associated with *MIDI* (musical instrument digital interface) synthesizers, this term refers to one of the individual sound recordings that occupy the synthesizer's table of sounds. Most patches represent recordings of musical instruments, but, owing to the 128-patch size of the *MPC* (multimedia personal computer) standard, most wave tables also include noninstrumental sounds such as applause, gun shots, and such esoterica as the "space voice" sound. The group of sounds that go into making up a particular wave table are often referred to as that player's "patch set."

pattern recognition: This term refers to the recognition of shapes and patterns by machine systems. As computing becomes increasingly visual, this form of machine intelligence will continue to take on a correspondingly heightened importance. Ultimately, the computer may be able to recognize individual faces, and thus be able to recognize people by sight.

PBX: Stands for Private Branch eXchange, a relatively high-end piece of communications hardware designed to manage large numbers of telephonic connections, usually between the denizens of a single office building and the rest of the world. This term has gained renewed popularity, because the device that it describes is being used as an analogy for *data communications* hardware that is now coming to market for use by cable operators to offer *movies-on-demand* services (hence, *video* PBX) to their residential clientele.

PCI: This term stands for Peripheral Component Interconnect and represents an open standard for *local bus* developed by Intel. Like other local *bus* technologies, PCI has been developed to help eliminate the inevitable bottlenecks that occur on traditional *ISA bus* personal computers when they attempt to move *mixed media data types* between the computer and its peripherals.

PCX: This venerable graphics file format is a *bit map*, or *raster file,* format that was originally the native format of the PC Paintbrush graphics development program. Paintbrush is a program now owned by Microsoft, and it is still offered as a utility program to all MS-DOS or MS *Windows* users—which, of course, accounts for its widespread use. Owing to both its age and its position in the mainstream of *desktop* computing, the PCX format has been revised numerous times over the years to keep pace with the continual enhancement of PC displays.

PDA: Stands for Personal Digital Assistant and represents a broad class of handheld personal computers (*HPC*) that many critics believe represent the next logical progression of the personal computing revolution. These devices will rely heavily on *wireless* forms of *transmission*, and will certainly grow to increasing levels of *multimedia* capability as they evolve. The Apple Newton was one of the early examples of a PDA. Personal digital assistants provide a form of *data communications* that is free from the *spatial* constraints of the computer or the telephone, enabling users to carry on data-processing activities anywhere they happen to be.

PDF: Stands for Portable Document Format, a file format (analogous to *HTML*) that can handle document file formats from a variety of *desktop* publishing applications. The PDF format was developed by Adobe Systems, which also developed the Adobe Acrobat Reader (similar to an HTML *browser*) to interpret and display PDF files. The Adobe Acrobat Reader is available for free from Adobe Systems. PDF is a flexible format for representing various types of files independent of the operating *platform* or software application. A PDF file can contain text, graphics, and images in a device-independent and *resolution*-independent format. PDF allows for a wide variety of fonts and colors.

peak cell rate: Also referred to as "PCR," this is the maximum *transmission* speed of an *ATM* connection as measured in *cells.*

pen plotter: This is a type of electronic drawing, or "plotting," device that works by moving a robotic pen carriage over a recording surface (paper, for example). The two basic types of pen plotter are *flatbed* and *drum*.

perceptual asymptotes: This term was coined by the French film theorist Andre Bazin. It refers to the process by which various media continue to be improved and refined in terms of the amount of information they deliver until they reach a point at which they exceed the human capacity to process that particular type of information. Once they reach that point, or asymptote, there is no further need to improve the information carrying capacity of the medium. The classic modern example of a perceptual asymptote has to do with CD audio, which, at a *sampling rate* of 44 MHz, has been refined to the point where it exceeds the capacity of the human ear to discern any further enhancements. Long since gone, Bazin was a true visionary, foreseeing the general tendency for all media to continuously add capability until they reach the limits of human perception.

perfect sound: This term was coined in the world of audio engineering to describe manufactured sound that cannot be distinguished from real sound, or speaking more generally, copies of an original that cannot be distinguished from that original.

performance animation: An outgrowth of research efforts in *virtual reality*, this term refers to a form of *animation* wherein the performance of the animated character is tied directly to the *real time* movements of an actual human. The technique relies upon human performers wearing special motion-tracking devices to drive all of an animated character's movements and expressions, including all of the mouth movements.

performance support system: Though it has not quite earned the status of an acronym (PSS) yet, this term is gaining ground as a concept for how to electronically structure an organization's information and training resources. A PSS is a computer-based system that provides on-the-job access to integrated information, advice, and learning experiences, thus improving worker productivity. Owing to their expansive goals, PSSs have numerous components and are actually starting to spawn their own vocabulary: they include advisory systems, *hypermedia* information bases, and libraries of *tutorials* and other indexed learning experiences. The central dream of PSS is to offer embedded, or just-in-time, training, giving workers just what they need, nothing more than they need, and all of this at precisely the moment they need it.

performance tracking: From the world of *educational software*, this term represents a concept that ranges from simple *answer analysis* (the learner answered a questioned correctly, or not) all the way to complex systems that track performance over long periods of time and across broad spans of curricula. In most cases, performance tracking is achieved by simply recording the learner's responses to various questions, and then by subjecting the accumulation of those responses to some form of analysis. With gaming software, tracking is a bit more indirect than it is in instructional situations, but basically it operates by assessing and then recording how well the user is responding to the game's central challenge. In many respects, the high end of performance tracking is akin to creating a database of someone's school transcripts and test results. The difference, though, is that by converting this, or any far-reaching span of performance data, into a machine-readable format, it makes it possible for the *instructional designer* to build sophisticated instructional systems. Using these long-term performance data, an instructional system can perform such sophisticated tasks as *strand management*, where specific content, and styles of presentation for treating that content, are matched to the user's diagnosed needs. This, in turn, helps the designer deliver on the long-sought promise of individualized instruction— *courseware* that analyzes learner need and prescribes instructional sequences that are specifically suited to meet that need. In large measure, performance tracking must be considered one of the frontiers of *interactive multimedia* and *instructional technology* because it represents the vanguard of *software engineering* efforts that seek to understand the needs of specific users.

persistence: A term used frequently in the domain of *object-oriented programming*, it refers to the ability of objects to persist through multiple sessions. For example, if data created during the running of a program do not last (persist) after the program session is terminated, then the data do not possess the characteristic of *persistence*. In contrast, data that do survive between sessions are persistent.

persistence of vision: From the realm of human perception, this term refers to the illusion of smooth, continuous motion that people experience when viewing *animation* or *video*. This illusion is created when the *sequence* of *frames* is played back rapidly enough that the viewer cannot discern the differences that exist between the individual images.

persistent connection: This is the type of *network* connection that remains intact even when users are away from their computers. The purpose of this type of connection is to facilitate the more or less continuous background updates that occur when one subscribes to a *push technology* vendor across the *Web*.

personal newspaper: Like *personal television*, this concept was developed at the *Media Lab*, courtesy of its founder, Nicholas Negroponte. Now a popular concept for the next *interface paradigm* (beyond the *desktop metaphor*, that is), the personal newspaper exploits the familiarity of the newspaper to present information in headline-and-column format that has been tailored to the individual's needs. As now conceived, the tailoring will be done by *intelligent software agents*, which are programs that self-navigate the *information superhighway* in search of information items that meet the needs and preferences of the individual. In its full-blown future—if that ever comes to pass—the contents of the personal newspaper will be *multimedia*, with the actual delivery medium for any given piece of information being determined by which one is best suited for that particular piece. Thus, for an essay written by, say, Tom Wolfe, the delivery medium would be plain old text. For an item that reports some sort of natural disaster, any *video footage* that is available would naturally be employed and would be shown in the type of window now used by the traditional newspaper for still images (a.k.a. photos).

personal television: A concept invented at the *Media Lab*, this is a future version of the television projected to operate by culling from public media sources just those items that are of personal interest to the viewer. The device will be programmed with an individual's information and entertainment needs and preferences. It will possess a soft copy of one's media profile. This information will be used to scan the mass of public media sources to construct a personal viewing *menu*. Personal television is already starting to take shape on the *Web*. With the concept of the *cookie*, which profiles user preferences, in conjunction with *push technology*, which provides customized data feeds to subscribers based on the contents of their cookies, the future may be closer than we think.

PGP: Stands for Pretty Good Privacy. It is one of the most secure *encryption* programs available for protecting *e-mail* and data files. Written by Phillip Zimmerman, it uses a public key encryption algorithm, called the International Data Encryption Algorithm, in conjunction with a random session key, and uses the *RSA* algorithm to encrypt the session key. PGP is available as *freeware,* or a low-cost commercial version can be purchased. The freeware version can be used for personal purposes, but cannot be used for commercial gain. If one wishes to use PGP in a business context, then the commercial version must be obtained from *Network Associates*. To use PGP, you either *download* the program or purchase it, and then you install it on your computer. Typically, it will contain a user *interface* that works with most popular *e-mail* programs. After installing the program, you must register your public key with a PGP public-key *server* so that the people you communicate with are able to find your public key. Network Associates also maintains a very popular public key server. PGP runs on all major *platforms*, is well featured and fast, with sophisticated key management (i.e., no secure *channels* are needed to exchange keys between users), *digital* signatures, data *compression*, and good *usability* design. A user guide exists in two volumes. In 1994, the U.S. Government prosecuted Phillip Zimmerman for exporting the PGP software from the United States. This case was of wide legal interest because all he did was post PGP to a bulletin board. The government hoped to establish that posting on a bulletin board, or *BBS*, was the equivalent of exporting. The case was dropped in 1996.

phong shading: This is one of the high-end forms of *polygon shading* associated with computer-generated graphics. Use of this technique can create extremely realistic computer images.

phosphor: One of the fundamental elements of *video* display technology, this term refers to the luminescent substance that is arrayed on the inside of the cathode-ray tube (*CRT*) display. When the electron gun of the CRT scans the array of phosphors, they are illuminated to form the patterns that are the video image.

photosensor: This device is capable of converting light energy to electrical energy. A common use of photosensors is to serve as the conversion mechanism that links *fiber optic transmission* to computing devices.

phototexturing: From the world of computer graphics, this sophisticated graphics technique is used extensively in *DTM* (digital terrain modeling) and works by draping real photos and satellite imagery over *polygon*al terrain data. It is heavily used for adding realism to *simulations* that incorporate a substantial amount of terrain scenery.

physics-approximate simulation: Is a form of computer *simulation* wherein models of the real world are created from a library of algorithms based on Newtonian physics. The term was coined by Marvin Minsky, considered one of the fathers of *artificial intelligence* and a visionary with respect to the future of technology.

pick-up: From the world of audio engineering, this term refers to one of the most common and simplest of recording devices, an electromagnet that *captures* acoustic vibrations and *converts* them to electrical *signals*.

PICT: This is a standard *bit-mapped* graphic file format for the Apple Macintosh.

picture planes: In seeking to understand how *multimedia applications* manipulate the screen, it is important to realize that most programs make use of a set of picture planes, arranged one behind the other. Today's standard is four planes: At the frontmost position is the *cursor plane*, a small area of up to 16 x 16 *pixels* that holds the current position of the *cursor*. Behind the cursor are two image planes, known as the *front plane* and *back plane*, respectively. These are the two most active and important planes and are used for executing most *DVE* (digital video effects), particularly the large subclass of *digital* effects known as *two-plane effects*. At the backmost position, behind these two center planes, is the plane referred to as the *backdrop*, which usually holds items such as screen background colors.

picturephone: Most communications experts believe that this term represents the next phase in remote, point-to-point, human communications. Early prototypes are already appearing that transmit *quasi-video* (very small screen sizes at very low *frame rates*).

PIM: Stands for Personal Information Manager, a type of software application responsible for helping individuals handle personal forms of data, such as names and *addresses*, phone numbers, and calendars. In recent years, PIM software has become strongly associated with *PDAs* (personal digital assistants), though software from this category is commonly used on all forms of personal and *desktop* computers.

PING: Stands for Packet InterNet Grouper, which is a *UNIX* program that sends a *network* message and waits for a reply. It has several uses, all of which are associated with testing aspects of network connections. It tests whether a certain computer is active on a network. "Ping tests" are used to help debug data *links* and the network layers of a connection. They are also used to produce network diagnostics by tracing the route from one computer to another.

pinna: This anatomical term refers to the soft, shell-like mass of skin that surrounds the ear. Psychoacoustic research in the area of *HRTF* (head-related transfer functions) has determined that the pinna plays a major role in the listener's perception of the direction from which sounds are emanating. Consequently, efforts to digitally *encode* and create *3-D sound* have begun to take stock of this role, often referred to as the "pinna effect."

PIP: Stands for Picture-In-Picture, a term that represents the migration of software *windows* concepts from the realm of personal computing to the world of television. Simply put, PIP is the appearance on a television screen of more than one *channel* at a time, a feat made possible by the creation of an on-screen window that overlays a portion of the current channel while playing *host* within its confines to a second channel.

pistol grips: This is a new form of input device being employed in proto-typical interactive movie theaters whereby the interactive moviegoer can vote on such issues as plot outcome.

pitch: From the world of sound engineering, this term refers to the repre-sentation of a sound wave's *frequency*, which is typically expressed in cycles per second. The higher the pitch, the higher the frequency of the sound waves.

pits and lans: For better or worse, the evolution of optical technology has ensured that these two terms are bound together for all time. They de-scribe the way in which binary (*digital*) information is *encoded* onto the surfaces of *optical storage* media. Simply put, pits are microscopic holes that are etched into the surface of an optical platter, while lans are areas that remain flat because they are not so etched. These two surfaces rep-resent the +'s and -'s of binary data of the *digital* world. When a *laser* beam is shone off of a pit it bounces back as a different value than when that laser beam is shone off of the flat surface of a lan.

pixel: This term was first coined to describe the smallest unit of a *video* screen and is a contraction of the phrase "picture element." With respect to *video* screens, the term refers to the small dots that, when taken alto-gether, make up the visual image that appears on the screen. The term's use has been recently expanded to describe the smallest elements of any system that represents data in the form of 2-D arrays of visual informa-tion (e.g., fax machines, copiers, *laser* printers). The term is typically used to describe the *resolution* or image quality of such devices (e.g., 480 x 640 *pixels* for *VGA* monitors—the higher the number, the higher or better the resolution).

pixel hold: From the world of *DVE* (digital video effects), this term refers to one of two types of effect that are known together as *mosaic effects*. Pixel hold works by extending the color and tone (*chrominance* and *luminance*) from one *pixel* to its neighbors in a process that continues until the screen appears to break up into a gathering of extremely coarse and hazy blocks.

pixel pusher: This is the insider term for a computer graphics artist.

pixel repeat: From the world of *DVE* (digital video effects), this term refers to one of two types of effect that are known together as *mosaic effects*. Pixel repeat works by *zooming* in on a portion of the screen, but without providing the additional detail needed to keep the on-screen image well focused. Thus, as the target portion of the screen continues to be enlarged, the image itself appears to be getting coarser, or more out of focus.

pixel thinning: Is a technique for compressing an image—thereby reducing its *bandwidth* requirements—by systematically discarding certain classes of *pixel*.

pixellation: One of the primary *artifacts* of *digital* forms of *video*, pixellation is the mosaic-like effect obtained by *zooming* in on portions of a *bit-mapped* image.

platform: Also known as "delivery platform," this term refers to the combination of hardware and software components that are assembled to deliver some sort of *multimedia application*. Because the industry is still so young, single devices that integrate all of the devices in a way that is transparent to the user have only recently appeared. And, for the most demanding *multimedia applications*, it is still often necessary to build a platform by assembling components, such as high-*resolution* monitors, *joysticks, video* drivers, and *DVD* players. In time, most industry experts believe that one or more single-device, integrated solutions will emerge. In fact, most believe that the *interactive television* (ITV) will be just such a device. When the ITV appears, we may no longer have to bother with this term.

platform strategy: Owing to the volatility in the *multimedia* hardware and software markets, most sane developers of *multimedia applications* devise a platform strategy very early in their design process. This strategy specifies the *platform*, or range of *platforms*, that the planned product will be able to run on. The growth of multimedia on the *Internet* adds a new element to this consideration. Due to the wide variety of potential configurations that may be found on the user (or client) end, developers must engineer mechanisms into their applications that address this unforeseeable range of differences as best they can. The specific identity and version of *browser* and the availability of *plug-in modules* are just two of the client-side variables that must be considered when developing a platform strategy for a Web-enabled multimedia application.

playfield: In the world of *electronic game design*, this term refers to the on-screen portion of the game *interface* where the action of the game takes place.

play-life: An important design attribute of *electronic games*, this term refers to the amount of play time the typical game player will enjoy with a particular game. Some games lose their allure after only a few hours of play, while others seem to provide almost endless enjoyment.

play-mechanic: In the world of *electronic game design*, this term refers to the actions, or series of actions, the player must perform to operate the game. It is also known as the *routine-of-play*, and more or less defines the rules of the game.

plug-and-play: High on the lexical scale of wish fulfillment, this term refers to the notion that getting a PC peripheral to operate as advertised should demand no more effort than that required to pull the device out of its box and plug it into the computer. As most PC users would attest, this is hardly the case. Compatibility problems riddle the PC industry, and often the most difficult part of acquiring a new peripheral—say, a *laser* printer, a *DVD* player, or a *scanner*—is just getting the _____ thing to work in the first place. To achieve the dream of plug-and-play, PC hardware and peripheral devices must be automatically configured by the operating system. The Macintosh environment has typically been credited with doing a better job of this than the PC (MS *Windows*), a tendency that owes to the stronger enforcement of software and *interface* standards that Apple can ensure because it controls the manufacture of both the hardware and the operating system. The lack of plug-and-play as an industry characteristic will be a nagging obstacle to the evolution of the *multimedia* market.

plug-in module: Often, well-constructed, or just plain popular, software, packages attract further development from third-party software developers, who seize the opportunity to enrich the target package by building some set of functions that that program is missing. For example, a *paint system* that is well received and popular might, for some unknown reason, be missing a good library of *fill* patterns (e.g., *radial fills, gradient fills*, etc.). A smart, third-party software developer might take advantage of this opportunity by filling that gap with a good library of fills, even before the original software manufacturer does. When this occurs, the gap-filling piece of software is often referred to as a plug-in module, indicating that the customer can simply plug the expanded functionality into the existing package without worrying about any compatibility problems. This term has become more important than ever with the advent of the *Web*, where *browsers* must frequently be updated and augmented with plug-ins to even run particular applications.

PLV: Stands for Production-Level Video and refers to one of two standard *video file* formats that comprise Intel's *DVI* (Digital Video Interactive) technology. PLV is a high-quality format that relies upon an *asymmetrical, interframe codec* that, like the *MPEG* (Motion Picture Experts Group) standard, demands a time-consuming and expensive encoding process. PLV stands in contrast to *RTV* (real-time video), the inexpensive, *intraframe* portion of the DVI *codec* canon.

PNG: Stands for Portable Network Graphics, which is a graphics format. PNG provides a well-defined format standard, freely available, for graphics with good *compression*. It was designed to replace the *GIF* format, thereby eliminating some of that standard's limitations, such as its inability to accommodate more than 256 colors. PNG was created in reaction to the decision by UNISYS, the holder of the patent for the GIF format, to start charging licensing fees seven years after Compuserve had made GIF freely available to the public.

point of demarcation: From the world of telecommunications, this term refers to the physical point where the phone company ends its responsibility for the wiring of phone lines.

pointer: A widely used programming technique, a pointer is a statement within a computer program that "points" to the location of another statement. Pointers are employed abundantly in such data structures as *VTOC*s (volume tables of contents), where they are used to point to the starting *addresses* of the files located on a particular storage device. In *hypermedia* programs, the *hyperlinks* that connect one portion of the document to another are, essentially, pointers—they point from the origin of the hyperlink to its destination.

pointing device: This computer input device enables the user to directly manipulate objects on the screen. The *mouse* has been the standard graphical user interface (*GUI*) pointing device, but *trackball*, graphic pen, and *laser* gun are all additional examples of this increasingly popular and important method of interacting with the computer.

point-of-sale systems: Refers to computer programs that replace the cash register where merchandise is sold. These programs keep track of electronic money (*e-money*) transactions, as well as product inventory, and are responsible for generating much of the data that wind up in corporate *data warehouses* and *data marts*. Also commonly referred to by the acronym "POS," these types of programs are integral to the evolution and growth of *e-commerce* on the *Internet*.

Polhemus Tracker: This is one of the first, and still most popular, forms of *magnetic positioning systems* developed for use with *virtual reality (VR)* systems. Created by Polhemus Navigation Sciences at Colchester, Vermont, this device uses a form of magnetic position sensing to enable virtual reality products to track the movement and position of VR users (cybernauts) as they move about within their *virtual worlds*.

policing: With respect to data communications, this term is now common parlance for a method of determining the level of compliance exhibited by *ATM cells* as they enter a *network*.

polygon shading: From the world of 3-D graphics, this term refers to a family of techniques used in conjunction with *polygons* to create the visual illusion of three-dimensional depth. *Gouraud* and *Phong shading* are two examples from this family.

polygons: With reference to computer graphics, especially those at the high end where *virtual reality* devices and *CAD* (computer-aided design) applications dwell, this term refers to a 2-D image segment manipulated in various ways (through *shading*, for example) to make up images of 3-D objects. For example, a 3-D cube is made up of six flat squares. Each one of these squares is a polygon. Obviously, the more polygons a particular image uses, the more realistic it can be made to look. However, as is typical with the cost-benefit downside of most computing applications, the more polygons one uses, the longer it takes to create the image.

polyphony: With regard to *MIDI* (musical instrument digital interface) synthesis (the dominant sound technology of the *MPC* [multimedia personal computer] standard), this term refers to the number of individual notes that a particular player is capable of playing simultaneously. Often referred to as the number of *voices* (e.g., 24-voice polyphony), the larger the polyphony, obviously, the richer the sound.

POP3: Stands for Post Office Protocol, and refers to an *e-mail protocol* used on the *Internet* to enable users to pick up their mail from anywhere on the Net, even if they are connected through someone else's account.

portability: Used frequently in the field of *software engineering*, this term refers to a desirable feature of software systems wherewith the system can be easily migrated, or ported, from one *platform* to another. This feature is desirable because it eliminates or reduces the considerable expense associated with reprogramming products to run on every popular platform in the market. The widely acclaimed move to *object-oriented programming* is at least partly motivated by this programming discipline's ability to accommodate the feature of portability. *Java*, the Web-oriented *high-level language* developed by Sun Microsystems, is another, more recent attempt at making portability a relatively easy goal to obtain. In fact, Java advertises itself as the "write once, play anywhere" programming language.

position tracking: Refers to a family of technologies being developed under the banner of *virtual reality (VR)* to keep track of the positions and orientations of users as they interact with the VR system. These technologies include mechanical, ultrasonic, magnetic, optical, and/or *image extraction* sensors.

postchannel world: This term describes the belief that in the near future our TV networks will be comprised of so many *channels*—will be capable of carrying so much *video bandwidth*—that the concept of an individual TV broadcast channel will become obsolete. In this brave new world, consumers will reign. Rather than being subject to the constraints of a viewing schedule prescribed for them by distant network executives, the viewing public will be afforded the luxury of viewing whatever they want, whenever they want it.

postproduction: In the traditional world of film and *video production*, this term refers to that phase of the product development cycle that covers all of the manipulation of the video after it has been produced or *shot*. Thus, this large segment of the development cycle covers all of the editing and the addition of all special audio and video effects (for example, *DVE* [digital video effects] such as the fades and *dissolves* that are used to produce *segues* between scenes). It is a common saying in the film industry that all of the filmmaking activity that occurs in advance of postproduction is nothing more than the making of raw clay, and that the real artistic shaping of the film occurs during the postproduction phase. Up until now, the postproduction phase of filmmaking has required the use of relatively expensive facilities and equipment, usually located in what are called "post-houses." The current flood of all-digital, *desktop video production* tools is all but threatening to cannibalize the postproduction industry by making the most sophisticated forms of editing and DVE available to artists at a fraction of the costs associated with traditional *analog* facilities.

PostScript: A page-description language that serves much the same role for documents that *MIDI* (musical instrument digital interface) serves for music. PostScript was developed by Adobe Systems and has now become the *defacto standard* for page-description languages. The value that it brings to the market is that it is a type of *display list* placed in a certain format that PostScript-compatible printers, regardless of brand, can read. By instructing the printer through code where to place its ink, a printer can re-create any image and any font without having to have that font loaded into memory.

post-symbolic communications: This phrase, originated by *virtual reality* visionary Jaron Lanier, describes a near-future form of communication in which the maturation of the various technologies surrounding virtual reality will make it possible for communicating parties to share ideas with one another, not so much by talking about the world, but rather by manipulating objects in a shared *virtual world*. Lanier also refers to this form of communication as "reality conversations."

POTS: Stands for Plain Old Telephone Service, still the *backbone* of the modern communications system, but plagued by an outmoded infrastructure.

POV: Stands for Point Of View, a term that describes the vantage point from which an act of communication is witnessed or perceived. Thus, in a film, POV typically refers to the positioning of the camera relative to the subjects being filmed. With literature, POV may mean much the same thing as it does with regard to film, that is, the physical vantage point from where the reader should imagine seeing a scene. But the term may also refer to a more abstract notion, such as a particular political point of view. However, when used as an acronym, the term usually refers to the physical vantage point for viewing a scene or situation. POV has always been one of the fundamental artistic considerations in building a piece of *video* or film. This lofty status should not change— in fact, it may actually grow in prominence—as we enter the era of interactive forms of entertainment.

PowerPC: This term refers to a multi-vendor family of *desktop* computing products introduced in 1994. Based upon a RISC (reduced instruction set computing) processor designed by IBM and fabricated by Motorola, and on an operating system developed by Apple, the PowerPC was intended to provide significant competition against the long domination of the *personal computer* market by machines based on the Intel 80 x 86 processors. Because the RISC architecture has been responsible in the early 1990s for some of the more powerful graphics workstations, the PowerPC's primary allure is its facilitation of *multimedia applications*.

PPP: Stands for Point-to-Point Protocol. PPP allows a computer running *TCP/IP* to connect to the *Internet* over standard telephone lines using a high-speed *modem*. It uses a method of encapsulating various *protocols*, including *IP*, into a serial *link* so that they can be sent over a modem. It supports *synchronous* and *asynchronous* lines, and is the successor to *SLIP*

prediction: In the world of *video codecs*, this term refers to a form of *motion compensation* in which a *frame* is constructed during *decompression* from the difference information between the original *frame* (determined during the *compression* process) and the preceding *key frame*. In other words, frames that follow the key frame have their contents predicted based upon the known contents of the key frame.

preference tracking: A close cousin to *performance tracking*, this concept drives *software engineering* efforts to create programs that understand the emotional preferences of the user. Examples of this might include programs that monitor preferences for style of TV programming (e.g., westerns versus whodunits, violent versus nonviolent programming), purchasing preferences, social styles, etc. The purpose for tracking preference is, of course, to then use that data to match system resources to the needs of the user. In the emergent phenomenon of *home interactive media*, preference tracking will serve as an *enabling technology* used to help deliver on the promise of *personal television*—a *smart TV* that knows the user's likes and dislikes and uses that information to build individualized evenings of entertainment.

preproduction: In the world of film and *video*, this term refers to that part of the development phase that lies in between the completion of the scripts and the commencement of the video shoot (also called *production*). Once a script is approved for production, the development team must first perform a number of preparatory functions before launching into the very expensive process of shooting the field *footage*. They must, for example, break out the scripts, identifying the characters, the props, the sets, and the locations. Then, if locations are to be involved in the shoot, they must scout for the best site(s). Also, they must conduct casting sessions, select the cast, and perform a large number of tasks associated with estimating and controlling the budget. In toto, these preparatory activities are referred to as preproduction. Because most *multimedia* budgets are still quite constrained when compared with those that are available for the typical film project, much of the video placed in multimedia titles is actually stock footage rather than originally produced video. By using stock footage and other forms of *clip media*, multimedia developers are able to dramatically reduce their costs of production. But as multimedia grows in stature, and as development budgets grow in corresponding fashion, so too will the various activities associated with preproduction become very important to the successful creation of interactive content.

PRI: Stands for Primary Rate Interface, which is a higher capacity form of *ISDN* connection than the more common *BRI* (basic rate interface). PRI has 24 *B-channels* for carrying data payloads, and is guided by a 64 *Kbps D-channel*, which carries control data. Thus, the maximum *transmission* capacity for PRI is 1,536 Kbps.

privilege: This term refers to a security key that is used to provide access on a *network* to some resource: a file, a program, or a service. It allows the owner or administrator to control who has access to the resource. On a networked computer system, every account is assigned a privilege level, usually one of three: user, admin, or guest. The user level typically allows access to applications, although special applications may require a corresponding set of special privileges. The admin level generally involves the widest set of privileges, allowing access to all applications, and to the highly sensitive administrative functions of the system. In contrast, the guest level permits a more tightly constrained set of privileges, typically involving a narrowly defined group of functions.

problem-based learning: From the realm of *instructional design*, this term describes an emerging school of thought that says that people learn best, not by deliberately studying educational materials, but by applying concepts and skills to the task of solving specific problems. This premise has major consequences for how the computer is employed as a teaching tool. The dominant, early model of computer-based instruction has been the study, or *drill-and-practice,* model. During the late 1980s and early 1990s, schools spent considerable funds on what were called "integrated learning systems." These broad-based, electronic curricula are dominated by the drill-and-practice model of instruction. The reliance on this model reflects, not so much a deep-seated belief that the study model of instruction is the secret to effective pedagogy, but rather a capitulation to the relatively easy nature of programming drill-and-practice programs, which amounts to little more than programming a succession of multiple-choice style questions. Advocates of the problem-based approach to learning oppose the extensive use of integrated learning systems and are promoting a move to problem-solving, game-oriented programs that go much further in terms of engaging the learner. *Educational software* is likely to move in this direction in the near future, and away from the drill-and-practice (also called "drill-and-kill") paradigm.

procedural knowledge: From the world of *artificial intelligence*, this is the form of machine knowledge responsible for modeling the *sequence* and nature of task completion. This form of machine knowledge draws heavily upon, but is independent from, declarative knowledge.

Proclamation 66: Considered a landmark case in the history of educational technology, this legislative act by the state of Texas made it possible for Texas school districts to purchase instructional *multimedia* products with funds that hitherto were limited to the acquisition of standard textbooks. To many, this act represents a breakthrough in thinking about what constitutes a "textbook."

production: In the world of film and *video*, this term refers to that most exciting of phases in the development process during which the director says "lights, camera, action." It is the phase that lies between *preproduction* and *postproduction*, and it is the penultimate act of film creation in which the actors and crew are assembled, and the original field *footage* is *shot*.

production chart: With reference to the *production* of a film/*video*/*animation*, this is a form that shows the status of every scene in the picture during the various stages of production.

progressive scanning: The standard form of scanning for today's television is termed *interlaced* scanning, which means that it takes two complete passes of a TV's *CRT* (cathode ray tube) electron gun to paint a single image on the screen. When a single screen image of NTSC-quality TV is transmitted, it is actually transmitted in two separate *frames*, each one containing every other line of the 525 *scan lines* that make up a television image. Thus, one frame will contain all odd scan lines (1, 3, 5, etc.), while the very next frame contains the even lines (2, 4, 6, etc.). This interlaced method is motivated by the need to conserve *bandwidth*. Progressive scanning is the more natural, but much more bandwidth-intensive technique whereby one frame equals one screen image. It is called progressive scanning because each scan line is followed, not by its next odd or even cohort, but rather by its next, and closest relative. Thus, scan line 1 is followed by scan line 2, which is followed by scan line 3, etc. One of the great debates over the nature of the *HDTV* (high-definition television) standard had to do with the inclusion of the progressive scanning method of *transmission*. This form of scanning eliminates many of the typical *artifacts* of normal TV broadcasts, such as interline *flicker* and certain distortions associated with rapidly moving objects. The penalty, of course, is that with progressive scanning, a transmitted image in the *video* stream requires twice as much bandwidth as is required by an interlaced image.

Project Jedi: This was a project undertaken by Lucasfilm with the goal of changing the way that movies get made. The primary intent of the project was to *convert* from a process that, historically, has relied entirely upon *analog* technologies, to a process that relies entirely on *digital* technologies. It is believed that the outcome of such a conversion will make possible unprecedented levels of ability to manipulate the visual image for artistic purposes.

proprietary: This term refers to any component of a software application, or other *media asset*, to which a company or individual has exclusive rights.

protocol: A very important term in the world of *data communications,* a protocol is a widely accepted set of rules that allow otherwise incompatible machines or software to communicate with each another. *TCP* and *IP* are both prime examples of data communication protocols. Without protocols, the large number of *platforms*, operating systems, and applications that make up the world of computing would be in such perpetual conflict with one another that the notion of networking would simply be a pipe dream.

protocol suite: A group of *protocols* in a *network* which function together to define a service or function between computers allowing them to exchange messages and other information. Each protocol defines a single aspect of the service.

prototype community: The costs of software development tend to be high. So too are the costs of creating high-quality media. When you combine the two—which is exactly what you do when you build *interactive multimedia*—the costs can be very high. Thus, it behooves *multimedia application* developers to create early prototypes of their programs, and to test them on at least one representative sample of their target market. This is no easy chore, because it involves organizing a willing and qualified community of users (viewers, gamers, or whatever). When such a community is organized, the organization who did the organizing tends to view them as a considerable asset and seeks to use them for extensive testing, perhaps of more than one product or system. The term prototype community is now being used to describe this community of users upon which prototypes are tested.

psychoacoustics: From the increasingly prevalent world of 3-D audio, this term refers to an academic discipline that concerns itself with the human perception and interpretation of sound. Most of the recent advances in the *digital* encoding of *HRTF* (head-related transfer functions) have grown out of research in this field.

public domain: Any item of *electronic content* (media or software) that is free of any *copyright*, trademark, or patent restrictions is said to be public domain. In the coming age of *multimedia*, where so much of our information will be assembled from myriad, and previously unrelated, sources (e.g., from *stock footage, clip media*, etc.), the need and demand for sources of public-domain content will be intense. The phrase public domain should not be confused with *freeware* or *shareware*, which is software that is *copyrighted*, but that is distributed without (advance) payment. With shareware you are expected to pay a fee, while freeware may have any number of other restrictions. Public domain means no copyright, and no exclusive rights.

public-switched telephone network: Also commonly referred to by its acronym, PSTN, this term refers to the massive telephone infrastructure to which everyone has common access rights. When someone wants to send information over a *channel* that is not private, they must access and use the PSTN. Thus, if someone is using a *LAN* (local area network), or a direct private line, they are not using the PSTN. But in almost every other conceivable case in which communications are occurring between geographically separate entities, they are making use of the public-switched telephone network.

pulse code modulation (PCM): PCM is done by *sampling* a waveform at a constant rate (*sampling rate*) of thousands of times per second to *convert analog* audio to *digital* audio. The minimum standard *MPC* (multimedia personal computer) samples sound at 11,025 Hz with 8 *bits* per sample, and plays back waveform audio at 22,050 Hz with 8 bits per sample. The sampling rate needs to be double the highest *frequency* of the sampled sound to produce the "Nyquest" frequency sound standard.

purging: In traditional data processing, this term refers to the very necessary process whereby files that have outlived their usefulness are removed—are purged—from the system's storage devices. Purging can be accomplished through either manual or automated procedures. Most automated procedures base their decision to purge a particular file or piece of information on the criterion of lack of use. In other words, if a file has not been accessed for a predetermined period of time, it is judged by the system to no longer be of use, and it is therefore eliminated from the system. In the era of *multimedia*, where file sizes are going to mushroom in order to handle the *mixed media data types*, the need to purge files in a logical and consistent way is apt to grow in importance.

push technology: This term refers to a relatively new method of providing information across the *Web*. Through most of the *Internet's* history, information was provided by simply making it available from a *Web site*. This practice places the onus for finding, accessing, and then making use of the information almost exclusively on the user. In other words, the information on Web sites was—and still is, for the most part—largely passive. It sits on the Web site waiting the attention of users. Push technology is a reversal of this method. First made popular by PointCast, and now emulated by many other organizations, push technology uses preselected criteria to automatically feed information to computer users. The information arrives as either a constant trickle, or via frequent dial-ups. The advantage for the information providers is that it lets them be more proactive, which is particularly important for those providers who are advertising goods and services. For users, the advantage lies in not having to search out information every time it is needed. Instead, most push technology providers send out many different types of information, and let their subscribers receive what portion of that information they want through the use of *information filters*. In essence, push technology is a direct descendent of the traditional media concepts of "broadcasting" and *channels*. Push technology is different than traditional TV channels, though, in that it provides the user with many different information flows, or streams, from within the same source (which could also be referred to as a channel). Many analysts view push technology as the leading edge of *personal television*, a highly customized form of *video* communications foretold by the *Media Lab*'s Nicholas Negroponte. See *SDI*.

Px64: This is a popular *videoconferencing* standard developed by the *CCITT* (Consultative Committee on International Telephone and Telegraph). It is primarily a *codec* (compression-decompression) standard, and facilitates the *transmission* of audio and *video* data over copper or fiber *channels*.

Users and developers will start with conventions that they understand—television, books, films, computer games, computer-aided instruction—and then discover new ways to use the multimedia technology environment.
  —SueAnn Ambron, Apple Computer, Inc.

QHY: Stands for Quantized High-resolution Y, a term that refers to a technique that elaborates on the *DYUV* (delta luminance color difference) *compression* scheme. QHY works by enhancing the *luminance* (or Y) *signals* of the image and interpolating them between the *chrominance* and luminance values already stored as a DYUV image. Wherever luminance varies greatly between two DYUV *pixel* values, QHY interpolates a correct value to achieve the effect of a sharper image.

QOS: Stands for Quality Of Service, a term of emerging importance in the world of *data communications*. QOS describes the quality of an end-to-end connection over a *network*, and is most commonly used to manage—and guarantee—a certain level of service between originating and receiving points in a high-*bandwidth* form of communication (such as *videoconferencing*).

quantization: In the process of *ADC* (analog-to-digital conversion), quantization is the step that immediately follows *sampling*, and is responsible for providing *digital* media with the binary-*encoded* numeric values that *capture* some or most of the properties of the original sensory *signal*.

quasi-video: As computing makes the painful transition from the alphanumeric forms of data to the higher *bandwidth* versions of data—audio, image, and especially *video*—it is being forced to *render* these presentational media in a compromised format. With regard to video, which has the highest bandwidth of the three, there have been three basic avenues of compromise. The first has to do with screen geography. Since all forms of *digitized* visuals are translated into a *pixel* format, and since each pixel represents some amount of memory requirement, the size and corresponding memory requirement of a piece of *digital* video is directly proportional to the amount of screen space on to which it is projected. Thus, many digital video applications are limited to a certain size *window*, so as to control the overall amount of computer data that must be moved through the system to create the motion picture. The second area of compromise has to do with *resolution*, i.e., with the number of pixels that must be represented to display a given image. Obviously, the lower the resolution, the smaller the amount of data that must be employed to represent the image. Thus, lowering the resolution is another way of lowering the memory and processing requirements associated with displaying video. Finally, the third factor of compromise has to do with how many frames per second (*fps*) are used to represent the motion picture. For television, the standard is 30 fps. In the first half of the 1990s, however, most makers of video hardware and software still found this *frame rate* to be a bit daunting. As a result, many "video files" were stored and played back at lower frame rates, the most common of which hovered in the 10–15 fps range. Taken together, these three compromises represent what many in the *multimedia* industry are referring to as the quasi-video of computing. It is important to note that, with time and the inexorable advance of hardware and software, the compromises of quasi-video will likely go away (taking with them—thankfully—the term).

queue: In the computer world, this term refers to a group of items waiting to be acted upon by the computer. The arrangement of items within the queue typically determines the processing priority.

QuickDraw: Introduced with the initial Apple Macintosh in 1984, this is Apple's library of software tools for developing static graphics. It made the *PICT* file format an industry standard for graphics files.

QuickRing: The *local bus* standard for Apple Macintosh, it is capable of moving up to 350 *Mbps*, making it one of the fastest local bus standards in the industry.

QuickTime: Introduced in 1991, this is Apple's library of system software tools for creating time-based data—audio, *animation*, and motion picture. At the heart of QuickTime, as with any motion-enabling software, is a *codec* (responsible for data *compression-decompression*), and so it seems inevitable that QuickTime will be compared against *DVI* (digital video interactive), *MPEG* (Motion Picture Experts Group), and other codecs. QuickTime has three major components: the movie toolbox, which makes it possible to play, edit, and otherwise manipulate the time-based data; the image compression manager, which is the high-level *interface* to QuickTime's codec; and the component manager, which is largely responsible for interfacing QuickTime resources to external system resources.

Stalking the future is a curious game.
**—Nicholas Negroponte,
Director, the Media Lab at MIT**

radial fill: From the world of computer *paint systems*, this term refers to a type of *fill* in which a pattern is projected from a center outward in all directions.

radio button: An *interface* element common to graphical user interfaces (*GUIs*) based on the *desktop metaphor*, radio buttons are typically placed in groups of three or more. Their principal distinction as a *mode* of selecting program functions is that they are mutually exclusive: you can only select one of them. Their name derives from the obvious metaphor with the dials on a radio.

RAID: Stands for Redundant Arrays of Inexpensive Disks and represents one of the latest incarnations of magnetic *disk* storage. This form of storage is gathering wide appeal among *multimedia* developers because it offers much higher capacities than traditional magnetic storage, and yet offers the far greater data transfer speeds that have always characterized magnetic as compared to optical *disc* (e.g., *CD-ROM* and *DVD*). Through a process called *file striping*, this form of storage also provides the desirable feature of redundancy, wherewith the failure of one *disk* in the array does not cause any loss of data because each file is duplicated on the other *disks* in the array.

random access: Of long-standing importance as a central concept in data processing, this term is often defined in relation to its opposite: *sequential access*. With information that is stored on a sequential access device, *access times* are typically longer because one has to pass over everything that intervenes to access the desired information. Tape storage is the classic example of a sequential access device. If you are at the end of a tape—one of your VHS tapes, for example—and want to access a scene near the beginning, then you must rewind the tape, searching all the while, until you get all the way to the front of the tape. In contrast, random access means that you can access any single piece of information as easily as any other piece of information, regardless of where any of it is stored on the medium. *Disk* storage is considered the classic example of a random access device. This random access capability is made possible by the use of directories, which enable read heads to find out the *track* and sector *address* of the desired information, and then move directly to that location.

raster file: As opposed to a *vector file*, a raster file is an image file generated either by using a paint program or by scanning an image. A raster file is stored in the form of a *bit map*. This is literally a "map," or two-dimensional array, of the display image containing the location of each *pixel* and its representative *grayscale* or color characteristics. Raster images are noted for their brilliant colors and high *resolution*, but also for their unwieldy size and resistance to flexible manipulation (e.g., resizing). Vector files, in contrast, are generated by *draw programs* and are laid out on the basis of mathematical equations, or *"vectors."*

raster image processor: Providing the *bridge* from *electronic content* (e.g., *ASCII* data) to image (e.g., *bit map*), this device transforms the *encoded* representation of a character into the desired pattern of *pixel* marks so that it may be laid down on paper. The quality goal of a raster image processor is to take the *encoded* character and transform it into a *pixel* pattern that *captures* that character's typefont, style, size, and orientation as accurately as possible.

raster-to-vector conversion: In the workaday world of *multimedia applications*, image files frequently need to be converted from one format to another. Raster-to-vector conversion is one of the most difficult of these conversions, demanding a great deal of the conversion software. This process requires the software to detect the presence of geometric shapes in a *bit-mapped* image, and then convert those shapes to *vectors*, or mathematical representations. Typically, this is done with a trace function that literally traces and redraws the image with mathematical vectors of the lines, shapes, and objects that make up the image.

ray tracing: This technique is used for creating realistic computer images by tracing rays from viewpoint to light source, which is, of course, the reverse of light rays. In other words, this technique traces the path of light as it bounces off of reflective surfaces. It calculates both hidden surfaces and *shading*. However, it tends to be *CPU-intensive*, requiring a relatively lengthy processing time for each image that is generated. The high cost in terms of *CPU* cycles is, however, offset by the high value that ray tracing provides to a graphical image. It is a technique that is used primarily to give computer-generated images a very realistic and subtle sense of lighting.

RBOC: Stands for Regional Bell Operating Company, a type of corporate entity that was established as a result of the 1984 antitrust suit that broke up the AT&T Bell System. There are seven RBOCs, or "baby bells" as they are sometimes called: Ameritech, Bell Atlantic, BellSouth, Nynex, Pacific Telesis, Southwestern Bell, and US West. The legislation that broke up the system prohibits the RBOCs from providing *video* services into their local market areas, but these restrictions are under severe legislative scrutiny and may be lifted at almost any time. In any event, the RBOCs are busy forming alliances with *CATV* (cable) operators, and are expected to become major providers of *multimedia* services as we enter the *age of interactivity*.

RDF: Stands for Resource Description Framework, an emerging *Internet* standard being advanced by the W3C (*World Wide Web* Consortium). The RDF is designed to provide a foundation for processing *metadata*. Its principal design goal is to enable *interoperability* between applications that exchange machine-understandable information on the *Web*. It emphasizes creating facilities to enable automated processing of *Internet resources* and should become instrumental in the further evolution of such key *enabling technologies* as *intelligent software agents* and *search engines*. At the core of RDF is a model for representing named properties and their values. These properties serve to represent both attributes of resources and relationships between resources.

RDS: Stands for Radio Data System, an innovation recently imported from Europe to the United States that offers interactive services to radio listeners through an FM *subcarrier channel*. Haled as the first major innovation in radio technology since the introduction of the FM *signal* in 1961, RDS offers a number of services not possible with conventional radio. A number of these features focus on the provision of text and graphics, which involves a small screen to display printed information like the station's call letters, the name of a song and its artist, traffic and weather bulletins, and possibly even advertising. Additional features include the ability to search the dial by format, rather than by station; a *hand-off function* for cross-country drivers that automatically switches to a stronger station for a broadcast being aired nationally (e.g., National Public Radio); and the ability to automatically interrupt any station with an emergency announcement, such as a weather warning.

real time: This refers to an operating *mode* for computers under which data are received and processed, and the results returned so fast that the process appears instantaneous to the user. Real-time modes are usually described in contrast to batch systems, where data are accumulated over time, and then submitted for processing all at once, often during late night hours when the real-time processing load placed on the computer system has diminished. As more and more of the processing load moves to managing the *user interface* in concert with the rise of *multimedia applications*, the pressure will grow on hardware/software to provide systems that feature real-time performance.

rear-projection: A form of projection system that has grown very popular in corporate America, rear-projection provides for significantly larger display areas than are feasible with conventional *video* monitors. Rear-projection works by reflecting the video image off of a mirror that stands behind a special screen onto which the image is cast. The use of this type of system for marketing and other corporate presentations has done a great deal to foster the speaker-support segment of the *multimedia* industry.

recognizer: From the world of *OCR* (optical character recognition), this term refers to a process that is the opposite of rasterizing. The recognizer takes the *pixel* image pattern of a character on a document, identifies the particular character that it represents, and then assigns it the appropriate computer code. In the PC domain, a recognizer *converts* a character stamped on a paper document into its appropriate *ASCII* code.

Red Book: This term refers to the original *compact disc* format standard established by Philips and Sony for *digital* audio, also known as *CD-DA* (compact disc-digital audio). When one buys a music CD at a retail center, it is a sure bet that the *disc* has been pressed in accordance with the Red Book standard.

redlining level: In the world of *digital* audio, this term refers to the *amplitude* of the loudest sound that a *digital* system is capable of expressing. For an audio engineer, the trick is to keep all events in the sound*track* beneath the redlining level of the digital system that is being used.

refresh rate: This is the rate at which the electron beam of an *RGB* (red, green, blue) monitor scans the screen, thereby restoring (refreshing) the image. Most computer displays—and TVs under the *NTSC* (National Television Standards Committee) standard—refresh the screen every 1/60th of a second.

relevance feedback: This term refers to an electronic search process that structures the search experience into steps. The first step allows the user to identify relevant documents in an initial search list. Then, in the second step, the search and retrieval system provides a new, and hopefully more *granular*, query based upon that initial search list.

remediation: From the field of learning theory, and more recently, from *instructional design*, this term refers to a teaching strategy that seeks to address learning deficiencies directly, rather than working on learning strengths. With the various forms of computer-based learning (e.g., *CAI* [computer-aided instruction], *CBT* [computer-based training], *educational software*, etc.), remediation is often used in direct response to an incorrect answer to a question.

render: One of the most *CPU-intensive* of all computer processes, rendering is the penultimate phase in the creation of 3-D graphics and *animation*. Prior to rendering, a graphic artist will create a 3-D model, which is, in essence, a *wireframe* representation of the graphical object (a chalice, for example). Once this model has all of the shape and size attributes the artist wishes, the rendering process will be launched. This process involves removing all of the jagged edges and hidden surfaces, followed by adding all of the object's *shading* attributes, such as *texture* and depth. Rendering is becoming an increasingly sophisticated aspect of *multimedia* production, and, along with the *compression* of motion pictures, represents one the strongest forces pushing chip manufacturers to build faster processors.

rendering engines: Are hardware/software systems powerful enough to generate illusion-sustaining landscapes, buildings, etc. An example of a rendering engine would be *DTM* (digital terrain modeling). The future of rendering engines is clear: they will play a role as one of the key automata involved in the creation of realistic settings for *virtual reality* and *interactive fiction* products.

repeater: A simple form of data-networking hardware, the repeater works by amplifying or refreshing the passing stream of data, thereby extending the distance the data can travel.

replication: Is a form of software functionality primarily designed to accommodate the distribution of documents and databases across the users and devices that make up a computer *network*. Replication works by synchronizing the contents of objects that are distributed across two or more *nodes* on a computer network. For example, a large corporation may create regional subsets of its sales database to be stored and accessed from departmental *servers* located in each geographic region. As these regional databases are changed to reflect local sales activity, they will temporarily fall *out of sync* with the master database located at corporate headquarters. The process of keeping those two copies of the same data in sync lies at the core of the software functionality known as replication. This form of functionality will be of increasing importance as firms all over the world strive to establish and manage their corporate *extranets*. Most sophisticated database management tools provide extensive replication features. Many *groupware* products—and particularly *Lotus Notes*—provide replication features for managing *DLOs* (document-like objects).

repurpose: Is becoming an important term in the world of *multimedia* content creation. Given that there are so many playback *platforms* in popular use today—such as the various flavors of *desktop* PC environment, the TV, etc. —it is important for content creators to build products that can be delivered on more than one, and hopefully all, of these platforms. In this way, the content creators can obtain the widest possible market for their programs. The process of taking a piece of content that was originally created for delivery on one specific platform and making it capable of being delivered on another is called repurposing. Hence, for example, most of the large movie studios will be seeking to repurpose their movies by converting them from *analog* to *digital* form for delivery on PC platforms that feature *DVD*.

rerecording: With regard to filmmaking, this term refers to one of the penultimate phases of *postproduction*, where the final sound*track* is rerecorded from its various components, which were either separated from one another at an earlier time so that they might receive individualized attention (e.g., the various *voice* tracks in a dialogue), or were recorded separately in the first place (e.g., the film's musical components). During this final *mix*, many things are done to perfect the audio track, such as balancing volumes, adjusting the *pitch* of the voices or sounds (treble/bass balance), and perhaps adding some special effects (e.g., a telephone filter, which makes a *voice* sound as if it is being heard over a telephone). As with so many aspects of media production, this process can benefit greatly from the *digitization* process, because it leads to the ability to analyze, separate, and recombine sounds, all on the same *platform*, and all without the traditional concern for handling many different types of physical media. The maturation of such technologies as *MIDI* (musical instrument digital interface) and *DSP* (digital signal processing) ensures that the process of rerecording will soon be done entirely within the *domain* of a computerized system.

resample: This process is undertaken to adjust the *resolution* of a *digital* image to match the capabilities of the current hardware *platform*. Resampling down discards *pixel* information in an image. Conversely, resampling up adds pixel information through *interpolation*.

resolution: In its most general sense, this term refers to the fineness of the detail represented by any form of media—audio, image, *video*, or even such exotic forms of media as *tactile feedback*. The most common use of the term today occurs with regard to the images shown on a *video* or computer display, where they are measured as a number of discrete elements per area—for example, *pixels* per square inch. The higher the number, the better the resolution and the higher the quality of the image.

resolution independence: This term refers to a highly desirable capability for computers to be able to output media—audio, image, *video*—at any *resolution*, regardless even of the resolution at which the original media was *captured* or *digitized*. This term is nearly synonymous with *scalability*.

retinal imaging: One of the more futuristic of new media devices being contemplated today, this technology represents the art of painting an image directly onto the retina of the eye. One strategy for doing this is for the computer to steer a low-powered *laser* beam around the retina, thereby activating rods and cones in the desired patterns and intensities.

reverb: Short for "reverberation," this audio engineering term refers to the natural echo that accompanies almost every sound as it bounces off of natural objects in the listener's environment. Because sound recordings that lack reverb are perceived as thin and unnatural, much effort is made by audio engineers to add this dimension to their finished work.

RFC: Stands for Request For Comment. RFCs are a series of documents about the *Internet* begun in 1969 (when the Internet was still *ARPANet*). RFCs are used to gather requirements and feedback regarding new Internet standards. They are easily obtained online via *FTP* from several *hosts*. Anyone can submit an RFC, and if it receives enough support, it will eventually become a standard. Thus, all Internet standards are originated as RFCs, but not all RFCs gain the acceptance needed to become standards. All RFCs are assigned a number, which, once published, cannot be changed. Modifications are given a new RFC number.

RGB: Stands for Red, Green, Blue and represents the most widely used representation of *video* images, wherein the constituent *pixels* are defined by their respective red, green, and blue color components.

rich data: This is one of the many industry terms that is used to label the *digital* forms of traditionally *analog* media—e.g., image, audio, and *video*. These newcomers to the digital domain lie at the very core of the move to *multimedia*, and are often contrasted with the conventional, alphanumeric forms of computer data, which require only a fraction of the *bandwidth* that is demanded by rich data. *Mixed media data types* is one of the many synonyms for rich data.

RIP: 1) Stands for Remote Imaging Protocol, a standard for transmitting computer-generated, *mixed media data types* over the television *transmission* infrastructure. It is created by TeleGrafix of Huntington Beach, California, and is intended to replace the long-standing *NAPLPS* (North American Presentation Level Protocol Standard) by making it possible for online services to transmit a much more media-rich form of content. 2) The RIP acronym also stands for Routing Information Protocal, which is a distance *vector* (as opposed to a *link* state) routing *protocol*, and an *Internet* standard *IGP* defined in STD 34, *RFC* 1058 (updated by *RFC* 1388). Distance vector protocols normally use only a single metric, such as *hop* count, to determine the shortest path for transmission, and they exchange all of their routing table information with all other *routers* on a *network* on a regular schedule.

Riven: The long-awaited sequel to *Myst*, created by the brothers Robyn and Rand Miller, and distributed by Broderbund.

RLE: Stands for Run Length Encoding and refers to a commonly used strategy for compressing data, especially data with black-and-white images, like those associated with paper documents. RLE works by counting the number of consecutive *pixels* that have the same visual value—such as occurs with the proportionally large white spaces in most documents—and then stores only the location and "count" of these consecutive pixels. This is in contrast to *bit-map* images, which supply the numeric, or *digitized*, value of each and every pixel in the image. It is important to note, however, that many RLE algorithms start with bit maps as their primary source of input, and then "compress them down" by *parsing*, counting, and then saving all of the segments in the *bit map* that possesses consecutive pixels with the same *digital* characteristics.

robot-based search engine: This term refers to a type of *Internet* search tool that relies entirely upon automated techniques for searching the

World Wide Web. These engines automatically navigate across the *Web*, searching for *hyperlinks*, retrieving relevant documents, indexing them, and creating databases out of them. *Yahoo!* and *AltaVista* are two well-known examples of robot-based search engines.

rogue agents: From the realm of *intelligent software agents*, this term refers to *agents* that act in harmful, and possibly illegal, ways as they perform tasks on behalf of their human owners. Rogue agents are *agents* that do not follow the accepted guidelines for *agent* behavior. They can be built specifically to cause trouble, or they may just become mischievous as a result of poor programming. Neophyte programmers, in particular, are likely to build agents that do not conform to guidelines for proper agent behavior, and may, for instance, program their agents to request thousands of *URLs*, thereby bringing any number of *host* sites to a crawl.

rolling demo: From the world of *multimedia applications*, this type of program is used almost exclusively in marketing situations, such as show or retail floor exhibits. With rolling demos, a *sequence* of screens/*video* segments is programmed to flow from one screen/segment to another with little or no need for human intervention. These demos are typically used to display key product characteristics and features. Their primary benefit is, of course, that they do not require the expensive services of a salesperson, and so can be left unattended at shows or in stores. Most rolling demos provide a feature that enables users to break out of the preprogrammed sequence and take direct control of the program's *media assets*.

room tone: From the world of audio production for film and *video*, room tone represents the natural sound of any location (e.g., the low buzz and clinking china of a restaurant crowd, the machine murmur of outside traffic). Room tone is used instead of blank film or tape for spaces in between sound takes, because every location has a sound, whereas film and tape do not. In the age of *multimedia* technology, an abundance of audio *clip media* is becoming available through companies that offer libraries of such sounds to video producers.

rotate: From the world of computer graphics, this term refers to a common function of *paint systems* and draw programs that allows images to be rotated, usually around the center of the object. Rotating turns the image in various directions around an axis.

rotoscope: In the world of feature *animations*, this is a machine made to project filmed images *frame* by frame onto the surface of a drawing board. The image is traced onto animation paper and used by the animator to achieve lifelike movement. In a sense, rotoscoping is a form of *data capture* for animation.

rough cut: From the world of filmmaking, this term refers to one of the first phases of the *postproduction* process wherein the director/*editor* team put together their first pass at building the finished movie. They do this by sequencing together an initial selection of takes and *shots* from the *production* phase. Depending upon many factors—e.g., the skill of the director as reflected in his or her choices during *production*—the rough cut will be either close to, or rather distant from, what the finished film will look like. Many of the more sophisticated electronic *video* editing products, such as Adobe's Premiere, make it possible for film developers to prepare their rough cuts entirely in a *digital* format. This means that, rather than coping with the problems associated with a potentially large and cumbersome number of *sequential access* video tapes, the editing crew can work entirely in *random access* or *nonlinear mode*. Of course, this also assumes the presence of some rather large storage devices, including a sizable volume of erasable media.

router: Is an *internetworking* device that is a step up in sophistication from a *bridge*. Unlike bridges, which connect *LAN* segments, routers are used to direct data traffic between LANs, and often involve remote destinations. Routers work by reading the *address* contained in the first few lines of each data *packet* they receive, and then computing how to best send that packet to its destination, taking into consideration how much traffic happens to be on various segments of the *network* at the time of the requested *transmission*. Routers function at layer 3—the network layer—of the *OSI* reference model.

routine-of-play: In the world of *electronic game design*, this term refers to the actions or series of actions the player must perform to operate the game. It is also known as the *play-mechanic*.

RSA: A public key *encryption* method, RSA was invented in 1977 by Rivest, Shamir, and Adelman. Its design is based on the notion that prime numbers are difficult to factor. An easy method for factoring large prime numbers can potentially break RSA. *PGP* uses the RSA algorithm, as does *Netscape Navigator.*

RTF: Stands for Rich Text Format, a Microsoft file-formatting standard that grew out of the Microsoft *Windows* software developer's kit. It was designed to enable software developers to create help files to accompany their software. Specifically, RTF enables developers to embed elements of document structure, such as tables of contents, index entries, *hyperlinks*, etc. Many popular word-processing packages now support the RTF standard, which is becoming something of a *de facto standard* for the formatting of text.

RTOS: Stands for Real-Time Operating System and refers to operating system(s), or OS components, that operate quickly and efficiently enough to manage direct user interaction. With the increasing movement of computer applications into the workaday world of noncomputer professionals, and with the addition of high-*bandwidth* (media) data types, the demands placed on operating systems to manage high volumes of information in *real time* will continue to grow. *CD-RTOS*, the operating system of Philips' once popular *CD-I* standard for *home interactive media*, provides a good example.

RTV: Stands for Real-Time Video, and refers to one of the two standard file formats that make up Intel's *DVI* (Digital Video Interactive) technology. RTV is an inexpensive, *intraframe codec* in which both *compression* and *decompression* can be executed on the fly, and stands in contrast to *PLV* (production-level video), the more expensive, interframe portion of the DVI codec canon.

rubberbanding: In this line-drawing technique, an "elastic" line is extended from one or more point(s) to wherever the screen *cursor* is located. This feature is used with many *paint systems* to enable an easy and flexible way for artists to reshape objects.

The computer de-routinizes, and routine is a sedative to the mind. The general relegation of trivial tasks to the mechanical periphery is perhaps the most explosive phenomenon of computerization.

**—Douglas Leebaert,
Professor, Graduate School of Business,
Georgetown University**

sample-rate converters: Because there are now so many forms and modes and standards for digitizing the various media (audio, image, *video*, etc.), there is often a need to *convert* a *signal* from one *sampling rate* to another. Sample-rate converters perform this function, and therefore can be said to be part and parcel of a *scalable architecture*. The need for sample-rate conversion commonly arises when transferring a *digitized signal* from one system to another. For example, an audio *signal* recorded at 48 kHz on a professional *digital* tape deck may have to be *converted* to 44.1 kHz for storage on a CD. Another obvious example has to do with digital telephone systems where, in order to carry the low-quality 8 kHz standard of the *public-switched telephone network* (PSTN), digital audio from almost any other digital source must be sampled down.

sampling: The first step in any form of *DSP* (digital signal processing), this process is responsible for converting the continuous, *analog* forms of *signal* known in the real world of nature to the discrete-time, binary forms of *signal* employed in the world of *digital* computing. In the process of *ADC* (analog-to-digital conversion), sampling precedes the step known as *quantization*, whereby the discrete-time *signal* obtained by sampling an analog signal is *converted* to a binary-*encoded* numerical value that *captures* some or most of the natural signal's properties.

sampling rate: This refers to the number of times per second that digitizing circuitry measures an *analog signal* to produce a *digital* value. With regard to digitizing various sources of media, this critical variable is virtually synonymous with quality, because it expresses the *resolution* at which the *ADC* (analog-to-digital conversion) takes place. All other things being equal, the higher the sampling rate, the finer the quality of the *digitized* media.

saturation: A technical characteristic of color, saturation refers to the purity of a color. Rich, intense colors are thus said to be highly saturated, while dull or diluted colors are characterized as not being very saturated. For example, pink is a low-saturation form of red.

SAW: Stands for Surface Acoustic Wave, which is an important *touch screen* technology used to enable such consumer applications as automated teller machines and information *kiosks*. With SAW, the screen is equipped with a molded glass panel. Surface acoustic energy is sent over the glass panel to receivers. When a finger or some other energy-absorbing device touches the screen, it absorbs a portion of the wave, a process that is then translated into *xy coordinates* to determine what section of the screen has been touched. SAW technology also provides for a third type of coordinate, known as the *z-axis*. The z-axis data are used to determine how much pressure is being applied to the screen, so that, for instance, an application can use greater or lesser degrees of pressure to control such behavior as *scrolling* velocity.

SBCELP: This acronym stands for an emerging standard in *voice coding*. The SB is short for Lernout & Hauspie Speech Products of Belgium, the firm responsible for developing the coding technique, while the *CELP* stands for Code-Excited Linear Prediction, a noun cluster that captures the essence of the technique's algorithmic makeup. SBCELP is routinely capable of creating *voice compression* ratios in the range of 30:1, and possesses a *codec* that requires about 12 *Mips* (millions of instructions per second) of computational power for compressing the voice *signal*, and about 1.5 Mips for decompressing the same signal. Numerous low-cost *DSPs* (digital signal processors) are now available that can perform these codec tasks.

SCADA: Stands for System Control And Data Acquisition and represents one of the emerging, large scale applications for *multimedia* technology. SCADA centers look like the War Room at the Pentagon. They feature large *video* displays and are connected to the world by abundantly equipped *broadband* communications facilities. Geographic information systems (GISs) that present *real-time* sources of data on brightly colored maps are perhaps the most common form of *enabling technology* used in conjunction with SCADA. Picture this: a fast food mogul stands before a GIS displaying real-time sales data and joyfully shrieks at the realization that there is a flurry of cheeseburger sales in Delaware.

scalability: A term of increasing importance in the world of computers and *multimedia*, scalability refers to the ability of a given technology to scale up or down in capability in conjunction with the differing capabilities of the technologies that surround and support it. For example, when used with reference to the fragmented world of *video codecs*, this term refers to a computer's ability to optimally adapt a *digital video* stream to the *data rate* of the playback system with which it finds itself working. If, on the one hand, the playback system has superior *resolution* (e.g., *SVGA*), then the codec should scale itself up so that the compressed image is decompressed to play at this high-quality resolution. But if, on the other hand, the playback system has antiquated display technology, the *codec* should decompress the image to play at the lower level of resolution.

scalable architecture: This term refers to any product designed so that buyers can upgrade their initially purchased items without having to replace those items. This term can be aptly applied to the personal computer market, where it is possible to upgrade one's initial purchase by, for example, adding internal memory chips, attaching new peripheral devices, or even replacing the machine's motherboard. In contrast, the television has, for the most part, failed to make scalability a part of its design: if a family has a black-and-white TV and now wants color, they must simply buy a new color television set. This term is much in vogue now, because as the industry contemplates the inevitable merger of the television and the computer, there is much hope that this new device— the *interactive television* or *smart TV* or *teleputer*—will feature a scalable architecture. Looking ahead, once televisions are actually built to be *scalable*, this architecture will make it possible for their owners to do such things as add new *disk* storage so that they can *download* more programming, or simply add more flatbed screen *cells* so that they can watch a bigger screen.

scan converter: Also referred to by the longer phrase "video scan converter," this device helps to *convert video signals* from one format to another, mediating format differences primarily between the worlds of TV and computer video. Unfortunately, this increasingly intense *interface* between the *analog* world of traditional media production and the *digital* world of computers is based upon a significant technical difference in the way the video signal is handled. For TV, the format has remained the same in the United States since the *NTSC* (National Television Standards Committee) standard was set for color television in the 1950s. In contrast, for computers, the standard seems to change with every new release of every make and type of computer, which means, of course, almost daily. When converting an image from computer to television formats, for example, a scan converter must change the image from digital to analog, and from *noninterlaced* to *interlaced*, plus it must match the *refresh rates* between the two. So long as the analog and digital worlds coexist in nervous parallel, the market for scan converters should remain a strong, but complex, one. Bring on the *teleputer*.

scan head: Is the part of a *scanner* that optically senses the text or graphic as it moves across the page.

scan lines: These are the parallel lines across a *video* screen, and along which the scanning spot travels from left to right when projecting the video information that makes up the picture on a TV screen or monitor. *NTSC* (National Television Standards Committee) standard video systems produce 525 of these scan lines on a screen.

scanner: This term refers to a data-capture device that creates a two-dimensional, *bit*-stream image of the object being scanned. Most commonly, scanners are used to *digitize* paper documents. The primary function of a scanner is to translate paper documents into electronic *pixel* or *bit-mapped* images. Typically, the scanning process involves reflecting light off of the target object in such a way that it can be *captured* or *converted* to *digital* data. The subcomponent within a scanner that is responsible for converting the light to digital data is the *CCD* (charge-coupled device).

scheme: In *Internet* parlance, this term refers to a plan that defines the format and order of a data object. Schemes are used to define the syntax or order to which the parts of a hierarchical object must conform. For example, *URLs*, *domain names*, and *IP addresses* are all objects that have several parts, and their respective schemes define the order and format for each of their different parts.

scientific visualization: This emerging field uses computer graphics to create visual models of physical processes and numerical data. This form of computer graphics is being used to depict a wide range of phenomena. Many scientists use it to create literal translations of nature, such as a visual, cross-sectional model of a volcanic eruption. Others use it to portray highly abstract concepts, such as a color-coded, *heat-mapped* depiction of a stock portfolio over the course of a trading session. Scientific visualization is an approach or a process that adds value by making it possible to distill huge amounts of numeric data into a single image, or into a series of images grouped together in the form of *animations*.

scope and sequence: From the hallowed halls of academe, this term refers to a significant step in the design of any educational program. It has become quite popular with *instructional designers*, who use this step to lay out the scope of the content to be covered in a particular piece of *educational software* (*courseware*), and to specify the most desirable sequence(s) in which that content should be experienced by the learner.

screen candy: This insider term refers to little visual rewards placed within an interactive program to dazzle the user.

screen capture programs: This term describes a family of software utilities, commonly used by *multimedia* developers in particular, which are used to quickly *capture* the current contents of the computer screen. These programs typically work by creating a snapshot, or *bit map,* of the current contents of the screen, and can usually be enacted by some form of simple command, such as a two-keystroke combination or command sequence. A very popular use of these programs occurs when they are used by *courseware* developers to capture computer screens for the purpose of building software *simulations*.

Script-X: One of the mission-specified projects of *Kaleida Labs* (the former joint venture between Apple and IBM), Script-X was a *multimedia* authoring language that embodied a number of very powerful software design principles, such as *object-oriented programming* and cross-platform compatibility. As originally envisioned, Script-X was to be to *multimedia* what Apple *PostScript* is to desktop publishing.

scroll bar: From the world of the desktop graphical user interface (*GUI*), the scroll bar is a common *interface* element used to change locations within a document. Typically, the scroll bar is a rectangle having on each end an arrow in a square box indicating direction of movement within the document. Inside the scroll bar is a scroll box, which is the item that the user drags in order to move within the document.

scrolling: A common technique in computer user *interface design* whereby all the displayed information on the screen is moved at once, either vertically or horizontally.

scrolling game: This is a somewhat pejorative term that has been used to label the dominant genre of *video* games in which the player-controlled protagonist is moved across the screen from left to right, encountering a succession of obstacles as different backgrounds scroll by.

SCSI: Stands for Small Computer Standard Interface and refers to a very important set of standards that was established to control the way that peripheral devices of virtually every kind (*scanners*, storage devices, printers, etc.) are connected to personal computers. Pronounced "scuzzy," this 8-*bit*, parallel standard makes it theoretically possible for any device, such as a *CD-ROM* player, to attach to any personal computer, provided of course that both have been equipped with a SCSI *interface*.

SDI: Stands for Selective Dissemination of Information, which is a practice that will become increasingly common among purveyors of *push technology* on the *Web*. SDI enforces a business process by which some type of selection criteria is used to build a list of *addressees*. A standard in the realm of *e-commerce* would apply some form of market segmentation logic to a list of potential broadcast candidates so as to filter out all but the most qualified customers. The *push technology* provider would then selectively broadcast its marketing message to just those candidates who appear on the filtered list of addressees. You can think of SDI, alternatively, as either a form of information filtering, or as an enabler of junk *e-mail* on the Web.

search engine: Is a program designed to search large amounts of text documents for specified *keywords* and return the *addresses* of documents that meet the selection criteria. Given that millions of *Web sites* populate the *Web*, without search engines it would be impossible for the ordinary user to access data needed on a particular topic. Search engines like *AltaVista*, *Yahoo!*, and others maintain large databases of cataloged entries based on keywords, titles, or the full text of the document for millions of Web sites. But even with this extensive coverage, they only manage to "be aware of" less than half the sites available. And with the exponential growth of the Web, even these high-profile search engines are getting further and further behind. This is a disappointing perspective, since the search engine must be viewed as our number one weapon in the war against *information overload*.

SECAM: Stands for Systeme Electronique Coleur Avec Memoire, and is the counterpart to the North American *NTSC* (National Television Standards Committee) standard for encoding TV *signals*. SECAM is used in France, Russia, and Eastern Europe, and makes use of 625 *scan lines* and runs at 25 frames per second (*fps*).

seek: This term is used most often in the *digital* world to refer to the positioning of a read head on a mass storage device in the correct location to read a particular file, or a particular piece of information.

seek time: This term represents a performance measure used most commonly with *disk* storage devices. It measures the time it takes for the *disk* read head to pick up from its current location and move to its next one. Obviously, seek time is controlled in large measure by how close the data from one read is relative to the next read. Thus, seek time as an official performance measure is usually recorded as an average over several types of read.

segue: Industry jargon from the world of *video production*, this term is used to describe the transition from one major theme, scene, etc., to the next.

selective dissemination of information: See *SDI*.

self-extracting program: This term refers to a type of program that is embedded within a compressed file, and is used to decompress that file once it arrives at its destination. On the *Internet*, where *bandwidth* is relatively scarce, many people use *compression* routines to reduce the size of the files that they transmit across the *Web*. The only problem with this practice is that these files need to be decompressed once they arrive at their destination. A self-extracting program is a *decompression* routine that extracts itself from the compressed file once it arrives at a destination, and then automatically performs the task of decompression on the file to which it was joined.

seller agents: From the realm of *intelligent software agents*, this term refers to *agents* that function on the *Web* by offering product information to prospective buyers, and then by consummating sales on behalf of their human owners. As envisioned by *e-commerce* visionaries, seller agents of the future will conduct most of their dealings with *buyer agents*, thereby creating a predominantly automated marketplace for certain types of products and services.

semantic retrieval: A new type of search technology that goes beyond conventional *keyword* searches. It works on the basis of a concept space, which includes all documents linked to a subject document. Semantic retrieval has been studied at *NCSA Mosaic* in conjunction with its *Digital Library* project. They have invested resources in pursuing this research initiative in the hope of creating more efficient *search engines*, which, as result, should help to reduce the problems associated with *information overload*.

sensorama: This was one of the earliest prototypes of *virtual reality*. Developed as a prototype arcade game in the mid-1960s by Martin Heilig, it was one of the first examples of a multisensory *simulation* environment that provided more than just visual input. This prototype featured a binocular viewing optics system, 3-D binaural sound, simulated vibration cues, wind *simulation*, and a chemical smell bank that generated simulated smells borne into the user's face by the wind simulator. The premise of the game was to create a first-person viewpoint of a motorcycle ride through New York City. Skeptics of *virtual reality* have derived from this project the pejorative phrase *smell-o-vision*, which they use to cast aspersions on the effort to build VR gear, a venture that the skeptics consider misguided and a waste of cultural resources.

sequence: Is a series of scenes that make up a definite episode in a story.

sequencer: In the world of *MIDI* (musical instrument digital interface) sound production, this term refers to a program feature that enables a composer or sound engineer to move musical and other sounds around, i.e., to rearrange them into the desired sequence. In many respects, the sequencer is highly analogous to the *cut-and-paste* features found in word-processing programs and *paint systems*.

sequential access: Of long-standing importance as a central concept in data processing, this term is often defined in relation to its opposite: *random access*. With information stored on a sequential access device, *access times* are typically longer than with a random access device. Tape storage is the classic example of a sequential access device. If you are at the end of a tape and want to access something near the beginning, then you must rewind the tape, searching all the while until you get to the desired information. In contrast, random access means that you can access any single piece of information as easily as any other piece of information, regardless of where any particular target item may be stored on the medium. *Disk* storage is considered the classic example of a random access device. This random access capability is made possible by the use of directories, which enable read heads to find out the *track* and sector *address* of the desired information, and then move directly to that location.

serial communication: From the world of *network* computing, this term refers to a *mode* of communicating data in which the *bits* are moved across the *transmission media* in a string, one *bit* at a time. Serial communication is often contrasted with parallel communication, where the data is moved in groups (e.g., 8 *bits* at a time) along *parallel transmission channels*.

serial port: Typically located on the backside of the personal computer, this port enables the PC to communicate with the many serial devices in the computer environment. Many printers possess a serial *interface*, and because the *modem* is a serial device, it makes this port the computer's main communication *channel* to the world. The serial port operates by converting data streams from the parallel structure they possess while moving across the computer's internal *data bus*, into the single-*bit* structure they must possess when traveling across the *transmission* lines that communicate with serial devices.

server: A term usually associated with *LAN* (local area network) and database technologies, a server is a centralized repository of shared database information. In a typical *LAN* configuration, the server is the largest machine in the *network*, and generally manages the *network* (plays host to the *network operating system*), as well as usually managing the network's largest collection of shared objects. Attached workstations make requests to the server, which then *downloads* the requested information to those workstations.

session layer: The session layer is the third layer from the top in the *OSI* seven-layer model. It uses the transport layer to establish a connection between processes on different *hosts*, while also handling security, and creating and managing the session.

SET: Stands for Secure Electronic Transaction, an emerging standard for enabling secure credit card transactions across the *Web*. The standard is being developed by Secure Electronic Transaction LLC, also referred to as SETCo, which is an organization set up by the major credit card companies. Once the standard has stabilized, SETCo will oversee its use in the marketplace by awarding SET Mark seals to companies whose software has passed a set of compliance tests. The SET standard is clearly a key *enabling technology* for the future of *e-commerce* on the Web.

set design author: With respect to the construction of *virtual reality* worlds, this term describes an emerging role for individuals who design and construct the *virtual* sets that make up the *virtual world*. For example, in the popular game *Myst*, the set design author was the person who designed the island on which the game takes place, including all of its natural elements and human-made *artifacts*.

set-top box: This term is fast becoming the center of one of the great technological debates of our time. While it is widely accepted that the computer will converge with the television in the long run, it is not at all certain which of these two venerable devices will win out in the near term. That is to say: we all know that the computer is becoming more like the TV, that it can now show TV-quality images, and that it can, in fact, be rigged with an *expansion board* that makes *pass-through video* possible. We also know that the TV is being made smarter all the time, and that, in fact, there are boxes that we can attach to the TV that provide it with most, if not all, of the intelligence of a computer. These boxes are now being called set-top boxes. They actually have quite a history, going back at least to the beginning of the *video* game industry. During that seminal period, companies like Nintendo and Sega were quite busy placing *CPUs* in their game machines, but avoided calling those devices by any name that might suggest the presence of a computer out of fear that any computer-like device would cause a phobic reaction among their buyers. Nevertheless, these set-top boxes had— and still have—CPUs, and so have all the essential ingredients of a computer. Moreover, their technical make-up is advancing rapidly, and with products like the 3D0 player, are approaching the power of a full-blown *desktop* computer. Thus, we have a controversy: will the set-top box become so powerful that it eliminates the need for a personal computer? Or, will the personal computer take on so many media capabilities that it will eliminate the need for a separate presentational device like the television?

SGML: Stands for Standard Generalized Markup Language, and is—at least historically—the leading standard among *tagging languages*. It uses special character sequences called *markup tags* to embed control information within streams of text data. These *tags* work by separating text to be processed in a specialized way—text to be boldfaced, for example— from the remainder of the text stream. The specific rules for how to interpret the various *markup tags* specified under SGML are set forth using *DTDs* (document type definitions). The greatest weakness of SGML today is that it has no facilities for handling nontext data. Consequently, it is not presently suited for handling the *mixed media data types* of *compound documents*. Indeed, its number one offspring, *HTML* (hypertext markup language), is performing this function for the *Internet*, and will, in all likelihood, supercede SGML as the number one tagging language in practice.

shading: Is one of the fundamental techniques for creating highly realistic computer-generated graphics. Shading occurs when a light source is added to the visual environment created by the computer. When this happens, areas that fall away from the light source are shadowed, and areas closer to the light source are highlighted. The problem with shading is that it tends to add significantly to the computational load, thereby slowing *frame refresh rates* significantly in most contemporary systems. *Gouraud* and *Phong* are two techniques that represent the high end of shading.

shareware: Is noncommercial software distributed free on the basis of an honor system. If a user likes the program and uses it, the understanding is that the user will pay for the shareware later. The author of the shareware usually requests a small fee. The fee is small because the creation of shareware does not involve the same business costs that are associated with the packaging and advertising of commercial software applications. Shareware is available from sources such as bulletin boards, online services, *archives* on the *Internet*, and sometimes via *CD-ROM* or floppy disks. Shareware is *copyrighted* and, therefore, should not be treated like *public domain* software.

sheetfed scanner: This type of *scanner* has fixed sensors and light sources. The documents are fed past the light sources like a fax machine. This type of scanner is generally used for high-volume applications, though there are now some small, personal-use models available.

shot: From the world of filmmaking, this term refers to the smallest logical unit of a film—to the fundamental unit of filmmaking. A shot represents the span of time in a film during which a single camera *POV* (point of view) is sustained. Obviously, shots vary widely in duration. Though moving from one shot to another has typically been considered an aesthetic decision to be governed entirely by the filmmaker's artistic goals, with the advent of *digital* processes, it is increasingly a decision that has significant technical and practical implications. The most powerful motion picture *codecs* (compression-decompression programs) work on the principle of finding and eliminating redundancy in successive *frames* of a film. To the extent that a piece of film moves in a hurried fashion, jumping quickly from one shot to the next in MTV fashion, a codec will have a difficult time achieving a high *compression ratio*. This is so because—on average—there will not be much redundancy over the groups of frames that make up the film. In contrast, films with a lazy pace (from the standpoint of how they are edited), featuring lots of extended shots where the camera stays focused on the same objects for long periods of time, are ideal for achieving high compression ratios. Slowly paced films will possess a great deal of visual redundancy (also called *temporal redundancy*).

shot list: From the world of filmmaking, this term refers to a list of the *shots* that must be executed based on the *blocking* of a particular scene in the director's mind. As such, it is one of the more important planning documents in the making of films. With the use of *authoring systems* that possess *time-line interfaces*, the *links* between the shot list and the finished shots can be automated, thus making it possible to automate at least the first phase of editing a picture. This, of course, assumes that the finished shots have all been *digitized*.

shovelware: Some jaded jargon from the realm of *hypermedia*, this term refers to *disks* loaded with so much poorly organized information that the user, seeking to *navigate* that information, is lost in an electronic morass of meaningless data.

shuttle: From the *analog* world of tape, this term refers to use of the fast-forward and rewind features of a tape deck to search for some specific part of a *video*. While using this *sequential access mode* of searching, *editors* must keep the picture visible so that they are able to find the scene or *shot* for which they are looking. Most tape decks designed for video *postproduction* purposes are equipped with a "shuttle knob," which speeds this process of seeking specific points in the tape. However, it must still be considered a brute force technique of searching. The pain and agony of shuttling is one of the reasons why many feel that *nonlinear, random access*, all-digital *video* is the wave of the future.

SIG: Stands for Special Interest Group, a term used by many professional associations and groups to describe smaller parts of their organizations dedicated to a particular subject or occupational interest. Often times, an SIG will grow to become an impressive organization in its own right. For example, SIGGRAPH, which hosts one of the most important trade shows in all of the *multimedia* industry, is an SIG of the ACM (Association for Computing Machinery) dedicated to computer graphics.

signal: In the world of *digital* media, signal refers to the physical properties of sensory information that change with time, especially those associated with the electromagnetic spectrum. Thus, in speaking about *DSP* (digital signal processing), it is customary to speak of the "*voice* signal" or the "*video* signal," etc.

signal processing: This is a near-synonym to *DSP* (digital signal processing).

signal reconstruction: This term is roughly synonymous with *decompression* in that it describes the reconstruction of an *analog signal* from its digitally *encoded*, compressed counterpart.

silence function: Often available with *digital audio production systems*, this function eliminates all sources of ambient sound and other unintentional noise in an audio *track* by enabling the audio *editor* to simply force all values in the selected passage to zero.

SIMNET: Short for SIMulated NETwork, this program represents the first serious effort at creating a networked *virtual reality simulation*, also referred to as *cyberspace*. SIMNET is a networked *virtual* battlefield funded by *DARPA* (Defense Advanced Research Projects Agency), and developed at the Institute for Simulation and Training at the University of Central Florida in Orlando. It enables geographically dispersed players to wage war with one another on a simulated and shared battlefield. It thus provides a prototype of the role of *equitagonist*. Each stand-alone simulator is in the form of a tank and contains a copy of the world database, including the terrain and the *virtual* representations of all of the other simulators—or equitagonists—engaged in the conflict.

simulation: This term refers to an increasingly popular form of *multimedia application*, used most often for providing educational experiences in the most realistic contexts possible. Simulations are based on the same goal-oriented, highly interactive design principles as *video* games, except they typically place the gaming challenge within some real-world, job-relevant context. Flight simulators, simulations of the stock market, software simulations, and war games are four fairly obvious examples of this highly sophisticated form of *multimedia*.

simultaneous-interpretation telephone: Conceived by Koji Kobayashi, former head of Japanese corporate giant NEC, this term refers to a telephone system that provides *real-time*, machine-generated translation between languages, thus making it possible for individuals to conduct a free and normal conversation even though they do not understand one another's language. Though this technology has yet to be achieved, it is commonly thought of as one of the key *enabling technologies* of the global village.

sine wave: Is a continuously varying, repeating *signal* characterized by *amplitude*, *frequency*, and phase. The sine wave is the primary mathematical symbol for *analog* phenomena, which include, of course, analog media.

skills management: Though this business practice is normally thought of as belonging to conventional data processing activities (and particularly those associated with human resources), it has great significance to the future of *multimedia* in the corporate world. Skills management is founded on a basic set of relations. First, job skills are correlated to skill assessments (i.e., tests, or other measures of knowledge and skill). The assessments determine where people have skill gaps, or shortcomings, in their job-related competencies. These skill gaps are then correlated to training *interventions* (i.e., courses or mentoring activities), which are designed to close those gaps, thereby enabling the individual to become better prepared for the job. Skills management is of considerable import to corporate multimedia because it is increasingly being used to automate the process of prescribing computer-based training (*CBT*), and other forms of instructional media, to workers who have demonstrated knowledge and skill gaps. Skills management is becoming, in fact, a *backbone* information system for supporting and promoting the use of *instructional technologies* such as CBT, *MBT*, and *WBT*, and is also considered a key *enabling technology* for both *knowledge management* and the achievement of the goals associated with becoming a *learning organization*.

skills management system: An information system designed to automate the activities associated with *skills management*: namely, the detection of skill gaps and the subsequent prescription of appropriate training *interventions*. The rise of skills management systems in large organizations should fuel the demand for computer-based (*CBT*), multimedia-based (*MBT*), and Web-based (*WBT*) training modules, and thus for the overall demand for *multimedia* development services. It is also a key technology enabler for *knowledge management*.

sliders: From the world of *interface design* (not baseball), this term refers to a type of on-screen control *icon* used to control functions—like sound volume, for example—that vary along a scale of values. As a general *interface* component, sliders are often contrasted with toggles, or toggle switches, which are used to control functions characterized by discrete on-off states.

SLIP: Stands for Serial Line Internet Protocol, which is software that allows the *Internet protocol* running on an *Ethernet network* to be used on a serial line. SLIP allows a PC to connect to the Internet via a telephone *link*, or *IP packets* to be transmitted over a serial link. SLIP is being replaced by *PPP*.

smart TV: One of the many emerging synonyms for *interactive television*, this term underscores the necessity for televisions to take on machine-based, or processor-based, intelligence as they become more interactive, and less passive.

SMDS: Stands for Switched Multimegabit Data Service, a *broadband technology* developed by Bellcore (the R&D branch of Bell Communications).

smell-o-vision: This is industry slang for a loser technology. It refers back to an early 1960s attempt at *virtual reality* called *sensorama*, in which the manufacturers tried to incorporate smell as a form of output. Obviously, this experimental technology did not pass the sniff test.

SMIL: Stands for Synchronized Multimedia Integration Language, an emerging standard sponsored by the *World Wide Web* Consortium (W3C) that will greatly facilitate *Webmasters'* ability to design and deliver *Web content* based on the *rich data* types of *multimedia*. While it has been possible for some time now to deliver audio, still image, and *video* across the *Internet*, in the world before SMIL, each media element had to be treated separately; it was only possible to coordinate, or synchronize, these elements with a great deal of programming effort. SMIL, which is pronounced "smile," will enable Webmasters to coordinate the timing of diverse media elements, even though they may be stored on and managed by separate *Web sites*. As envisioned, SMIL will be a relatively straightforward extension to *HTML*. The first public draft of SMIL was made available in November 1997, and many industry analysts believe that it will become one of the key *enabling technologies* of *interactive television*.

SMPTE: Stands for Society for Motion Picture and Television Engineers, and is pronounced "simp-tee." It is a professional society that has been responsible for establishing a number of standards for motion picture and television equipment. The most widely known of these standards is the SMPTE *time code*, which, like the *MPEG codec*, is often simply referred to by the sponsoring organization's acronym.

SMTP: Stands for Simple Mail Transfer Protocol, a *server* to server *protocol*, which is the *TCP/IP* standard for transferring electronic mail messages between computers, usually over *Ethernet*.

snail mail: From the emerging culture of *cyberspace*, this derisive bit of slang refers to the conventional, paper-and-envelope mail of the U.S. Postal Service.

snap-to grid: One of the many *accuracy aids* now used in computer graphics programs, this term refers to an underlying and often transparent *grid* that works to force alignment of objects at a microscale within a graphics development environment. Thus, for example, this tool is often embedded in *paint systems* so as to force alignment of bullet points and other forms of lettering that the artist would normally want to have aligned with a common vertical or horizontal edge. Every once in while, this otherwise useful tool can get in the way by forcing alignment where the artist wants rough edges. As with most software features, though, the artist can typically circumvent this problem by simply turning off the snap-to grid feature, or by making adjustments to the spacing between the elements of the grid.

sneakernet: This is slang term used to describe the lowest form of local area network (*LAN*), which is actually no form of *network* at all. With sneakernet technology, data communication between computers occurs by first copying files onto a diskette, and then by walking (that's the sneaker part) the diskette over to another computer, where the files are copied onto the target machine through its diskette drive. Sneakernet technology is particularly ineffective with *multimedia*, where the typically large data files are often too big to fit on one, or even several, diskettes.

SNMP: Stands for Simple Network Management Protocol, which is a *network* management *protocol* used almost exclusively in *TCP/IP* networks. Like most basic network management tools, SMNP provides a means to monitor and control network devices, and to manage configurations, statistics collection, performance, and security.

SNR: Stands for Signal-to-Noise Ratio, which is a measure of quality for any form of *digital signal*. For example, with regard to audio, where this ratio is most often applied, SNR refers to the clarity of sound in relationship to ambient noise.

socket: This term refers to a software feature that was designed at Berkeley for the *UNIX* system as an *interface* between standard application *I/O* and the *network* communication facilities. It allows *application programs* to use *TCP/IP* to connect to remote computers in order to send and receive data.

soft robot: A term coined in 1984 by Alan Kay, it refers to much the same software design concept as does the term *interface agent*. A soft robot is a computer-based *agent* that represents a system made up of software routines. When given a goal (by a human user), this system is capable of carrying out the details of the appropriate computer operations and of asking for, and receiving, advice in human terms when it gets stuck.

software engineering: One of the most demanding and valuable enterprises of the information age, this discipline is responsible for designing, coding, testing, implementing, and integrating the myriad software applications that account for the pervasive ascent of machine intelligence in our time.

SONET: Stands for Synchronous Optical NETwork, which is a *CCITT* (Consultative Committee on International Telephone and Telegraph) standard that defines a number of levels of *digital telephony* service over *fiber optic transmission* lines. SONET is often associated with the *backbone* of the American communications *network* and ranges in carrying capacity from 1.544 megabits per second (Mps) up to 2.4 gigabits per second (Gps).

sound placement DSP: This technology permits audio producers to position apparent sound sources anywhere in space around prospective listeners: front, back, left, right, above, below. Based on digital signal processing (*DSP*) technology, sound placement *DSP* is a foundational technology for creating the 3-D, *surround sound* systems critical to the success of many *high-intensity amusement attractions.*

sound-space resolution: This term is used to describe how many sound source positions can be simulated in a *3-D sound* system.

spam: The original meaning of the term was to "crash" a program by loading a data file larger than the fixed length *buffer* of that file. With the rise of *Usenet newsgroups* over the *Internet*, spam has taken on a new, though related, meaning. It now means to deliberately or accidentally cause a *newsgroup* to be flooded with inappropriate or irrelevant *e-mail* by posting a provocative message or an advertisement, which leads to a large number of irrelevant responses. Another way to spam is to cross-post a message to two antagonistic newsgroups, thereby provoking a large amount of cross-attack mail between the two groups. The best way to respond to a spam is to *e-mail* the sender personally, while at the same time copying the postmaster at the same *address.* Sending a reply to the newsgroup only increases the spam. By its very nature, spam causes more spam.

spatial: When used in conjunction with the world of *video codecs*, this term refers to actions that are performed on an individual *frame.* In this sense, spatial is nearly synonymous with the term *intraframe*. Spatial is often used in contrast to *temporal*, which refers to *codec* actions that are taken over the span of two or more video frames, and in this sense, the contrast between spatial and temporal techniques is synonymous with the contrast between intraframe and *interframe* modes of *compression*.

spatial positioning: From the realm of *3-D audio*, this term refers to the ability of *3-D sound* systems to expand the conventional stereo sound field, so that sounds appear to originate from locations beyond the left and right speakers.

speckles: From the world of document and image scanning, this term refers to any dots or gray patches found on scans, faxes, or copies. They represent a form of background *noise*.

specular light: Is directional light from a specific source that reflects directly off the surface of an object without entering it. This form of light is a key concern of advanced graphics programs that are seeking to create increasingly realistic visual representations of the world.

speech font: A projected future technology for *multimedia*, wherein one is able to use sophisticated *text-to-speech* and speech synthesis technologies to shift between different styles of computerized speech (e.g., male/female, bass/alto, etc.) with the same ease and flexibility characteristic of changing fonts in today's word processors. Imagine a day when you are able to request that your computer speak to you in the voice of Humphrey Bogart or Lauren Bacall.

Sphinx-II: Is a *voice recognition* device developed by Microsoft, which allows the user to speak directly to the computer. It recognizes words by matching recorded sounds to a list of 27 speech sounds, and then by searching through a 20,000-word vocabulary. Its error rate is currently about 12.5 percent . An improved version of this product is known as *Whisper*.

spline: From the realm of *3-D animation* and modeling, this term refers to one of the fundamental elements upon which most commercial *animation* packages are based. A spline is a mathematical representation of a curve. Spline-based graphics are, therefore, pictures built from numerous mathematically defined curves.

split bar: From the world of graphical user interface (*GUI*) design, this term refers to the bar, or separation marker, that splits one *window* from another. Thus, for example, if a user has opened up two documents and has made both of them visible on the screen at the same time, with one in each of two windows, respectively, the bar that separates those two windows is called the split bar.

sprites: From the realm of computer *animation*, a sprite is a small image, stored in libraries of such images, which is movable under program control. In many respects, sprites are the computer animator's version of a subroutine library, representing reusable graphical elements. Sprite libraries normally range in content from character sets used in representing text on screen to sets of characters used in animating computer games.

square: In the realm of *DVE* (digital video effects), this everyday word takes on the specific meaning of a *two-plane effect* where the image on the *front plane* becomes a square opening or closing, revealing the image on the *back plane*.

stand-alone system: This term is used to describe a self-contained computer system not connected to either a *network* or a larger computer.

star topology: From the realm of computer networking, this is one of three dominant *network* topologies. The other two are ring and *bus*, and both of these differ from "star" in that they connect all of the workstations on the network over a single *transmission* line. In contrast, the star topology features a separate *transmission* line for every workstation, and all transmission lines emanate from the *server*. Star topology is on the ascendance because it is the only one of the three topologies well suited for handling the large, continuously flowing streams of data characteristic of *multimedia* applications.

steadicam: From the world of filmmaking, this relatively recent invention is a device that makes it possible for the camera to make rock-solid, "steady" *shots*, even when mounted on something moving, such as a plane, a roller coaster, or even the shoulder of a person who is running. In many instances, the steadicam has been used to create for the film viewer the sense of being "in" the movie, of being in the shoes of one of the characters. This ability to place the viewer in the action will have growing significance as filmmakers turn to *interactive cinema* as an artform. Thus, whether or not the steadicam continues to be of practical use in our technological future, it should at least be remembered for the technical goals it successfully achieved.

step frame: This term refers to a feature of certain *video* manipulation devices, such as *frame-accurate* tape decks and *laserdiscs*, which permits the user to move backward and forward in the video stream one *frame* at a time.

stereo pairs: These are pairs of overlapping images *shot* by cameras from slightly different vantage points for the purpose of creating stereoscopic, 3-D forms of visual media.

stereoscopic glasses: By rapidly displaying slightly offset images alternately in both lenses, these early *virtual reality* devices create for their wearers an illusion of three-dimensional depth. In the future, these devices may become as light and unobtrusive as eyeglasses, with increasing *resolution* and separation accuracy.

stereoscopic vision: Is the sensing of a single 3-D image by binocular vision of two perspective images generated from different vantage points.

stock footage: In the world of filmmaking, this term refers to film *footage* that represents commonly used scenes, or filler, such as trains, planes, or automobiles in transit. These scenes can be acquired from companies that collect and sell such categorized film segments as their core business. "Stock footage houses" provide filmmakers with catalogs that provide an indexed listing of the contents of their libraries. By making use of these libraries, filmmakers can decrease the cost of making a particular film by an amount commensurate with what it would cost to shoot the scenes they buy as stock footage. Given the high costs of original film *production*, the savings from using stock footage can be considerable. Many of these stock footage firms are now *digitizing* their libraries, laying them down on *CD* and *DVD*, and thereby broadening their markets by a considerable degree to include the growing number of *desktop video* producers. In the emerging *multimedia* industry, these newly digitalized vendors of *clip media* are being referred to as "content vendors." It is possible to visualize a day when commercially successful films will be comprised entirely of stock footage, or clip media segments—artfully stitched together.

storage place: This term is used in the context of describing the storage feature of a highly literate form of *multimedia,* such as an art gallery *kiosk*. The term represents the shift in perception of electronic storage from that of a physical or logical phenomenon to that of a cultural phenomenon. Like the burial place of archaeological concerns, it is a relatively simple futuristic leap to imagine that our children's children will remember their ancestors by storing their media representations—a *video* biography, for example—rather than, or in addition to, some form of their physical remains.

storage virtualization: This term refers to the ability to make storage devices appear as if they have unlimited capacity. A *network*-implemented concept, this is done by transparently migrating inactive files through a series of "migration steps" to *servers* located (theoretically) anywhere across a network. The steps for implementing storage virtualization are controlled by network administrator–defined rules, which are transparent to users.

store-and-forward: This term describes a commonly offered data-communications service, wherein data messages (broadly defined) containing *address* information about their destinations are temporarily stored, and then later transmitted onto their respective destinations. *Voice mail* and *e-mail* are two common types of store-and-forward service.

story cube: This term is a play on the *linear video* design term *storyboard*, and it represents a design presentation tool used by interactive designers to provide a high-level, graphical representation of the structural aspects of their programs.

storyboard: A term co-opted into the interactive field from the world of film and *video*, it refers to a piece of panel material on which is placed one or more sketches that present the look and feel of a proposed screen or story *sequence*. Storyboarding has become an integral part of the planning of any program that possesses a significant visual component.

storymercials: Many analysts and industry pundits have wondered upon the problem that will face advertisers when our prospective *information superhighway* makes all forms of entertainment available based entirely on consumer demand, thereby eliminating the one-minute advertising slot altogether. Obviously, such an eventuality creates a form of TV in which all *channels* would be operated like the contemporary premium (pay-per-view) cable channels, such as Showtime or HBO. As an advertiser's antidote to this possibility, one idea that has surfaced is that products will become "embedded" in the entertainment, illustrating their benefits by virtue of how they are used by the story's protagonists. The term being offered to cover this idea is that of storymercial.

STP: This term stands for Shielded Twisted-Pair, an expensive, high-end form of *transmission media* used in networking data applications that require high levels of capacity and reliability.

strand management: From the realm of *instructional technology* and *educational software*, this term refers to the body of design principles that specify how educational segments (*courseware*, for example) can be organized and sequenced in an automated fashion. In well-designed programs, the strand management logic is governed by software routines that track and assess performance and *learning styles* so as to match the learner's knowledge, skill level, and learning preferences to appropriately designed educational sequences. When this occurs, the educational software can be accurately credited with obtaining the long-sought dream of individualizing instruction. Though the concept of strand management has been around for years, its implementation has been very difficult and expensive to achieve. The biggest barrier has been the costs associated with creating a large and rich enough repository from which to build the educational segments so that the software can be truly responsive to every learner's needs. Programs that possess strong elements of strand management are commonly referred to as "adaptive learning systems." They can adapt on the fly to whatever problem or deficiency the learner exhibits. As a concept with wide transferability, strand management has much to offer producers of sophisticated *video* games and other types of interactive entertainment.

stream management: From the world of computer networking, this term is on the rise, as it describes a type of service demanded of any *network management system* that would manage the flow of the large, continuously flowing streams of data that characterize *digital video* and other high-bandwidth sources of audiovisual data.

streaming: Is a technique that allows *video* to be played as it is *downloaded* from the *Internet*. As such, streaming is time sensitive. The conventional *packet switching networks,* which may route *packets* by different routes and must, therefore, wait until all *packets* arrive, is generally unsuitable for use with streaming data, like *video*. In contrast, the sophisticated *network* technology *ATM* provides the necessary *bandwidth* and *connectivity* to support the streaming of *video*.

street-fighting games: This term describes a genre of *electronic game* in which the central *play-mechanic* features a protagonist, controlled by the player, who moves up and down a street while fending off a procession of evil-doing foes.

stretch target: This term from the business management school of process innovation refers to projects that enable the sponsoring organization to stretch its current capabilities in a dramatic fashion. As organizations large and small begin to implement such enterprise-wide *multimedia* solutions as *performance support systems*, they will, by definition, be setting stretch targets for themselves.

structured graphics: This term refers to a way of describing an image using a set of simple geometric primitives. These primitives (e.g., lines, arcs, rectangles, ellipses, etc.) are the building blocks that construct the image. Structured graphics represent a distinct approach to treating visual data, and are often referred to as *vector* graphics and contrasted with *bit-mapped* graphics. With structured graphics, the image is stored and drawn as an array of *pixels*. Thus, every *pixel* in an entire image is given a value that represents its visual characteristics (*brightness*, color, etc.). When high levels of image quality are sought (defined in terms of numbers of pixels and permissible colors), bit-mapped images can become large and difficult for a computer system to store and transmit. Bit-mapped graphics store the image itself. In contrast, structured graphics store a set of instructions for drawing the objects that comprise the image. This system saves considerable storage, and it is the chief advantage of this approach. Structured graphics, however, usually require complex display software, which must contain a module that can interpret the structured graphics instructions and draw the appropriate objects.

student model: From the realm of intelligent *CAI* (computer-aided instruction), a student model is a software component that records and maintains an information base on such learner characteristics as preferred learning *mode* and current level of skill mastery. A well-designed student model contains common student errors and misconceptions compiled by classroom teachers and cognitive scientists. The overall goal of the student model is to make interactive forms of training more responsive to the individual needs of the student.

style sheet: Originating from the field of document design, but now a major player in the look and feel of *Web pages*, a style sheet is a definition of a document's appearance in terms of such standard elements as font size, style and color, columnar layout; front matter structure; line spacing and margins; and so forth.

stylus: This pencil-shaped graphical input device is used with a *data tablet* to enter data and commands into some form of graphics software package.

subcarrier: This term is used with reference to radio and television broadcasting to describe small portions of a given station's broadcast *channel* not used for radio or television *signals*, respectively. As we enter the age of interactive radio and television, this hitherto unused resource is now being viewed as a potential *carrier* of data *signals*, i.e., as a *narrowband* path along which users can interact with the broadcasting source to express such things as content or format preferences. This term is nearly synonymous with *backchannel*.

subject index: A *controlled vocabulary* used by indexers of information objects to enforce standardization of *cataloging* and retrieval practices. The subject index is rapidly emerging as an item of interest for those involved in the databasing of *multimedia* assets, because *digital images*, graphics, audio clips, and the like must be *tagged* with some class of textual identifiers in order to become searchable. The subject index is also referred to by library science specialists as a *thesaurus*. There are two major types of subject index: the vertical thesaurus, which is oriented toward particular industries or other domains of interest; and the horizontal thesaurus, which is cross-functional in its orientation and is therefore applicable across a range of user communities.

subject indexing: A topic that until recently was only of interest to library science specialists, subject indexing is fast becoming of ever-widening interest, particularly to that segment of the *multimedia* industry concerned with databasing, and otherwise managing, large collections of *digital media*. When images, graphics, audio and *video* clips, and the like are *digitized*, they become digital media, and are capable of being moved across *networks*, like the *Internet*, and played on computing machines, such as PCs. However, when these traditional analog media become digitized, they do not immediately lend themselves to being managed in large collections, as is the case with the conventional forms of computer objects like transaction data and personnel records. In order to manage large collections of digital media—that is, to make these media objects available to users for search and re-use—it is necessary to assign text descriptors to each digital object (i.e., to each digital image or digital audio clip). When you assign text items to digital media, you are indexing those objects. Most early attempts at managing large collections of digital media objects—also referred to as *clip media*—have permitted a free-form process of indexing the objects. Basically, whoever was given the responsibility of indexing the objects was allowed to use whatever terms came to mind. This technique has not proven useful owing to the lack of standards used in indexing the media objects. Put simply, users who are not directly involved in the original indexing of the objects are often unable to find what they are looking for. This is the case even if suitable objects are stored in the database, because the users do not apply the same language to describing the materials as was used by the indexers. To counteract this problem, library science specialists are attempting to impose standards in the indexing of media objects through the use of *controlled vocabularies*, which are also known as subject indexes. It is hoped that through the wide and repeated use of subject indexing standards, the proposition of databasing multimedia objects will become more useful and profitable to the world of users.

submarining: This term refers to an *artifact* common to *LCD* screens in which the *cursor* disappears briefly during a rapid move. The problem is caused by the relatively slow response times of *pixels* in a *LCD* screen.

subnet: This term refers to a portion of a *network* that is defined as a smaller independent network, for the purposes of *IP addresses* or for other network delineation needs.

SUI: Stands for Sound User Interface, and refers to an *I/O* (input/output) *interface* specialized for processing *voice* and other forms of audio. SUIs will become common components on DSP-equipped *MPCs* (*digital signal* processing-equipped multimedia personal computers).

superscalar: From the realm of computer processor design, this term refers to a feature present in many of the latest processors, including the Pentium line of microchips from Intel, in which two or more arithmetic operations are executed at the same time. Superscalar chips tend to have very high performance with respect to floating-point math, which is particularly important for graphics processing.

surfing the net: This refers to a casual type of *browsing* on the *Internet*, in which the user meanders from page to page, from *Web site* to Web site, with no particular destination or research goal in mind. Many spouses are acutely aware of this phenomenon. Hours and hours pass by, family members feel alone and left out, while our subject surfs the net, moving from one point of interest to another, presumably finding nuggets of information all along the way.

surrogate travel: This is one of the first applications of *interactive video* and *virtual reality* to have rightfully earned the status of a *multimedia* genre. Simply put, surrogate travel programs are designed to create the illusion that users can move through geographically remote areas as if they were there. Common subtypes are the *moviemap*, wherein users can travel the streets and byways of remote territories, and the *walkthrough*, wherein users can *navigate* the rooms and hallways of simulated buildings.

surround sound: This is a general commercial term for describing *3-D audio* products. The "5.1 channel sound" provides a representative example of surround sound products. It has five audio *channels:* left, right, and front-center channels, plus separate left and right rear effects channels. In corresponding fashion, use of this product requires five speakers. It also possesses a subwoofer *signal*, which represents the ".1" portion of the product title.

SVGA: The acronym for Super Video Graphics Array, it refers to a high-*resolution RGB* (red, green, blue) color monitor designed to support a PC Super Video Graphics display driver. An SVGA monitor supports at least 256 colors in its highest graphics *mode* (1024 horizontal *pixels* x 768 vertical pixels). This standard is set by *VESA* (Video Electronics Standards Association).

S-VHS: Stands for Super-VHS, a high-quality extension of the VHS tape format for home *video* creation. This higher quality format provides for clearer images and high-fidelity stereo audio. Low-cost standards like S-VHS advance the mission of lowering the barriers to entry for those wanting to produce professional video. And by virtue of a quick leap of faith, it also lowers the barriers creating professional *interactive multimedia*.

S-video: Offering a higher quality *signal* than composite *video*, but a lower quality than *component video*, this mid-level format divides the *signal* into two *channels: luminance* and *chrominance*. It is also referred to as *Y/C*, where the "Y" stands for luminance, and the "C" for chrominance.

switched 56: From the world of telecommunications, this term refers to a service often compared with *ISDN*. Offered by local telephone carriers and *IXCs*, switched 56 traffic can travel over the same physical infrastructure that supports ISDN at rates of up to 56 *Kbps*.

switching node: From the realm of data communications, this term refers to any relay or *interface* between *network* systems not connected by the same physical cable. Such a *node* implements the lower three levels of the *OSI* reference model, the physical, data *link,* and network layers, respectively.

Sword of Damocles: Credited with being the first ever head-mounted display, this device was created in 1968 by *virtual reality* pioneer Ivan Sutherland, while he was a student at Harvard University. This device got its name because it was hung from the ceiling by a large and ominous-looking arm that served as a mechanical *position tracking* device.

symmetric multiprocessing: A term of growing significance in the computer industry, it refers to a type of operating system that works in a *multiprocessing* environment such that it allocates code to run on any free processor in the multiprocessor computer. Thus, it views all of the processors as being equivalent, nonspecialized resources for performing the processing requirements of the system. Asymmetric *multiprocessing* systems, in contrast, typically contain specialized processors that are not equally adept at performing all functions, and that, therefore, contribute in varying fashion to the tasks at hand. An asymmetric system, for example, might have a processor specialized in handling audio data, and would not make use of this audio processor unless the application had audio content. Also referred to by the acronym "SMP," symmetric multiprocessing systems are generally perceived to provide better overall throughput and greater availability than do asymmetric systems.

sync: Short for synchronize, this term refers to the need to create a precise sense of unison between picture and sound elements in a *video sequence*.

synchronous: With regard to data processing, synchronous refers to processes or interactions that occur at the same time, as opposed to those that occur at various points in time (and that are, thus, in *asynchronous mode*). Often, *distance learning* is referred to as either *asynchronous* or synchronou*s*, depending upon whether the instructor and learners are communicating via the *Internet* at the same time (synchronous) through *chat* sessions, or at various times (asynchronous) through *e-mail* or through the viewing and posting of information to classroom *Web sites*.

synthespians: Are computer-generated actors, especially prominent in animated forms of *interactive fiction*, who may perform the roles of *interface agents*.

system emulation titles: A genre of interactive *CD-ROM* titles that seek to engage users in environments that simulate selected real-world economic and/or physical systems. SimCity by Maxis, which engages users in a game where they, in effect, manage and build a simulated city, is considered the exemplar, or core example, of this genre.

systems analyst: Considered the lead design role in the creation of computer systems, the systems analyst is generally charged with the design, specification, feasibility, and implementation of computer systems for business. Relative to the world of *multimedia*, this role is roughly analogous to those of *game designer, instructional designer,* or a creative director of an interactive application.

systems integration: One of the major disciplines of modern data processing, this term refers to the often challenging task of making dissimilar system elements, such as two or more *application programs* created by different manufacturers, work together to achieve a coordinated set of business goals. For example, getting an *e-mail* program developed by an outside vendor to work harmoniously with an organization's homegrown billing system would require a work effort in systems integration.

The stammering newborn work will always be regarded as a monster, even by those who find experiment fascinating.

**—Alain Robbe-Grillet,
French Avante-Garde Novelist**

tactile acuity: Is a measure of the *resolution* of a *tactile feedback* device, such as VPL Research's *DataGlove*.

tactile feedback: One of the new frontiers of human-machine communication, this form of "touch and feel" feedback is emerging from *virtual reality* research labs. It has to do with delivering feedback in a form perceived in a meaningful way by the human *haptic system*. The *DataGlove* and *DataSuit* developed by VPL Research are two early attempts at creating the tactile *interface*.

tag: Is used in *HTML* documents (and other *tagging languages*) to specify the format requirements for size, color, position, and method of display for the content marked.

tagging language: This is a general term for languages that make use of *markup tags* to impart complex formatting characteristics to text documents and *DLOs* (document-like objects). They are essential to programs, such as *desktop* publishing systems, that are specialized for creating highly formatted documents. *SGML* (standard generalized markup language) is perhaps the best known example of a tagging language. Another example is *HTML* (hypertext markup language).

tape autoloader: This form of *near-line storage* makes use of robotic arms to move tapes between a storage area and a unit that reads from, and writes to, the magnetic tape cassettes. This type of alternative storage is gaining popularity, because it accommodates some of the enormous storage requirements of large-scale *multimedia* applications, such as *VOD* (video on demand).

Targa file format: Also commonly referred to by the three-character identifier "TGA," this term refers to a file format standard for *bit-mapped* images that dates back to 1984. The format was established for using the Targa *video* board developed by Truevision. The so-called Targa board was one of the first specialized PC *expansion boards* designed for enhancing the computer's ability to handle visual data.

taxels: An obvious *analog* to the *pixels* of the visual display world, this term is a contraction for tactile display elements. Taxels are the fundamental units of *tactile feedback* and are used in various *virtual reality* devices, such as the *DataGlove*, to deliver "touch and feel," or haptic sensations to the user.

T-carrier system: A breakthrough component in the history of *digital* communications, the T-carrier system was the first successful implementation of digital *voice transmission*. Introduced in the 1960s by the Bell System, its original transmission rate was 1.544 *Mbps*, and was offered in the form of *T1 lines*. Later, the *T3 line* was introduced, featuring a rate of 44.736 *Mbps*. In today's environment, T1 and T3 lines are frequently used by *ISPs* to gain high-speed connections to the *Internet*.

TCO: Stands for Total Cost of Ownership, an economic concept that has become increasingly associated with the raging debate over the relative merits of the *NC* (network computer) versus those of the PC *desktop* computer. Because personal computers are relatively complex pieces of business machinery, requiring frequent software updates and involving steep learning curves, they are said to have a relatively high TCO. In contrast, because it is a relatively simple piece of computing equipment, and is managed almost entirely across the *network* by one or more *servers*, the NC is viewed as having a dramatically lower TCO. This, in fact, is the very foundation of the argument for promoting widespread adoption of network computers. Stay tuned.

TCP: Stands for Transmission Control Protocol (see *OSI* model, layer 4), and is the most common transport layer *protocol* used on *Ethernet networks*, or on the *Internet*. It runs on top of *IP*, Internet protocol, to provide reliable communication, flow-control, *multiplexing*, and a *full-duplex* stream service to the Internet, thereby ensuring complete delivery of the entire message or file.

TCP/IP: Stands for Transmission Control Protocol/Internet Protocol. It is the suite of *protocols* which defines the computer-to-computer communication for the *Internet*. TCP ensures the correct transfer of data. IP receives data from TCP, organizes it into *packets*, and sends it to another *network* within the Internet. TCP/IP is a routable protocol, which means that each *frame* carries a logical *address* containing *pointers* to both the destination network and the destination station. At run time, this logical address is *converted* into a physical *address*, which the various pieces of networking hardware can then use to route each message to its appointed destination safely. TCP/IP was developed at the University of California for the U.S. Department of Defense, originally to run under *UNIX*. Owing to popular demand, it is now available for all major operating systems. (See also *TCP, IP, OSI.*)

TDMA: Stands for Time Division Multiple Access, one of two emerging standards for *digital wireless* communications. TDMA is modeled after a popular method of data communications known as *multiplexing*, whereby a single communication *channel* facilitates the *transmission* of several messages by time-dividing the message stream into units that can be shared by multiple users. The accepted analogy is that TDMA places everyone wishing to communicate into the same room, but allows them to only speak one at a time and only in short *bursts*. Because it represents a new form of transmission capacity, TDMA—along with its sister technology, *CDMA* (code division multiple access)—is thought to be part of the solution to the emerging *bandwidth* crisis that is part and parcel of the coming age of *multimedia*.

tear-off menu: From the world of *interface design*, this term refers to a *menu* that can be removed from the *menu* bar and moved around the screen like a floating *window*. What makes it useful is that it remains fully extended, even after it has been detached, so the user does not have to click it open every time a selection is needed. This feature is extremely popular with graphic artists when they are working with *paint programs*, because it affords them such conveniences as being able to move a color *palette* close to the object they are colorizing. In a more general sense, the tear-off menu is intriguing as an interface design element because it suggests a *mode* of *interactivity* in which objects carry with them, wherever they go, their own user-selectable options.

TEI: Stands for Text Encoding Initiative, which is an international project set up to define a set of generic guidelines for encoding electronic text material. It is a five-year project funded by numerous agencies in the United States, Europe, and Canada. The impetus for this project has come from the need of the research community to access large quantities of data in *electronic form.* "Text," in this context, includes not only text in all forms, but also graphics and audio, all integrated in a seamless vehicle of *digital* information (i.e., into a *compound document*). While printed material uses fonts, chapter headings, and other visual cues to indicate text features, electronic documents need to be coded with *markup tags* to make explicit the various features of the document. *HTML* is an example of a markup language used for *Web pages*. The guidelines developed by TEI provide a generalized *scheme* for markup tags to be used with all kinds of material. *SGML* is used as the base language for TEI, and the full package contains definitions for over 400 different text features grouped into sets. These are documented in *Guidelines for Text Encoding for Interchange*, available to the public since May of 1994.

telecommuting: This now-popular term refers to the practice of performing gainfully employed work from a location that is geographically separated from the employer's place of work. Typically, at the center of any telecommuting situation will be some form of *network* connection between the remote office and the workplace. Increasingly, the network infrastructure supplied by the *Internet* is being used to facilitate the practice of telecommuting. Most telecommuters work from home, and therefore "commute" to work via the electronic connection. Most employers promote telecommuting because it reduces the business *overhead* of having to supply office workers with continuous access to an office.

teleconferencing: The audio precursor to *videoconferencing*, this term refers to a form of communication in which the *enabling technologies* of *POTS* (plain old telephone service) are exploited to allow three or more parties to engage in the same *voice* conversation.

telemetry: This refers to the control of machine processes from remote locations. With the emergence of audio and visual recognition systems, this *multimedia* technology will play an increasing role in the remote control of all types of machines and processes.

telephony: This umbrella term is used to describe the totality of technologies associated with the telephone.

telepresence: A birthplace of many *virtual reality (VR)* products and concepts, this term refers to a field of research and development that is devoted to technologies that enable users to operate equipment, or otherwise exert their presence, in environments from which they are physically separated. The primary purpose of the technology is to enable remotely situated operators to receive enough sensory feedback to feel like they are really at the location where they are trying to perform one or more tasks. As an example, one of the first attempts at developing a telepresence visual system was done by the Philco Corporation in 1958. With this system, operators could see an image from a remote camera on a *CRT* mounted on their head in front of their eyes, and could control the camera's viewpoint by moving their head. A contemporary example would be the use of telepresence technology to manipulate a deep-sea probe, perhaps to upgrade or repair a transoceanic cable, or to seek out buried treasure (such as was depicted in the movie *Titanic*).

teleputer: George Gilder uses this term for the device he predicts will come to serve the function of *interactive television*. He prefers this word because it better captures the sense that this new communications device will embody the convergence of the television, the telephone, and the computer.

telerobotics: One of the key components of *telepresence*, this term refers to the remote manipulation of robotic devices. Though useful in its own right, telerobotics can also be viewed as an engine for *multimedia applications*. By fulfilling the goals of specific telerobotic projects, researchers often stumble across technological serendipities that have much to offer to the manufacturer of *virtual reality* devices. One of the reasons for this is that some of the most interesting and innovative elements of telerobotics can be used to experience the world in ways for which humans are not equipped. For example, though human sight is not equipped to handle the infrared portion of the electromagnetic spectrum, researchers are capable of creating robotic sensors that can see infrared, and from that source, create a representation (e.g., a color-enhanced, partially transparent overlay) that can bring the representation within our visible spectrum.

TeleTact Glove: This *virtual reality* device was developed at the National Advanced Robotics Research Center in conjunction with Airmuscle Ltd., both of which are located in the United Kingdom. This glove is used in tandem with the *DAG* (data acquisition glove), developed by using the same principles. The TeleTact is essentially a virtual reality, *force feedback output device*. When users wear this glove, it makes their hands feel as though they are grasping any number of real-world objects. To do this, the DAG records *digitized* patterns of force feedback. Each pattern is associated with grasping a particular object under a given set of circumstances. Then, the TeleTact re-creates this *force pattern* in a process roughly analogous to the DAC (digital-to-analog conversion) that occurs with *digital* audio devices.

teletext: One of the earliest attempts at providing *multimedia* services to the residential (consumer) market, teletext works by transmitting textual information over the same *transmission* channels that serve television. Largely considered a failed, "bleeding edge" experiment, teletext has been relegated in recent years to supplying public service types of information.

Television Explorer: This is Microsoft's *browser* designed for use with *digital* TV, and obviously a companion product to the company's widely used *Internet browser, Internet Explorer.* An integral part of the *Windows* 98 operating system, Television Explorer is able to gather information from a variety of online TV programming guides—cable, satellite, and broadcast—and display it in a single *grid* on the screen. By thusly exploiting its built-in *search engine*, this product strives to achieve Nicholas Negroponte's (of the MIT *Media Lab*) vision of *personal television.*

Telnet: This term refers to the *Internet* standard *protocol* that allows a user to sign onto a remote time-sharing system. Telnet runs on top of *TCP/IP.* Programs exist under different operating systems to implement this *protocol* by performing *terminal emulation* for the remote system. Like most time-sharing systems, Telnet requires a valid user name and password, and it allows users to enter commands to a *server* as though they were at the console of that server.

template matching: From the realm of *OCR* (optical character recognition), this term refers to one of the most commonly used techniques for recognizing the characters that lie on the original, scanned document. It works by comparing a character with a stored template of the same character. Its primary weakness is that the system can only possess a library of templates with a finite number of font shapes, sizes, and styles. When there is a match, the system will generate the *ASCII* code for the character. When no match is found, the character must be submitted to manual recognition. This technique of template matching is often compared with *feature extraction*, a more powerful, but more expensive, alternative for implementing character recognition.

temporal redundancy: This term is frequently heard in *codec* technology circles, where it is used to describe the tendency for large amounts of information to be repeated from one *frame* to the next in motion picture *sequences.* This tendency is what makes possible a class of *compression* technologies, called *interframe codecs*, that dramatically reduce the amount of visual information required to represent a particular motion sequence by capturing just those elements that change from one frame to the next.

terabyte: This next level of *digital* storage capacity may cause eyebrows to raise, but only in degrees of diminishing astonishment. Once thought to be obtainable only by the very largest organizations, a terabyte of information represents 1,000 *gigabytes* (or one million, million *bytes*; or one trillion *bytes*). As organizations undertake more and more *multi-*

media-oriented projects, such as the mammoth *backfile conversion* projects to transfer all of their paper documents into image data, the use of terabyte-size storage systems will become increasingly common. In today's market, many systems possessing this level of storage capacity come in the form of *optical juke boxes*.

terminal emulation: A throwback to the earliest days of the PC revolution, this term refers to the process of enabling a personal computer to function like a *dumb terminal* connected to a mainframe. Basically, terminal emulation is made possible by a software program that re-creates the behavioral properties of the terminal that it is emulating. Because the *Internet* provides access to such an enormous variety of computers and *networks*, some of which are quite old, the process of terminal emulation is still somewhat in demand.

tertiary memory: This term is used to describe low-speed, high-volume memory, such as *optical juke box*, tape, and other forms of *off-line* and *near-line* mass storage.

texel: From the realm of computer graphics, this term refers to a single colored point in a *texture* map. Conceptually, it is analogous to such fundamental graphical elements as *pixels* and *voxels*.

text search and retrieval: This term refers to the core of competencies that have emerged from the field of *software engineering* over the years to define the manner in which items of information are sought for and found from within our culture's mass of textual documents (e.g., magazines, newspapers, etc.). This is a very important frontier for the entire information industry, because how we learn to organize, and then find, textual items will establish the scientific bases for how we organize and search for other forms of information. In general, an information retrieval system may be thought of as a form of structured memory where items are stored and then *tagged* or indexed for later retrieval. With text, unfortunately, most of the information is contained in documents that possess a form which is very poorly organized from the standpoint of facilitating computer searches. Indeed, only tabular forms of data, such as are found in databases, are well suited for implementing rapid and accurate lookup. Thus, much of the effort associated with text search and retrieval has to do with making text documents more readily searchable. The longest standing method for organizing the contents of documents for searchability has been that of appending to the document a header record, or summary file, and then filling that data structure with *keywords* that describe the contents. Thus, a header record appended to the contents of this book would undoubtedly contain entries such as *multimedia*, "interactive," and the like. Using this method, at least some portion of the document is structured for search and retrieval; and, in any event, the presence of the header record obviates the need to search the entire document, which can prove to be an extremely *CPU-intensive* and costly undertaking. Of course, the crux of indexing is whether or not the index entries successfully represent the contents. The issue is further complicated when we recognize that different groups and constituencies (lawyers versus college professors, for example) will define what is important in a particular document in entirely different ways. Suffice it to say that as we move into an era where it becomes increasingly important that other forms of media are effectively indexed, as is already becoming the case with *clip media* and *stock footage* libraries, the techniques and knowledge we derive from the ongoing practice of text search and retrieval will grow steadily in importance.

text-to-speech conversion: This emerging medium of the *MPC* (multimedia personal computer) relies upon *DSP* (digital signal processing) technology to process *ASCII* text, generate a phonetic transcription, and then produce synthetic speech. In other words, with this technology, the computer becomes able to "read aloud" any document stored in the industry-standard ASCII format. This technology has been available for some time in such products as IBM's Primary Editor Plus, a word processor for children, which, among other things, is capable of reading back anything that the child (or other user) has typed. Most existing systems provide rather crude and mechanical interpretations of human speech. But as *voice* synthesizers become more lifelike, computers will increasingly communicate by speaking in natural human tones (see, for example, *speech fonts*).

texture: When used in conjunction with computer graphics, this term refers to a two-dimensional *bit map* that is pasted onto objects, or *polygons*, to add realism. Many *clip media* vendors sell libraries of common (and not-so-common) textures for use with *paint systems*. These libraries may include various wood surfaces (e.g., oak, mahogany), natural surfaces (e.g., grass and clay), or human-made substances (e.g., brick and cement).

texture mapping: Is a common feature in *paint systems*, and refers to the mapping of *digitized* surface *textures* (e.g., a brick pattern) onto a *wireframe* surface to create a more refined and realistic image.

TGM: Stands for Thesaurus of Graphic Materials, which is a *subject index* that provides a substantial body of terms for the indexing of pictorial materials, particularly the large general collections of historical images found in many libraries, historical societies, *archives*, and museums. As with any subject index, the intent of the TGM is to promote standardization in image *cataloging*. Developed by the U.S. Library of Congress, TGM stands as a prototype for the *multimedia database* and *clip media* industries.

thesaurus: The conventional meaning of this term is, of course, that of a dictionary devoted to listing synonyms and antonyms. Recently, however, this term has been annexed into the realm of *subject indexing*, where it is used to name any instance of a *controlled vocabulary* used for indexing particular classes of information objects. This term is important to *multimedia* because it is now being used to describe widely accepted controlled vocabularies, such as the *TGM* (Thesaurus of Graphic Materials), which are used to standardize the *cataloging,* or databasing, of multimedia objects such as *clip media.*

thin client: This term has become nearly synonymous with the *NC*, which is a *desktop* computer that relies upon connections to one or more *network servers* for most of its functionality and sophistication. The adjective "thin" is used to describe these machines because they typically lack many of the components that characterize today's "fat" personal computers; i.e., they tend not to have any *expansion boards* or *disk* drives, and do not feature a very powerful *CPU*. Often, this term is used more restrictively to refer to just the software that resides on a network-connected computer. In this case, a thin client is a program that possesses minimal software functionality, and therefore does not demand much in the way of local computer resources (e.g., memory, disk space, CPU cycles).

3-D animation: From the high end of computer graphics, this term refers to a form of *animation* that relies upon the on-screen movement and interaction of 3-D objects. From a *production* standpoint, the creation of 3-D animation presents many thorny problems; the most significant of which is that it is both *CPU-* and memory-intensive. Because of this, 3-D animation tends to be quite expensive to develop, deliver, and support.

3-D digitizing: This emergent, sophisticated form of data generation works by capturing (*digitizing*) the x, y, and z coordinates of a real object, thus creating a 3-D representation of that object. These data can then be used to create, for example, a holographic image. The fundamental unit of information *captured* by 3-D digitizing is often referred to as a *voxel*, the 3-D equivalent of a *pixel*.

3-D sound: This term refers to sound systems that produce convincingly directional, 360-degree *spatial* motion and support acoustics. The implementation of 3-D sound usually involves stereo earphones that make use of *DSP* (digital signal processing) to deliver complementary audio *signals* that reconstitute sonic volume and motion.

thresholding: From the world of document and image scanning, this term refers to a process used to create clean images from dirty, faded originals. The user sets a limit of contrast—a threshold—beneath which the *pixel* will be reproduced as white, and above which it will be reproduced as black.

thumbnails: This term refers to the postage-stamp sized reductions of *digital* images that are rapidly taking a prominent place in the design and implementation of graphical user interfaces (*GUIs*). The term was originally coined because these image reductions tend to be about the size of a human thumbnail. This size is justified because it is large enough to make the visual contents discernible to the human eye, but small enough to conserve screen geography and memory consumption. The most common use of thumbnails in today's *multimedia* market is to supply visual summaries of images stored in some type of collection (e.g., *clip media* collections, *digital libraries, multimedia databases*). Thumbnails are also commonly used in digital *video* editing tools to represent the *frames* in a video sequence. In this capacity, they enable *editors* to manipulate portions of a videostream by simply clicking on, or *dragging* and dropping, the thumbnails.

TIFF: Stands for Tagged Image File Format, an industry standard for *bit-mapped* images, originally developed by Aldus Corporation. This standard uses *tags* (i.e., labels) to define the structure of graphics images that have been *captured* by *digital scanners* for processing. It supports black-and-white, grayscale, pseudocolor, and true-color images in any *resolution*, all of which can be stored in a compressed or uncompressed format. TIFF was designed as an industry standard in the 1980s when transferring graphic images between applications and/or *platforms* had represented a substantial problem.

timbrality: With respect to *MIDI* (musical instrument digital interface) synthesizers—perhaps the key audio technology of the *MPC* (multimedia personal computer) standard—this term refers to the number of different instruments that a given MIDI device can play simultaneously. Obviously, the greater the number of simultaneous instruments, the more resonant the sound.

timbre: Pronounced "tam-bur," this term refers to one of the key components in a musical sound. Typically distinguished from *pitch* and loudness, timbre establishes the distinguishing quality of a musical sound (in much the same way that *hue* distinguishes a color). With regard to many of the emerging and sophisticated *digital* audio production tools, timbre is an element that is typically isolated so that it can be more directly manipulated by the composer or audio engineer. *MIDI* (musical instrument digital interface) composition tools are particularly adept at manipulating timbre.

time code: This term refers to a code embedded in a *video* sequence so as to facilitate editing and synchronization. Each *frame* in the *video* is given a time offset (or *address*) from the beginning of the sequence, thus enabling *editors* to specify precise entry and exit points from which to start and end scenes, respectively. In the soon-to-be-extinct realm of analog video, time codes are actually burned into a spare *track* on the videotape (see *BITC*), where they remain until the penultimate stages of *postproduction*. In the rising realm of *digital* video, time codes will be just another digital element in the video data stream, and will be responsible for enabling *random access* and the databasing of video content.

time stamp: Is information added to a message, record, or other unit of data indicating the time at which it was processed by the system.

time-line metaphor: This term refers to the most commonly used *interface design* for *media integrators* and other computer presentation systems. These *interfaces* use a columnar, almost spreadsheet-like structure, with the columns calibrated in terms of time slots. The rows represent the various media sources (audio/*voice* clips, music, image, *video* sequences, etc.). By using this specialized, time-based, tabular structure, the time-line metaphor makes it easy for *multimedia application* developers to synchronize a wide variety of media types by controlling their appearance, their "performance," and their disappearance with reference to a shared time line.

title depth: This is a descriptive term that connotes one very important aspect of a *CD-ROM* or *DVD* title's quality: namely, its depth of content, which can be largely discerned from how many times the user is inclined to use it. A "shallow title" is one that users discard after using only once or a few times, and would therefore be characterized as having very little depth. In contrast, a title with depth will have, generally speaking, many layers of content and will inspire its users to reuse the program over and over again. Because it possesses a strong multiplay quality, *Myst*, by Broderbund, is said to have excellent title depth.

titling: Refers to the process of laying down text overtop of a *video signal*. Now an integral function in most *desktop* video systems, standard applications of titling include the placement of *video* text for company logos on advertising pieces, and the *production* of titles and screen credits for movies and TV broadcasts.

T1 line: A *digital* telephone line—commonly used for *distance learning*, among other things—the T1 line transfers digital information at the relatively high rate of 1.544 megabits per second. The T1 line is made of two twisted-pair copper cables. Much of the *Internet backbone* is made up of T1 lines leased to various subscribers.

topology: This term describes the physical layout of a *network*, the computers on the network, and the *links* that join them.

torque: In the field of *animation*, this term refers to the twisting of parts of the body in contrast to each other. It is believed that by paying close attention to such relational aspects of body motion as torque, animators are better able to create *life quality* in their *productions*.

touch screen: A popular form of effecting human-computer interaction, especially with *IVD* (interactive video disc) applications, this technology makes it possible for users to interact with computer programs by simply touching designated *hot spots* on the screen. Touch screens work under much the same principle as the *mouse* input device, except that, rather than clicking on the desired hot spot, the user simply touches it with a finger. (See also *SAW*.)

track: With regard to the storage of *digital* information, a track is a *linear*, spiral, or circular path on which information is placed. This term is equally applicable to magnetic and optical forms of storage. This term is also used in the film/*video* community to refer to any single component of a finished video, such as the sound track.

track analysis: In film and *video production*, this refers to an examination of a sound*track* by the *editor* to determine exactly where various sounds occur.

trackball: From the world of computer input devices, this device uses a ball that is free to move around within a fixed mounting. As the user rotates the ball, receptors inside the fixed mounting record the movement and translate it into on-screen *cursor* movements.

tracking devices: A category of *virtual reality* gear, tracking devices calculate the user's movements within a *virtual world* based on that user's actual physical movements. The *Polhemus Tracker* is an example of a tracking device.

transceiver: This term refers to a communication device that possesses both a receiver and a transmitter in the same unit. Transceiver devices are heavily relied upon to equip most *wireless* communication infrastructures.

transfer rate: In computing, this general term refers to the rate at which information is moved between any two devices, particularly from *online storage* into RAM. Currently, an important transfer rate is that between *servers* and clients across the *Internet*, because it represents a bottleneck, making it difficult for producers of interactive programs to create many of the audio-visual effects taken for granted in the arena of traditional, *analog video productions.*

transmission: Is a general term for both the act of sending or receiving an object and the object itself, such as a fax. The word can be qualified by the control *protocol*, which defines the format of the transmission. It can also be qualified by the type of medium, which is used to carry the transmission, as in *baseband* transmission in which one *signal* is carried at a time, or *broadband* transmission in which many signals are carried at one time. Most communications between computers use baseband transmissions.

transmission media: Is a general term for describing the physical media that are used to facilitate a given form of communications. Though most of the public takes them for granted, transmission media are an extremely important part of our national infrastructure. At present, many large corporations in the communications industry are making huge investments in transmission media, particularly in *fiber optic cable*, primarily to help establish their place in the emerging *NII* (National Information Infrastructure) and *GII*. See also *cabling*.

transparent GIF: This term refers to a *GIF* image whose color background is made to appear clear, so that the GIF background essentially disappears into the background color of the *Web page* itself, where it is being inserted. Various *shareware* tools for making GIFs transparent are available at *TUCOWS* and other *Web sites*.

transponder: This important device is used in satellites and plays a critical role in the provision of *DBS* services. A transponder basically operates like a mirror since it receives a signal from earth (an *uplink*) and retransmits that same information back to earth (a *downlink*).

treatment: A term derived from the world of film and TV, it refers to a general or high-level description of a proposed program, an outline of sorts. It is generally used as the first step in the business planning process to interest potential clients, programmers, publishers, etc.

trucking: In film and *video production*, this term refers to the movement of the camera toward or away from the scene. "Trucking in" means that the camera is being moved closer. "Trucking back" means that the camera is being moved further back. These terms are near-synonyms for *panning* and *zooming*.

TrueType: Developed by Apple Computer, this widely used standard defines a set of outline-based typefaces that are used to create display and printer fonts.

TSR: This software acronym stands for Terminate-and-Stay Resident, and it is used to describe programs that load themselves into memory with the intent of staying there. TSRs are typically represented by software utilities, such as *screen capture programs*, which developers, in particular, like to have at their disposal.

T3 line: A *digital* line facility used to transmit a DS3 formatted digital *signal* at 44.736 megabits per second, ample capacity for carrying full-screen, full-motion video (*FMV*).

TUCOWS: Stands for The Ultimate Collection Of Winsock Software. TUCOWS is a *Web site* that provides a horde of *shareware* software, all of which can be *downloaded* from the *Internet*. (The *address* is "http:// www.tucows.com".)

tunneling: When users establish a secure path through the *Internet*, they are said to be tunneling. With security being such a pervasive concern with respect to using the Internet for critical and *proprietary* forms of information exchange, the notion of being able to establish one, or even a *network* of, private—and therefore secure—pathways is enormously appealing. The *IETF* has proposed a standard for setting up Internet tunnels called PPTP, or point-to-point tunneling protocol, which, among other things, should enable organizations to have VPNs, or *virtual* private networks, on the Internet.

tunneling router: From the world of the *Internet*, this term refers to the process of *encrypting* and decrypting information that flows to and from untrusted computer *networks* for security purposes.

Turing Test: This refers to the frequently cited test described by Alan Turing in his justly famous 1950 article "Computing Machinery and Intelligence." In that article, he proposed that the only way for a computer to prove itself to be truly intelligent (in the human sense) was if it could respond to the questions asked by a human interviewer in such a way that the answers would be indistinguishable from those that one would expect to receive from a human. In other words, a computer may finally be deemed intelligent when—and only when—it can carry on a normal conversation with a human being. As we progress further and further into the recesses of the age of *multimedia*, the ability for *interface agents* to pass the Turing Test may become a key technological *benchmark*.

tutorial: Borrowed from the world of academe, this term is used by *instructional designers* to refer to a form of *multimedia application* that seeks to pull learners through a highly constricted sequence of interactive experiences designed to convey a narrowly defined set of learning objectives. Software tutorials and *drill-and-practice* math programs are two fairly obvious examples of this type of *educational software*.

TV tuner boards: This category of *expansion board* enables the user to receive broadcast *video* and display it in a *window* on the PC monitor. This type of *board* simplifies the process of using the computer to view video segments because it causes the video stream to bypass the PC's internal graphics subsystem, playing it directly from its *analog* source (e.g., directly from a VCR).

TVRO: Stands for TeleVision Receive Only, and is used to describe antennae (dishes) that are used to receive *signals* from a satellite. TVROs are the principal form of subscriber equipment in the *DBS* (direct broadcasting by satellite) market.

TWAIN: This term refers to an established *interface protocol* that seeks to standardize the way various image *capture* devices, such as *scanners* and *frame grabbers*, are accessed by application software. As an example, any *scanner* that is "TWAIN-compliant" can be directly accessed from within software that supports TWAIN devices. Not to be confused with Mark Twain, the nineteenth-century American writer.

twitch-and-shoot fantasy: An obviously derogatory term, this phrase describes the dominant genre in the first generation of *video* games that focuses on violent themes and the user's ability to respond quickly to various forms of animated threat by merely blasting those threats to smithereens (or its electronic equivalent).

two-plane effects: From the realm of *DVE* (digital video effects), this term refers to a broad family of effects used primarily to effect a visual transfer from one screen to its successor. Fades and *dissolves* are common types of this effect. Two-plane effects are so called because they operate on two visual planes, with the image held on the uppermost, or *front, plane* being replaced by the image held on the lower, or *back, plane*.

txt: This term refers to a popular *file extension* used with files that hold "vanilla" text, most often *encoded* in the *ASCII* character set. This file format has long been the lowest common denominator among text documents because it ensures that the file does not possess any invisible control characters.

Our methods of transmitting and reviewing the results of research are generations old and by now are totally inadequate for their purposes.
**—Vannevar Bush,
Conceptual Pioneer of "Hypertext"**

UDP: Stands for User Datagram Protocol, which is a connectionless *protocol* that *NFS* (Network File System) utilizes to make it stateless, that is, each request is an independent transaction.

ultrasonic position sensing: This is an experimental form of *position tracking* being investigated in *virtual reality* research. Basically, the technology works by placing some form of ultrasound emitter on an object (such as a human being). As this emitter moves around within the *virtual world*, ultrasound sensors (microphones) keep track of its position by *sampling* the location of the transmitter.

underlay: In the world of *animation*, this terms refers to a section of the background that is mounted on the *cel*. Adopting an object-oriented approach to animation, underlays, like other constituent elements of the animated world, can be stored in libraries for continual re-use.

undo: An important graphical user interface (*GUI*) application *menu* choice in most quality applications, this command permits users to reverse their most recently performed actions. Utilization of this option fulfills the maxim: "to err is human, to forgive divine."

unicast: As opposed to *multicast*, this term refers to sending messages to a single, specified *host* over the *Internet*.

universal readership: One of the most democratic principles of the modern *Internet*, this term refers to the goal of making it possible for any information available on the *Web* to be accessible from any type of computer in any geographical location by any authorized party.

UNIX: This popular and venerable multi-user, multitasking computer operating system is commonly used by *Internet servers*. Originally developed at Bell Labs in the early 1970s, it was not a *proprietary* operating system owned by one company. As a result, it attracted many different *software engineering* firms, and evolved into a very robust, network-oriented product. Among its many favorable characteristics, the *TCP/IP* suite is fully integrated with UNIX.

uplink: The opposite of *downlink*, this term represents the first path segment of a satellite communication in which a terrestrial *signal* is beamed from a ground station to a satellite in orbit.

upload: To upload a file of programs or data is to transfer it over a *digital* communications link from one computer to another. One generally uploads from a client or smaller computer to a *server*. *FTP* is commonly used to upload files. Uploading is the opposite of *downloading*.

URC: Stands for Uniform Resource Citation. URC is a form of *metadata* describing a document on the *Web*. It consists of pairs of data, i.e., a field name plus a value, which give an attribute about the file. Some of its fields include: *URIs*, author, publisher, data type, date, and *copyright* status. A URC is not considered a character string, but rather a set of fields with values in a free format.

URI: Stands for Uniform Resource Identifier. URI is a generic term for all types of names and *addresses* referring to objects on the *Web*. A *URL* is one kind of URI.

URL: Stands for Uniform Resource Locator. It is the standard for specifying the absolute *address* of a resource on the *World Wide Web*. The access *scheme* or *protocol* for a URL is the first part before the colon. The format of the rest of the URL depends on the *protocol*. For "http" it includes the *host number* or a *domain name*, path, the resource or file, and optionally, attributes or a command. For example, if we look at the following URL address: "http://wagner.princeton.edu/foldoc/cgi-script?NCSA"—"http" is the protocol, "wagner.princeton.edu" is the domain name, "foldoc" is the path, "cgi-script" is the program file, and "?NCSA" is a query string. The "?" indicates a fragment identifier or a specific location in the document. However, one of the persistent problems associated with the URL standard is that if the file is moved, then the access is broken. Unless someone kindly provides a *forwarding address*, the user trying to access this URL will receive a "file not found" error message. URLs are used extensively on the *Web*. They provide the destination addresses for all *hyperlinks* specified in *HTML* documents. Other values for the protocol may be *FTP, telnet, gopher, WAIS*, etc. Use of partial URLs may lead to a successful connection. If only a file name is given, the *browser* assumes the same *host* and directory as the previous call.

URN: Stands for Uniform Resource Name. URN is a concept proposed originally in 1991, but it is still under development by an *IETF* working group. The concept is being developed to provide a more durable means of addressing resources on the Net. The widely used *URL* fails if a file has been moved to another directory or *host*. URNs will require *servers* on the *network* to provide the current *address* of all resources, much as the *IP* server does today for *host* addresses. The format of a URN is still being discussed. *Browsers* will recognize a URN as another form of *protocol*, and pass them to a server to be resolved into an absolute address.

usability: In the world of computer programming, this term refers to that quality of an application that makes the software easy for the user to understand, learn, and use. A *systems analyst* can incorporate several components into a software program to heighten its usability. Online reference and procedural information, typically in the form of a *PSS* (*performance support system*), enables an application user to obtain just-in-time, *context-sensitive help*. *CBT* (or *MBT* or *WBT*) provides in-advance training that can get the user off to a good start with the application. And last but not least, the quality of the graphical user interface (*GUI*), as reflected in the clarity and expressiveness of its *icons* and other *interface design* elements, and in the clarity and completeness of its workflows, will be the ultimate determination of usability for a software application.

usability evaluation lab: In the early 1980s, IBM Corporation began focusing its efforts on small-systems development, as well as on developing complementary business application software to run on these *platforms*. In an effort to improve the *usability* of the software *interface design*, as well as the design of the supporting documentation and training materials, IBM devoted its efforts to building *usability* labs. Rather than testing for software bugs or hardware human factors glitches, as had been previously done, this lab concerned itself with the design elements that enabled a new user to understand, learn, and use the business applications. A team in Atlanta, Georgia, composed of M. Mehal, R. Autry, P. Smith, Dr. J. Morgan, and Dr. D. Leonard, developed the IBM Atlanta Usability Lab, as well as a usability lab evaluation process for planning, designing, running, analyzing, and reporting evaluation results. From that seed, IBM and its business application customers began to think about and evaluate software from a usability perspective. Through another IBM Atlanta effort, the Multiples Marketing Program, IBM disseminated to its hardware and software customers the knowledge, expertise, and process for conducting usability lab evaluations worldwide. As a result, many companies now have usability labs in which end users, sitting in a control room, perform various tasks with the software in development. These users are observed by developers in an observation room and are filmed, interviewed, surveyed, and essentially brought into the development process solely for the purposes of improving the usability of the software and its supporting materials. Quantitative data extracted from these tests include the tasks performed successfully, task performance time, number of errors, and error recovery time. Qualitative data extracted include (through observations, written surveys, and interviews) evaluation subject preferences, problems, solutions, and overall emotional responses to the software. Hopefully, the usability lab evaluation process will also be employed for the development of *hypermedia applications* and *multimedia* applications.

USB: Stands for Universal Serial Bus, which is a *"plug-and-play" interface* between a computer and various peripheral devices attached to it, including audio players, keyboards, printers, *scanners*, telephones, and the like. The USB standard is a joint development of DEC, IBM, Intel, Microsoft, NEC, and Northern Telecom. It is available at no cost to all computer and peripheral vendors.

Usenet: Is a worldwide, or distributed, bulletin board system (*BBS*) containing more than 15,000 *newsgroups* or forums covering any topic your heart could possibly desire. It was developed in 1979–1980 at Duke University by Steve Bellovin, Jim Ellis, Tom Truscott, and Steve Daniel for *UNIX* machines. Today, it is accessed from the *Internet,* and from many other online services, by subscribers from government agencies, high schools, and businesses. It has become a focal point for technical articles, news *discussion groups*, *chats*, and *flames*. Newsgroups can be moderated or unmoderated, i.e., censored or not censored.

user interface: A term that has gradually taken on great importance for *multimedia applications*, user interface refers to the point of contact between a human user and the contents of a computer system. Traditionally, this term was used to denote the devices through which a user would communicate with the computer, e.g., the keyboard, the *joystick*, etc. As the computer has become more knowledge oriented and media oriented, and as these devices have become more sophisticated (e.g., with the use of *tactile feedback* devices, such as the *DataGlove* and *DataSuit*), the role of the user interface and its design will continue to grow and expand in significance. Concepts such as the *interface agent* and *avatars* lie at the cutting edge of thinking that is now taking place with regard to the user interface.

UTP: Stands for Unshielded Twisted-Pair, a term that refers to the least expensive, lowest capacity form of *transmission media* used in the *transmission* of data. Formed by twisting pairs of copper wires—typically in groups of four—UTP is just one step above telephone cable. By twisting the copper wires, this technology reduces some of the electrical interference that can occur from proximity to motors, computers, etc. Owing to its low cost, UTP is a very popular medium for networking computers and is often cited as a difficult-to-hit, but desirable, target for implementing networked *multimedia applications.*

UUencode/UUncode: This term refers to a set of algorithms for converting files into a series of *7-bit ASCII* characters for *transmission* on the *Internet.* UUencode stands for "UNIX-to-UNIX encode," a term that owes to this software utility's *UNIX* origin. Today it is a universal *protocol* used to transfer files between different *platforms* including UNIX, *Windows*, and Macintosh.

Reading entails the possibility that we may formulate ourselves and so discover what has previously seemed to elude our consciousness.
—**Wolfgang Iser, Literary Theorist**

vanity board: In the world of *electronic game design*, this term refers to a game screen used mostly in arcade games to present accumulated high-score information.

variable-length records: This refers to a way of organizing a database such that the sizes of records containing the data need not be uniform. With the move to media-based forms of data (to audio, image, and *video* databases), the need for variable-length records will grow. One of the carryovers from the alphanumeric-only days now being adapted for this use is the so-called *memo field*. With a memo field, only the *address* of the record is stored in a fixed-length format. The content of the field is open-ended and, in fact, may be stored on a separate device from the one that holds its address.

VBI: Stands for Vertical Blanking Interval, which is the black bar in between *frames* of a television broadcast. The limited *bandwidth* capacity of VBI has been used in recent times to carry the small amounts of control information associated with early attempts at interactive forms of television. Information transmitted through VBI is limited to text, simple graphics, and information for positioning on-screen objects. In the 1980s, *teletext* services offered news and other information through a VBI *signal* on broadcast television. Of note to the curious, the plans for building the inter-stellar transport vehicle featured in the film *Contact* were sent via the VBI of the extra-terrestrial *transmissions* sent to earth.

VDU: Stands for Visual Display Unit, a very general term that refers to the now-diverse universe of *video* displays (e.g., *LCDs*, *CRTs*, etc.).

vector: This term is used in the realm of computer graphics to refer to the mathematical representation of a geometric object contained within a computer image. Vectors are typically used to represent "primitive" objects such as circles, arcs, and lines. Their use in this context reflects an effort to create an abstract representation of *digitized* images, thereby reducing the storage space and *transmission bandwidth* required to handle visual forms of data.

vector file: As opposed to raster, or *bit-map,* files, vector files are made up of mathematical equations—also referred to as *vectors*—that provide an easily manipulated representation of an image. *Raster files,* in contrast, are typically large, because they are composed of a bit map that possesses a value (or set of values) for every *pixel* in the image. Though they are more readily manipulated, vector files typically do not possess the high-image quality found in most raster files.

vector-to-raster conversion: In the everyday world of *multimedia applications,* a veritable explosion of paint and image manipulation software tools has created a frequent need to *convert* files from one format to another. Vector-to-raster conversion is one of the easiest conversion processes to perform. This sort of translation effectively takes a picture snapshot of a *vector file* and organizes it into a *bit map.*

Veronica: Developed at the University of Nevada, Veronica (which stands for Very Easy Rodent Oriented Net-wide Index to Computerized Archives) is a database of the items on (almost) every *menu* on thousands of *gopher* services. It is updated regularly and provides *keyword* and subject searches of gopher menu titles in the *gopher space.*

versioning: This term refers to the process of naming, finding, and manipulating different versions of files or documents in a *digital library.*

vertical correlation: Also referred to as "vertical redundancy," and closely related to the concept of *horizontal correlation,* this term refers to an element of redundancy present in most sources of visual information. If, for example, two *pixels* located next to one another in the vertical plane of a picture have the same visual characteristics (i.e., the same color and *brightness*), then they may be said to possess vertical correlation. This form of redundancy, like all other forms of visual redundancy, is important to the process of *video compression.* If a whole vertical string of *pixels* have the same visual characteristics (in a background depicting the sky, for example) then they may be easily compressed down to a simple mathematical formula. This formula will express the shared visual characteristics of that string of *pixels* only once, accompanied by a multiplier that represents the number of consecutive pixels possessing those characteristics (a compression technique known as *RLE* [run-length encoding]).

VESA: This is the acronym for one of the *multimedia* industry's leading standard-setting associations. It stands for Video Electronic Standards Association, and it is represented by a set of software and hardware manufacturers with a common concern for establishing standards for graphic and *video* display adapter cards.

VESA VL Bus: The *VESA* stands for Video Electronics Standards Association, and the term refers to one of the early standards set for overcoming the bottlenecks associated with handling *video* on traditional PCs. The VESA VL Bus, which was featured on a number of *video adapter cards*, is a 32-bit *bus* capable of operating as fast as a *CPU's* memory access speeds. This standard was designed to enable faster operating speeds of video display and hard *disk* subsystems at affordable prices.

VFW: Stands for Video for Windows, Microsoft's package of system and authoring software for integrating *video* files into Microsoft *Windows*.

VGA: An acronym that stands for Video Graphics Array, it refers to the medium resolution *RGB* (red, green, blue) color monitor designed to support a PC Video Graphics display driver card. Now largely an historical curiosity, VGA is a display standard that was originally developed by IBM in 1987 for its PS/2 line of computers and supports 16 colors in its highest graphics *mode* (640 horizontal *pixels* x 480 vertical pixels).

VGA-to-NTSC boards: This class of *board* product takes the *signal* from a PC's graphics adapter and *converts* it to a *composite signal* (e.g., SuperVHS) so that it can be recorded onto an *analog* medium such as a videocassette. Some of these products also offer *genlocking* and *overlay* capabilities, making it possible for the user to combine PC graphics with the *video* before it is sent to the tape.

victory conditions: In the world of *electronic game design*, this term refers to the threshold of performance that the player must achieve to "win" the game.

video: Is a system of recording and transmitting visual information by converting moving or still images into electrical *signals*. These signals can be broadcast through high-frequency *carrier* waves or sent through cables on a closed circuit.

video adapter card: A family of *expansion cards* designed to enhance the PC's ability to manipulate *video*, these cards work by off-loading many of the video processing functions from the *CPU* to the card itself.

video bandwidth: One of the key components in measuring the tractability of a *multimedia application* (i.e., the ability to process the amount of information at an acceptable rate), video bandwidth is a measure of the size of a *digitized video* data stream. Four major elements go into determining video bandwidth: 1) the *aspect ratio* of the picture; 2) the scanning method (*interlaced* versus *progressive*, with the latter requiring twice as much *bandwidth* as the former); 3) the picture's repetition rate (i.e., the *frame rate*), which is usually expressed as frames per second, such as the 30 *fps* of *NTSC* (National Television Standards Committee) television; and 4) the number of *scan lines* in each *frame* (which is the dominant component in determining the picture's *resolution*).

video Christmas card: This metaphoric term represents one of those future exemplars of how we may use the high-*bandwidth networks* of the future to communicate with one another at holiday events, or whenever. An example is when Dave in *2001: A Space Odyssey*, by Stanley Kubrick, receives a visual birthday greeting from his parents while he is on board the spaceship headed toward one of Jupiter's moons.

video dial-tone: A concept associated with the *picturephone*, the video dial-tone is functionally analogous to the telephone *dial-tone* in that it provides the individual user with some sort of visual pattern that signifies that *bandwidth* has been made available for purposes of placing a *video* phone call.

video dictionary: A subclass of *hypermedia applications*, this term refers to programs that feature the alphabetically organized collection of information items, primarily in the form of *video* clips.

video digitizer: Typically, this refers to a board-level product that accepts *analog video* input from standard *video* sources, such as VCRs, videocameras, *laserdiscs*, and cable TV, and displays it on the monitor screen, converting the *signal* into a binary (*digital*) file on cue. Some of these products display the video signal in its native *interlaced* format, where the screen is painted in two passes. Other boards reconstruct a frame in memory before displaying it as a *noninterlaced* image, which offers the advantage of less *flicker* and more clarity.

video fax: This term is nearly synonymous with *movies-on-demand*, a term that refers to an emerging service, whereby consumers access movies of their own choice from a central database of films. The term video fax describes the technical process that controls how users make use of *movies-on-demand* services. After accessing the database of movies, and making a selection, the consumer waits a short period of time while the *digital* form of the film is *downloaded* from the central database to the *interactive television* playback unit. Thus, envisioned in this fashion, movies-on-demand may work much like the ubiquitous document fax does today: The entire contents of the document (movie) are transmitted and received before the user begins to consume any part of it.

video PBX: Nearly synonymous with *video server*, this term refers to communications hardware that serves as the intermediary between residential consumers and databases of *video* product. It is called a *PBX* (private branch exchange), because it operates much like a telephonic PBX in making large numbers of point-to-point connections. In most cases, equipment worthy of this term is relatively high-end (e.g., mainframe) computing hardware owned and operated by the cable companies.

video segmenting: This process lies at the cutting edge of *multimedia* technology. It employs various forms of visual pattern recognition to automate the process of intelligently segmenting *video* content into manageable and purposeful chunks. To date, the most common form of video segmenting has to do with automated scene-change detection. To perform this function, algorithms have been constructed that scan each *frame* of a video *sequence* to determine which ones represent a boundary between one scene and another. Clearly, one of the key detection variables for scene detection has to be simply that of the absolute amount of change—or delta—that occurs from one frame to the next. The purpose of such algorithms, obviously, is to automate the process of breaking *digital* video sequences into scenes. Future—and more meaningful—applications of video segmenting might include visual detection algorithms that are capable of identifying particular actors, thereby enabling the process of segmenting a video into scenes in which a particular actor appears. Imagine, for example, a video segmenting program that could scan an entire *archive* of films, generating a list of mark-in and mark-out points for every segment in which Cary Grant or Marylin Monroe appears—or where they appear together.

video server: This term refers to a specialized portion of a *LAN* (local area network) set aside to handle the unique demands of providing sources of *digital video* to LAN clients in much the same way as traditional LAN *servers* provide data and application services to those same clients. A video server must cope with the unique challenges associated with the large, continuously flowing streams of data (i.e., *streaming* data) necessary to play compressed digital video or other high-*bandwidth* audiovisual data types. These *mixed media data types* are time dependent, and thus, in addition to requiring a continuous (uninterrupted) connection between client and server, possess several key differences relative to the traditional sources of data that move over LANs. These traditional sources are characterized by relatively small file sizes, and thus, possess the need for only momentary and intermittent dominance of the *network channel* capacity. As a consequence, most traditional *LAN protocols* are contention based and are designed to handle *bursty traffic* over a shared *transmission* line on the network, where only one *client/server*, or workstation-to-workstation connection is being accommodated at any given moment. Typically, these data conversations are so brief, that the individual users are unaware that their requests are being handled out of a *queue*. In contrast, *multimedia* data flows demand relatively long and continuous connections, and so are not well suited to the traditional network *protocols*. Instead, most video servers demand dedicated, point-to-point connections with each of their clients, an arrangement referred to as a *star topology*. Additionally, because the transmission resource (the wire connecting server to client, for example) is not normally a shared resource, the network protocols for networked video are not normally based upon contention *schemes*, but rather rely on conversational protocols more typical of *telephony*.

video teleconferencing, videoconferencing: Possibly one of the earliest and largest markets for *multimedia*, this application essentially applies the technologies associated with *picturephone* to group situations. Despite the relatively high cost of transmitting *video* in *real time*, video teleconferencing is viewed as being affordable when used to hold high priority, corporate-style meetings where face-to-face contact is seen as a critical element in the communications. Several standards have cropped up to *encode* the *quasi-video signals* that are typically used in video teleconferencing, the most notable being the *H.261* standard.

videodisc: Like the old format war that was fought between Betamax and VHS over who would be king (the standard, that is) in the VCR industry, the videodisc standard was once compared against *CD-ROM* as an alternative for delivering interactive forms of media. The videodisc standard is physically larger than CD-ROM (about the size of an LP album) and is double-sided, and its *data rate* and rotational speed are higher. However, it had one serious drawback that ultimately destined it to go the way of Betamax. Though its control information is stored in *digital* format, its program information—the images and other media—is stored in *analog* format. Thus, its primary form of storage is at odds with the digital format of computers. With the advent of *DVD* (digital video-disc), the moribund fate of videodisc technology is all but sealed.

videodisc levels: Now little more than a historical footnote, *videodisc* was traditionally divided into five levels of technology/interactivity, ranging from the modest interaction of switching the machine on and off, up through the sophisticated branching and presentation strategies allowed by integrated systems of *CPU* and *disc* player. Those layers are: Level zero: *linear* play of *videodisc*, i.e., those designed to play only videodisc versions of movies. Ironically, this simplest form of videodisc has had the longest run as a viable playback medium in the marketplace. Level one: a player with still/*freeze frame*, picture stop, *frame* and chapter stop addressability, and dual-*channel* audio, but with no programmable memory. All functions are initiated by manual inputs from the player's keypad. Picture stop and chapter stop codes are put on the *disc* during *mastering*. Level two: a player with on-board, programmable memory. The player's memory is programmed from information contained in audio channel two of a level-two *encoded* videodisc, or is programmed manually from the player's keypad. Inputs are made from the keypad. Level three: any videodisc player controlled by an external computer. This is the level that characterized the preponderance of programs termed *IVD* (interactive videodisc) programs. Level four: A videodisc-and-computer system in which the videodisc is used to store computer-readable *digital* data as well as *analog video* and sound information. The videodisc player functions as an *optical storage* drive to the computer, as well as the source of analog picture and sound.

videot: This is slang for a *video* game junkie.

videowall: Seen frequently at large trade shows, videowalls are large assemblages of monitors stacked together to form a single display area. Typically, they are controlled by a computer, which does the work of taking a single image and splitting it up so that the picture can be spread across all of the monitors.

view: In the simplest sense, the term view refers to what is seen—that is, what is visible to the user—within a *window* on a PC's graphical user interface (*GUI*). But this term means much more. It is one of those tip-of-the-iceberg terms. Put simply, it is one of the most important and central concepts in all of *multimedia*. Moving on to one of its still-simple, but abstract, meanings, a view is one way of seeing a particular set of data. Critical to the concept of a view is that there are many different ways of looking at the same set of data. Thus, for a simple table of numerical data—representing, say, sales figures listed by a salesperson—one can take a view of that data which is the table itself; or, one can take a view that represents the same data in the form of a bar graph, or maybe a pie chart. One might also take that data and write a narrative around it, describing how the various salespeople are doing, based solely on the sales figures contained in the table.

The point is, there are many different ways to view the same information. As one addresses more complex datasets, where it is only possible to consider portions or summaries of the data at any one moment, then the concept of view takes on another dimension, that of scaling up or down relative to the object being considered. Thus, as one scales up, the view takes in a wider scope, but contains less detail. As one *zooms* in, the scope narrows, but the detail is increased. In a sense, the notion of view takes stock of the perceptual limitations of the human mind relative to the volume of information that can be considered at any moment in time. And this notion of presenting digestible views, within the context of a "view-generating system" that can switch flexibly and quickly between many different views, is a core concept, a sort of gestalt that drives the entire enterprise of *human interface design, GUI,* and *usability*. It is also an extremely important design component with respect to the development of *data warehouses* and *data marts*.

viewer polling: This is one of the prototypical forms of *interactivity* that is already being experimented with in anticipation of the coming of *interactive television*. As the term implies, viewer polling works by actively soliciting the opinions and attitudes of viewers. In today's technology context, viewer polling is conducted by using the telephone as the means by which viewers communicate their opinions back to the broadcasting source. Obviously, this is a contemporary *kludge* that uses two separate technologies. More recently, several TV broadcasters are using their *Web sites* to augment the use of *telephony* in implementing viewer polling campaigns. Under this model, TV viewers are provided with the broadcaster's *URL* while watching TV, and then use that information to access the Web site, where they fill out some type of form that captures the data for which the poll was designed. As envisioned for true interactive television, though, future forms of viewer polling will involve the user's direct interaction with the TV (by clicking on an on-screen *icon*, for example) which, in turn, will communicate back to the broadcasting source via some form of data *backchannel*.

viewport: A term for programmers, it refers to a rectangular portion of the screen onto which the *window* and its contents are mapped.

VIMS: Stands for Visually Induced Motion Sickness, a unique form of motion sickness that is a result of some of the more powerful *virtual reality* entertainment environments. Almost exactly the opposite in cause from normal motion sickness, VIMS occurs when there is a compelling sensation of self-motion without any corresponding visceral cues. Research shows that this form of nausea tends to occur during a user's initial exposure to a particular *simulation*, especially in cases where there are many motion cues.

virtual: Virtual in computer terminology means not real, but conceptual. For example, *virtual memory* allows applications to execute as though they had more memory than is physically present. The operating system manages this fete in a way that is transparent to the user by swapping programs and data in and out of *RAM* from the *hard disk* as more memory is needed, a process that is referred to as "paging." In another typical form of usage, the term virtual implies a *simulation* technology that permits the user to experience something without needing its physical presence, e.g., a virtual theme park.

virtual communities: This term describes subsets of Marshall McLuhan's global village, groups of geographically dispersed people who communicate with such intensity that they form what could be properly called communities. Obviously, these communities will make heavy use of *multimedia* technology, as the capacity of our public *networks* expand to accommodate the higher *bandwidths* associated with moving *mixed media data types* between remote locations. The *Internet* has certainly begun to realize McLuhan's idea of creating strong communities composed of geographically dispersed members. Such communal entities as *chat* forums, *listservs*, *distance learning* classes, and the like, are nothing if not virtual communities.

virtual corporation: Is an organization, or an arrangement, whereby employees and contractors work together via the *Internet* and the telephone, typically in a *telecommuting mode*, to achieve some set of business goals. Most virtual corporations are formed because none of the participating business entities are capable of achieving the business goals by themselves, and are therefore willing to share the kinds of intimate and intense interaction that characterize the business processes of a single corporation. Most virtual corporations are, however, temporary in nature, and tend to dissolve quickly after the project(s) for which they were initially formed are brought to completion. The rise of the virtual corporation is very important to the continued evolution of *multimedia* and *Web* technologies, because it typically generates a strong set of business needs for intense interaction between a geographically separated set of players.

virtual mall: This term refers to one of the emerging visions for how interactive shopping will be presented as an *interface paradigm* once *mass deployment* of an all-digital, National Information Infrastructure (*NII*) occurs. Under this interface paradigm, the at-home shopper will fly through an electronic version of a mall, using the input device to steer and stop as the salivary glands of shopping dictate. Early versions of the virutal mall concept are already starting to appear on the *Internet*, as department stores and other retailers set up *Web sites* to provide aggregated access to wide bodies of retail items. It is fully anticipated that the concept of virtual mall will be at the very center of the rapid evolution of *e-commerce*.

virtual memory: This term represents one of the older software design technologies and perhaps the first use of the word *virtual* in the computer world. Virtual memory is a fairly sophisticated technique used in computer systems as follows. First, an application is divided up into discrete chunks. In most cases, these chunks are regular in size and are called "pages." When an application is running, it typically uses only a few pages of the program in a given time *frame*. These active chunks are referred to as the working set of pages. Since only a few pages are being used at any one time, a large program can waste a great deal of memory in a system with inactive pages that may never be used at all. To ensure the efficient use of memory, a computer can be programmed to load only the working set of pages into memory and still be able to run the application, even though much of its code is absent from memory. If the application requires a page not currently in memory (for example, when branching to a different part of the program that lies outside of the code represented by the current working set), a page fault is generated by the computer hardware. At this point, the computer chooses a page not being used, swaps it out to hard *disk*, reads in the required page, and then continues executing the application. This process is totally transparent to both developers and users alike. Thus, since no "out of memory" error ever confronts either of these two groups, even though they may be working with extremely large program files, the computer appears to have a limitless supply of memory. This apparent extension of capability beyond what is real is what has given rise to the use of the term virtual. In the era of *multimedia* technology, where an explosion of file sizes of all sorts will soon be upon us, expect virtual memory to be one of the more important forms of virtual for quite some time.

virtual presence: Refers to a branch of *virtual reality* that allows the user to manipulate and sense remote objects. This form of VR technology has grown out of research sponsored primarily by NASA, which uses it to enable mission-related activities that require direct manual labor, but for which it is not practical to have a human present. For instance, NASA used virtual presence technology to repair the Hubble space telescope.

virtual private network (VPN): VPN is a private data *network* that uses the public telecommunications infrastructure for secure data *transmissions*. It maintains privacy and security through *tunneling*. VPN is regarded as a low-cost solution for corporate *extranets* and *intranets*, because it uses the *public-switched telephone network*, and therefore does not incur the costs associated with leasing private lines from a public *carrier*.

virtual reality (VR): VR is primarily a *real-time* graphics and *animation* technology that immerses users into alternate worlds, ones that are intended to seem as real as the real world of nature. Through a combination of sensing and *interface* devices, and software, VR systems provide direct interaction with computer-generated models of the world. In its purest form, virtual reality is a computer-generated, surrogate environment that allows users to experience the full sensory/tactile feedback of a place in space and time that is different from the one in which the user is presently located. As the famous French film critic, Andre Bazin, said over 50 years ago with respect to cinema: "it is the presence of an absence." Thus, virtual reality relies on many of the same illusionary forces so critical to our various narrative traditions (e.g., the novel and the movie). Recently, there has been such an expansion in the uses and technologies associated with VR, that there are now all sorts of VR systems, ranging from *environmental VR* to *full immersion VR* to many different forms of partial VR. Taken as a whole, virtual reality should be viewed as the leading edge of interactive *multimedia* technology—potentially the most sophisticated, demanding, and engaging medium of the information age. To "enter" a virtual reality, a user in today's technological environment will typically don special gloves, earphones, and goggles, thereby submitting three senses to be "managed" by the computer system. As with film and *video*, the most powerful form of machine-controlled feedback in VR systems is still the full-motion video (*FMV*) image. With today's technology, most VR systems struggle mightily to keep the flow (the *frame refresh rate*) of FMV data up to date as the user moves about within a *virtual world*. VR applications have been developed for a wide range of industries, including entertainment, science, medicine, business, architecture, and education. One of the most useful, and economically defensible, applications of VR technology is the *simulation* of business situations and tasks that are very dangerous, but that are mission-critical to the sponsoring industries and organizations. Thus, for example, VR systems can be used to simulate dangerous flight and air traffic situations for the airline industry.

virtual surreality: This is a term coined by the philosopher Daniel Dennett in his 1991 work, *Consciousness Explained*. Dennett joins a widening group that is skeptical of the various meanings implied in the term *virtual reality*. According to Dennett, the experiences one has while garbed in the paraphernalia of VR systems are at best something a user might imagine as real for only a short span of time.

virtual VCR: This term was coined by those in the know about *interactive television*. Basically, it is a synonym for *movies-on-demand*, a term that describes one of the early interactive TV services, whereby the consumer orders a movie from a large *menu* of choices. The actual movies are stored on a large *video server*, located on the facilities of the cable or *DBS* operator.

virtual world: This term refers to the immersive environment that is created by any *electronic game* which makes extensive use of *virtual reality* equipment. This term is very similar in meaning to the concept of a "microworld," which is commonly used by literary critics. That is, just as novelists create for their readers an all-encompassing environment that is of their own imaginary making, so too do manufacturers of VR games create worlds that are entirely their "creations." Thus, a virtual world is the sum total of the visual, auditory and tactile stimuli, plus the cognitive qualities of the *play-mechanics*, that comprise the environment of the VR game. One measure of how well the VR industry is maturing will be the quality of the virtual worlds it creates.

virus: Is a potentially nasty electronic bug or program created by *hackers* to wreak havoc on as many computers as possible. Often these programs are self-duplicating, and users have little control over their spread once they have penetrated a computer's operating system. Users can purchase anti-virus programs to detect viruses early on and remove them from their computer systems. Unfortunately, the *Internet* represents a vast opportunity for the quick spread of computer viruses.

VIS: Stands for Visual Information System, which was Tandy's entrant into the home *CD-ROM* player market. Rather than being designed as a PC peripheral, VIS was more like Philips' *CD-I* system, in that it was designed as a television accessory. Now largely a historical curiosity, VIS made use of a stripped-down version of Microsoft's *Windows*, known as *Modular Windows*, and was intended for use by couch potatoes wielding remotes.

visual workbench: This term refers to a *human-factors engineering* application for *virtual reality*, whereby physical environments are modeled/simulated for purposes of conceptual trial and error. A contemporary example is provided by the University of Washington's Human Interface Technology (HIT) lab. HIT developed a *simulation* of a new runway for SEATAC airport, complete with simulated sound, so that stakeholders could test out the impact of various design strategies.

visualization for planetary exploration: This is one of the most prominent applications of *virtual-reality* technology for purposes of exploration not yet undertaken. This project, being developed at NASA's *Ames Research Center*, involves taking topographical data generated from satellites and space probes to create 3-D models of portions of planet surfaces from around the solar system. The system makes it possible for users to *fly* over mountains and down into valleys on, for example, the Martian surface. As better *rendering engines*, and more accurate data, become available, the system is planned for *scalability*, such that one day people may be able to partake of systems that simulate flight through photo-realistic versions of planetary surfaces.

VIVID: Stands for VIdeo, Voice, Image and Data, and refers to the range of media types that must now be handled in their respective *digital* formats by *multimedia applications*.

VLDB: Stands for Very Large DataBase, and at this stage of the Information Age, it is definitely a moving target. When originally conceived, this term was used to describe traditional databases, most of which were associated with transaction data, that had grown into the multi-*gigabyte* range in terms of their size. However, with the advent of the *mixed media data types*, and particularly in view of such applications as video on demand (*VOD*), the metrics for what constitutes a VLDB have definitely shifted by an order of magnitude and now clearly occupy the *terabyte* space. For example, just a modestly sized *digital library* of feature films (encoded in, say, the *MPEG* 2 format) requires between 5 and 12 terabytes of storage. To help make the distinction between VLDBs that are composed of good old alphanumeric data (as most corporate databases still are), and those that have grown to enormity by virtue of storing *multimedia* objects, the industry has generated a special purpose version of the acronym. Many analysts now use "VLMMDB," which stands for Very Large MultiMedia DataBase.

voc: This somewhat dated file format for *digital audio* represents the original sound format for the SoundBlaster card, itself one of the older and more venerable *expansion boards* in the history of *multimedia* computing. Voc files are still quite popular with the PC versions of *electronic games*.

vocabulary switching: From the world of *artificial intelligence* and *digital libraries*, this term refers to the ability of computers to distinguish different meanings for the same word. For example, vocabulary switching can be used to distinguish Paris, the city in the country of France; from Paris, the city in Texas; from Paris, the classical god of myth; from plaster of Paris.

VOD: Stands for Video On Demand and is nearly synonymous with *movies-on-demand*. Many industry critics see true VOD as still lying somewhere out there in the near, but as yet unobtainable, future. Its immediate predecessor, *NVOD* (near-video on demand), will make use of the rapidly growing *bandwidth* of the cable TV and *DBS* (direct broadcasting by satellite) infrastructures to supply users with so many starting times for a particular film that wait times will never exceed a very short duration, say 10 minutes at the most. It's like a bus schedule where the buses are running with very high frequency. VOD should follow on the footheels of NVOD, and not only allow viewers to pick out a program and choose just when they want to view it, but will also enable them to start, stop, and pause each program without affecting any of the other programs available to, or being viewed, by others.

voice: This everyday word has recently moved into the world of *digital* audio, where it has taken on the meaning of an independent *channel* in a multi-channel, *digital audio production*. Thus, you may find it written in one of the trade journals that the sounds produced by a particular musical instrument, say a horn, make up one of the voices in a 24-voice production.

voice annotation: A concept associated with *hypermedia applications* and the *compound document*, this term refers to the practice of annotating reference documents with *voice* messages. Obviously, voice annotation is one application of voice *digitization*.

voice coding: Refers to methods of digitally encoding and compressing *voice signals*, optimized to the spectral patterns characteristic of *voice*.

Techniques like *SBCELP*, developed by Lernout & Haupsie Speech Products of Belgium, are making 30:1 *compression ratio*s for voice signals possible. Such medium-specific specialization in algorithm development is a reflection of the growing maturity of *multimedia* technology.

voice grade: A term used to describe the relatively low-quality audio *signal* that typifies dial-up telephonic communications. Voice grade has a relatively modest *bandwidth* of 3,000 Hz.

voice mail: Though not usually thought of as such, this *store-and-forward* service is a precursor to the *compound document*, which may become one of the dominant forms of *multimedia* technology. Because they store messages in an audio format, and are typically controlled by computers, voice mail systems are clearly a form of multimedia technology.

voice recognition: A long sought-after goal of the computer intelligentsia, voice recognition is a form of user input whereby the computer is able to respond in a meaningful fashion to human speech. This form of input has long been held back by the lack of a thorough understanding of human speech, a scientific deficiency that has made it impossible for programmers to create the algorithmic foundations for what is often referred to as *natural language processing*. This *mode* of software intelligence is required by computers so that they might be able to "understand" normal, conversational speech. Today's voice-recognition systems are confined to the use of fairly limited vocabularies. Most systems can only recognize vocabularies under a thousand words. These systems are based on a technology whereby the words spoken by a human are first *digitized*, and then submitted to a look-up function, which attempts to match the digitized instances of human speech against a table of stored speech patterns. It is expected that as our scientific knowledge of human speech progresses, the vocabularies supported by voice-recognition systems will expand apace, ultimately reaching the long-awaited dream of continuous speech recognition.

voomies: These are *virtual reality* movies designed to be experienced in a 3-D movie theater. Among media futurists, it is anticipated that the first voomies will be exploratory virtual realities, where audience members can move through the *virtual worlds* (i.e., 3-D environments) and watch the dramatic action of the story from whatever perspective they choose.

voxel: This volume element can be thought of as the 3-D equivalent of a *pixel*. It is used, for example, to describe the *spatial* display elements in a 3-D *scientific visualization* system.

VRAM: Stands for Video Random Access Memory, and is pronounced "vee-ram." It is a special type of memory used with high-end, high-performance *accelerator boards* to speed up the processing of visual (display) information in personal computers. Its most distinguishing characteristic, and the thing that separates it from standard dynamic RAM, is that it allows the computer to write new information to a memory location, even while the old information is being read.

VRML: Stands for Virtual Reality Modeling or Markup Language. It is a standard for describing 3-D objects and *virtual reality* worlds on the *Internet*. Owing to the *bandwidth* constraints of the contemporary *Web*, evolution of the market for VRML *authoring systems* and *Web sites* based on VRML-defined content may be a bit slower than other segments of the online marketplace. However, media futurists fully expect that this standard—or whatever may replace it—will soon become a key *enabling technology*, and will have broad influence over the nature of *Web* design in the near future. Design concepts, such as the *virtual mall*, are already being widely discussed and will rely heavily upon the VRML standard to achieve anything close to to their full potential.

VRML repository: Is a resource for the dissemination of information on *VRML*. It is maintained by the San Diego Supercomputer Center (SDSC), located on the campus of the University of California at San Diego; and is funded by the National Science Foundation (*NSF*). The content of the VRML repository is in the form of *URLs* annotated and organized by topic. There is a strict standard of quality control applied to this repository, as content is checked regularly to ensure relevance to VRML, and dead entries are eliminated in a timely manner.

VTOA: Stands for Voice and Telephony Over ATM. This term refers to the standard method for sending voice *transmissions* over an *ATM network*. In essence, this standard serves the purpose of blending the old (*telephony*) with the new (the *broadband technology* of *ATM*).

VTOC: Stands for Volume Table Of Contents. This is a critical portion of any form of data storage *disk*. Its contents include the *disk* (or volume) name, *copyright* information, *pointers* to datablocks, multi-volume sequence numbers, and version numbers. In essence, it is a combination of the disk's *address* system and *metadata* repository, and is used extensively by the operating system to manage the disk's resources (e.g., the opening, closing, and deleting of files).

Historical accident has kept programmers in control of a field in which most of them have no aptitude: the artistic integration of the mechanisms they work with.
—**Theodore Nelson, Distinguished Fellow, Autodesk, Inc.**

WAIS: Stands for Wide Area Information Server, pronounced "ways." WAIS is a retrieval system for distributed information. It uses a simple language input, offers indexed searching with *keywords*, and provides *relevance feedback* to enhance future searches. WAIS is also a *protocol* name which can be used in a *URL*. In terms of its genealogy, it is a contemporary of *gopher*, and a predecessor of *HTTP/HTML*.

WAIS Gateway: Allows access to *WAIS* stations; it is a networking *protocol* converter for the *WAIS* data retrieval system.

walkthrough: This is a subtype of the *surrogate travel* genre, wherein one is able to navigate the hallways and rooms of remote, or even nonexistent, buildings. Walkthroughs rely heavily on *CAD*-based (computer-aided design-based) libraries of algorithms. They use 3-D *algorithms* and objects to create rooms and hallways on the fly as users exercise their software-encoded, navigational freedom to move about within the simulated building. Common applications include *human-factors engineering* and real estate marketing.

WAN: Stands for Wide Area Network, a term which refers to computer *networks* that are not limited to a geographic area within a range of 10 km, as are *LANs* (local area networks). WANs often use common *carrier* facilities.

water cooler syndrome: For the sociologist of media, this term refers to the tendency for people to talk the next day about what they watched on TV the night before. In the age *multimedia*, what will people talk about the morning after?

wav: This is the file extension for the standard adopted by Microsoft and IBM for *multimedia* sound applications. Wav files contain audio data based on the *pulse code modulation (PCM)* waveform. If you scan a *disk* directory and see entries possessing a wav *filename extension*, you can be certain that those files contain *digital* audio.

wave table synthesis: One of two primary forms of *MIDI* (musical instrument digital interface) synthesis (the other being *FM synthesis*), wave table is generally considered to be the superior of the two. It uses a store (or table) of digitally recorded instrument samples, and then blends those sampled sounds together on the basis of the *sequence* of *MIDI* commands it receives to create the programmed music or sound effects. The table of sounds—or *patches*, as they are sometimes called—are usually stored in a custom-developed form of read only memory (ROM). Wave table players have ROM sizes that range in size from 1 to several megabytes, with the obvious quality advantage going to the larger tables, which hold correspondingly more, longer, or more intricate instrument samples. For playback, wave table players are measured in terms of two quality factors: 1) how many instruments they can play simultaneously, a feature called *timbrality*; and 2) how many different notes they can play at the same time, a feature called *polyphony*.

wavelet image compression: A sophisticated variant of *DCT* (discrete cosine transform) this is one of the frontier *compression* technologies; it is now receiving a considerable research and development effort.

WBT: Stands for Web-Based Training, and refers to electronic *courseware*, or *CBT* (computer-based training) that is offered to learners across the *Web*. In most contemporary instances of WBT, the training is being delivered across a corporate *intranet* to an internal audience of employees. However, media futurists anticipate that WBT will become a major business opportunity, enabling *content providers* to offer educational products on any number of subjects to market segments spread across the entire range of demographic groups.

Web: One suspects that this will be remembered as the most fashionable root word in the English language at the turn of the century. See also *World Wide Web*, for which this term is the short form.

Web node: Is any addressable hardware device connected to a *network*: a computer, a printer, etc. A Web node can also be a *hypertext* document.

Web page: Is a single file, formatted using *HTML* (hypertext markup language), and containing digitally *encoded* text, graphics, sound, and/or *video*, all of which can be viewed using a suitably configured *browser* on the *World Wide Web*.

Web site: As ubiquitous as rain, the Web site is the location for *Internet* content provided by the largest corporations, as well as by untold thousands of small companies and individuals seeking to have their information viewed by millions (they hope) on the *Web*.

Webcasting: Nearly synonymous with *push technology*, this term refers to a *mode* of receiving information from across the *Web* that is, fundamentally, a reversal of how users have obtained *Internet resources* historically. Traditionally, users have initiated access to *Internet resources* through their own direct actions—by *browsing*, by *downloading*, or by *bookmarking*. With Webcasting, types of Web content are unobtrusively and periodically downloaded to the user's machine through a set of prearranged linkages. Though, for the most part, the user establishes those linkages in the first place, the ongoing update of the information—news, weather, sports, etc.—is handled automatically, in an unattended *mode*. Most Webcasting arrangements require a *persistent connection* to the *Internet*. Pointcast and Backweb represent two early examples of Webcasting technology.

Webmaster: One of the meteoric professions of the information age, there are actually two key areas of competency associated with this new occupation. On the one hand, there is the "creative" side of Webmastering, which is responsible for designing, constructing, and managing the information content of an organization's *Web site*. On the other, there is the technical side of Webmastering, which is responsible for managing the programming and other technical aspects of the Web site *server*. In all but the smallest organizations, these two roles will reside in separate individuals. In the larger organizations, entire Webmaster teams will be responsible for managing these functions. As the world of business turns increasingly to corporate *intranets* for managing internal corporate communications, and to *e-commerce* for handling external sales and marketing, the responsibilities and rewards associated with Webmastering will continue their dramatic rise.

WebTV: This brand name represents the combined products and services of Sony, Philips, and WebTV Networks (now a subsidiary of Microsoft). It also represents one of the first legitimate steps in the direction of the long-awaited convergence of television and the *personal computer*, or what George Gilder refers to as the *teleputer*. Sony and Philips are manufacturing *set-top boxes* that connect TVs to the *Internet,* through either a standard *modem*, or the higher *bandwidth* device known as a cable modem. WebTV Networks sells and manages the access service. Users of WebTV will browse the *Internet* using a standard *browser* and a handheld control. An optional keyboard is available, which becomes extremely handy when users start interacting with their *e-mail* using Web TV.

whisper: Stands for Windows Highly Intelligent Speech Recognizer, which is an improved version of *Sphinx-II* developed by Microsoft. It offers continuous speech recognition, speaker independence, online adaptation, noise robustness, dynamic vocabularies, and grammars. It can be scaled to fit different PC configurations. See also *voice recognition.*

White Book: Developed by Philips and JVC in 1993, this standard enables the storage of *MPEG* (Motion Picture Experts Group) *video* on *CD-ROM.*

white pages: A collective term (noun) used to refer to the universe of all *Internet* directory programs. For reasons of sheer volume, no one directory contains every name and *address.*

whiteboard: Also referred to as "electronic whiteboard," this device is one of the key *enabling technologies* of *document conferencing.* After two remote users establish a *desktop*-to-desktop connection, the session software presents a whiteboard *window* that both participants are permitted to view and manipulate. With the typical implementation of this concept, *bit maps* of the whiteboard are being transmitted back and forth over the *network* as each participant makes changes to the contents. Most implementations also enable either participant to save snapshots of the whiteboard for future reference.

wide shot: From the world of filmmaking, this term refers to a *shot* that provides a broad *view* of all, or a large part, of the action in a scene.

wide-fast SCSI: Is an advanced version of the *SCSI* (small computer standard interface) *bus* for moving data within PC-based systems. It accommodates 32-*bit* performance and is a welcome addition to machines that are seeking to perform such challenging *multimedia* roles as that of a *video server.*

windows: From the world of graphical user interfaces (*GUIs*), this widely used term refers to independent regions created on the computer screen to segregate different functions and/or forms of information. Windows are made possible by the growth in *bit-mapped* displays, and, in turn, make it possible for several applications to display results on the same screen simultaneously. Thus, windows represent two basic graphical user interface design (*GUI*) and *human interface design* principles: 1) people desire to, and are capable of, working on more than one task at a time; and 2) to maintain cognitive order during such multitasking activities, it is advisable to create a visible way of segregating, or compartmentalizing, one task from another. The most ubiquitous windows graphical *user* *interface* application is the operating system by Microsoft, otherwise known as Microsoft *Windows*. Most other operating systems of our time, such as the Macintosh OS and IBM's OS/2 are based on the *interface design* principles associated with the use of windows.

Windows: Microsoft's graphical user interface (*GUI*) extension to their MS-DOS operating system, now an industry standard. It represents Microsoft's implementation of the *desktop metaphor interface* that flowed from the early 1980s pioneering work of the *Xerox PARC* research group on graphical *user interfaces*.

WindowsCE: Microsoft's "thin" version of its *Windows* operating system, designed primarily for small computing devices, such as *HPCs* (handheld personal computers) and *palmtops*. It is also designed to handle the operating needs of *embedded PC* environments, such as those associated with consumer electronics and automobiles. Also referred to as "WinCE," or just "CE," this operating system offers a scaled-down version of the Windows95 *GUI*, a number of *PIM* applications, and some scaled-back editions of the Microsoft Office applications (e.g., Excel and Word). WindowsCE is also projected for use in the personal *navigation* systems of automobiles, for use with the navigational features of *DTV*. In general, this extension must be viewed as representing a central role in Microsoft's credo of "Windows everywhere."

Winsock: This is an application programming interface (*API*) that runs between the following: an *application program* such as *Netscape Navigator*; the windock.dll program, which is part of *Windows*; and *TCP/IP* and your *modem* or *network* card in your *personal computer*. Winsock is, in essence, a convention for connecting with and exchanging data between several programs on a computer or a network. A number of companies provide Winsock programs, along with a set of *IP protocols* and applications.

Winsock 2: This is the 32-*bit* version of *Winsock*, which offers enhanced performance, an *interface* to *wireless networks*, and support for *multicasting*.

wipe: From the world of *DVE* (digital video effects), this is a transitional effect wherein one scene supersedes another by wiping it off the screen. As with the other transitional effects, the more sophisticated *paint programs* and *authoring systems* now supply entire libraries of wipes, e.g., from side-to-side, top-to-bottom, etc.

wire speed: From the realm of *data communications*, this term refers to the data *transmission* speed achieved when the origin and destination sites of a communication are directly connected, either through dedicated wires or circuits. This term is important because it bears a significant technical distinction. Many forms of data communications are slowed because they must be routed through many communication *nodes*, where each traversing of a node requires the computer *overhead* associated with opening up the data package (also known as a data *packet*) to determine the *protocol* and destination *address* of that packet. Performing this *overhead* activity takes time, of course, and thereby reduces the speed of transmission. However, when a dedicated wire or circuit has been put in place between the sender and receiver of the data *packet*, there is no such overhead to slow the communication. Thus, the packet is able to move at the theoretical speed limit of the wire or circuit that connects the two sites, thereby achieving wire speed. Many communication firms generate revenue by setting up dedicated circuits for their customers.

wired glove: This category of *virtual reality* gear is used to create a crude sense of touch for users immersed in *virtual worlds*. Also referred to frequently by the brand name, *Data Glove*, these devices rely upon computer-connected sensors in the glove to measure the bending of fingers. VR systems represent the glove in the graphics display of the virtual world, usually in the form of a disembodied hand. With most wired gloves being employed today, the user is free to move the hand and grab both virtual and real objects.

wireframe: In graphics, this is a 3-D outline image displayed as a series of connected *line segments*, including all of the hidden lines. In the standard *methodology* for 3-D graphics development, the step of building the wireframe image immediately precedes the phase known as *texture mapping*, during which the wireframe structures become layered with the visual "coatings" that make them look like real objects.

wireless: This term refers to our history-making return to the radio airwaves for *transmission bandwidth*. Technologies such as *TDMA* (time division multiple access) and *CDMA* (code division multiple access) are being heralded as providing a substantial portion of the bandwidth required to feed the voracious appetite for, first, personal communication services, and then later, for *interactive multimedia* services. If wireless does prove to be as rich a source of *bandwidth* as experts are predicting, our TV set-tops will be visited once again by devices that are the futuristic equivalent of the rabbit ears that the baby boomers grew up with. Indeed, *DBS* (direct broadcasting by satellite) may be seen as a return-generation of just exactly that: the original *mode* for delivering television *signals* into the home. Of course, these modern technologies are distinguished from their forebearers by being based on *digital*, rather than analog, encoding of the transmitted information. Wireless technologies will also enable the widespread use of *PDAs* (personal digital assistants), and other handheld communications/computing devices.

wizard: A common *interface design* element of performance support systems (*PSS*), a wizard is a series of interactive steps that "walk" the user through the process of completing a particular software task. Increasingly, wizards are being viewed as an essential ingredient in the *usability* of popular commercial software applications.

workflow management: One of the emerging application *domains* of the 1990s, workflow management is a sophisticated *groupware* feature designed to facilitate and accelerate the flow of work products—primarily documents—between the individuals and the automated tasks comprising a work team. *Lotus Notes* is an example of a software application that facilitates workflow management.

working plane: With respect to high-end visual modeling systems, this term refers to a visual reference system, a *grid* laid down on the screen at the outset of a given development project. This grid, or working plane, offers a *spatial* reference model to which items can be positioned, a feature also referred to as a *snap-to grid*. It is also very useful for scaling, wherein the feature is employed for sizing visual objects to fit a given context.

World Wide Web, WWW: The World Wide Web (WWW) is a *client/server* retrieval system for distributed information in a *hypertext* format using the *Internet* for transport. It was developed at *CERN*, the high-energy physics laboratory in Geneva, Switzerland, to meet the needs of scientific researchers. WWW uses the *HTTP* for sending and retrieving documents formatted with *HTML tags*. The most significant design feature of the WWW is the hypertext model, which calls for a system that enables the linking of documents distributed over the entire Internet. This ability to dynamically *link* to almost any location on the Internet is made possible by the ubiquitous *hyperlink*. A hyperlink is a *hot spot* that has been embedded in the active document. It contains a *URL*, which is the *address* of another, presumably related, document on the *Internet*. The user can retrieve the linked document by clicking on the hyperlink.

Through such links, a network of related documents can be accessed from a terminal anywhere on the Internet. To read HTML documents, the user needs a *Web browser* such as *Netscape Navigator*, Microsoft's *Internet Explorer,* or *Mosaic*. See also *gopher, WAIS*.

In 1994, the World Wide Web Consortium (W3C) was founded to develop common *protocols* to help guide the evolution of the World Wide Web. The W3C is an international industry consortium, jointly hosted by the Massachusetts Institute of Technology Laboratory for Computer Science (MIT/LCS) in the United States; the Institute National de Recherche en Informatique et en Automatique (INRIA) in Europe; and the Keio University Shonan Fujisawa Campus in Asia. The Consortium is led by Tim Berners-Lee, director of the W3C and creator of the World Wide Web and Jean-François Abramatic, chairman of the W3C. The consortium is funded by commercial members.

world-building software: This emergent term is used by practitioners of *virtual reality* to describe the *authoring systems* that they use to create simulated portions of the world, or entire *virtual worlds*. As the *Internet* continues to grow in popularity, many first-generation world-building tools are migrating from their *proprietary* beginnings to the use of such widely accepted *Web* standards as *Java* and *VRML*.

WORM: Stands for Write Once, Read Many, and refers to a standard form of *compact disc* technology that permits users to write their own data to CD, albeit only once. In effect, WORM technology turns the CD *mastering* process over to the users. This enablement of the user stands in stark contrast to the traditional way of doing things with respect to *CD-ROM*, where, historically, the mastering has been done at specialized facilities that employ expensive equipment. Though far less expensive than these capital intensive facilities, WORM drives have remained beyond the financial reach of most *desktops*, and have typically been bought only by those organizations who have a high volume of CD mastering they must perform. As with almost every other kind of *digital* technology, though, this expense factor is subject to change, as WORM drives are becoming increasingly affordable. Most contemporary WORMs permit *multisession* recording, which means that you cannot reuse the same *disc* geography, but you can take more than one session to make use of the entire geography of the disc. The Kodak Photo CD consumer technology is multisession, which makes it possible, for example, for families to make use of small chunks of a single CD as their photo libraries grow over time, thus keeping the overall expense of the technology under check.

worm: Is a program similar to a *virus*. It infects computers by replicating itself continuously until all space is filled and the system crashes.

WYSIWYG: Stands for What You See Is What You Get and is pronounced "wizeewig." This term dates back to the earliest attempts to upgrade the graphical capabilities of personal computers so that users could get a realistic view of what their output would look like once it was committed to hard copy. For example, owing to the limited graphical capabilities of early computer monitors, first-generation word-processing programs were unable to display any of the special formatting characteristics that the word-processing software permitted, such as bold facing and underlining. To see these effects, early PC users had to wait until they printed the document. Obviously, they were often surprised (with "surprise" being a pejorative term in this context) with what they wound up getting. As the graphical capabilities of computers began to improve, the word-processing programs were able to display these effects on the screen, thereby initiating the phrase what you see is what you get, and, with it, this endearing acronym. As an interesting historical note, early *HTML editors*, which came along at least a decade after most word processors had fulfilled the WYSIWYG promise, were not able to provide WYSIWYG functionality. These authoring tools are, of course, in enormous demand by *Webmaster* teams everywhere, and have now integrated WYSIWYG capabilities. But this early "step back" is very typical of large-scale technological advances, such as the *Internet*. A new skeletal structure is put in place that has broad business appeal, but in its early stages, this new infrastructure lacks many of the common comforts that are already well established on the systems that it is replacing.

At PARC we coined the phrase "user illusion" to describe what we were about when designing user interface.
—**Alan Kay, Apple Fellow, Apple Computer**

Xanadu Project: Launched in the mid-1960s by Ted Nelson—the man also credited with coining the term *hypertext*—this project was responsible for conducting breakthrough research on the impact of the computer on the entire enterprise of text creation. The obvious allusion that gave birth to this project's name is the magical place of creative imagination described in the nineteenth-century poem, *Kubla Khan,* by Samuel Taylor Coleridge, in which seemingly discordant images are intermixed to create an other-worldly realm of "A Sunny Pleasure Dome with Caves of Ice!" One of the key concepts to emerge from this project is that of intermixing and matching portions of text from various sources to form composite works. Of obvious applicability to hypertext systems, Nelson has used the term "xanalogical storage" to refer to the shared document space that results from such intermixing of textual works. In 1988 the Xanadu Project was taken over by Autodesk, the California software maker most famous for its AutoCad and other visual processing tools. In many obvious ways, this project fully anticipated most of the visionary features that we now take for granted on the *Internet.*

Xerox PARC: The acronym stands for Palo Alto Research Center. Established in 1971, this now-famous R&D facility was responsible for developing some of the earliest prototypes for the personal computer. However, what has earned this center a rightful place in the creation myth of *multimedia* was its central role in devising some of the earliest concepts and standards for the design of graphical user interfaces (*GUI*). The fruits of this effort were first brought to market in the form of the Apple Macintosh and Microsoft *Windows desktop user interfaces.* PARC was also largely responsible for developing the Smalltalk programming language, the *high-level language* commonly given the credit for launching the object-oriented paradigm in software design. Of its more recent research projects, the most noteworthy to the continued progress of multimedia technology appears to be the Information Theater. This project is aimed at enhancing *text retrieval* technologies, and at breeding a new form of presentation technology referred to as *information visualizers.*

X.400: This is a somewhat complex messaging standard that is frequently compared against the more popular, though less officially sanctioned, alternative, *SMTP.* The X.400 standard is specified by the *ITU,* and is quite popular in Canada and Europe. Its primary purpose is that of establishing a structure for specifying *e-mail addresses.*

xy coordinates: Within the realm of computer graphics, these are the horizontal (x) and vertical (y) *addresses* of any particular *pixel* on a screen. With reference to *Web pages* located on the *Internet,* each clickable area on an *image map* has a particular set of xy coordinates relative to the upper left-hand corner of the graphic image as it appears on the *Web site.* Clicking on a particular xy coordinate takes you to a particular file or *link* below the image map.

Thus the computer has called attention to itself as a medium, as have all media before it.
—**Rob Swigart, Novelist**

Yahoo!: Is the first and most prominent WWW *search engine* and directory of *Web* sites. It is organized into a hierarchy of topic categories, such as arts and humanities, business and economy, computers and *Internet,* education, etc. It began in 1994 as a *bookmark* list of Drs. David Filo and Jerry Yang, two electrical engineering Ph.D. candidates at Stanford University. Yahoo! Inc. is now a publicly held company, with a market capitalization of close to two billion dollars, and with a number of important corporate Internet partners, including Netscape Communications, Inc.

Y/C: More commonly referred to as *S-video,* this *video* type provides a quality of signal that lies between *composite* and *component video.* The Y stands for *luminance,* and the C for *chrominance.* These visual components represent the two *channels* into which the form of video signal is broken.

Yellow Book: Is the Philips/Sony technical specifications reference for the physical structure and data layout of *CD-ROM discs.* These specifications are based on the *Red Book's* description for audio CDs, also known as *CD-DA.* The Yellow Book standard has two modes: mode 1 is the basic specification based on CD-DA; and mode 2, also known as *CD-ROM-XA*—the XA standing for extended architecture—which involves the *interleaving* of audio and graphic data, critical to enabling the *synchronization* of audio and visual components.

YUV: This is the industry standard way of transmitting and storing *video* information. Under this method, the *RGB* (red, green, blue) data for each *pixel* is *converted* to a format that uses one *channel* (Y) to represent the *luminance,* or overall intensity of that pixel, and two channels (UV) to represent the *chrominance,* or color. The advantage of this technique is that it makes it possible to reduce the overall volume of data required to represent a *video* image by lowering the UV *resolution* relative to that of the Y. This process takes advantage of the universally accepted principle that the human eye is less sensitive to color than it is to *brightness.*

Discovery favors the well-prepared mind.
—Jerome Bruner, Educational Philosopher

z-axis: This term refers to a technology that is associated with *touch screen* applications. Whereas *xy coordinates* are used by touch screen applications to determine what portion of the screen a user has touched, the z-axis is used to determine how much pressure has been applied. Applications featuring a z-axis are then able to use that information to control such functions as the speed by which the user *scrolls* through the on-screen information. The *SAW* (surface acoustic wave) category of touch screen technology is well known for featuring z-axis capabilities.

Zip Drive: Prompted largely by the need to exchange large, *multimedia* data files, the Zip Drive is a small portable *disk* drive with a capacity of 100 *megabytes* (MB). Trademarked by the Iomega Corporation, Zip Drives are also commonly used to *archive* valuable but infrequently used PC files.

ZMODEM: Is a *protocol* for transferring one or more files in *packets* over a dial-in *serial port* to a variety of programs running on PC-DOS, CP/M, *UNIX,* VMS, or other operating systems. It has a relatively simple *user interface* and provides error correction with high-speed *modems,* satellite *transmissions,* wide area, and packet *networks.* It also adds value by modifying packet size depending on phone-line traffic and quality, thereby helping to reduce network *latency.*

zoom: In *video* and photography, this term refers to the capability for enlarging (to zoom in on) or reducing (to zoom out from) an area of an image. As a piece of the accepted cinematic nomenclature, the term zoom more precisely describes the enlargement of the film subject relative to its context or setting. This term is often contrasted with *pan,* which means to pull away from the subject. In most graphics development software (e.g., *paint systems*), the term zoom is also commonly used to describe a similar type of software functionality with which the artist is able to zoom in and out with reference to some portion of the image.

POSTSCRIPT

*This day before dawn I ascended a hill, and
look'd at the crowded heaven,*

*And I said to my spirit "When we become the
enfolders of those orbs,*

*and the pleasure and knowledge of every thing
in them, shall*

we be fill'd and satisfied then?"

*And my spirit said "No, we but level that lift to
pass and continue*

beyond."

—*Walt Whitman, poet of* **Leaves of Grass,**
from *"Song of Myself"*

ANNOTATED BIBLIOGRAPHY

I n concert with the overall increase in interest regarding multimedia, the Internet, and the Web, we have witnessed a spate of written, and now online, material over the past decade which hits in and around these subjects. Books on multimedia, interactive multimedia, virtual reality, cyberspace, the Internet, and the World Wide Web are proliferating at an increasingly accelerated rate and now threaten to take up entire stacks in libraries and bookstores across the country. News magazines and trade journals (both in print media as well as those available electronically on the WWW) that are entirely devoted to the subjects of multimedia, the Internet, and the Web have appeared in the last several years. Many long-standing publications in related areas have begun to re-orient their content so that they are now invading the same conceptual turf. As if in a magnanimous gesture to its own cannibalizing forces— to its own executioner, if you will—the print and publishing industry is certainly doing its part to inform the public about the coming of multimedia and the rise of the Internet and the World Wide Web.

Additionally, while it might be gratuitously facile to say that the intellectual foundations for multimedia and the Web start with Plato, or thereabouts, it would be accurate to say that serious people have been giving serious thought to the various forms that new media might take for at least the majority of this century. This vein of genetic thought leads, in particular, to the likes of Vannevar Bush, Marshall McLuhan, and Ted Nelson, among others.

The entries in this book owe something to all of these sources, recent and otherwise. In this annotated bibliography, we attempt to give the reader some form of shoehorn into this now burgeoning bundle of source materials, both paper and online. We have broken down the annotated bibliography into three sections: a section devoted to books and key articles (drawn from scholarly periodicals), a second greatly expanded section devoted to trade journals and magazines (some available in both paper and online form), and a third section devoted to electronic publication collections that are essentially online newsstands that contain links to a multitude of Webzine resources. With regard to the second section in particular, we have decided to treat the magazines as a whole, even though it should not be concluded from this that their individual feature articles are not as valuable as they might be. In fact, one of the happier trends in the industry right now is the appearance of some very high-quality trades, to which—it should be pointed out—the authors have culled from and synthesized information to build the content for many of the entries of this book.

Given the wealth of material available in print and online, we make no claim of being comprehensive, or even of being close to comprehensive. Rather, we merely hope that this bibliography is somehow representative, and that it can lead the reader through a systematic swath of the mounting literature on multimedia and the Web.

Books and Scholarly Articles

Ahuja, Vijay. *Secure Commerce on the Internet*. Boston: Academic Press Professional, 1996.

> This book presents the issues, technologies, and methods for achieving security for electronic commerce on the World Wide Web. A manager of network security products at IBM, Ahuja provides in readable, nontechnical prose, information on the history of the Internet, a chronology of major Internet break-ins, as well as specific data on the current hardware, software, and services available for protecting electronic information disseminated across the World Wide Web.

Allen, Thomas B. *War Games*. New York: Berkley Books, 1987.

> Though this book does not make a single mention of multimedia, it is of note to the interactive community because it covers a subject that is of mounting importance to the future of media. The author points out that at, or near, the pinnacle of all of the branches of America's armed forces there is a penultimate form of training that is called "war games." These games strive to create as much of the complexity of the real world as possible and are perhaps more accurately referred to as simulations. But, then again, the difficulty we have in naming this highest form of military training may be a further reflection of the underlying instability and change that is part and parcel of the emerging age of multimedia. For the sake of fostering worthwhile reflection, this book is worth a read.

Ambron, Sueann, and Kristina Hooper. Editors. *Interactive Multimedia: Visions of Multimedia for Developers, Educators, & Information Providers*. Redmond, WA: Microsoft Press, 1988.

> This work is the third in a trilogy of readers published by Microsoft Press in conjunction with Apple Computer to pronounce the coming of multimedia. Of the three, this book does the best job of dealing with issues of interactive design and content development. The foreword by John Sculley and articles by Stephen Weyer and Sueann Ambron are particularly noteworthy.

Aukstakalnis, Steve, and David Blatner. *Silicon Mirage: The Art and Science of Virtual Reality*. Berkeley, CA: Peachpit Press, 1992.
> This is a very competent survey of the enabling technologies and applications that are making virtual reality the cutting edge of multimedia. It does a fine job of explaining the scientific principles that are making the creation of such new and immersive technologies as force feedback possible. It also lays out an industry-by-industry survey of the current applications of virtual reality. Put simply, the book does its part to establish the legitamacy of VR.

Benedikt, Michael. Editor. *Cyberspace: First Steps*. Cambridge, MA: MIT Press, 1992.
> An excellent reader on the emerging subdiscipline of virtual reality known as "cyberspace," this book does more than any other in the industry thus far to explore the philosophical implications of new media. In particular, articles by the editor and by Michael Heim lay out some of the dimensions of the deep structure of cyberspace. For those with an academic orientation, this book represents a good vehicle for placing the cutting edge of multimedia technologies in perspective.

Benford, Tom. *Introducing Desktop Video*. New York: MIS Press, 1995.
> The exploding demand for digital video and knowledge about how to create and manage it has produced considerable confusion in the the multimedia marketplace. This book provides a strong introduction for practitioners, i.e., for people who want and need to create digital video for commercial purposes. After covering the fundamentals of digitizing video, the book treats desktop video production tools, the myriad codec (compression-decompression) standards, the popular transitional process known as morphing, and some tips regarding how to optimize original video production in anticipation of the special needs of digitizing video.

Brand, Stewart. *The Media Lab: Inventing the Future at MIT*. New York: Viking, 1987.
> When neophytes ask what book they should read to get their bearings with respect to multimedia and the Web, this is the one that we almost always recommend. It is a pleasurable, anecdotal read. But it also examines with considerable clarity the roots of new media thinking, if for no other reason but that it explores the background of Nicholas Negroponte, the founder of the Media Lab and one of the industry's true visionaries. What is most heartening about this book is that, while all of the projects it describes were intended by virtue of the Lab's mission statement to conjure communications technologies 30 years out, several of them are actually starting to be implemented today. In particular, Negroponte's concept of "personal television" would appear to be just around the corner and will likely arrive—full-blown, virtually as conceived—about a decade ahead of sched-

ule. Written by the author of *The Whole Earth Catalog*, this book is both fun and informative.

Brockman, John. *Digerati: Encounters with the Cyber Elite.* San Francisco: Hardwired, 1996.

From August 1995 through April 1996, Brockman interviewed 36 of whom he considered to be important developers and commentators of cyberspace. The results are presented in this book, in which the "digerati" discuss their work, their vision of cyberspace, and the future of cyberspace. Included herein are Stewart Brand, Steve Case, John Dvorak, Bill Gates, Scott McNealy, Howard Rheingold, among many others.

Bush, Vannevar. "As We May Think." *Atlantic Monthly.* (July 1945), pp. 101–08.

Any bibliography that purports to cover multimedia and the Web is obliged to include this entry. This article is typically credited with being the first to articulate "hypertext." It would probably be a bit more accurate to say that it is the first description of the implications of hypertext, even though it predates the first use of that term by roughly two decades. Bush bemoaned the antiquated state of our library information systems (if you could have called them that in the 1940s) and foresaw a day when all of the contents of all of the world's print-based information would be inter-connected by associational links. Researchers and browsers alike would be able to traverse this structured labyrinth of information by simply following these links, either on the bases of their immediate research needs, or their current intellectual whims. Bush called this future haven of interlinked literature the "memex." As concepts go . . . long live the memex.

Chawla, Sarita, and John Renesch. Editors. *Learning Organizations: Developing Cultures for Tomorrow's Workplace.* Portland, OR: Productivity Press, 1995.

In setting out to define the boundaries of multimedia, the danger always lurks that one will go too far away from the obvious core industries of film and video, computing, and telecommunications. However, we include this book for your consideration because it represents one of the key business drivers for fueling the evolution of multimedia. No craft can mature without the expenditure of economic resources, and probably no other basic trend at work in today's economy will have as much to do with drawing economic resources to the production of multimedia than the growing preoccupation among executives toward corporate learning. As the Information Age hastens on, every organization is feeling the pinch of keeping its workforce up-to-date. This book of collected essays does a good job of surveying the concerns and methods associated with the corporate response to the crucial need for accelerated learning.

Chorafas, Dimitris N. *Intelligent Multimedia Databases.* Englewood Cliffs, NJ: Prentice-Hall, 1994.

When surveying any category of literature having to do with computer software, there is one thing of which you may be fairly certain: if the work has "intelligent" anywhere in its title, then the topics contained therein will be pushing the limits of either what is known or practical, or both. This whirling dervish of a book covers a number of mainstream topics having to do with the inexorable need to extend the traditional model for relational databases, but then it also delves into most of the cutting edge concepts associated with our time. Topics such as semantic modeling, intelligent software agents, and distributed multimedia keep things interesting.

Dodds, Philip V.W. Editor. *Digital Multimedia Cross-Industry Guide.* Boston, MA: Focal Press, 1995.

One of the great difficulties in working in the field of multimedia is the rather painful job of defining it. Simply put, no one seems to be quite able to comfortably perform this necessary task. We all know that the field is an admixture of converging disciplines, but just exactly which of the many candidate traditions should we consider as belonging to this new club? This structured collection of essays makes a bold attempt at identifying just exactly the collection of industries that rightfully belong to the field of multimedia. The book includes individual essays on broadcast TV, cable TV, consumer electronics, handheld computing devices, computer hardware, computer software, the ATM broadband technology, and telecommunications. Whether or not this is precisely the "right" collection of industries is a subject for which the debate is a long way from being resolved—by anyone. But the effort is appreciated, and the whole argument is well framed in an introductory essay by Philip Dodds, the editor.

Eddings, Joshua. *How the Internet Works.* Emeryville, CA: Ziff-Davis Press, 1994.

This beautifully illustrated book is actually one in a fairly extensive series of heavily illustrated books that seek to provide basic introductions to computer-related topics. This particular book assumes absolutely no prior knowledge of the Internet, working through such basic concepts as how e-mail works, how one sets up a connection to the Internet, and how the whole addressing infrastructure of the Web is pieced together. For anyone who is a visual learner, this book—and the entire series of which it is a part—should hold substantial appeal.

Gadecki, Cathy, and Christine Hechart. *ATM for Dummies.* Foster City, CA: IDG Books Worldwide, Inc., 1997.

This book provides invaluable information about ATM and its use with the Internet as a means for electronic commerce. It specifically provides information on the practical uses of ATM, as well as related transmission protocols.

Gardner, Howard. *Frames of Mind: A Theory of Multiple Intelligences.* New York: Basic Books, 1983.

Like a number of other entries in this bibliography, this one may seem a bit tangential. However, learning theory is one of the core competencies of one of the core applications of multimedia and the Web. Howard Gardner's contribution to learning theory has been considerable, and we could have included almost any of his works here. This one, though, ranks among his most memorable and should be required reading for anyone who wishes to practice the emerging profession of instructional design.

Greenfield, Patricia Marks. *Mind and Media: The Effects of Television, Video Games and Computers.* Cambridge, MA: Harvard University Press, 1984.

Though this book predates most of the speculation over the coming of multimedia, it does a great deal to both anticipate it and light its way. Greenfield offers an excellent survey of the literature and research that occurred during the 1960s and 1970s pertaining to the comparative value of different learning media. She is absolutely prescient in her assessment of potential instructional benefits of the video game genre and lights the way in 1984 to the recent emergence of edutainment titles.

Hale, Constance, Editor, and the Editors of Wired. *Wired Style: Principles of English Usage in the Digital Age.* San Francisco: Wired Ventures, 1997.

This helpful guide includes the latest jargon, acronyms, and software titles for many of the concepts and major players associated with the explosive growth of the Internet. This book also provides definitions and tips for English usage within electronic documents.

Hanclosky, Walter. *Principles of Media Development.* White Plains, NY: Knowledge Industry Products, Inc., 1995.

This book provides information on media design, production, and management. Hanclosky includes in his discussion the incorporation of graphics, photography, video, and film into multimedia applications. He provides examples from training and development, sales and promotion, documentation, and other areas of industrial communication and media.

Holsinger, Erik. *How Multimedia Works.* Illustrated by Nevin Burger. Emeryville, CA: Ziff-Davis Press, 1994.

This is the best exemplar of books that most successfully employ graphics and text to explain computer hardware and software technology. It succinctly and clearly defines and illustrates "how multimedia works" and is part of the Ziff-Davis "How It Works" series. Hats off to author, illustrator, and editorial staff for bringing an understandable view of multimedia to the masses.

Horn, Robert. *Mapping Hypertext: Analysis, Linkage, and Display of Knowledge for the Next Generation of Online Text and Graphics.* Waltham, MA: The Lexingtion Institute, 1989.

This book provides data on how to map and structure information for hypertext and multimedia. In particular, Horn explains the ways to logically link various types of information: e.g., categorical, chronological, geographical, and task based.

Jacobson, Linda. Editor. *Cyberarts: Exploring Art and Technology.* San Francisco: Miller Freeman, 1992.

This interesting reader ranges across a broad range of topics that are currently impacting the multimedia industry. The book is particularly useful in its coverage of the many categories of software that impinge on the interactive multimedia authoring process. Of particular note are entries that cover MIDI/MSC and the low-cost, all-digital alternatives to high-end professional video that are now entering the market at a rapid pace. This book also contains a gem from Ted Nelson, who takes about 10 rich pages to describe the current status of his life-quest Xanadu Project.

Katz, Arnie. *Inside Electronic Game Design.* Rocklin, CA: Prima Publishing, 1996.

More than anything else, this book addresses a topic that has been crying for treatment for a long time. No other aspect of multimedia design is so crucial to the industry's maturation and well-being as is the design of electronic games. Though one might have hoped for a slightly more academic treatment of the subject, this book does a credible job of sketching the history of the electronic game industry, and of describing the basic structural elements that make up an electronic game. Arnie Katz is most convincing when he discusses the methodology of preparing a game-design document, which is a far more involved process than the typical layperson might imagine. A solid third of the book is devoted to interviews with accomplished game designers.

Kearsley, Greg P. Editor. *Artificial Intelligence & Instruction: Applications and Methods.* Reading, MA: Addison-Wesley, 1987.

Heavy sledding, as they say, but this is a worthwhile read for those who have an interest in the many academic projects launched during the 1970s and 1980s to explore the pedagogical potential of machine intelligence.

Keyes, Jessica. *Webcasting: How to Broadcast to Your Customers over the Net.* New York: McGraw-Hill Companies, 1997.

This book provides current information about using the Internet for electronic commerce. It is a comprehensive guide that provides information on the integration of television, radio, print, telephone lines, and computers. The book also offers tips with regard to utilizing the Web for advertising messages, via multimedia, to the vast Internet audience.

Khoshafian, Setrag, A. Brad Baker, Razmik Abnous, and Kevin Shepherd. *Intelligent Offices: Object-Oriented, Multi-Media Information Management in Client/Server Architectures*. New York: John Wiley & Sons, 1992.

This is one in a series of very sound books published by John Wiley to explore the promising new conceptual areas in computer science. This book provides a synthesis of object-oriented software design, the integration of media into traditional applications, the design of graphical user interfaces, and the deployment of operational/computing resources over distributed, client-server architectures. For those interested in the technological foundations of multimedia—the enabling technologies—this is an excellent survey.

Lambert, Steve, and Suzanne Ropiequet. Editors. *CD ROM: The New Papyrus*. Redmond, WA: Microsoft Press, 1986.

This is the first in a trilogy of readers published by Microsoft Press in conjunction with Apple Computer to pronounce the coming of multimedia; as you would expect, this title does the best of the three to frame the overall context of the emerging multimedia industry. The foreword by Bill Gates does much to illustrate how much he was in tune with the graphical/media orientation of computing, even before he was able to successfully implement his *Windows* graphical user interface in the Intel-dominated PC world.

Laurel, Brenda. Editor. *The Art of Human-Computer Interface Design*. Reading, MA: Addison-Wesley, 1990.

Of all the multimedia readers that have appeared over the past decade or so, this is probably the most representative of the industry's true range of interests. It is also distinguished by the general quality of its contributors—just about every industry thought leader has an entry in this volume. Perhaps the most noteworthy article is the editor's treatment of the exciting and complex concept of "interface agents."

Leebaert, Derek. Editor. *Technology 2001: The Future of Computing and Communications*. Cambridge, MA: The MIT Press, 1991.

Though this reader gives only scant treatment of multimedia, per se, it does an excellent job of speculating on the technical agenda of the industry's major enabling technologies: computer architectures, office automation, tele- and data communications, etc.

Lieberman, Debra A. "Learning to Learn Revisited: Computers and the Development of Self-Directed Learning Skills." *Journal of Research on Computing in Education*. Vol. 23 (Spring 1991), pp. 391–95.

> This scholarly article does a good job of relating the leading trends in learning theory to the use of instructional technology in school programs. Though there is a tendency in our country to be highly critical of our primary and secondary schools, this article is indicative of some of the cutting edge thinking that is going on with regard to the application of educational software.

McCoy, John. *Mastering Web Design: Tools of the Trade from Industry Leaders*. San Francisco: Sybex, 1996.

> By focusing on the methods, the emerging genres, the design principles and the tools, this book does a solid job of establishing Web design as a design discipline in its own right. Indeed, if the industry continues to progress in its present direction, developers of multimedia may soon forget that there was any other form of design. This work does a good job of offering explicated examples from the Web.

McLuhan, Marshall. *Understanding Media: The Extensions of Man*. New York: Mentor, 1964.

> McLuhan had a unique ability to identify the large historical arcs associated with media. And now that the forces of change have accelerated the forward evolution of media, McLuhan is being quoted with increasing frequency, particularly from the point of view represented in this book.

Mast, Gerald. *Film, Cinema, Movie: A Theory of Experience*. Chicago: University of Chicago Press, 1983.

> As we labor to contemplate the future of media, it will no doubt be prudent for us to understand where we have been. Gerald Mast is one of the best film theorists going, and this is probably his most insightful discussion of the film medium—the medium, I think we all agree, to which the interactive arts will owe the most.

Maybury, Mark T. Editor. *Intelligent Multimedia Interfaces*. Cambridge, MA: MIT Press, 1993.

> Round up the usual cutting-edge suspects when describing the contents of this reader: natural language processing, virtual reality, knowledge representation, etc. This book also devotes one of its three major sections to automated presentation design, and has an intriguing essay on the use of multimedia to assist car drivers. Each of its 15 entries contains an abstract.

Miller, Mark A. *Internetworking: A Guide to Network Communications LAN to LAN; LAN to WAN,* second edition. New York: MIS Press, 1995.
Though highly technical, network engineers swear by this book as one of the cornerstones of a competent education in the subject of internetworking. It provides detailed coverage, not only of all the major networking protocols (including TCP/IP), but also of a wide range of specific networking products. From time to time, the book reads a bit like much of its text was too strongly derived from product marketing literature and press releases.

Minoli, Daniel. *Internet & Intranet Engineering: Technologies, Protocols, and Applications.* New York: McGraw Hill Companies, Inc., 1997.
This book provides information on many of the tools and technologies used for creating and integrating multimedia into Internet and intranet development. HTML, commercial services, broadband communications, browsers, and future trends are also covered in the work.

Nelson, Theodore Holm. "The Hypertext." *Proceedings of the World Documentation Federation.* (1965).
The first use of the term "hypertext" appears in this article and stands as the virtual starting gate for one of the most fecund intellectual careers in what is now being called multimedia.

Nielsen, Jakob. *Hypertext and Hypermedia.* Boston: Academic Press, 1993.
This book delves into hypertext and hypermedia theory. In this seminal piece of work, Nielsen discusses the history, applications (in business, education, and entertainment), navigation, usability, and future of hypertext and hypermedia.

Owen, Trevor, Ron Owston, and Cheryl Dickie. *The Learning Highway: A Student's Guide to Using the Internet in High School and College.* Toronto: Key Porter Books Limited, 1995.
This book provides information on how to research information through the Internet. It provides important information for multimedia in regard to interactive tools used to handle multimedia over the Web.

Pagan, Kevin, and Scott Fuller. *Intranet Firewalls.* Research Triangle Park, NC: Ventana Communications Group, Inc., 1997.
This work provides security information for controlling access from inside and outside company networks. The guide is a practical reference for providing network security so that users can utilize the Internet for electronic commerce with the knowledge that security precautions are in place.

Papert, Seymour. *Mindstorms: Children, Computers, and Powerful Ideas.* New York: Basic Books, 1980.

> One of the earliest works to examine the use of computers in education, this book is notable for a number of reasons. It details the LOGO language, a high-level language developed explicitly for use by children for the sake of exploring math and science concepts. It covers a number of issues in instructional design that, if anything, are even more pertinent today than they were when they were written. Most notably, though, it captures the essence of Seymour Papert, a man who has been at the forefront of the entire computer revolution by virtue of his association with the MIT Artificial Intelligence Lab and his ability to contribute to and articulate the thinking that has taken place therein.

Parsaye, Kamran, Mark Chignell, Setrag Khoshafian, and Harry Wong. *Intelligent Databases: Object-Oriented, Deductive, Hypermedia Technologies.* New York: John Wiley & Sons, 1989.

> One in a series of books published by John Wiley, it explores some of the emerging concepts in computer science. This book does an excellent job of exploring the key issues in software engineering, particularly those having to do with object-oriented programming and hypermedia design, both of which impact very heavily on the enterprise of multimedia. It possesses one of the industry's most intelligent discussions of Ted Nelson's Xanadu Project and does an excellent job of analyzing the issues associated with designing and building knowledge bases.

Pfaffenberger, Bryan. *Internet in Plain English.* Second Edition. New York: MIS Press, 1996.

> This book provides practical references for the many facets of the Internet. In particular, the book defines a comprehensive list of terms, acronyms, and emerging Internet trends and concepts. Included in the discussion are the following topics: technology, physical media, programs and tools, standards and protocols, as well as history and context of the Internet.

Rada, Roy. *Interactive Media.* New York: Springer-Verlag, 1995.

> Rada's book provides analysis of the organizational impacts that result from implementing hypermedia, groupware, and network applications. The book spans both industry and education. Several case studies are included of hypermedia systems in business, teaching, research, and medicine.

Resnick, Lauren B., and L.E. Klopfer. "Toward Rethinking the Curriculum." In *Toward Rethinking the Curriculum.* L.B. Resnick and L.E. Klopfer, editors. Arlington, VA: Association for Supervision and Curriculum Development, 1987.

> This article is one of many possible entries for Lauren Resnick, perhaps the leading American thinker in the field of educational reform. Through-

out her canon of work, one finds a steady theme: curriculum needs to move away from the industrial-age traditions of drill-and-practice emphasis on specific content and other forms of regimentation, and in the direction of pedagogies that stimulate higher order thinking, problem solving, and the acquisition of process knowledge. These pedagogies are much more difficult than their traditional forebears to encoded interactive multimedia programs . . . but so be it.

Robbe-Grillet, Alain. *For a New Novel: Essays on Fiction.* New York: Grove Press, 1965.

For anyone who sees the production of interactive forms of art as a mission against which are stacked incalculable odds, these essays from Robbe-Grillet will prove comforting, if not insightful. Though his fictional works were never widely accepted in his own time, Robbe-Grillet stands as probably the most inventive practitioner of the narrative arts in our century. These essays articulate the rebellious, iconoclastic vision that is so abundantly present in his novels. Had he "bloomed" during the 1990s, we have no doubt that Robbe-Grillet would be devoted to interactivity and the cyberarts.

Ropiequet, Suzanne. Editor. *CD ROM: Optical Publishing.* Redmond, WA: Microsoft Press, 1987.

The second in a trilogy of readers published by Microsoft Press in conjunction with Apple Computer to pronounce the coming of multimedia, this one has the stongest orientation of the three toward the engineering issues associated with CD-ROM technology.

Schneiderman, Ben. *Designing the User Interface: Strategies for Effective Human-Computer Interaction.* Reading, MA: Addison-Wesley, 1986.

This work serves as a de facto standard in the area of interface design, a discipline that possesses near-complete overlap with the field of interactive multimedia design. Schneiderman's text is particularly insightful in its treatment of the concept of "direct manipulation."

Steinmetz, Ralf, and Klara Nahrstedt. *Multimedia: Computing, Communications & Applications.* Upper Saddle River, NJ: Prentice-Hall, 1995.

This 800+ page volume provides as comprehensive a coverage of the myriad topics associated with multimedia as you are apt to find. It is particularly strong in the technical areas, devoting about 75 percent of the book to dealing with such issues as digital video compression, the networking of multimedia data, and optical storage technologies.

Tilton, Eric, Carl Steadman, and Tyler Jones. *Web Weaving: Designing and Maintaining an Effective Web Site.* New York: Addison-Wesley Publishing Co., 1996.

This book provides information on Web site design, server security, advertising on the WWW, site maintenance, and site style information. It also provides reference material on HTML, VRML, and Java scripting languages.

White, Mary Alice. *What Curriculum for the Information Age?* Hillsdale, NJ: Lawrence Erlbaum Associates, 1987.

This is an excellent treatment of educational concepts that should deeply concern everyone in the multimedia industry.

Winograd, Terry. Editor. *Bringing Design to Software.* New York: ACM Press, 1996.

This collection of essays brings together a very interesting mix of perspectives and, in particular, forces the issues associated with the convergence of software engineering and the visual arts. Thus, one of the primary foci of the book is graphical user interface design. It also focuses on how MIS organizations can reorganize to ensure that visual and human factors concepts get the attention they deserve in the design and development of mainstream business applications. Far from being just a collection of essays, Winograd provides copious interstitial notes and comments to give this work a strong sense of cohesion.

Magazines and Trade Journals (in paper form and on the World Wide Web)

America's Network. Published by Advanstar Communications, 201 Sandpoint Avenue, Suite 600, Santa Ana, CA 92707-8700. Available on the WWW from the <http://www.americasnetwork.com> site.

This highly specialized print publication and its online counterpart evaluate emerging technologies from a business case perspective, including the design, development, operation, and maintenance of public networks including the Internet. The target audience for this slick, but content-rich, publication includes engineers and managers. The content may also be of interest to the multimedia developer, as it covers competitive access providers, cable TV companies, wireless networks, telecommunication industry suppliers, and local/long distance telephone companies.

Boardwatch Magazine: Guide to Online Information Services and Electronic Bulletin Boards. Published by Boardwatch Magazine, 8500 West Bowles Avenue, Suite 210, Littlewood, CO 80123. Available on the WWW at the <http://www.boardwatch.com> site.

With publication that began in March 1987, this magazine covers electronic bulletin boards, commercial online services, and the Internet and calls itself "the guide to Internet access and the World Wide Web." Though there is little that is related strictly to multimedia, this is a good source for general information about what is new with Internet-related trends and technologies.

Byte. Published by McGraw-Hill, One Phoenix Mill Lane, Peterborough, NH 03458. Available on the WWW at the <http://www.byte.com> site. From its inception, *Byte* established itself as the most credible technical read in the small systems (desktop) world. For those in the multimedia industry responsible for following technical trends, this is the key journal. In recent years, with the rise of multimedia, *Byte* has become exceptional at following relevant technical trends in computer architectures and software engineering.

CD-ROM Professional. Published by Pemberton Press, Inc., 407 Kingston Avenue, St. Paul, MN 55117–2424.
This magazine has gained a high level of credibility with multimedia content developers. Appropriate to its name, the magazine focuses on technical and marketing issues having to do with CD-ROM as a delivery medium for multimedia content.

CD-ROM Today. Published by Imagine Publishing, Inc., 1350 Old Bayshore Highway, Suite 210, Burlingame, CA 94010.
This magazine offers a slick presentation with no skimping on content. Topics covered are education, entertainment, reference, and applications. A typical issue includes information on techniques, upgrade strategies, shopping, and many reviews and ratings of CD titles. The features are big on multimedia including evaluating components to support multimedia systems. The focus is on using and buying, not so much on developing multimedia presentations, though a developer will certainly find much of interest here as well. The magazine calls itself the "home guide to PC and Mac multimedia."

CD-ROM World. Published by Mecklermedia, 11 Ferry Lane West, Westport, CT 06880.
Though this magazine covers much of the same ground as the other multimedia trades, it does seem to be developing a specialization in one area: the review of CD-ROM titles. In an industry that is crying for standards of criticism, this orientation is a welcome one.

Computer Graphics World. Published by PennWell Publishing Company, 10 Tara Boulevard, Suite 500, Nashua, NH 03062–2801.
Increasingly, this magazine is becoming a must-read for those involved in the authoring of multimedia content. From a tradition heavily focused on specialized computer graphics programs, *CGW* has transitioned into the center of the multimedia industry by reorienting its feature articles so that they deal with the cutting edge of authoring technologies. The magazine is

particularly strong in the field of nonlinear, all-digital software tools, a hotbed of activity that is leading Hollywood in the direction of a collision with Silicon Valley perhaps a year or two ahead of the schedule set by the San Andreas fault.

ConneXions Online (an online publication that was formerly the print magazine *ConneXions, The Interoperability Report)*. Published by The Interop Company, a Division of Softbank Expos, 303 Vintage Park Drive, Foster City, CA 94404. Available on the WWW at the <http://www.interop.com> site.

Since 1987, the print version of this publication tracked current and emerging technology within the computer and communications industry, particularly interoperability issues, the Internet suite of protocols (TCP/IP), OSI, and related LAN/WAN technologies and protocols. It also provides information about call for papers, announcements, technical white papers, and conference announcements for relevant not-for-profit events such as SIGCOM and IFIP. No advertising appears. After 10 years, the report retired as a print publication and since 1996 has been a Web-based publication only. It also publishes in-depth technical tutorials on aspects of networking. Though little appears on topics directly related to multimedia, the publication gives a good overview on networking and data communications issues related to the Internet.

Desktop Video World. Published by TechMedia Publishing, Inc., 80 Elm Street, Peterborough, NH 03458.

A relative newcomer, this trade journal focuses on issues surrounding the use of digital media on desktop machines, primarily the PC, Mac, and Amiga platforms.

Film & Video: The Production Magazine. Published by Optic Music, Inc., 8455 Beverly Blvd., Suite 508, Los Angeles, CA 90048.

Though the main features of this monthly film industry publication are devoted to the latest movie releases, the magazine focuses most of its space to covering the technical trends in the film and video community. This also means that they are on top of the transition to digital media, particularly as it relates to digital technologies for postproduction. Many of the features are also devoted to dealing with how new digital technologies are exploited in the making of high-end feature films.

IEEE Multimedia. Published by IEEE Computer Society, 10662 Los Vaqueros Circle, P.O. Box 3014, Los Alamitos, California 90720-1314.

This magazine provides up-to-date information on multimedia hardware and software and includes product descriptions, product reviews, book reviews, and upcoming conference announcements.

Information Week. Published by CMP Media Inc., 600 Community Drive, Manhasset, NY 11030. Available on the WWW at the <http://www.informationweek.com> site.

Like *Byte*, *PC Magazine*, and a number of other technically oriented publications, this magazine has drifted in the direction of multimedia and the Web in step with the industry. Indeed, this weekly publication has become almost preoccupied with the Internet and such related topics as e-commerce. It has also gathered strength as a credible source of insight, offering numerous survey-based features and its own set of lists. In keeping with the times, it also offers a push media option. For business and technology managers, this is an excellent source of up-to-date information on industry concepts and trends.

Interactions, New Visions of Human Computer Interactions. Published by the Association for Computing, 1515 Broadway, New York, New York 10036.

This bimonthly publication has a scholarly bent and speaks to issues facing HCI practitioners, including design, evaluation, and understanding of the field. Included is information about tools, case studies, usability evaluations, business methods, and design as well as coverage of conferences, symposiums, and book reviews. Multimedia is included in the scope of coverage.

Inter@ctive Week. Published by Inter@ctive Enterprises LLC, 100 Quentin Roosevelt Blvd., Suite 400, Garden City, NY 11530. Available on the WWW at the <http://www.interactive-week.com> site.

This weekly publication focuses mostly on technical issues having to do with the Internet, corporate intranets, and the infrastructure that supports both. It is well suited for engineers and managers who need to keep up with product and industry trends.

Internet Magazine. Published by Greater London House, Hampstead Road, London NW17QZ.

Calling itself "Britain's best selling Internet magazine," this publication features news; information on Internet providers; tips on creating Web sites; and reviews of software, sites, and hardware. Information on multimedia is also included in the magazine.

Internet Magazine. Published by Matrix News, 1106 Clayton Lane, Suite 500W, Austin, TX 78723.

This monthly newsletter is about cross-network issues including conferencing systems, USENET, UUCP, and BITNET. Included is an occasional article about use of multimedia across the Internet.

Internet User. Published by Ziff-Davis Publishing Company, One Park Avenue, New York, NY 10016. Available on the WWW from the <http://www3.zdnet.com> site.

This electronic magazine includes product reviews of items such as authoring tools, browsers, plug-ins, servers, and site management and communication tools. It also includes articles of interest about trends and technologies, as well as software to download. There is no information specifically about multimedia, but it is a good source of information about Internet-related issues.

InternetWorld. Published by Mecklermedia Corporation, 20 Ketchum Street, Westport, CT 06880. Available on the WWW at the <http://www.internetworld.com> site.

Launched in 1993 this magazine covers noncommercial and commercial uses of Internet and the National Research and Education Network. It offers information and analysis about trends and technologies and profiles key companies, people, and products that impact the Internet's growth and development. *Circulation Management Magazine* named *InternetWorld* 1995's highest growth magazine in terms of circulation from a field of 500 consumer publications tracked. It touts itself as the "#1 Internet authority." Articles on topics related to multimedia do appear often in *InternetWorld*.

Macworld. Published by Macworld Communications, Inc., 501 Second Street, San Francisco, CA 94107. Available on the WWW at the <http://www.macworld.com> site.

So long as the Macintosh continued its two-to-three-year lead over the PC platform with respect to media capabilities, this magazine found itself in the center of the multimedia industry almost by default. Now that this situation has changed, this historically excellent publication must struggle to keep its audience. Though its product range has always been narrow, this was a superb magazine for following developments in multimedia, particularly with respect to the many authoring tools that have become frontrunners through their historical tie to the Macintosh platform. *Macworld* has also done an excellent job through the years of illustrating basic computer concepts for the neophytes, possessing perhaps the best art department in the trade magazine industry.

Macworld Online. Published by Macworld Communications, Inc., 501 Second Street, San Francisco, CA 94108. Available on the WWW from the <http://www.macworld.com> site.

This electronic magazine is full of information and downloadable software and is an excellent complement to the paper magazine. Plus, this impressive Web site allows viewing of the equally impressive Macworld paper magazine as well as mechanisms for searching through back issues.

MediaZine. Available at the <http://www.mediazine.com> site. Published by Creative Digital Media.

> This online magazine is targeted at providing information about and tools for multimedia use on the Internet. It covers many aspects of graphics, multimedia, and the Internet including: getting started with multimedia, project/resource planning, news and commentary, animation techniques, interactive media, managing media, 3-D modeling, software tutorials, reviews, and authorware. There is much of interest here that may warrant frequent visits for both new and experienced multimedia and Internet developers. The site is published by a company involved in multimedia consulting and training.

Morph's Outpost (on the Digital Frontier). Published by Morph's Outpost, Inc., P.O. Box 578, Orinda, CA 94563.

> Appropriately, this tabloid-style publication is one of the most unusual trade journals in the industry. Its content profiles *NewMedia* fairly closely, though it possesses a somewhat stronger orientation to content creation and interviews. This publication may validate the long-held suspicion about the screws and bolts rattling free in California.

Multimedia and Technology Examiner. Published by CompuServe Corporation, 5000 Arlington Center, Columbus, OH 43220. Available over the CompuServe Information Service (CIS) to CIS members, with an introductory page on the WWW at the <http://ourworld.compuserve.com/homepages/THE_MULTIMEDIA_AND_TECH_EXAMINER> site.

> Started in 1993, this online newsletter provides an impressive array of news articles, product reviews, and tutorials concerning PC-based multimedia, desktop video production, telecommunications, home/business automation, and consumer/professional/broadcast electronics. Some detailed topics include evaluations of CD-ROM titles, including games, applications, and development tools and reviews of multimedia tools, laser disk titles, and Nintendo news. This is another of the electronic publications representing a movement from print to online with an element of interactivity.

Multimedia Schools. Published by Information Today, Inc., 143 Old Marlton Pike, Medford, NJ 08055.

> Claiming to be "a practical journal of multimedia, CD-ROM, online and Internet in K–12," this publication includes reviews and results of tests of items such as interactive encyclopedias, case studies of use of multimedia in educational settings, and sections on technology planning. The focus of the publication is on the needs of school practitioners. It includes articles, reviews, columns, and information on electronic resources.

Multimedia Today. Published by IBM Multimedia Solutions, 4111 Northside Parkway, HO4L1, Atlanta, GA 30327.

This publication raises the concept of consultative selling to an art, using a trade journal to showcase and explore IBM's multimedia product offerings. The magazine is particularly strong on case studies, and each issue provides an extensive, detailed catalog of IBM business partner multimedia products, including sections on courseware and production tools.

Multimedia World. Published by PC World Communications, Inc., 501 Second Street, #600, San Francisco, CA 94107.

Brought to us by the same people who publish *PC World*, this magazine is positioned in the same approximate niche as *NewMedia*. Its content—to use the term *du jour*—is not of the same consistency or quality.

NetGuide Magazine. Published by CMP Media Inc., 600 Community Drive, Manhasset, NY 11030. Available on the WWW at the <http://www.netguide.com> site.

Dealing with issues covering the "online world," including online services, bulletin board systems, and the Internet and claiming to be "the #1 source to everything for the Internet," this magazine gives information on Web page development and includes a Webmaster forum. The publication does run articles on multimedia-related resources. It also provides tutorials and reviews of sites, tools, and hardware and software products.

Network, Strategies and Solutions for the Network Professional. Published by United News and Media, 600 Harrison Street, San Francisco, CA 94107. Formerly *LAN, The Network Solutions Magazine.* Available on the WWW at the <http://www.Network-Mag.com> site. Also available from the Compuserve network forum at GO NMAG.

Targeted for an audience of network professionals and managers, this publication provides a good perspective of issues related to networks, specifically regarding new developments and trends in applications using networked computers. Typical subjects include the Internet, emerging technologies, case studies, intranets and LANs, network and system management, and tutorials. The magazine also features a yearly "Network Buyers Guide" issue.

NewMedia Magazine. Published by Hypermedia Communications, Inc., 901 Mariner's Island Boulevard, Suite 365, San Mateo, CA 94404. Available on the WWW at the <http://www.newmedia.com/NewMedia/newmedia.html> site. Also accessible from *Hyperstand* at the <http://www.newmedia.com> site, which provides access to the paper magazine as well as to back issues, software downloads, and related items of interest.

In many respects, this magazine has become the *Byte* of multimedia. Its lead features are uniformly strong and strike at the key issues facing the industry. Their annual *Multimedia Buyer's Guide* represents a substantial contribution to the industry, not just because it helps organize the information about who is selling what, but also because the editors have taken the effort to have it help categorize the exploding media phenomena that are multimedia.

Newspage. Published by Individual, Inc., 8 New England Executive Park West, Burlington, MA 01803. Available on the WWW from the <www.newspage.com> site.

Chock full of Internet business and technology-related articles, this electronic magazine claims to be the "Web's leading source of daily business news." Included is news about the Internet, software, hardware, communications, and a section on multimedia.

PC Magazine. Published by Ziff-Davis Publishing Company, One Park Avenue, New York, NY 10016. Available on the WWW from the <http://www3.zdnet.com> site.

A stalwart of the PC industry, this magazine has its fair share of multimedia articles as well as articles regarding the Internet, in parallel with the overall industry trends in these directions.

PC Magazine Online. Published by Ziff-Davis Publishing Company, One Park Avenue, New York, NY 10016. Available on the WWW from the <http://www3.zdnet.com> site.

This includes all the content that is in the print version of this magazine, plus Web site and shareware links.

Scientific Computing and Automation. Published by Gordon Publications, a Cahners Publishing Company, a member of Reed Elsevier Inc., 301 Gibraltar Drive, Morris Plains, NJ 07950. Available on the WWW at the <http://www.scamag.com> site.

Calling itself "the Scientific and Technical Community's Leading Source for New Technology," this magazine provides news and information for people working in various fields of scientific computing. It covers computing and automation applications and products for the laboratory and features product news, company profiles, an events calendar, and links to WWW sites. It covers multimedia under the category of software products. Some of the multimedia categories include audio editors, compression software, multimedia authoring tools, and video editors.

SunExpert. Published by the Computer Publishing Group, 1330 Beacon Street, Brookline, MA 02146.

> Covering topics related to UNIX client/server networks and published monthly, this magazine is written by veteran UNIX gurus with regular columns including the popular "Ask Mr. Protocol." Articles concern issues facing the system administrator and network managers. Monthly editorials include news and technology; communications and protocols; understanding the basics of the UNIX operating system; applications development in a client/server world; system administration; techniques for mixed UNIX networks; new products and services; and buyers guides to hardware, software, and peripheral communications gear.

Technical Communication, Journal of the Society for Technical Communication. Published by the Society for Technical Communication, 901 North Stuart Street, Arlington, VA 22203.

> Written and produced primarily by members of the technical communication community from both academia and business, this quarterly publication includes information about advanced technologies, technical and visual communications, and multimedia-related issues including tips on project management. Special issues occasionally deal with the Internet and the development and dissemination of online information over the WWW.

Upside. Published by the Upside Publishing Company, 1159–B Triton Drive, Foster City, CA 94404. Available on the WWW at the <http://www.upside.com> site.

> This magazine has a well-executed focus on technology issues as they relate specifically to investment. Though the topics range primarily in the direction of general computing and telecommunications, it is an excellent source for those in the investment banking business, or for those who are investors in the stock market.

Videomaker. Published by Videomaker, Inc., PO Box 4591, Chico, CA 95927.

> As media production equipment becomes increasingly digital, magazines such as these become an excellent source even for those members of the multimedia development team who are looking from a scholarly perspective. Refreshingly, many of the articles come with detailed footnotes and bibliographies.

Visual Developer. Published by The Coriolis Group, Inc., 7339 E. Acoma Drive, Suite 7, Scottsdale, AZ 85260.

> There is excellent coverage in this magazine of a variety of topics related to programming that include tools and techniques for Internet applications, games, hardware issues, Windows applications, and delivery systems in general.

Web Magazine. Published by Web Magazine, PO Box 56944, Boulder, CO 80322.

> Reflecting the lighter, entertainment-related side of the Web world, this magazine features a Web guide to travel, film, sports, music, TV, and other entertainment-type topics.

Web Week. Published by Mecklermedia Corporation, 20 Ketchum Street, Westport, CT 06880. Available on the WWW at the <http://www.webweek.com> site.

> Addressing the concerns of businesses operating or contemplating a home page on the World Wide Web, this weekly publication proclaims itself as being the "Newspaper of Web Technology and Business Strategy." It offers news, product analysis, and information. While there is not a great deal about multimedia technology here, there is information about the business side of working on the Web, including an Internet stock report.

Yahoo Internet Life. Published by Ziff-Davis Publishing Company, One Park Avenue, New York, NY 10016. Available on the WWW from the <http://www3.zdnet.com> site.

> With a name referring to the Yahoo! search utility, this electronic magazine claims to be a "guide to what is the best of the Web." It includes reviews of sites, information about and downloads to sites considered worth visiting, coverage of what is new on the Web, computer-related news, humor, useful sites, travel, and entertainment.

ZD Internet Megasite Magazine. Published by Ziff-Davis Publishing Company, One Park Avenue, New York, NY 10016. Available on the WWW from the <http://www3.zdnet.com> site.

> Impressive offerings appear in this weekly electronic magazine that claims to be "the definitive source for Internet and intranet computing." The magazine covers online trends, demos, downloads, search tools, a Web coach with tutorials, a news watch, and information about companies of note. There is nothing specific about multimedia here, but there is information to give a good idea of Internet-related news and trends.

Electronic Publication Collections

Ecola's Newsstand. Available from the <http://www.ecola.com/news/computer/> site.

> Includes newspapers, magazines, and computer publications and allows browsing of groupings such as general computer, applications, and product development (including digital media, systems and networks, and telecommunications).

Electronic Newsstand. Available from the <http://www.enews.com/zones/tech/> site.

A collection of online magazines with search capabilities and an interesting selection of technology-related publication reviews and features.

Global Computing—Computer Publications. Available from the <http://www.globalcomputing.com/pubhp.html> site.

A large collection of e-zines that allows for impressive browsing and searching.

Internet Magazines. Available from the <http://www.yahoo.com/Computers_and_Internet/Magazines/> site.

A collection from Yahoo! of electronic publications on computer- and Internet-related issues that allows for browsing and searching.

Media Central. Available from the <http://www.mediacentral.com/> site.

A collection of media, marketing, and telecommunications online publications from Cowles Business Media.

WWW Magazines. Available from the <http://www.yahoo.com/Business_and_Economy/Products_and_Services/Magazines/Computers/Internet/World_Wide_Web/> site.

A collection from Yahoo! that gives links to numerous online publications including the "top 30 magazines and newspapers published on the World Wide Web."

ZD Net. Available from the <http://www3.zdnet.com/> site.

A collection from Ziff-Davis, a major publisher of numerous publications on technology-related subjects.

ACRONYMS

Acronym	Meaning
A/D	analog to digital
ADC	analog to digital conversion
ADF	automatic document feeder
ADPCM	adaptive delta pulse code modulation
ADSL	asymmetrical digital subscriber line
ALU	arithmetic logic unit
ANSI	American National Standards Institute
API	application programming interface
ARM	Argonne Remote Manipulator
ARPA	Advanced Research Projects Agency
ARPANet	Advanced Research Projects Agency Network
ASCAP	American Society of Composers, Authors and Publishers
ASCII	American Standard Code for Information Interchange
ATM	asynchronous transfer mode
AVI	audio video interleaved
BBS	bulletin board system
BITC	burned in time codes
BLOB	binary large object
BMP	bit-mapped file
BPS	bits per second
BUFR	binary universal form for representation
CAD	computer-aided design
CAI	computer-assisted instruction
CATV	community-antenna-television
CAV	constant angular velocity
CBR	content-based retrieval
CBT	computer-based training
CCD	charge coupled device
CCITT	Consultative Committee on International Telephone and Telegraph
CDF	channel definition format
CD-DA	compact disc-digital audio
CD-I	compact disc-interactive
CDMA	code division multiple access
CD-R	compact disc-recordable

Acronym	Meaning
CD-ROM	compact disc-read only memory
CD-ROM-XA	CD-ROM extended architecture
CD-RTOS	compact disc-real time operating system
cel	celluloid
CELP	code excited linear prediction
CERN	Conseil Europeen pour la Recherche Nuceaire
CFD	computational fluid dynamics
CGA	color graphics adapter
CIE	commercial Internet exchange
CIRC	cross interleaved reed-solomon code
CIX	commercial Internet exchange
CLUT	color lookup table
CLV	constant linear velocity
CNIDR	Clearinghouse for Networked Information Discovery and Retrieval
codec	compression-decompression
com	commercial
CPU	central processing unit
CRT	cathode ray tube
CSLIP	compressed serial line Internet protocol
CSU	channel service unit
CUI	character user interface
CWIS	campus-wide information server
DAC	digital-to-analog conversion
DAG	data acquisition glove
DARPA	Defense Advanced Research Projects Agency
DATV	digital advanced television
DBS	direct broadcasting by satellite
DCA	directory client agent
DCE	data communications equipment
DCT	discrete cosine transform
DDN	Defense Data Network
DIB	device independent bit map
DICOM	digital imaging and communications
DLL	dynamic link library
DLO	document-like objects
DMA	direct memory access
DNS	domain name server (or system)
DPI	dots per inch

Acronym	Meaning
DSA	directory server agent
DSP	digital signal processing
DSS	decision support system
DSU	digital services unit
DTD	document type definitions
DTE	data terminal equipment
DTH	direct to home
DTM	digital terrain models
DTVC	desktop videoconferencing
DVE	digital video effects
DVI	Digital Video Interactive
DXF	drawing interchange format
DYUV	delta luminance color difference
EDI	electronic data interchange
EDL	edit decision list
edu	education
EGA	enhanced graphics adapter
EISA	extended industry standard architecture
ERDAS	earth resource data analysis
EVL	electronic visualization lab
FAQ	frequently asked questions
FAT	file allocation table
FDDI	fiber distributed data interface
FDX	full duplex
FIF	fractal image format
FM synthesis	frequency modulation
FMV	full-motion video
FPS	frames per second
FQDN	fully qualified domain name
FTP	file transfer protocol
GIF	graphics interchange file
GII	global information infrastructure
gov	government
GUI	graphical user interface
HDF	hierarchical data format
HDTV	high definition television
HMD	head-mounted display
HRTF	head-related transfer functions
HTML	hypertext markup language

Acronym	Meaning
HTTP	hypertext transport protocol
I/O	input/output
IAB	Internet Architecture (Activities) Board
IAP	Internet access provider
ICAI	intelligent computer-assisted instruction
ICMP	Internet Control Message Protocol
IESG	Internet Engineering Steering Group
IETF	Internet Engineering Task Force
IFF	interchange file format
IGES	initial graphics exchange specification
IGP	interior gateway protocol
IICS	International Interactive Communication Society
IID	interaural intensity differences
IITF	The Information Infrastructure Task Force
IMA	Interactive Multimedia Association
IMAP	Internet messaging access protocol
Internic	Internet Network Information Center
IP	Internet protocol
IRC	Internet relay chat
IRIS	Institute for Research on Information Systems
IRTF	Internet Research Task Force
ISA Bus	industry standard architecture bus
ISDN	integrated services digital network
ISO	International Standards Organization
ISOC	Internet Society
ISP	Internet service provider
ITD	interaural time differences
IVD	interactive video disc
JBIG	Joint Bi-Level Image Experts Group
JFIF	JPEG File Interchange Format
JPEG	Joint Photography Experts Group
LAN	local area network
LBE	location-based entertainment
LCD	liquid crystal display
LED	light-emitting diode
LLC	logical link control
LOD	level of detail
LV-ROM	laser vision—read-only memory
MARBI	Machine Readable Bibliographic Information Committee
MARC	machine readable cataloging

Acronym	Meaning
MBT	multimedia-based training
MCC	Microelectronics and Computer Technology Corporation
MCF	meta content format
MCI™	Media Control Interface
MIDI	musical instrument digital interface
mil	military
MILNET	military network
MIME	multipurpose Internet mail extension
MIPS	millions of instructions per second
MPC	multimedia personal computer
MPEG	Motion Picture Experts Group
MSC	MIDI show control
MSCDEX	Microsoft CD-ROM extensions
MUD	multi-user dimension or dungeon
NAPLPS	North American Presentation Level Protocol Standard
NCSA	National Center for Supercomputing Applications
NDL	National Digital Library
NFS	network file system
NIC	Network Information Center
NII	National Information Infrastructure
NNTP	network news transfer protocol
NOC	network operations center
NOS	Network Operating System
NREN	National Research and Education Network
NSF	National Science Foundation
NSFNet	National Science Foundation Network
NTSC	National Television Standards Committee
NVOD	near video on demand
NVRAM	nonvolatile random access memory
OCLC	Online Computer Library Center
OCR	optical character recognition
OLE	object linking and embedding
OPAC	Online Public Access Catalog
org	nonprofit organization
OSI	open systems interconnection
PAL	phase alternating line
pan	panorama
PAS™	Performance Animation System
PBX	private branch exchange

Acronym	Meaning
PCI™	Peripheral Component Interconnect
PCM	pulse code modulation
PCX	PC Paintbrush Graphics File Format Exchange
PDA	personal digital assistant
PDF	portable document format
PGP	pretty good privacy
PICT	bit-mapped picture graphics file format for the Mac
PING	packet Internet groper
PIP	picture-in-picture
PLV	production-level video
PNG	portable network graphics
POP	post office protocol
POTS	plain old telephone service
POV	point of view
PPP	point-to-point protocol
QHY	quantized high-resolution Y (luminance) compression
RAID	redundant arrays of inexpensive disks
RBOC	Regional Bell Operating Company
RDS	radio data system
RFC	request for comment
RGB	red, green, blue (video images)
RIP	remote imaging protocol
RIP	Remote Imaging Protocol
RLE	run length encoding
RSA	Rivest, Shamir, Adelman (invented) encryption method
RTF	rich text format for help files
RTOS	real-time operating system
RTV	real-time video
S-VHS	super-VHS
SBCELP	SB is short for Lernout & Hauspie Speech Products of Belgium code-excited linear prediction algorithm
SCADA	system control and data acquisition
SCSI	small computer standard interface
SDI	selective dissemination of information
SECAM	Systeme Electronique Coleur Avec Memoire
SGML	standard generalized markup language
SIG	special interest group
SIMNET	simulated network virtual reality battlefield
SLIP	serial line Internet protocol

Acronym	Meaning
SMPTE	Society for Motion Picture and Television Engineers
SMTP	simple mail transfer protocol
SNMP	simple network management protocol
SNR	signal-to-noise ratio
SONET	synchronous optical network
spam	stupid person's advertisement
STP	shielded twisted-pair
SUI	sound user interface
SVGA	super video graphics array
sync	synchronize
TCP	transmission control protocol
TCP/IP	transmission control protocol/ internet protocol
TDMA	time division multiple access
TEI	text encoding initiative
TGM	Thesaurus of Graphics Materials
TIFF	tagged image file format
TSR	terminate-and-stay resident
TUCOWS	The Ultimate Collection of Winsock Software
TWAIN	technology without an important (interesting) name
txt	text file extension
UDP	user datagram protocol
URC	uniform resource citation
URI	uniform resource indicator
URL	uniform resource locator
URN	uniform resource name
UTP	unshielded twisted-pair
UUencode/ UUuncode	Unix to Unix encode / Unix to Unix uncode
VBI	vertical blanking interval
VDU	visual display unit
Veronica	Very Easy Rodent Oriented Net-wide Index to Computerized Archives
VESA	Video Electronic Standards Association
VFW™	Video for Windows
VGA	video graphics array
VIMS	visually induced motion sickness,
VIS™	Visual Information System
VIVID	video, voice, image, and data
VOD	video on demand

Acronym	Meaning
Voomies	virtual reality movies
VR	virtual reality
VRAM	video random access memory
VRML	virtual reality modeling or markup language
VTOA	voice and telephony over ATM
VTOC	volume table of contents
WAIS	Wide Area Information Server
WAN	wide area network
WAV	sound wave file
WBT	Web-based training
Whisper	Windows Highly Intelligent Speech Recognizer
WORM	write once, read many
WWW	World Wide Web
WYSIWYG	what you see is what you get
Xerox PARC	Xerox Palo Alto Research Center
Y/C	Y for luminance channel signal; C for chrominance channel signal
YUV	Y for luminance channel signal; UV for two chrominance channel signals